Radicalization in Theory and Practice

RADICALIZATION IN THEORY AND PRACTICE

Understanding Religious Violence in Western Europe

Edited by
Thierry Balzacq and
Elyamine Settoul

University of Michigan Press
Ann Arbor

For questions or permissions, please contact um.press.perms@umich.edu

Published in the United States of America by the
University of Michigan Press
Manufactured in the United States of America
Printed on acid-free paper
First published December 2022

A CIP catalog record for this book is available from the British Library.

Library of Congress Cataloging-in-Publication data has been applied for.

ISBN 978-0-472-07514-0 (hardcover : alk. paper)
ISBN 978-0-472-05514-2 (paper : alk. paper)
ISBN 978-0-472-90283-5 (open access ebook)

https://doi.org/10.3998/mpub.12202059

An electronic version of this book is freely available, thanks in part to the support of libraries
working with Knowledge Unlatched (KU). KU is a collaborative initiative designed to make
high quality books Open Access for the public good. More information about the initiative
and links to the Open Access version can be found at www.knowledgeunlatched.org.

The University of Michigan Press's open access publishing program is made possible
thanks to additional funding from the University of Michigan Office of the Provost and the
generous support of contributing libraries.

Cover image courtesy Unsplash.com / Jr Korpa

Contents

List of Illustrations   vii

Acknowledgments   ix

Radicalization and Religious Violence in Western Europe:
An Introduction   1
Thierry Balzacq and Elyamine Settoul

PART I. THEORIES

1. Economic Perspectives   23
Daniel Meierrieks and Tim Krieger

2. Social Movement Research   46
Daniela Pisoiu

3. Islamic Doctrines: Theorizing Radicalization through the
Concept of "The New Spaces of Jihadism"   68
Mohamed-Ali Adraoui

4. Conversion Models   93
Juliette Galonnier

5. Social Psychology   119
John F. Morrison

PART II. PATTERNS OF RADICALIZATION IN WESTERN EUROPE

6. Belgium   143
    Sarah Teich

7. France: Joining Jihad and Joining the Army—A Comparison   166
    Elyamine Settoul

8. Germany: Individual Variations in Relational Mechanisms
    of Radicalization   186
    Robert Pelzer and Mika Moeller

9. Spain: Profiles and Patterns of Jihadist Radicalization   212
    Rut Bermejo-Casado

10. United Kingdom: Islamist Radicalization in a Spatial Context   237
    Tahir Abbas

Concluding Remarks   255
    Valérie Amiraux

Contributors   265

Index   273

Digital materials related to this title can be found on
the Fulcrum platform via the following citable URL:
https://doi.org/10.3998/mpub.12202059

Illustrations

Figures

1.1 Terrorism in Western Europe, 2000–2015   25

1.2 The Interplay of Demand for and Supply of Radical Activities   37

6.1 Educational Achievement of Muslims in Belgium   145

8.1 Timeline of Events Related to Millatu Ibrahim and Total
     Number of Videos Posted on its Website, Al-Ghurabaa   195

Tables

1.1 Socioeconomic Conditions and Support for Islamist Terrorism   34

6.1 Select Cases of Radicalized Belgians   155

6.2 McCauley and Moskalenko's Radicalization Mechanisms   161

Acknowledgments

Radicalization in Theory and Practice was submitted to the University of Michigan Press in 2019. This was an unfortunate timing. Like many publications submitted to presses and journals during the pandemic, the book found itself in the pipeline longer than we had imagined. Each step took such energy and time that, absent the constant commitment and patience of contributors and editors at the University of Michigan Press, this book would never have seen the light of day. We are very grateful for their generosity and professionalism. Every time we went back to contributors with very complex queries from reviewers, they responded, sometimes by doing extra research. The main credit goes to them.

We were also lucky to have benefited from the expertise of several very rigorous reviewers. They offered extensive comments and generous suggestions for how to effectively carry out the changes they found important in order to enhance the quality of the book. By any stretch of mind, we do not think the book would have taken this shape without their careful reading. Due to our own limitations, there are points we couldn't address to the extent they may have demanded. So, they cannot be blamed for any remaining issues; they only deserve our gratitude and readers', as what they will read herein is—in important part—the result of conversations with the reviewers.

At the University of Michigan Press, this project was remarkably shepherded by Elizabeth Demers. We also want to thank Haley Winkle, who conducted the production phase with kindness and professionalism.

Finally, many other people provided incredible help along the way. Benjamin Puybareau and Elise Rousseau at the University of Namur were instrumental in organizing the authors' workshop in Belgium. The Namur Advanced Research College provided generous funding to support the workshop. In the final stages of the project, Balzacq moved to Sciences Po. He wants to thank his colleagues for welcoming him to Sciences Po and making him feel at home.

Radicalization and Religious Violence in Western Europe

An Introduction

Thierry Balzacq and Elyamine Settoul

The most general aim of this book is to advance, if a little, our understanding of radicalization as it relates to jihadi terrorism. This calls for a word of caution, however. While our empirical cases focus on jihadi manifestations and consequences of radicalization, our conceptual chapters drive home a set of ideas, assumptions, and logics that are not unique to jihadi radicalization or violence. In other words, while the book emphasizes Islam-inspired radicalization, it acknowledges that radicalization boasts different meanings and has an equally powerful bearing on other types of beliefs (e.g., political and economic). The book sits, therefore, between conceptual apparatuses with a broader scope and reach and case studies that vet their relevance in specific contexts.

A caveat is not a substitute for stating a book's backbone. This book can also, and most obviously, be read as an attempt to explicate the various ways in which radicalization sometimes leads to violence. Contributors want to account for conditions under which some individuals holding radical views resort to violence. Our cases confirm that many do not. The book is about the others that do, and it draws attention to the diversity of motives and circumstances that push or pull them toward violent action.

Whatever their point of departure, the essays brought together in this volume are not meant to discover "root causes" of terrorism to slake a predictive policy desire. They are, rather, concerned with exploring processes of radicalization in their different facets in order to augment our understanding of the conditions under which violence becomes the privileged option for interactions.

Studying radicalization remains controversial. Although most intelligence agencies in Europe seem to have their attention fixated on jihadism, it is worth stressing that every ideological system, be it political or religious, is likely to embody manifestations of violent radicalization. To capture how radicalization takes shape, Bertjan Doosje and colleagues (2016) single out five forms of radicalization, and none, according to them, assumes a violent character a priori: nationalistic, extreme right-wing, extreme left-wing, single issue, and religiously motivated types. Beyond their obvious distinctive concerns, these different groups are described as sharing a set of basic common elements: One, these categories defend a cause that is not, or is insufficiently, dealt with by political institutions. Two, these groups believe their values to be legitimate and superior to those of others. Three, they are all receptive to the efficacy of the use of violence (Wieviorka 1993).

Be that as it may, most analysts acknowledge that the concept of radicalization is debatable and can be a source of confusion (Sedgwick 2010). Many criticisms outline its subjectivity and arbitrariness. Not unlike the word "terrorism," radicalization catalyzes infighting over meaning and is therefore highly political. Peter Neumann observes, for instance, that someone called a terrorist by some is a freedom fighter to others (Neumann 2013, 878). The same goes for groups categorized as "radical." This label carries a stigma (Goffman 1963) that contains a sort of performativity, for at the slightest mention of "radical" in the political context, the state narrative can either bring these groups into disrepute or glorify them. It can also adjudicate on the normal and the abnormal, the acceptable and the unacceptable within the political arena. Unsurprisingly, being labeled as "radical" carries implications for infighting within the said radical groups (Collovald and Gaïti 2006, 23), as it can strengthen the commitment and reinforce the allegiance of some, or conversely convince others to quit. The label "radical" produces contingent outcomes.

To recast the argument, this book is not a treatise on all forms of radicalization, but a work on jihadi radicalization and its link with violent action, an important problem that tends to be skirted by extant studies because the causal relation between radical opinion and violence is mostly assumed rather than tested. It is further concerned with how, and in what sense, current theories enable us to account for not only the properties of all violent radicalization, but also what (if any) are specific to violent radicalization, that is, the distinctive character of radicalization that violent jihadism expresses. The book can, then, be taken as a comparative theoretical-empirical study of violent radicalization processes. Against this backdrop, this introductory chapter now attends first to the concept of radicalization, next to the salient features of jihadi radicalization, and finally to this book's overall structure.

The Concept of Radicalization

Before discussing how radicalization manifests itself, we need to come to terms with the different meanings pressed under the label "radicalization." To that effect, this section outlines three conceptions of radicalization: etymological, descriptive, and critical. Doing so, we hope, furthers the cause of conceptual accuracy and ameliorates this book's use of the concept. Students of critical and descriptive views are usually different people, but they all appropriate the etymological tone of the concept. This distinction suggests, among other things, that it is primarily the divide between critical and descriptive/analytical accounts of radicalization that matters (Fadil, Ragazzi, and de Koning 2019; Patel 2011; Coolsaet 2008). There are possible variations in an individual author's commitment to either, but, as it happens, critical and descriptive approaches do not ask the same questions, and when they do, their answers spring from different diagnoses and foreground distinctive prescriptions.

The etymological study of the word "radicalization" does not shed much light on the topic, as the Latin origin of the word, *radix*, also means "root." It follows that being radical means, figuratively, "returning to one's roots." In fact, this difficulty in grasping what is "radical" pertains to the fact that the adjective is used to define ideas, practices, and beliefs in a relative way that is contingently related to time and space. What is radical clearly depends on the historical and geographical context. For instance, up until recently, same-sex marriage used to be a very radical idea in many societies, and in fact this perception still prevails in many parts of the world. In short, the authors tend to agree that radicalization is a catch-all term that means many things and refers to a variety of frames of reference. That is, its intension is large and its extension is difficult to delimit. This concern with the content and remits of radicalization leads to what we call, for lack of a better word, a descriptive/analytical understanding of radicalization. Here, it is the degree and intensity of the relation between radical opinions and violence that rivet scholars' attention. Farhad Khosrokhavar, for instance, defines radicalization basically as the "convergence of an extreme ideology and moving into action" (2014, 8. Our translation). For others, like Charles Allen, the term encompasses more and pertains to "the process of adopting an extremist belief system, including the willingness to use, support, or facilitate violence, as a method to effect societal change" (2007, 4). Despite the lack of consensus, many researchers set out to differentiate cognitive from violent radicalization. Cognitive radicalization is the process through which individuals adopt ideas in opposition to dominant norms, oppose the social order in place, and seek to replace it with another one based on a different belief system. Violent radicalization, which concerns a much smaller group of people, appears when individuals use every means possible to implement cognitive radicalization's ideas and beliefs. It should nonetheless be noted that the adoption of a radical ideology is neither a necessary nor sufficient condition that compels violent action. This reading parts ways with interpretations that assume radicalization and violence go hand in glove. For example, Eitan Alimi, Chares Demetriou, and Lorenzo Bosi (2015, 11) refer to radicalization as a processual leap from "nonviolent tactics of contention to tactics that include violent means." In this context, then, radicalization and violent action are one and the same. The problem, however, is that this view might end up countenancing policies that blur the line between holding radical beliefs and privileging violence as a legitimate recourse for action. The shortcut is alluring, but misleading. Hence, contributors to this volume demonstrate, in different environments, that ideology does not always translate into action (Borum 2011; Horgan 2006; Victoroff 2005).

Critical scholars situate the concept of radicalization within the political context that saw it rising to prominence. In the aftermath of 9/11, studies that sought to examine the root cause of terrorism were cast as a commiserating look at terrorist violence. Radicalization came across as an actionable concept able, as it were, to point policy-makers toward the "making" of a terrorist. In the words of Neumann (2008, 4), "In the highly charged atmosphere following the September 11 attacks it was through the notion of radicalization that a discussion about the political, economic, social and psychological forces that underpin terrorism and political violence became possible again." That is, radicalization was quickly adopted by various law enforcement agencies because, in the main, it empowered them to carry out certain forms of policing based on predictive models that the growing scholarship on radicalization would make available. Arun Kundnani (2012,

5) argues that the new paradigm of radicalization that took shape between 2001 and 2004 was primarily if not exclusively oriented toward a question with discriminating currents in its wake: "Why do some individual Muslims support an extremist interpretation of Islam that leads to violence?" Because, so the argument goes, such extremist violence is inspired by dangerous appropriation of Islamic thought by some Muslims, it is on that ideology and the associated community that the intellectual and policy gaze ought to focus (Silber and Bhatt 2007). Taken to its logical conclusion, this book, too, could be treated as reinforcing this trend. Three responses could possibly be offered, without calling off continual attention to the matter.

To begin with, this book is not about discovering "indicators" of radicalization that would allow, or better encourage, a distinctive kind of policing. Instead, contributors were asked to investigate relational features that characterize radicalization, examine the extent to which local events reverberate globally, and ascertain the merit of available conceptual apparatuses in shedding original light on the case at hand. Second, some contributors to this volume are Muslims. They have an experiential understanding of biases that a poor handling of the radicalization concept can unleash. Social scientists need to cultivate a robust ethical and reflexive attitude when they study such questions. However, they should not forsake the analysis of the subject altogether because their work might be interpreted or employed for aims other than scientific progress. The study of radicalization cannot be an indictment against all Muslims any more than the study of white supremacists is an indictment against all white people. Social scientists should recognize the danger while exploring such sensitive questions and tread the path with rigor and ethics. By the way, isn't it what serious research standards command? Third, our book has not been supported by any funding agency and is not meant to respond to a policy-oriented tender. It is not critical, however, in the sense of critical theory. The book is analytically critical, as it questions explorations of radicalization that emphasize mono-causality at the service of prediction. Further, the book is theoretically eclectic; that is, empirical cases exhibit more varieties in the trajectories to violence than are often acknowledged by studies that are driven by the imperative of pinning down the root causes of radicalization.

Theorizing Radicalization

The term "radicalization" has just been—if briefly—introduced. Essays in this volume will unpack it more fully, though each would involve it in a different manner. Indeed, by employing radicalization, these essays lift the veil on other rather less obvious but by no means marginal conceptions of radicalization. For now it is well to note that studies are not only using the term in distinctive fashions but are also putting forward different approaches to the phenomenon. We shall, therefore, be concerned in this section with theoretical frameworks about radicalization and the kind of inquiry they tend to be associated with.

Part of the gulf that separates approaches to radicalization stems, we think, from what they consider as the primary determinant of the transition from nonviolent to violent forms of action. Although the conceptions of radicalization found in the scholarship might be manifold, for the purpose of this book, we can, in a rough and ready way, identify three main accounts of radicalization. One focuses on the drivers and causes of radicalization; the second is concerned with circumstances or conditions that facilitate radicalization; and the third turns the arrow of investigation toward uncovering the mechanisms that sustain radicalization processes. It is in this sense that we might summarize these accounts by arguing that the first deals with "why" questions about radicalization while the second and the third are interested in the "when" and "how" questions, respectively (compare Bloom 2005; Bartlett and Miller 2012; Bergesen 2007; McCormick 2003).

When they look for root causes scholars treat radicalization as the effect of a number of factors that stand in a relation of constant co-occurrence with it. The aim is to identify processes and the underlying multifactorial causes that drive individuals with deeply implanted belief systems to engage in violence. To use David Mandel's words, it is about understanding "what goes on before the bomb goes off" (2010, 25). These causes are both cognitive (e.g., ideology, identity crises, memories of stigmatization) and material (e.g., social grievances, inequalities). One of the pending uncertainties is whether it is possible to establish an exhaustive list of causes that underlie radicalization. Moreover, sometimes researchers who inquire into causes entertain high hopes about their ability to derive predictions from causal explanations (Juergensmeyer 2005; Stern 2003). The general problem here is collapsing explanation into prediction. Finally, the observation of an instance of regularity is not an explanation of why something happened. That many of those who were involved in the Paris attack on November 13, 2015, had suffered from the absence of a paternal authority does not tell us why they chose violence as a means to express their radical beliefs. Many children without fathers do not become radicalized, and those who do are not all terrorists. What regularity offers is a better understanding of patterns of outcomes, but it doesn't fare well in answering the question "why?"

Causal accounts of radicalization, in view of the problems raised above, have transformed the search for causes into an examination of precipitating or facilitating factors. Thus, what appears as a facilitating condition, that is, a factor that sometimes gives a causal force its impetus, becomes a cause in itself. The danger here lies with the propensity to call any factor that bears even the slightest effect on the emergence of violent political action a "cause." Thus, the framework designed by Tore Bjorgo (2005) features no less than four causes, including structural, accelerating (or facilitating), motivational, and triggering causes. Realizing the oddity of calling all these factors "causes," the study, rather than scaling down the number of genuinely causal elements, proposes to further amplify the list of causal factors up to 14.

Studies that focus on pathways seek to combine an interest in causal factors with an overture toward broader facilitating conditions. John Horgan (2008) provides a good illustration of this line of research. Distancing himself from the sketchy studies of profiles, he proposes to look at pathways to radicalization and investigate the factors driving individuals to join or, conversely, leave these movements. He thus points to the influence of a number of macro-, meso-, and micro-factors in pathways of radicalization: macro refers to the broader societal environment in which individuals move about; meso relates to the role of socialization processes (e.g., family) and the influence of other group dynamics (e.g., friends, clans); and micro pertains to the personal attributes of people, including their predispositions as well as the way they perceive reality.

However, the analysis of disposition of a cultural or psychological tone reduces terrorism to ideational factors attached to the individual or given group. As a consequence, any political grievances or material circumstances that might account for violent radicalization are jettisoned (Laqueur 2004, 1987). Beneath a psychological view of radicalization is the creed that knowing a person's or group's pattern of beliefs is a reliable proxy for ascertaining their likely association with terrorist violence. One could appreciate why such account might seduce counterterrorist services. It provides them with a straightforward route to prediction, though it lacks explanatory traction.

Be that as it may, this combination of different levels of analysis crystallizes a wide array of theoretical approaches that tend to focus on very different matters: some focus solely on the individual and their psychology, when others emphasize the role played by socialization processes (Silke

2008; Cottee 2011). However, understanding pathways of radicalization raises the difficult question of how to effectively differentiate objective elements from very subjective ones (micro). If experiences of economic marginalization and political exclusion can be measured and have an objective reality, experiences involving emotional components such as indignation, humiliation, and many other psychological responses to discrimination are not quantifiable.

Despite the fact that there are many pathways to radicalization, and that many personal psychological and sociological features influence individual trajectories, a growing cluster of theories is moving toward a "processual" understanding of radicalization. But processes are underwritten, according to Charles Tilly (2003, 20), by mechanisms, that is, "similar events that produce essentially the same immediate effects across a wide range of circumstances." The study of mechanisms does not have to be linear, but a vast tract of scholarship on radicalization employs a mechanism-based approach in order to establish "what follows what" (Alimi, Demetriou, and Bosi 2015, 35). And here is the rub. In general, these views embrace linear models arguing that radicalization follows a number of distinct stages or steps that enable us to situate individuals on a scale of radicalization (Haggerty and Bucerius 2020; Bergesen 2007). Some draw on this view to bypass explanatory systems as they search for a potential existential crisis that could have sparked the radicalization process (McCauley and Moskalenko 2008).

More often than not these studies use the metaphor of a staircase to describe the gradual escalation of ordinary people taking a step too far. Fathali Moghaddam (2005), for instance, offers a six-step checklist, according to which individuals check off all the boxes when they commit violent acts such as suicide attacks. Quintan Wiktorowicz (2005) describes for his part a three-step process that starts with a "cognitive opening" that leads to "religious seeking" and ends with the "construction of a sacred authority," during which the frame of thought of the individual finally aligns with the group's ideology. How exactly do these steps matter? Cognitive opening, to start with, indicates when an individual is amenable to extremist ideas. It can be either created by a moral shock undergone by the person or prompted by external cues generated by radical entrepreneurs. Cognitive opening transports the individual into religious seeking, which is meant to heal the crisis by making an individual feel significant. In this way, religious seeking accounts for a quest of meaning, which religion is held to provide. This is what Arie Kruglanski, Jocelyn Bélanger, and Rohan Gunaratna term "significant quest theory." As they argue, the need for "personal significance—the desire to matter, to be 'someone,' and to have meaning in one's life—is the dominant need that underlies violent extremism" (2019, 37). The third step that endeavors to capture why some Muslims are drawn to religious violence is the construction of sacred authority around the figure of a charismatic leader (Appleby 2012).

Each step tells us something worth heeding, but linear models convey the powerful but false idea that individuals move across different steps and, necessarily, must first experience cognitive opening before embarking on a quest for religious meaning. Linearity, we know, is a one-way street. But, as some essays in this book demonstrate, it might well be that there is no clearly discernible order of precedence among the three steps. In our view, then, it improves matters to consider cognitive opening, religious seeking, and the construction of a sacred authority as contributing factors, not as consecutive steps arrayed toward extremist violence.

Still other models—linear in their explanatory timbre—assume that the key element resides in the organization of violent groups, as many similarities can be drawn with the modus operandi of sects. During a process of psychological and social conditioning, individuals are stripped of their multiple affiliations and brought to embrace solely the group's identity. The group will devise a worldview that fundamentally dehumanizes and demonizes the enemy (Flannery 2015; Stahelski 2005). Unlike linear models, Tinka Veldhuis and Jorgen Staun (2009) assume that these mental processes systematically lead up to the creation and reinforcement of a dichotomist and Manichean representation of the world. If they are helpful to model standard trajectory, these processes are nevertheless contested insofar as they only work retrospectively, if they have been completed (i.e., when individuals are fully radicalized), and they ignore individuals with similar social and psychological predispositions who have not joined the spiral of radicalization.

Jihadi Radicalization

When Mark Sedgwick (2010) uses the term radicalization, he traces how it rose in importance after the attacks carried out in Western European capitals of Madrid (March 11, 2004) and London (July 7, 2005). This allows him to emphasize the deeds of homegrown terrorists. In fact, in contrast to the attacks perpetrated by smaller foreign groups in the previous decades, the post-2004 terrorist actions have been predominantly committed by individuals born and socialized in the very Western countries they have attacked.[1] This specificity has since become a defining pattern, and European citizens are most likely involved in the most recent attacks (Hafez and Creighton 2015; Silber and Bhatt 2007). Indeed, the burden of this argument is that radicalization is primarily a Western phenomenon. Thus, policies that aim to address it ought to be geared toward "communities of believers on the outskirts of London, Paris, and other European cities, where Islam is already a growing part of the West" (Kepel 2004, 8).

As tempting as the development of an all-encompassing analytical model to decipher the dynamics of jihadi recruitment can be, important hurdles remain that must be overcome, the first of which is the great sociological diversity of the actors involved. Various surveys have brought to light the wide and protean array of motivations among those who wished to go to Syria and Iraq. Before the Islamic State was created in 2014, it appears that humanitarian reasons and a readiness to help played a large role in the motivations of some young Westerners to go and assist, as Syrian populations were being shelled by the regime of Bashar al-Assad in response to the 2011 popular uprising. Others joined in owing to religious beliefs to complete hijrah,[2] that is, to migrate to Muslim land. Recurring answers to surveys also include a quest for identity, a search for an adrenaline rush, and a morbid fascination with death. Explanatory theories of jihadi radicalization is a good reflection of the plurality of these trajectories. In France, the debate is fierce. Some paradigms seek to establish a causal relation between religious extremism and processes of violent radicalization. Gilles Kepel (2015) for instance believes that the rising Salafism of Western-based Muslim communities fuels the spread of jihadism. He argues for a "radicalization of Islam" and insists on looking into the scope and meaning of Islamic concepts (Kepel 2015, 51), thus assuming that Salafism is a gateway to jihadism (Adraoui 2020). Other researchers disagree. They focus instead on the social markers of terrorists and most of all on the rather weak degree of religious socialization. For Khosrokhavar (2014), indeed, jihadism takes root most and foremost in a deep sentiment of humiliation and on stigma that in turn becomes "sacralized in hatred," as shown in the social trajectory of numerous young members of the most violent groups that is characterized by a criminal record, time spent in

---

1. There are exceptions. The attacks carried out in Paris in 1995 were perpetrated by Khaled Kelkal, a young Frenchman who grew up in the suburb of Lyon. Yet this case remains marginal, and Algerian services are suspected to have been involved.

2. The term *hijrah* originally refers to the journey of the Prophet Muhammad from the city of Mecca, where he had been physically threatened, to the city of Medina, and by extension designates Muslims returning to Muslim dominated lands.

prison, involvement in social networks online, and more often than not an absent paternal figure (see also Dittrich 2007, 57; Ranstorp 2006).

While subscribing to this line of inquiry, Olivier Roy nonetheless emphasizes the generational dimension of the phenomenon (2016, 2004). He argues that Islam appears today as the last transnational utopia available on the market of radical dissent. According to him, then, nihilism and a fascination with death are the markers of the jihadi modus operandi, and they stand at odds with the fundamentalist practices of religious Salafists. If death has always been a lurking possibility when engaging in Islamist terrorism, it never used to be its sole purpose, all the less so that it violates Salafist principles that "condemn suicide as it interferes with God's will" (Roy 2016, 12). Roy explains that for this generation of jihadists, there is no plan B, no fleeing strategy. The perpetrators of terrorist acts are systematically looking for law enforcement forces for the ultimate confrontation, seeking a widely broadcasted death. In a way, then, they embrace Bin Laden's creed, "we love death more than we love life,"[3] when they deliberately choose death as the end game.

Marc Sageman (2004) departs from this interpretation. Specifically, he turns his gaze toward the importance of social networks such as religious diasporas. Sageman finds that radicalization originates from new types of networks that focus on breaking individuals' personalities in order to give rise to new non-hierarchical radical groups, and he rejects the idea that there could be a spontaneous phenomenon emanating from a bunch of individuals surfing the web. Even if some psychopaths can feel at ease with the terrorist movement's narrative, Sageman stresses that all terrorists do not fit the same psychopathological profile (Baele 2014). Others still concentrate on what a terrorist organization says. This is clearly seen in the work of Scott Atran (2016), whose research focused on Islamic State (IS) fighters and suggested that jihad provides youth with something they cannot find in Western societies, that is, the excitement of fighting for a sacred cause and achieving the kind of boundless power that comes with omnipotence. Atran rules out nihilism and prefers defining radicalization as an attempt to produce sacred values. In this view, groups such as Daesh are powerful countercultural movements, which provide youth with a "good fight" and a way to become heroes.

---

3. Quote from an interview of Bin Laden by Peter Arnett in March 1997. "Transcript of Osama Bin Laden interview by Peter Arnett." InformationClearinghouse.info: "We love this kind of death for Allah's cause as much as you like to live."

Global Phenomenon, Local Dynamics

A key part of the puzzle and a driving force behind this book is still missing: the crucial role played by local influences on this global phenomenon. Consider, once more, the case of Daesh. While there is no denying that Daesh was a global phenomenon based on the number of nationalities represented in its recruits, it is important to stress the extent to which its development relied on local sociological specificities. In fact, a growing number of researchers is taking an interest in questioning these variations. Why has Belgium provided more jihadi fighters per capita than any other European country? Why have Tunisia and Morocco provided the Islamic State with respectively 6,000 and 1,200 combatants when the bordering country of Algeria has only produced 200? (The Soufan Group 2015, 8–9) The same observation holds true when one zooms in and notices that some Tunisian, Belgian, and French regions have been remarkably prolific purveyors of jihadi fighters in comparison with others.[4] There are similar discrepancies between countries when it comes to the proportion of converts who joined these movements. Hypotheses covering a wide spectrum have been ventured to explain these territorial variations. Some trace the source of these national disparities back to the presence of high numbers of recruiters and propagandists in the territory. Those, like Raymond Taras (2012), who highlight the ethnic and religious minority integration policies and the need to review them, refer mostly to the way in which the state has been managing Islam, to the issue of Islamophobia and to the scale of discriminations that continue to plague Western societies (Khosrokhavar 2016). Still others call for a geopolitical interpretation of the phenomenon, stressing the impacts of transnational Islamic networks, lurking Western imperialism, and Western policies in the Middle East (e.g., interventions, conflict between Israel and Palestine). Finally, some analyses assume a causal relationship between the rationale for radical commitment and the consequences of colonial history. French colonization in particular has bred many forms of violence, be it cultural, linguistic, or symbolic, that only intensify the identity malaise experienced by the descendants of postcolonial migrants (Roy 2016).

In this context, a comparative approach becomes heuristically relevant to identify continuities and ruptures across time and space. Clark McCau-

---

4. Ben Gardane, a town of 65,000 inhabitants in the south of Tunisia, has provided nearly 15% of all Tunisian jihadists. In Belgium, 75% of Belgian jihadists come from Brussels and Antwerp. In France, the city of Nice has produced proportionally more jihadi fighters than the average of the other towns.

ley and Sophia Moskalenko (2011) offer one of the first attempts at doing this when they highlight the recurrences among the different forms of radicalization that have existed throughout history. By identifying common ground shared by movements as diverse as the 19th-century Russian anarchist organization "People's Will" and the contemporary jihadi movements such as Al-Qaeda, they shed light upon the mechanisms through which ordinary people come to commit extraordinary acts (McCauley and Moskalenko 2011, 6). In the same comparative line of work, the report entitled *Jihadist Hotbeds: Understanding Local Radicalization Processes* stresses for its part the importance of local territorial specificities on the jihadists' decision to engage (Varvelli 2016).

This book expands on similar works wherein local features of radicalization are accorded significant attention (Coolsaet 2008). But we contribute to that—still underdeveloped—tract of scholarship by ascertaining how and when local characteristics intersect, trump, or give way to global factors. Such a project relies on inductive reasoning, one which enables us to better understand how the contours of local dynamics both affect and/ or are affected by a global phenomenon.

Book Structure and Chapter Summaries

This book aims to understand and explain patterns of radicalization in Western Europe, with an eye toward developing more robust accounts of the phenomenon. It therefore has both theoretical and empirical objectives. Theoretically, *Radicalization in Theory and Practice* combines in-depth analyses of the most advanced theoretical approaches to radicalization with focused case studies. Thus, these theories are examined, compared, and assessed as they apply to different points in time and different political and cultural environments. Theories are examined in part I.

Empirically, the book identifies the mechanisms that explicitly link radical religious beliefs and radical actions. In doing so, it develops a richer view of the processes that underpin radicalization than has been previously achieved. Analyzing some 260 publications that came out between 1980 and 2010, Scott Kleinmann and Peter Neumann conclude that if the vast majority of them used qualitative methods, many demonstrate what the authors deem to be poor methodological rigor (2013). The sensitivity of the issues at stake in this research is seen as impeding the access of researchers to primary data, when it does not discourage them altogether from using quantitative methods. As a consequence, theoretical generalization becomes most unlikely, as these publications offer mainly descriptive and partial conclusions (Dalgaard-Nielsen 2010). By dwelling primarily on firsthand empirical investigations, the book aims to build a new framework of analysis from the ground up. In this light, the goals of the book are: (a) to encourage the quality of theorizing in this area; (b) to enhance the quality of methodological inquiries; and (c) to articulate security studies insights with broader theoretical debates in different fields, including sociology, social psychology, economics, and religious studies. Cases are discussed in part II.

Part I: Theories

The narratives on radicalization often focus on discrete theories, examining the nature of radicalization, the factors that drive it, and whether radicalization is a condition or a process. This book also discusses the nature of radicalization, but nudges it into a new direction: It posits that radicalization is less a condition than the result of a family of processes, and the book foregrounds a range of theories that are often overlooked by existing accounts of radicalization, including social psychology and conversion theories. The book starts with rational choice views, which offer a contrasting picture against which other approaches situate themselves. The section moves from generic theories that are often employed in explaining a variety of violent contentions to more specific approaches that deal with jihadi kinds of violence. However, the chapter on social psychology comes at the end of part I because it makes explicit some of the connections that are left implicit in the previous chapters.

In chapter 1, Daniel Meierrieks and Tim Krieger consider the concept of radicalization using an economic approach. The authors ground their analysis on concepts derived from the economic domain and which revolve around the idea of a rational agent and notions of costs, strategies, and profits. They note in their analysis, however, that the influence of socioeconomic factors varies widely depending on the stage reached in the process of radicalization. In chapter 2, Daniela Pisoiu highlights the relevance of theories of social movements in interpreting radicalization. These theories, widely used in historical analysis of left-wing and nationalist movements, allow radicalization to be connected with more classical types of political violence. They underline the logic of confrontation between the state and certain groups, or between rival groups. Pisoiu nonetheless stresses that phenomena of jihadi radicalization have specificities that these theoretical tools cannot comprehensively account for.

The next two chapters deal with approaches derived directly from the study of religious forms of violence. Specifically, in chapter 3 Mohamed-Ali Adraoui examines Islamic doctrine as a way to grasp the connection between the religious imagination and geopolitical developments. He identifies the emergence of a new type of jihadism in the form of a mass counterculture in which propagation is no longer based on a *command*-type logic but a *viral* one. In chapter 4, Juliette Galonnier explores the complex relationships between phenomena of religious conversion and radicalization. In addition to highlighting the overrepresentation of converts in radicalized populations, she favors an approach that analyzes this phenomenon as a special sub-category in the factors behind conversion. This method takes into account common denominators between conversion and radicalization, notably in terms of how the individuals work on their own bodies or the importance of the social environment in influencing their path in society. As John Morrison shows in chapter 5, these interrelationships play a particularly important analytical role in terms of social psychology. This approach underscores the profound links between psychological and sociological factors (micro/macro). Individuals going through this process are seeking a positive identity, a grand cause and meaning in a welcoming social environment. According to this logic, they tend to be absorbed by a group that offers them a form of psychological and emotional stability.

Part II: Patterns of Radicalization in Western Europe

The book adopts a comparative international approach to identify and characterize the patterns that, going beyond the specific contexts of individual countries, enable us to structure our understanding of these social trends. More specifically, each chapter addresses the following questions: What elements of continuity and variations can we observe from one national territory to another among European countries? Where can we see the signs of cohesion or division from one national territory to another? What aspects can be defined as local dynamics, and which are of a global or transnational nature? What does the case teach us about the mechanisms and theories discussed in part I? One of the persistent problems in radicalization studies is that many authors often draw on secondary data, assembled by others, sometimes for different purposes, in order to answer specific questions. Thus, a distinctive feature of *Radicalization in Theory and Practice* is that the authors brought together draw primarily on data they collected themselves, through intensive fieldwork.

What is the rationale behind our case selection? The different empirical cases chosen allow the scope and validity of the theories set out previously (in part I) to be verified. At the same time, they enable us to test the role of local, contextual variables in the phenomenon. These variables relate to social integration policies targeting the most vulnerable populations, the particular counterterrorist policies developed at a national level, or specific approaches in managing religious diversity. Statistics show that half of the Western fighters who joined Daesh came from three countries: France, Britain, and Germany. Belgium and Spain offer contrasting cases that ameliorate the comparison further. Belgium stands out insofar as it exported the most jihadi fighters per capita than any other European country, it experienced the first terrorist action of the Islamic state in Europe,[5] and finally the country served as a logistical support base for the attacks that targeted Paris in November 2015. In chapter 6, Sarah Teich shows how the Belgian case is striking for the dynamism of its Islamic organizations. Religious groups such as Sharia4Belgium have played a prominent role in the recruitment of Belgian jihadi fighters for Daesh. She explores the dynamics of radicalization in Belgium by using concepts from the social movement theories. The contribution concerning France focuses on the diverse motivations of French jihadists who left France to join the Islamic State. In chapter 7, Elyamine Settoul investigates the similarities that can be drawn between jihadi engagement and enrollment in a national army. The comparison between these two types of enrollment borrows methods from social psychology and suggests a shift away from a purely ideological-religious interpretation of jihadi engagement. Drawing on the theory of social movements, Robert Pelzer and Mika Moeller illustrate in chapter 8 the variety of factors that lead a group to radicalize or not. Through a comparative analysis of the development of two Islamists, Denis Cuspert and Hasan Keskin, they show how the actions of the state and the psychology of the subjects influence the process of radicalization. Like Belgium, Spain offers an interesting case to understand the generational element involved in radicalization, since it is only recently that the Muslim community has come back to this country. Thus, in chapter 9, Rut Bermejo-Casado analyzes the radicalization experiences of Spanish jihadists. She establishes sociological points of comparison between members of the Euskadi Ta Askatasuna (ETA), the perpetrators of the attacks in Madrid on March 11, 2004, and those who carried out the attacks in the Barcelona area in 2017. She observes that most jihadists had experienced a rather successful social

5. Attack against the Jewish Museum on May 24, 2014, perpetrated by Mehdi Nemmouche in Brussels.

integration. Further, she notes the crucial role of recruiters from terrorist organizations (e.g., Al-Qaeda, Islamic State) and of prison experience in the social development of certain jihadists. Finally, Bermejo-Casado observes a shortening of the period of radicalization among the perpetrators of the 2004 and 2017 attacks.

In chapter 10, Tahir Abbas also underlines the social and political aspects of religious radicalism in the United Kingdom. Deindustrialization combined with spatial relegation and declining social status have favored inward-looking forms of identity among the most marginal groups. Abbas highlights the processes of mutual self-reinforcement between the public, headline-grabbing discourse of the far right and the attraction of Islamist ideology for populations in a state of anomie.

In the concluding chapter, Valérie Amiraux summarizes the argument of the book, weaves the threads, and sketches research paths that the foregoing studies open. She returns to the central themes explored in the volume, including disciplinary and theoretical innovations as well as empirical issues, which enable this work to bring to light how different factors, contexts, and commitments—not all of which are known—account for a similar outcome (Schanzer 2014, 599). Amiraux argues that it is in the nature of the label "radicalization" to alter the perception of certain people and transform interactions between actors. Thus, if the scholarship on radicalization is to ameliorate our understanding of a phenomenon whose sources and dimensions remain irreducibly diverse, it needs to stand against the "consensual varnish" around the issue and stray from the "'solvent' effect," that is, "diluting [various phenomena] within a unifying and standardized term [namely, radicalization]" (Amiraux, this volume). As such, our understanding of radicalization must be more specific than often assumed. This book, then, constitutes a step toward clarifying the shape of the territory radicalization occupies and in exploring the concepts and theories within and through which research is conducted. With detailed case studies, Amiraux argues, researchers are not captive to the concepts and theories they have conceived. The conclusion's final section sets out prominent ethical questions that stalk research in radicalization.

REFERENCES

Adraoui, Mohamed-Ali. 2020. *Salafism Goes Global: From the Gulf to the French Banlieues*. Oxford: Oxford University Press.

Alimi, Eitan Y., Chares Demetriou, and Lorenzo Bosi. 2015. *The Dynamics of Radicalization: A Relational and Comparative Perspective*. Oxford: Oxford University Press.

Allen, Charles E. 2007. "Threat of Islamic Radicalization to the Homeland." U.S.

Senate Committee on Homeland Security and Governmental Affairs, March 14.

Appleby, R. Scott. 2012. "Religious Violence: The Strong, the Weak, and the Pathological." *Practical Matters Journal*, March 1. http://practicalmattersjournal.or g/?p=231

Atran, Scott. 2016. "The Devoted Actor: Unconditional Commitment and Intractable Conflicts across Cultures." *Current Anthropology* 57 (13): 192–203.

Baele, Stéphane J. 2014. "Are Terrorists 'Insane?': A Critical Analysis of Mental Health Categories in Lone Terrorist Trials." *Critical Studies on Terrorism* 7 (2): 257–76.

Bartlett, Jamie, and Carl Miller. 2012. "The Edge of Violence: Towards Telling the Difference between Violent and Non-Violent Radicalization." *Terrorism and Political Violence* 24 (1): 1–21.

Bergesen, Albert J. 2007. "A Three-Step Model of Terrorist Violence." *Mobilization* 12 (2): 111–18.

Bjorgo, Tore. 2005. *Root Causes of Terrorism: Myths, Reality and Ways Forward*. London: Routledge.

Bloom, Mia. 2005. *Dying to Kill*. New York: Columbia University Press.

Borum, Randy. 2011. "Radicalization into Violent Extremism." *Journal of Strategic Security* 4 (4): 7–36.

Collovald, Annie, and Brigitte Gaïti. 2006. "Questions Sur Une Radicalization Politique." In *La Démocratie aux Extrêmes*, edited by Annie Collovald and Brigitte Gaïti, 19–45. Paris: La Dispute.

Coolsaet, Rik, ed. 2008. *Jihadi Terrorism and the Radicalization Challenge in Europe*. Aldershot: Ashgate.

Cottee, Simon. 2011. "Jihadism as a Subcultural Response to Social Strain." *Terrorism and Political Violence* 25 (3): 730–51.

Dalgaard-Nielsen, Anja. 2010. "Violent Radicalization in Europe: What We Know and What We Do Not Know." *Studies in Conflict and Terrorism* 33 (9): 797–814.

Dittrich, Mirjam. 2007. "Radicalization and Recruitment: The EU Response." In *The European Union and Terrorism*, edited by David Spence, 54–70. London: John Harper.

Doosje, Bertjan, Fathali M. Moghaddam, Arie W. Kruglanski, Arjan de Wolf, Liesbeth Mann, and Allard Rienk Feddes. 2016. "Terrorism: Radicalization and De-Radicalization." *Current Opinion in Psychology* 11: 79–84.

Fadil, Nadia, Francesco Ragazzi, and Martijn de Koning, eds. 2019. *Radicalization in Belgium and the Netherlands: Critical Perspectives on Violence and Security*. London: I.B. Tauris.

Flannery, Frances L. 2016. *Understanding Apocalyptic Terrorism: Countering the Radical Mindset*. London: Routledge.

Goffman, Erving. 1963. *Stigma: Notes on the Management of Spoiled Identity*. London: Penguin.

Hafez, Mohammed, and Creighton Mullins. 2015. "The Radicalization Puzzle: A Theoretical Synthesis of Empirical Approaches to Homegrown Extremism." *Studies in Conflict and Terrorism* 38 (11): 958–75.

Haggerty, Kevin D., and Sandra M. Bucerius. 2020. "Radicalization as Materialization: Towards a Better Appreciation for the Progression to Violence." *Terrorism and Political Violence* 32 (4): 768–88.

Horgan, John. 2008. "From Profiles to Pathways and Roots to Routes." *ANNALS of the American Academy of Political and Social Science* 618 (1): 80–94.

Horgan, John. 2006. "Understanding Terrorist Motivation: A Socio-Psychological Perspective." In *Mapping Terrorism Research: State of the Art, Gaps and Future Direction*, edited by Magnus Ranstorp, 106–26. London: Routledge.

Juergensmeyer, Mark. 2005. *Terror in the Mind of God: The Global Rise of Religious Terrorism*. Berkeley: University of California Press.

Kepel, Gilles. 2015. *Terreur dans l'Hexagone: Genèse du Jihad Français*. Paris: Gallimard.

Kepel, Gilles. 2004. *The War for the Muslim Minds: Islam and the West*. Cambridge, MA: Belknap Press of Harvard University Press.

Khosrokhavar, Farhad. 2016. "Jihad and the French Exception." *New York Times*, July 19, 2016.

Khosrokhavar, Farhad. 2014. *Radicalization*. Paris: Éd. de la Maison des Sciences de l'Homme.

Kleinmann, Scott, and Peter Neumann. 2013. "How Rigorous is Radicalization Research?" *Democracy and Security* 9 (4): 797–814.

Kruglanski, Arie, Jocelyn Bélanger, and Rohan Gunaratna. 2019. *The Three Pillars of Radicalization: Needs, Narratives, and Networks*. Oxford: Oxford University Press.

Kundnani, Arun. 2012. "Radicalization: The Journey of a Concept." *Race & Class* 54 (2): 3–25.

Laqueur, Walter. 2004. "The Terrorism to Come." *Hoover Institution: Policy Review*, August 1, 2004. https://www.hoover.org/research/terrorism-come

Laqueur, Walter. 1987. *The Age of Terrorism*. Boston: Little, Brown.

Mandel, David R. 2010. "Radicalization: What Does it Mean?" In *Home-Grown Terrorism: Understanding and Addressing the Root Causes of Radicalization among Groups with an Immigrant Heritage in Europe*, edited by Thomas M. Pick, Anne Speckhard, and Beatrice Jacuch, 101–13. Brussels: IOS Press.

McCauley, Clark, and Sophia Moskalenko. 2011. *Friction: How Radicalization Happens to Them and Us*. New York: Oxford University Press.

McCauley, Clark, and Sophia Moskalenko. 2008. "Mechanisms of Political Radicalization: Pathways toward Terrorism." *Terrorism and Political Violence* 20 (3): 415–33.

McCormick, Gordon H. 2003. "Terrorist Decision-Making." *Annual Review of Political Science* 6: 473–508.

Moghaddam, Fathali M. 2005. "The Staircase to Terrorism: A Psychological Exploration." *American Psychologist* 60 (2): 161–69.

Neumann, Peter. 2013. "The Trouble with Radicalization." *International Affairs* 89 (4): 873–93.

Neumann, Peter. 2008. "Introduction." In *Perspectives on Radicalisation and Political Violence: Papers from the First International Conference on Radicalisation and Political Violence*. London, 17–18 January. https://www.nonviolent-conflict.org/wp-content/uploads/2016/11/Perspectives-on-Radicalisation-Political-Violence.pdf

Patel, Faiza. 2011. *Rethinking Radicalization*. New York: Brennan Center for Justice at New York University School of Law.

Ranstorp, Magnus, ed. 2010. *Understanding Violent Radicalization: Terrorist and Jihadist Movements in Europe*. London: Routledge.

Ranstorp, Magnus. 2006. "Introduction: Mapping Terrorism Research—Challenges and Priorities." In *Mapping Terrorism Research: State of the Art, Gaps and Future Direction*, edited by Magnus Ranstorp, 106–26. London: Routledge.

Roy, Olivier. 2016. *Le Djihad et la Mort*. Paris: Le Seuil.

Roy, Olivier. 2004. *Globalized Islam: The Search for a New Ummah*. London: Hurst.

Sageman, Marc. 2004. *Understanding Terror Networks*. Philadelphia: University of Pennsylvania Press.

Schanzer, David H. 2014. "No Easy Day: Government Roadblocks and the Unsolvable Problem of Political Violence: A Response to Marc Sageman's 'The Stagnation in Terrorism Research.'" *Terrorism and Political Violence* 26 (4): 596–600.

Sedgwick, Mark. 2010. "The Concept of Radicalization as a Source of Confusion." *Terrorism and Political Violence* 22 (4): 479–94.

Silber, Mitchell D., and Arvin Bhatt. 2007. *Radicalization in the West: The Homegrown Threat*. New York: NYPD Intelligence Division.

Silke, Andrew. 2008. "Holy Warriors: Exploring the Psychological Processes of Jihadi Radicalization." *European Journal of Criminology* 5 (1): 99–123.

Stahelski, Anthony. 2005. "Terrorists Are Made, Not Born." *Cultic Studies* 4 (1): 1–10.

Stern, Jessica. 2003. *Terror in the Name of God: Why Religious Militants Kill*. New York: HarperCollins.

Taras, Raymond. 2012. *Xenophobia and Islamophobia in Europe*. Edinburgh: Edinburgh University Press.

The Soufan Group. 2015. *Foreign Fighters: An Updated Assessment of the Flow of Foreign Fighters into Syria and Irak*.

Tilly, Charles. 2003. *The Politics of Collective Violence*. Cambridge: Cambridge University Press.

Varvelli, Arturo, ed. 2016. "Jihadist Hotbeds: Understanding Local Radicalization Processes." *Instituto Per Gli Studi Di Politica Internazionale*, July 15. https://www.ispionline.it/it/pubblicazione/jihadist-hotbeds-understanding-local-radicalization-processes-15418

Veldhuis, Tinka, and Jorgen Staun. 2009. *Understanding Radicalisation: A Root Cause Model*. The Hague: Netherlands Institute of International Affairs Clingendael.

Victoroff, Jeff. 2005. "The Mind of the Terrorist: A Review and Critique of Psychological Approaches." *Journal of Conflict Resolution* 49 (1): 3–42.

Wieviorka, Michel. 1993. *The Making of Terrorism*. Chicago: University of Chicago Press.

Wiktorowicz, Quintan. 2005. *Radical Islam Rising: Muslim Extremism in the West*. Oxford: Rowman & Littlefield.

PART I

Theories

ONE

Economic Perspectives

Daniel Meierrieks and Tim Krieger

This chapter provides an *economic perspective* on the *radicalization process*, with terrorism as the most extreme outcome of this process. The term "radicalization" has no generally agreed-upon scientific definition; instead, its meaning is fluid and contains many security-loaded negative connotations (Pisoiu 2014). Our analysis is based on two definitions of the term "radicalization" that appear particularly fitting: According to Peter Neumann (2013, 874), radicalization is "the process whereby people become extremists"; extremism here referring to "'radically' different ideas about society and governance . . . [or] the (often violent or coercive) actions in which those ideas result" (2013, 875). Similarly, Anja Dalgaard-Nielsen (2010, 798) defines "violent radicalization" as "a process in which radical ideas are accompanied by the development of a willingness to directly support or engage in violent acts."

At the heart of any economic analysis of radicalization is a *behavioral model* that explains why people decide in a particular way or, more specifically, why they choose one out of several options under a resource constraint. For instance, economic analysis seeks to answer why a person spends (scarce) time on becoming an extremist rather than earning money or starting a family. As a first step, our economic analysis aims at uncovering the theoretical mechanisms that explain human behavior turning toward radical actions. We ask whether radicalization is a rational choice that ultimately leads to a "supply" of radical activity. Second, we study how *terror-*

ism entrepreneurs, that is, semi-professional organizations and their leaders that conduct and organize radical activities, guide individual radicalization. These entrepreneurs "demand" radicalized new members. Demand and supply for radicalism meet on the "market" for radicalism, where its (relative) price determines total radical activity (and, arguably, the number of people who start to radicalize). Third, economic analysis confronts theoretical predictions with empirical evidence. We especially focus on the role of *economic determinants* in explaining violent extremism. Here, the primary focus is on empirical evidence related to *terrorism*. There are several reasons for this focus. First, Neumann (2013) argues that the phenomenon of radicalization is intimately linked with the phenomenon of terrorism, especially after the 9/11 attacks. What is more, terrorism—as an outcome of radicalization processes—produces noticeable negative economic effects; the economic consequences of "cognitive radicalization" (Neumann 2013, 873), that is, of the genesis and proliferation of radical ideas, are far less tangible and thus more difficult to examine.[1] For another, terrorism is a measurable outcome (indicated by, e.g., the number of terrorist incidents occurring in a given country and year); this allows for the application of quantitative methods (e.g., regression analysis) commonly used in economics. By contrast, empirical analyses of behavioral changes toward radicalism are still rare in economics. Finally, *economic models of (processes toward) deviant behavior* (rather than of deviant ideas) already exist, most famously Gary S. Becker's (1968) economic-rational model of crime. It seems appropriate to apply—and subsequently refine—earlier economic models of crime to another form of illicit behavior: terrorism.

Radicalism and terrorism as the outcomes of radicalization processes remain serious threats to security. For instance, figure 1.1 shows the extent of terrorism in Western Europe between 2000 and 2015, with the data drawn from the *Global Terrorism Database* (LaFree and Dugan 2007). Each year, Western Europe saw dozens (if not hundreds) of terrorist attacks with dozens (if not hundreds) of victims, with 2015 being a particularly gruesome year (most prominently due to the November 2015 Paris attacks). In recent years, such attacks have become increasingly associated with Islamist radicalism, while former hotbeds of nationalist-separatist terrorism (especially Northern Ireland and the Basque country) have become

---

1. Statistical analyses of the economic consequences of terrorism have shown that terrorism negatively affects, for example, domestic investment, vulnerable economic sectors (e.g., tourism, transportation, etc.), and international trade, ultimately hurting economic growth and development. We refer to Sandler and Enders (2008), Meierrieks and Gries (2013), and Gaibulloev and Sandler (2019) for a further discussion of this issue.

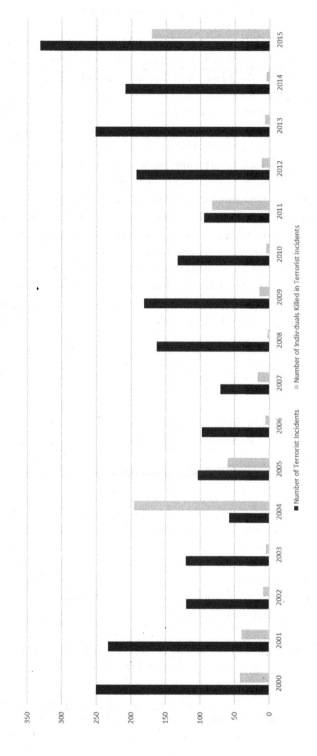

Fig. 1.1. Terrorism in Western Europe, 2000–2015

more peaceful. What is more, citizens of Western European countries have been attracted to joining foreign terrorist organizations (most prominently, *Al-Qaeda* and the *Islamic State*) in considerable numbers in recent years (Hegghammer 2013).

This chapter is organized as follows.[2] The second and third sections are devoted to a supply-side analysis. In the second section, we introduce a simple model of radicalism that is based—as common in economics—on behavioral concepts such as rationality, utility maximization, incentives, and cost-benefits analysis. We discuss the predictions of this model with respect to the role of socioeconomic factors (e.g., income, education) in determining radicalism and terrorism. Furthermore, we highlight the shortcomings of the radicalism model when it comes to explaining why people radicalize. Therefore, we also sketch an economic model of the process of radicalization. In the third section, we present an overview of empirical studies on the socioeconomic determinants of terrorism at the individual and country level. From this review, we learn that empirical evidence is too ambiguous to be explained by supply-side considerations only. This is why the fourth section separates the concepts of supply and demand for radicalism and terrorism by introducing the idea of terrorist entrepreneurs. The fifth section concludes.

The Supply Side: An Economic-Theoretical Framework of Radicalization and Terrorism

Radicals as Rational Actors

Economic models of deviant behavior resemble models of labor supply, in which there is a trade-off between (legal) individual labor supply and the *supply of illegal activities* (e.g., crime, terrorism, etc.). Models of this type rely—like all standard models in economics—on the representation of human behavior in accordance with the idea of the "economic man" or *homo economicus* whose behavior is characterized as follows (e.g., Kirchgässner 2008; Sandler and Enders 2004; Becker 1968):

1. When an individual has to decide between different actions, they take into account *preferences* and *restrictions*.

---

2. Note that this chapter draws in parts on Krieger and Meierrieks (2017; 2013; 2011), Krieger (2013), Meierrieks (2014), and Schneider, Brück, and Meierrieks (2015).

2. In accordance with this *economic calculus*, the individual chooses the action that maximizes utility (or expected utility).
3. This utility-maximization behavior implies *rationality*. It assumes that individuals follow their own intentions (i.e., their own preferences) so as to act to the best of their (relative) advantage given certain constraints.

Thinking of radicals or terrorists as rational actors seems to run counter to public perception, where radicals and terrorists (especially suicide terrorists) are usually deemed "irrational." However, psychological studies of terrorist behavior provide little evidence that terrorists routinely suffer from mental incapacities (Victoroff 2005). As summarized by Marc Sageman (2004, 83), the "failure of mental illness as an explanation for terrorism is consistent with three decades of research that has been unable to detect any significant pattern of mental illness in terrorists."

What is more, rationality in the context of the economic analysis of radicalism and terrorism does not imply that the *homo economicus* operates like a human computer. Rather, it suggests that a rational individual is able to gauge their freedom of action and consequently choose an action that is to their relative advantage. If circumstances change, the individual will *systematically* (i.e., in a predictable way) change their behavior (Kirchgässner 2008). This will still be the case when radicals and terrorists behave in ways that are "boundedly rational" (Simon 1955), which implies that they decide rationally only up to the point where a sufficient (but not the maximum) level of utility has been achieved.

The Radical's Calculus

Most economic models compare different equilibrium outcomes but tend to ignore the dynamics of moving from the old to a new equilibrium. More specifically, the economic analysis of radicalism typically compares states of the world with more or less (supply of) radical activity; how a person turned into a radical in the first place (that is, the process of radicalization) is rarely considered. In the following, we will first turn to the standard economic approach and investigate the factors that explain why the number of radical actions may change between two points in time. Afterward, we will make the radicalization process explicit and explain it using a broader economic approach that includes the possibility of boundedly rational behavior.

Our economic analysis starts with an examination of the *radical's calculus* that models the decision of "being" a radical or not. For our discussion, we suppose a (potential) radical may choose between two actions:

1. A non-radical activity that is associated with a specific level of utility. For instance, utility may arise from the consumption of a commodity that is purchased from a wage earned from employment (i.e., the supply of labor as a non-radical activity).
2. A radical activity that is associated with a specific level of utility. For instance, utility from (the supply of) radical behavior may be produced when such behavior induces political concessions from a government opposed by the radical.

Following our economic perspective, we expect the radical to consider the advantages (benefits) and disadvantages (costs) of these alternatives and choose the action corresponding to the higher net utility, where this decision implies (economic) rationality. If the radical activity is expected to maximize personal utility, the decision-maker ultimately chooses to conduct an (observable) radical activity.

The potential radical's economic calculus consists of three components. Each of these components is expected to influence their decision to behave radically or opt for the alternative (e.g., earn a living from regular employment).

First, the *direct or material costs* of being an extremist are one element of the radical's calculus. For instance, these costs are associated with joining a radical organization (which, e.g., may involve high information acquisition costs), perpetrating (potentially illicit) radical activities, and evading government punishment or surveillance (Schneider, Brück, and Meierrieks 2015).

Second, we have to consider the *benefits* of being a radical. These benefits are synonymous with the utility produced from the radical behavior. For one, benefits may accrue from achieving the long-run political, economic, religious, or social goals that underlie radicalism. For instance, government concessions (e.g., basing legislation on religious doctrine or refraining from foreign policy actions in the Islamic world) ought to benefit the members of radical groups (Schneider, Brück, and Meierrieks 2015). For another, radical actions may also produce "incidental benefits," such as donations from sympathizers and media attention that facilitates recruitment (Schneider, Brück, and Meierrieks 2015).

Third, the decision between two actions implies that the foregone utility (i.e., the *opportunity costs*) associated with the action not chosen has also been taken into account. For instance, given the choice between being a radical or not, the rewards from radicalism (e.g., political concessions) have to be weighed against the rewards from non-radicalism and non-violence, such as wages (and consumption) from participation in the ordinary economic life.

The idea of an economic calculus of a (potential) radical finally allows us to make a number of theoretical predictions: A person is more likely to supply radical activities when (1) the material costs of radicalism decrease, (2) the benefits of radicalism increase, or (3) the opportunity costs of radicalism decrease. In all these cases, the *relative price of radicalism* is affected in a way that makes radicalism more attractive. What is more, boundedly rational behavior may contribute to distorting the calculus in predictable ways. For instance, potential radicals may underestimate the costs of radicalism or overestimate its benefits (Abrahms 2006).

Economic Determinants of Radicalism: Theoretical Predictions

How can the theoretical framework outlined here predict radicalism (as the outcome of radicalization processes) and the supply of radical activity that is due to socioeconomic factors (as indicated by, e.g., poverty, unemployment, low levels of education)? Using an economic rational-choice representation of radicalism, we can make the following three predictions:

1. Poorer socioeconomic conditions reduce the direct costs of radicalism. For instance, operating a radical organization and evading government surveillance (e.g., via the establishment of safe houses) ought to become less expensive when socioeconomic conditions are unfavorable. This is because popular support for terrorism is expected to increase when economic conditions are poor and more potential radicals start to radicalize, which ought to dilute counter-radicalism efforts.[3]
2. Poorer socioeconomic circumstances are expected to increase the benefits of radicalism. For example, the potential payoff from radical activities (e.g., political concessions that alleviate socioeconomic hardship) is comparably more attractive during poor economic times.

---

3. Here, the idea is to also model the behavior of radicalization/terrorism *sympathizers* in an economic-rational fashion. In other words, the willingness to support rather than outright join radical organizations (e.g., through donations, the provision of information) is also subject to (opportunity) cost-benefit considerations. A further discussion of this idea can be found in Freytag et al. (2011).

3. Most important, poorer socioeconomic conditions affect the opportunity costs of radicalism. As stressed previously, these opportunity costs refer to the foregone utility associated with non-radical activity (e.g., from consumption of commodities purchased from wage income earned in the ordinary economic life). Arguably, poor socioeconomic conditions can be expected to constrain economic participation and consequently make the alternative (radicalism) a more attractive option for an economic-rational agent.

In sum, the predictions of an economic rational-choice model with respect to deteriorating socioeconomic conditions are straightforward. As argued by authors such as S. Brock Blomberg, Gregory D. Hess, and Akila Weerapana (2004b) and Andreas Freytag and colleagues (2011), *poorer socioeconomic conditions ought to translate into more radical activity* because they reduce the material costs of radicalism, increase its (expected) benefits, and, arguably most important, reduce its opportunity costs. At the individual level, this ought to lead to more potential radicals who actually start to radicalize.

An Economic Perspective on the Radicalization Process

Our simple model of radicalism has focused so far on the choice between non-radicalism (and thus, economic activity) and radicalism, thereby comparing two equilibrium states with and without radical activities. The definitions of radicalization presented in the introduction suggest, however, that radicalization is a *process with multiple steps*. In order to provide a sufficiently simple and intuitive economic analysis of the radicalization process, we follow Erik Pruyt and Jan Kwakkel (2014) by assuming that the process of radicalization can be split into different stages that can be analyzed separately. Here, in its first stage the radicalization process leads from non-activism to *political activism*, in the second stage from political activism to *extremism*, and in the final stage from extremism to *violent extremism* or terrorism. Individuals at these stages of radicalization are assumed to respond differently to economic incentives, exhibiting different economic calculi.

At the first stage of the radicalization process, the calculus is clear-cut. When economic conditions deteriorate, incentives for political activism increase. Given that the costs of political activism are—particularly in democracies—very low, we expect socioeconomic contractions to result in more political activism.

At the second stage of the radicalization process, the calculus changes. In particular, it becomes more costly to join an extremist radical organization (e.g., compared to joining a legitimate political party) because such organizations are rarer and information about the costs and benefits of membership are less clear. Furthermore, there is a *collective action problem* (Olson 1965) because many political activists—while supporting extremist ideas—consider active participation too costly. In plain terms, these persons free-ride on other extremists' activities, shying away from carrying the costs themselves.

At the final stage of radicalization, the calculus adjusts again. For one, the information costs associated with joining a *violent* extremist organization (e.g., with respect to finding such a clandestine organization in the first place) may become prohibitively high. Furthermore, we can expect violent extremists (i.e., terrorists) to be less responsive to socioeconomic incentives. In particular, the set of choices for violent radicals is limited. They cannot easily re-join the ordinary economic life even as economic conditions improve. Rather, their choice is between punishment (e.g., prison) and continued violent extremism. Facing these two choices, a violent extremist may very well choose a continuation of violence.

In sum, conceptualizing radicalization as a process and applying the economic concepts of full and bounded rationality (the latter being closely related to the issue of information acquisition costs) may further explain how socioeconomic variables are related to radicalism and terrorism. Radicalization involves changes in the calculus of individuals undergoing this process. Hence, an economic theory of the radicalization process adds valuable insights into why and how specific empirical outcomes emerge.

Economic Determinants of Radicalism: Empirical Evidence

Empirical studies that analyze whether socioeconomic variables and radicalism are related are usually carried out at the individual or the country level.[4] The former approach correlates data on the socioeconomic circumstances of individuals (e.g., their employment status, personal income) with the likelihood of them becoming radicals (e.g., joining an Islamist terror-

---

4. For the sake of brevity, we largely disregard variables that may matter at the meso level (i.e., at the level of the radical organization such as group dynamics, network effects, or the organizational structure of a radical organization). Analyses of radicalism and terrorism at the group level can be found in, for example, Cronin (2006) and Blomberg, Gaibulloev, and Sandler (2011).

ist organization) or supporting radicalism. The latter approach means to correlate macroeconomic data (e.g., on unemployment rates or per capita income) with the number of terrorist incidents occurring in a country during a specific period of time.

Individual-Level Evidence

A first set of empirical studies focuses on the individual characteristics of radicals and terrorists. For one, these studies examine the role of socio-demographic (non-economic) factors, such as marital status, age, religion, ethnicity, or sex, in explaining participation in radical groups. For instance, participants in terrorism are usually male and rather young (e.g., Gambetta and Hertog 2016). For another, they account for the role of socioeconomic variables, most importantly employment status, personal wealth, and income, as well as levels of education. In line with our prior theoretical discussion, we would expect sound socioeconomic circumstances (i.e., being employed, well-off, and well educated) to negatively predict participation in radicalism and terrorism.

Interestingly, though, these predictions are not in line with the empirical evidence on the individual level. Rather, higher standards of living and levels of education are *positively* associated with the individual decision to participate in terrorism (e.g., Krueger 2008; Berrebi 2007; Krueger and Malečková 2003). For instance, Alan Krueger and Jitka Malečková (2003) find that terrorists active in the Arab-Israeli conflict are in fact fairly well-off and educated. At a minimum, the evidence suggests that active terrorists do not especially suffer from socioeconomic deprivation.

Focusing more specifically on Islamist radicalism, similar patterns emerge. For instance, studying a sample of homegrown U.S. Islamic terrorists in comparison to non-radical U.S. Muslims, Krueger (2008, 295) finds that the "alleged homegrown Islamic terrorists that were studied [do] not appear especially deprived." Similarly, based the characteristics of 77 homegrown Islamist terrorists in the United Kingdom, Yener Altunbas and John Thornton (2011, 263) find that the homegrown Islamist terrorists "are often drawn from well educated, middle-class or high-income families." Diego Gambetta and Steffen Hertog (2016, 10), in a study of 497 individuals who have been active in Islamist militant groups, find that "violent Islamist radicals . . . are vastly more educated than their compatriots," with almost half of the individuals studied having a degree in engineering. The researchers (2016, 33) conclude "that university students and graduates generally are vastly overrepresented among Islamist radicals . . .

[implying that] the core of the Islamist movement emerged from would-be elites, not from the poor and the dispossessed."

Overall, terrorist activity appears to be supplied by members of the middle and upper classes who are relatively highly educated (Sageman 2004). Crucially, the finding that sound socioeconomic circumstances (especially education and income) positively predict participation in radical activities is at odds with our economic rational-choice model of radicalism.

Popular Support for Islamist Terrorism

There also exist a number of empirical studies analyzing the individual correlates of support for Islamist terrorism. This support is a first step for potential radicals toward entering a radicalization process. We provide an overview of the various findings in table 1.1. Here, answers to specific survey questions (regarding an individual's level of support for suicide terrorism, anti-American terrorism, and Islamist terrorism in general) are correlated with socioeconomic and non-economic characteristics of the survey respondents.

As shown in table 1.1, most studies reviewed suggest that poorer individual socioeconomic circumstances do not translate into stronger support for Islamist militancy. In other words, similar to active participation in violent extremism, socioeconomic circumstances also only have limited explanatory power to predict passive support for violent extremism by Islamist militants. If we assume that potential terrorism supporters and sympathizers behave at least as rationally as their more violent counterparts, the findings reported in table 1.1 are again not consistent with a rational-choice representation of radicalism.

Macro-Level Evidence

Another (much more extensive) set of empirical analyses investigates the effect of socioeconomic conditions on the emergence of radicalism and terrorism at the country level. For one, these studies use data on socioeconomic variables measured at the country level (indicating, e.g., per capita income, poverty levels, unemployment, or economic growth rates). For another, these empirical analyses also control for non-economic factors that may also be associated with terrorist activity, such as political or demographic variables (indicating, e.g., a country's political regime and population size).

Considering the socioeconomic determinants of terrorism, a first strand

TABLE 1.1. Socioeconomic Conditions and Support for Islamist Terrorism

Study	Scope	Main Results
Fair and Shepherd (2006)	14 Muslim countries, 2002	Unclear influence of economic conditions on support. Low socioeconomic status (lack of food) negatively predicts support; measures of high socioeconomic status (access to computers) positively predicts support.
Bueno de Mesquita (2007)	13 Muslim countries, 2002	Support for terrorism not correlated with education and personal economic situation.
Tessler and Robbins (2007)	Algeria and Jordan, 2002	Support for terrorism not dependent upon personal economic situation or personal assessment of country's economic situation.
Shafiq and Sinno (2010)	6 Muslim countries, 2005	Effects of income and education vary across countries and interact with political dissatisfaction.
Mousseau (2011)	14 Muslim countries, 2002	Approval of Islamist terrorism linked to urban poverty but not with other measures of poor socioeconomic circumstances (e.g., lack of education, poverty, income dissatisfaction).

of the literature is indeed consistent with the rational-choice theory of radicalism and terrorism outlined previously. That is, a number of studies find that higher levels of income and lower levels of poverty are obstacles to the production of terrorism (Caruso and Schneider 2011; Freytag et al. 2011; Blomberg and Hess 2008). For instance, Freytag and colleagues (2011) find that countries with higher per capita income levels are less likely to experience terrorism. Furthermore, there is evidence connecting solid short-run economic conditions (especially sound economic growth) with less political violence (Freytag et al. 2011; Blomberg, Hess, and Weerapana 2004a). For instance, Blomberg, Hess, and Weerapana (2004a) find that economic downturns correlate with increased terrorist activity.

A second strand of the literature establishes indirect linkages between socioeconomic conditions and the emergence of terrorist activity. First, these studies argue that policies of economic integration and liberalization tend to reduce terrorism by fostering economic growth and development. For instance, Quan Li and Drew Schaub (2004) show that higher levels of economic integration (e.g., trade openness) are negatively related to terrorism through their beneficial effect on economic development. Second, social welfare policies and functioning social safety nets are associated with less terrorism by removing economic grievances (Krieger and Meierrieks 2010; Burgoon 2006). Third, economic policies that counter economic discrimination of minorities lead to less terrorism, as such discrimination may have otherwise motivated terrorism (Piazza 2011). In other words, these findings are in line with rational-choice expectations in that socioeconomic progress (induced by specific policies that promote economic liberalization, economic non-discrimination, and economic security) affects the calculus of radicals in ways that make violence (observed at the macro level) less attractive.

A third strand of the literature, however, is far more skeptical about the pacifying effects of socioeconomic development. In fact, the empirical mainstream (as, e.g., outlined in Gaibulloev and Sandler 2019; Gassebner and Luechinger 2011; Krieger and Meierrieks 2011) does not support the idea that terrorism has strong economic roots. These empirical studies (e.g., Basuchoudhary and Shughart 2010; Abadie 2006; Kurrild-Klitgaard, Justesen, and Klemmensen 2006; Piazza 2006; Tavares 2004; Krueger and Malečková 2003) instead find that *political and institutional variables* trump economic ones in statistical analyses. That is, even though these studies control for the effect of the economy on terrorism, they do not find that it matters once politico-institutional factors come into play. Rather, these studies find that (1) unfavorable politico-institutional conditions (e.g., political instability) offer opportunities for violent extremism, (2) a lack of political participation and poor institutional quality constitute root causes of terrorism, (3) international political factors (e.g., foreign policy) matter to terrorism, again suggesting that such factors matter more than socioeconomic variables, and (4) demographic stress (signaled by, e.g., large populations) is conducive to the emergence of conflicts. For instance, Atin Basuchoudhary and William Shughart (2010) find that ethnic tensions promote transnational terrorist activity.

Notably, the empirical studies discussed above investigate the relationship between terrorism, radicalism, and socioeconomic development *in general*. That is, these studies do not only focus on religious terrorism, arguably the current most dangerous and prominent form of terrorism, but instead use data on other kinds of terrorism as well.[5] However, a few studies (Brockhoff, Krieger, and Meierrieks 2016; Kis-Katos, Liebert, and Schulze 2014; Robison, Crenshaw, and Jenkins 2006) have analyzed whether there are distinctions between different (with respect to their ideological background) kinds of terrorism, also regarding their respective socioeconomic

---

5. As noted by, for example, Meierrieks and Gries (2013) and Gaibulloev and Sandler (2019), earlier waves of terrorism have been dominated by anarchist, nationalist-separatist, and left-wing agendas. The end of the Cold War coincided with the end of the wave of left-wing terrorism, with Islamist terrorism becoming more prominent.

roots. Here, the evidence suggests that there are differences but also commonalities in the causes of Islamist and non-religious (e.g., ethnic or left-wing) terrorism. Most important for our discussion, there is no evidence that Islamist terrorism responds differently to the socioeconomic environment than its non-religious counterparts. Thus, we can very well extrapolate from the evidence presented thus far to the specific subset of Islamist radicalism and terrorism.

Empirical Puzzles

In sum, the findings introduced in the last section do not outright invalidate our previously introduced rational-choice theory of radicalism. However, the evidence is generally inconclusive. In detail, our overview of the empirical literature on the economic determinants of radicalism at the individual and country level has unearthed two empirical puzzles concerning the predictions of our economic model of radicalism and terrorism:

1. On the micro level, socioeconomic status (e.g., income, education, etc.) may positively predict participation in and support for radical activities rather than deter it.
2. On the macro level, the evidence is generally inconclusive. In any case, poorer socioeconomic conditions do not automatically translate into more radicalism and terrorism.

In the next section, we discuss how these empirical puzzles can be reconciled with our economic model by considering demand-side effects. As we discuss next, the inconclusive evidence does not suggest that the economic model is incorrect but rather *incomplete*, particularly at the micro level.

Reconciling Theory and Evidence: The Demand Side of Radicalism and Terrorism

How can we explain that—at the individual level—better socioeconomic status (i.e., more wealth, higher incomes, higher levels of education) tends to positively predict active participation in violent radicalism? A promising way to solve this puzzle is to also consider the *demand side* of radicalism and terrorism. Here, the demand side refers to understanding terrorist organizations as *terrorist firms* and the leaders of those organizations as *terrorist entrepreneurs*. This accounts for a basic insight from economics, namely

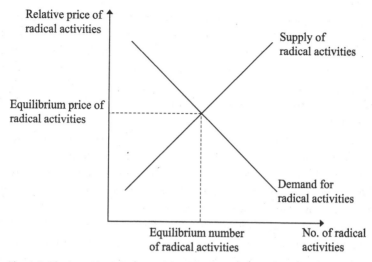

Fig. 1.2. The Interplay of Demand for and Supply of Radical Activities

that equilibrium prices and production (in our case, of extremism) result from the interaction of supply and demand (in our case, the supply of and demand for radical activity or, simply, extremists). Figure 1.2 shows how demand and supply determine the "market equilibrium."

Conceptualizing terrorist groups as firms and terrorist leaders as entrepreneurs and thus interpreting terrorist activity as a "business" or "enterprise" is a perspective taken by a number of academic contributions (e.g., Abdukadirov 2010; Zelinsky and Shubik 2009). Indeed, terrorist groups such as the *Islamic State* exhibit a number of characteristics they share with ordinary businesses. For instance, the Islamic State has an internal bureaucracy (e.g., designated to fighting, recruitment, propaganda, etc.), produces franchises (called "provinces" such as *Islamic State of Iraq and the Levant—Caucasus Province*), and exhibits an organizational hierarchy (with the "caliph" and a leadership council at the top).

Again, the economic analysis of the behavior of conventional firms and entrepreneurs rests on the well-known assumption of rationality.[6] Crucially, the actions of firms and entrepreneurs (e.g., with respect to choosing prices, levels of production) are chosen so that profit is maximized (e.g., Baumol 1968). This implies that production inputs (e.g., workers) are selected in a way that is conducive to *profit maximization*.

---

6. If one considers firms as impersonal entities, concepts like bounded rationality do not apply to them by definition.

The same mechanisms can also be expected to matter to the "production" of radicalism. That is, radical organizations are interested in maximizing their "profit," where this "profit" may be generated by donations from supporters, income from criminal activity (e.g., the drug trade), media attention, political concessions from the government, or the production of public goods to maximize political influence (e.g., Abdukadirov 2010; Ferrero 2005).

If we consider terrorist groups and their leaders to operate as businesses and business leaders, respectively, we can then examine how the socioeconomic profiles of prospective terrorist recruits matter to such profit-maximizing businesses. First, labor-economics considerations strongly suggest that education raises productivity, and this productivity gain is reflected in higher wages and profits (e.g., Becker 1962). An ordinary firm is thus expected to recruit more educated workers that raise productivity so as to maximize the firm's profit. Similarly, we expect that radical organizations trying to get people to radicalize would have available a large pool of potential radical followers from which members can be recruited so as to maximize "terrorist profits." This suggests that terrorist organizations will especially recruit the educated because educated members of radical organizations are more reliable and productive (e.g., with respect to "producing" violent extremism) than non-educated followers. Indeed, Efraim Benmelech and Claude Berrebi (2007), for example, find that Palestinian suicide bombers are more educated than the population average. They also find that more educated suicide bombers are more successful in producing damage (that is, they are more productive). Conversely, a violent extremist organization ought to be less interested in employing poorly educated or trained individuals.[7]

In sum, conceptualizing radical organizations as firms that produce an output in a way that maximizes their "profit" may help understand why participants in violent extremist groups tend to be rather well educated and well-off. Even though the supply side of radicalism may offer a pool of potential recruits with diverse socioeconomic backgrounds, the demand side (i.e., the radical organization and its leaders) ought to favor those recruits who are more educated, thus exhibiting a higher (expected) "terrorist productivity." Given that an individual's educational profile tends to closely correlate with their income (and also with the income/wealth of their family), we would expect to see—purely due to demand side

---

7. For instance, following this "business logic" it is not surprising that the Islamic State tends to use foreign recruits (who lack language skills and combat expertise) as expendable "cannon fodder."

considerations—participants of violent extremist groups to be on average better educated and having rather sound economic backgrounds.

This reasoning corresponds well to the model of radicalization stages introduced above, in which—at different stages—there are different levels of supply of radical activities that now meet different demands, expressed by different recruitment strategies. Today, for instance, initial contact with "would-be radicals" often takes place online, while actual recruitment for positions in a radical organization happens on a personal level.

Still, statistical analyses of the recruitment decisions of radical organizations remain—due to obvious data constraints—very scant, opening avenues for future research. For instance, it could be interesting to study what happens to those individuals (i.e., the less educated and thus poorer) who are "not in demand" by "terrorist firms" but still want to engage in extremist violence. One option may be that they self-radicalize and become lone wolf terrorists, but they could also be frustrated from being rejected by the terrorist group and reveal the group to counter-terrorism agencies.

Yet another interesting question is how boundedly rational or cognitively biased individuals respond to demand for radical services by extremist organizations. Economic theories of consumer marketing suggest that not fully rational potential radicals could be influenced by propaganda for the extremist cause. The same theories may provide valuable insights on whether and how it will be possible to undermine the extremists' strategies through appropriate countermeasures (e.g., counternarratives) at the different stages of the radicalization process.

Conclusion

Do radicalism and terrorism have socioeconomic roots? Why do individuals start to radicalize? As discussed in this chapter, economic theory provides interesting insights to these questions and shows how they are related. One important insight is that the answer to the first question should be yes. Socioeconomic improvements ought to make radicalism a less attractive option, especially by increasing the opportunity costs of radicalism. This prediction is derived from a simple economic model of radicalism that considers a radical to be a rational actor (i.e., a *homo economicus*) who maximizes utility and chooses radicalism over non-radicalism when the direct costs, benefits, and opportunity costs associated with radicalism are more favorable (i.e., utility-improving) compared to the (opportunity) costs and benefits of non-radicalism.

Empirical analyses of participation in and support for violent extremism (terrorism), however, show that the correlation between socioeconomic conditions and terrorism is rather weak at the country level and tends to be positive at the individual level. To reconcile these empirical findings with our theoretical deliberations, we discuss how our simple economic-rational model can be amended by relaxing the rationality assumption (to allow for bounded rationality) and—to provide an answer to the second question outlined above—by taking a closer perspective on the actual radicalization process. We also introduce the demand side of radicalism (where radical organizations favor the recruitment of educated members) to investigate the "market for radical activity"; only the combination of demand and supply effects can fully describe the radicalization process.

We argue that individual radicalization processes are complex and provide different incentives at different stages. These incentives are shaped by the "supply side" (i.e., potentially radicalized individuals and their living conditions) but also by the "market demand" for radical recruits. Regarding the first, there is no clear-cut relationship between socioeconomic factors and participating in violent extremism; regarding the latter, empirical evidence indicates that radical groups operate as "terrorist firms" that are interested in attracting well-educated (and thus comparatively better-off) recruits in the first place.

Underlying our reasoning is the question of whether socioeconomic variables do influence radicalization and, as its outcome, terrorism. If this is the case, economic and social policies could be employed to counter extremism. Based on our discussion, we advocate a more nuanced perspective on the role of economic factors in radicalization and terrorism. By explicitly analyzing the dynamics of the radicalization process from an economist's perspective, we are able to better recognize that socioeconomic deprivation may very well be important at the outset of the radicalization process but becomes less important as radicalization progresses. For instance, before joining the Islamic State, many European jihadists had criminal careers, suggesting that economic hardship was prominent in their lives and making them more susceptible to the radicals' call (Basra and Neumann 2016). However, and in accordance with our more elaborate model of radicalization, economic considerations are likely to matter less strongly the more radicalized individuals become (e.g., as they join an extremist mosque or even a terrorist organization) because the benefits of ordinary economic activity can be reaped less easily (e.g., as individuals have committed crimes during the radicalization process), while the benefits specific to radicalism (e.g., spiritual redemption; see Basra and Neumann 2016) begin to materialize.

What are the policy implications of our discussion? First, *after* radicalization has occurred (so that a country actually witnesses violent extremism, e.g., in the form of terrorism), policy measures that emphasize socioeconomic improvements may not be appropriate. Rather, government policies ought to influence the radical's calculus in different ways. As summarized by Friedrich Schneider, Tilman Brück, and Daniel Meierrieks (2015), the government may aim at raising the material costs of radicalism and terrorism by, for example, constraining access to weapons and explosives or raising penalties for extremist and terrorist offenses. It may also focus on reducing the benefits of extremism by, for example, denying a radical group media attention. However, during (and especially at the beginning of) the radicalization process socioeconomic improvements induced by political action (e.g., through redistribution, social welfare, and economic policies that promote economic growth) are more likely to be helpful. This is because we can expect non-radicals to be much more responsive to economic incentives than their already radicalized counterparts.

REFERENCES

Abadie, Alberto. 2006. "Poverty, Political Freedom, and the Roots of Terrorism." *American Economic Papers and Proceedings* 96 (2): 50–56. https://doi.org/10.1257/000282806777211847

Abdukadirov, Sherzod. 2010. "Terrorism: The Dark Side of Social Entrepreneurship." *Studies in Conflict & Terrorism* 33 (7): 603–17. https://doi.org/10.1080/1057610X.2010.484011

Abrahms, Max. 2006. "Why Terrorism Does Not Work." *International Security* 31 (2): 42–78. https://doi.org/10.1162/isec.2006.31.2.42

Altunbas, Yener, and John Thornton. 2011. "Are Homegrown Islamic Terrorists Different? Some UK Evidence." *Southern Economic Journal* 78 (2): 262–72.

Basra, Rajan, and Peter Neumann. 2016. "Criminal Pasts, Terrorist Futures: European Jihadists and the New Crime-Terror Nexus." *Perspectives on Terrorism* 10 (6): 25–40.

Basuchoudhary, Atin, and William F. Shughart. 2010. "On Ethnic Conflict and the Origins of Transnational Terrorism." *Defence and Peace Economics* 21 (1): 65–87. https://doi.org/10.1080/10242690902868343

Baumol, William J. 1968. "Entrepreneurship in Economic Theory." *American Economic Review Papers and Proceedings* 58 (2): 64–71.

Becker, Gary S. 1962. "Investment in Human Capital: A Theoretical Analysis." *Journal of Political Economy* 70 (5): 9–49. https://doi.org/10.1086/258724

Becker, Gary S. 1968. "Crime and Punishment: An Economic Approach." *Journal of Political Economy* 76 (2): 169–217. https://doi.org/10.1086/259394

Benmelech, Efraim, and Claude Berrebi. 2007. "Human Capital and the Productivity of Suicide Bombers." *Journal of Economic Perspectives* 21 (3): 223–38. https://doi.org/10.1257/jep.21.3.223

Berrebi, Claude. 2007. "Evidence about the Link Between Education, Poverty and Terrorism among Palestinians." *Peace Economics, Peace Science and Public Policy* 13 (1): 18–53. https://doi.org/10.2202/1554-8597.1101

Blomberg, S. Brock, and Gregory D. Hess. 2008. "From (No) Butter to Guns? Understanding the Economic Role in Transnational Terrorism." In *Terrorism, Economic Development, and Political Openness*, edited by Philip Keefer and Norman Loayza, 83–115. New York: Cambridge University Press.

Blomberg, S. Brock, Gregory D. Hess, and Akila Weerapana. 2004a. "An Economic Model of Terrorism." *Conflict Management and Peace Science* 21 (1): 17–28. https://doi.org/10.1080/07388940490433882

Blomberg, S. Brock, Gregory D. Hess, and Akila Weerapana. 2004b. "Economic Conditions and Terrorism." *European Journal of Political Economy* 20 (2): 463–78. https://doi.org/10.1016/j.ejpoleco.2004.02.002

Blomberg, S. Brock, Khusrav Gaibulloev, and Todd Sandler. 2011. "Terrorist Group Survival: Ideology, Tactics, and Base of Operations." *Public Choice* 149 (3–4): 441–63. https://doi.org/10.1007/s11127-011-9837-4

Brockhoff, Sarah, Tim Krieger, and Daniel Meierrieks. 2016. "Heterogeneous Terrorism: Determinants of Left-Wing and Nationalist-Separatist Terrorism in Western Europe." *Peace Economics, Peace Science and Public Policy* 22 (4): 393–401. https://doi.org/10.1515/peps-2016-0038

Bueno de Mesquita, Ethan. 2007. "Correlates of Public Support for Terrorism in the Muslim World." Washington: United States Institute for Peace. https://www.usip.org/sites/default/files/May2007.pdf

Burgoon, Brian. 2006. "On Welfare and Terror: Social Welfare Policies and Political-Economic Roots of Terrorism." *Journal of Conflict Resolution* 50 (2): 176–203. https://doi.org/10.1177/0022002705284829

Caruso, Raul, and Friedrich Schneider. 2011. "The Socioeconomic Determinants of Terrorism and Political Violence in Western Europe (1994–2007)." *European Journal of Political Economy* 27 (Supplement 1): S37–49. https://doi.org/10.1016/j.ejpoleco.2011.02.003

Cronin, Audrey Kurth. 2006. "How Al-Qaida Ends: The Decline and Demise of Terrorist Groups." *International Security* 31 (1): 7–48. https://doi.org/10.1162/isec.2006.31.1.7

Dalgaard-Nielsen, Anja. 2010. "Violent Radicalization in Europe: What We Know and What We Do Not Know." *Studies in Conflict & Terrorism* 33 (9): 797–814. https://doi.org/10.1080/1057610X.2010.501423

Fair, C. Christine, and Bryan Shepherd. 2006. "Who Supports Terrorism? Evidence from Fourteen Muslim Countries." *Studies in Conflict & Terrorism* 29 (1): 51–74. https://doi.org/10.1080/10576100500351318

Ferrero, Mario. 2005. "Radicalization as a Reaction to Failure: An Economic Model of Islamic Extremism." *Public Choice* 122 (1–2): 199–220. https://doi.org/10.1007/s11127-005-5792-2

Freytag, Andreas, Jens J. Krüger, Friedrich Schneider, and Daniel Meierrieks. 2011. "Cross-Country Estimates of Socioeconomic Determinants of Terrorism."

European Journal of Political Economy 27 (Supplement 1): S5–16. https://doi.org /10.1016/j.ejpoleco.2011.06.009

Gaibulloev, Khusrav, and Todd Sandler. 2019. "What We Have Learned about Terrorism since 9/11." *Journal of Economic Literature* 57 (2): 275–328. https://doi .org/10.1257/jel.20181444

Gambetta, Diego, and Steffen Hertog. 2016. *Engineers of Jihad: The Curious Connection Between Violent Extremism and Education.* Princeton: Princeton University Press.

Gassebner, Martin, and Simon Luechinger. 2011. "Lock, Stock, and Barrel: A Comprehensive Assessment of the Determinants of Terror." *Public Choice* 149 (3–4): 235–61. https://doi.org/10.1007/s11127-011-9873-0

Hegghammer, Thomas. 2013. "Should I Stay or Should I Go? Explaining Variation in Western Jihadists' Choice between Domestic and Foreign Fighting." *American Political Science Review* 107 (1): 1–15. https://doi.org/10.1017/S0003 055412000615

Kirchgässner, Gebhard. 2008. *Homo Oeconomicus.* Tübingen: Mohr Siebeck.

Kis-Katos, Krisztina, Helge Liebert, and Günther G. Schulze. 2014. "On the Heterogeneity of Terror." *European Economic Review* 68 (May): 116–36. https://doi .org/10.1016/j.euroecorev.2014.02.009

Krieger, Tim. 2013. "Calculating the Costs of 9/11." In *Beyond 9/11: Transdisciplinary Perspectives on Twenty-First Century U.S. American Culture*, edited by Christian Kloeckner, Simone Knewitz, and Sabine Sielke, 123–39. Frankfurt: Peter Lang.

Krieger, Tim, and Daniel Meierrieks. 2010. "Terrorism in the Worlds of Welfare Capitalism." *Journal of Conflict Resolution* 54 (6): 902–39. https://doi.org/10.11 77/0022002710367885

Krieger, Tim, and Daniel Meierrieks. 2011. "What Causes Terrorism?" *Public Choice* 147 (1/2): 3–27. https://doi.org/10.1007/s11127-010-9601-1

Krieger, Tim, and Daniel Meierrieks. 2013. "Terrorism: Causes, Effects and the Role of Money Laundering." In *Research Handbook on Money Laundering*, edited by Brigitte Unger and Dan Van der Linde, 78–92. Cheltenham: Edward Elgar.

Krieger, Tim, and Daniel Meierrieks. 2017. "How to Deal with International Terrorism." In *International Law and the Rule of Law under Extreme Conditions*, edited by Thomas Eger, Stefan Oeter, and Stefan Voigt, 223–47. Tübingen: Mohr Siebeck. https://papers.ssrn.com/sol3/papers.cfm?abstract_id=2479161

Krueger, Alan B. 2008. "What Makes a Homegrown Terrorist? Human Capital and Participation in Domestic Islamic Terrorist Groups in the U.S.A." *Economics Letters* 101 (3): 293–96. https://doi.org/10.1016/j.econlet.2008.09.008

Krueger, Alan B., and Jitka Malečková. 2003. "Education, Poverty and Terrorism: Is There a Causal Connection?" *Journal of Economic Perspectives* 17 (4): 119–44. https://doi.org/10.1257/089533003772034925

Kurrild-Klitgaard, Peter, Mogens K. Justesen, and Robert Klemmensen. 2006. "The Political Economy of Freedom, Democracy and Transnational Terrorism." *Public Choice* 128 (1): 289–315. https://doi.org/10.1007/s11127-006-9055 -7

LaFree, Gary, and Laura Dugan. 2007. "Introducing the Global Terrorism Database." *Terrorism and Political Violence* 19 (2): 181–204. https://doi.org/10.1080 /09546550701246817

Li, Quan, and Drew Schaub. 2004. "Economic Globalization and Transnational Terrorism: A Pooled Time-Series Analysis." *Journal of Conflict Resolution* 48 (2): 230–58. https://doi.org/10.1177/0022002703262869

Meierrieks, Daniel. 2014. "Economic Determinants of Terrorism." In *Understanding Terrorism: A Socioeconomic Perspective*, edited by Raul Caruso and Andrea Locatelli, 25–49. Bingley: Emerald Group Publishing. https://doi.org/10.1108 /S1572-8323(2014)0000022002

Meierrieks, Daniel, and Thomas Gries. 2013. "Causality between Terrorism and Economic Growth." *Journal of Peace Research* 50 (1): 91–104. https://doi.org/10 .1177/0022343312445650

Mousseau, Michael. 2011. "Urban Poverty and Support for Islamist Terror: Survey Results of Muslims in Fourteen Countries." *Journal of Peace Research* 48 (1): 35–47. https://doi.org/10.1177/0022343310391724

Neumann, Peter. 2013. "The Trouble with Radicalization." *International Affairs* 89 (4): 873–93.

Olson, Mancur. 1965. *The Logic of Collective Action: Public Goods and the Theory of Groups.* Cambridge, MA: Harvard University Press.

Piazza, James A. 2006. "Rooted in Poverty? Terrorism, Poor Economic Development, and Social Cleavages." *Terrorism and Political Violence* 18 (1): 159–77. https://doi.org/10.1080/095465590944578

Piazza, James A. 2011. "Poverty, Minority Economic Discrimination, and Domestic Terrorism." *Journal of Peace Research* 48 (3): 339–53. https://doi.org/10.1177/00 22343310397404

Pisoiu, Daniela. 2014. "Radicalization." In *The Oxford Handbook of European Islam*, edited by Jocelyne Cesari, 770–801. Oxford: Oxford University Press. https:// doi.org/10.1093/oxfordhb/9780199607976.013.9

Pruyt, Erik, and Jan H. Kwakkel. 2014. "Radicalization under Deep Uncertainty: A Multi-Model Exploration of Activism, Extremism, and Terrorism." *System Dynamics Review* 30 (1–2): 1–28. https://doi.org/10.1002/sdr.1510

Robison, Kristopher K., Edward M. Crenshaw, and J. Craig Jenkins. 2006. "Ideologies of Violence: The Social Origins of Islamist and Leftist Transnational Terrorism." *Social Forces* 84 (4): 2009–26. https://doi.org/10.1353/sof.2006.0106

Sageman, Marc. 2004. *Understanding Terror Networks.* Philadelphia: University of Pennsylvania Press.

Sandler, Todd, and Walter Enders. 2004. "An Economic Perspective on Transnational Terrorism." *European Journal of Political Economy* 20 (2): 301–16. https:// doi.org/10.1016/j.ejpoleco.2003.12.007

Sandler, Todd, and Walter Enders. 2008. "Economic Consequences of Terrorism in Developed and Developing Countries: An Overview." In *Terrorism, Economic Development, and Political Openness*, edited by Norman Loayza and Philip Keefer, 17–47. Cambridge: Cambridge University Press. https://doi.org/10.1017/CBO 9780511754388.002

Schneider, Friedrich, Tilman Brück, and Daniel Meierrieks. 2015. "The Economics of Counterterrorism: A Survey." *Journal of Economic Surveys* 29 (1): 131–57. https://doi.org/10.1111/joes.12060

Shafiq, M. Najeeb, and Abdulkader H. Sinno. 2010. "Education, Income, and Support for Suicide Bombings: Evidence from Six Muslim Countries." *Journal of Conflict Resolution* 54 (1): 146–78. https://doi.org/10.1177/0022002709351411

Simon, Herbert A. 1955. "A Behavioral Model of Rational Choice." *The Quarterly Journal of Economics* 69 (1): 99–118. https://doi.org/10.2307/1884852

Tavares, José. 2004. "The Open Society Assesses Its Enemies: Shocks, Disasters and Terrorist Attacks." *Journal of Monetary Economics* 51 (5): 1039–70. https://doi.org/10.1016/j.jmoneco.2004.04.009

Tessler, Mark, and Michael D. H. Robbins. 2007. "What Leads Some Ordinary Arab Men and Women to Approve of Terrorist Acts Against the United States?" *Journal of Conflict Resolution* 51 (2): 305–28. https://doi.org/10.1177/0022002706298135

Victoroff, Jeff. 2005. "The Mind of the Terrorist: A Review and Critique of Psychological Approaches." *Journal of Conflict Resolution* 49 (1): 3–42. https://doi.org/10.1177/0022002704272040

Zelinsky, Aaron, and Martin Shubik. 2009. "Research Note: Terrorist Groups as Business Firms: A New Typological Framework." *Terrorism and Political Violence* 21 (2): 327–36. https://doi.org/10.1080/09546550902771993

TWO

Social Movement Research

Daniela Pisoiu

Social movement research on what we now call "radicalization" was somewhat taken by surprise as the term emerged and took over in force the main discussions around involvement in terrorism and political violence. Social movement research already had a solidly established tradition of research on political violence, which included, for example, the left-wing terrorism of the 1970s—yet was not necessarily called *radicalization*. Indeed, social movement scholars initially avoided and even heavily contested both terms, terrorism and radicalization, on the reasoning that these phenomena are not sui generis, but rather types of political violence that emerged as further developments or consequences of other types of political violence. Complicating matters even more, the kinds of radicalization processes leading to terrorism had of course already been covered by the existing literature on (the psychology) of terrorism (Horgan 2004; Post, Sprinzak, and Denny 2003). Adding to this of course was also the specific, inherent focus of social movement literature on groups and movements, rather than individuals, whereas the "radicalization" literature specifically looked at individuals (see, e.g., Coolsaet 2013; Ranstorp 2010; and thousands more). As a result of these developments and constellations, the social movement research on radicalization—thus called—emerged a decade later and aimed to bridge classic social movement research and concepts, including on political violence, with terrorism and radicalization research concepts. The focus remains on groups and movements, though the individual also emerges at times—see for example the following definition: "a shift towards more violent forms of action, analyzed in particular at the level of groups or movements but also with respect to individual trajectories towards militant activism, and embedded in its social and political context as well as broader processes of contention" (Malthaner 2017, 373). More specifically, the social movement literature on radicalization places itself in the broader social movement approach categorized as "relational"—that is, emphasizing interaction and process, and which in turn emerged out of the "contentious politics" school. Although formally placed in a different discipline, some of the findings, concepts, and theoretical models developed here very much parallel socio-psychological ones, in particular regarding the relevance of (immaterial) rewards and selected group mechanisms. They also parallel those found in political science, especially concerning the behavior of groups among themselves and in relation to the state. Broadly speaking, social movement literature sees actors within a rational choice paradigm (thus dismissing structures as causal factors); however they also consider the role of context and ideology as scripts for action at a certain point along the radicalization process.

This chapter will thus deal to a fair extent with the social movement *relational* literature on radicalization and discuss its merits and pitfalls. Secondly, I approach a separate branch of social movement research that has concentrated more particularly on "culture" and has more or less resorted to social movement concepts. Thirdly, I outline how other disciplines and mixed social movement research on this topic have often resorted to concepts outside its field proper, in particular psychology and social psychology. Finally, I outline a series of apparent irregularities that require additional empirical research and possibly theoretical revisions. Before engaging in these topics, it is important to outline the work of a scholar who can be credited with not only placing the stepping stone of the social movement research on terrorism—in the specific jargon, political violence or "clandestine" political violence—but also whose work rises beyond the boundaries and limitations of particular paradigms.

How Everything Began: The 1990s Looking Back at the '70s

One of the most often quoted drawbacks of terrorism research is the lack of primary data (Silke 2001). On the reverse, classical works that have used large amounts of primary data and analyzed them systematically—such as the one funded by the German Ministry of the Interior in the 1980s, exploring the biographies, ideologies, and socio-psychological processes of the Red Army Faction (BMI 1981)—are highly regarded and often referenced, especially when evidence is needed to confirm or disprove a new theory. One such classical work is *Social Movements, Political Violence, and the State: A Comparative Analysis of Italy and Germany* by Donatella della Porta (1995). At the time, the author spent a relatively large amount of time arguing why social movement research and theory should also go over the topic of political violence, rather than solely dealing with the "good" social movements such as human rights, democracy, and so forth. This innovative study then set out to mobilize the (at the time) state-of-the-art Social Movement Theory, namely political process theory, to explain the emergence and activities of two major modern terrorist groups in Europe: the Red Army Faction and the Red Brigades. Political process theory reunites three strands of theory that developed as a reaction to the initial "strain" approach social movements. What these critiques started with was the observation that grievance is ubiquitous, whereas protest is not. The three strands were: *resource mobilization*, *political opportunities*, and *framing*. To this day, these remain the classical approaches to the study of social movements, and they have been to a lesser or a greater extent also applied to political violence.

More recently, Anthony Oberschall (2004) reunited these three approaches in reference to terrorism and argued that terrorism is a form of collective action that can be explained in the same way as other forms of collective action, like social movements, guerrillas, dissidents, or insurgencies. He applied the four dimensions of collective action to terrorism and argued that each of the following dimensions was a necessary factor for a group to become active as a terrorist collective. These are: (1) discontent, (2) ideology-feeding grievances, (3) the capacity to organize, and (4) political opportunity. Firstly, there has to be widespread discontent and a lack of relief. Discontent furthermore demarcates a terrorist group from a criminal gang, which only acts in the pursuit of personal goals. Secondly, there must be an ideology that frames discontent into grievances, and this must be spread widely throughout the population. It holds political elites responsible and justifies violence as a means to change the status quo. The legitimization of the terrorist cause is important, as it secures the cover for the group among the population. Thirdly, there must be the capacity to mobilize and organize to recruit new members, acquire funds and weapons, hide safely, coordinate, and communicate with each other. This, Oberschall argues, is only possible if the group is perceived by the population as legitimate and not deviant. Finally, there must be a favorable political climate, a political opportunity, or public support by allies or (foreign) states that facilitates the collective action of a terrorist group.

In a later work, della Porta (2013) expanded her model both in depth and breadth to develop a series of new mechanisms of engagement and applied them to right-wing Islamist and separatist clandestine organizations. These mechanisms are: escalating policing, competitive escalation, and the activation of militant networks, followed by organizational compartmentation, action militarization, ideological encapsulation, and militant enclosure. *Escalating policing* essentially summarizes the interaction between social movements and the state and is in effect the central explanatory mechanism for the emergence of clandestine political violence.

> Political violence throughout the world is intertwined with state responses to social movements in a sort of macabre dance. A mechanism of escalating policing can be identified at the onset of clandestine political violence in both democratic and authoritarian regimes. In the cases analyzed in this text, a reciprocal adaptation brought about an escalation of protest forms and approaches to policing. Policing was in fact perceived as tough and, especially, indiscriminate and unjust; transformative repressive events contributed to justifying violence and pushing militant groups toward clandestinity. (della Porta 2013, 33)

Della Porta (2013, 36) goes on to argue that the protest becomes further radicalized mainly due to policing. This mechanism was indeed first developed drawing on the developments associated with left-wing terrorism in the 1970s, and it could also credibly be applied to the Euskadi Ta Askatasuna (ETA) and Islamist movements in Egypt. When discussing the case of Al-Jamaa, della Porta demonstrates an apt example for this mechanism within the Salafist spectrum: namely that the repression of the Muslim Brotherhood and its subsequent transformation toward using peaceful means of protest strengthened Al-Jamaa, as the more radical activists started to turn to militancy and action as a way to reach their political goals (2013, 58). The complex account of how this mechanism impacts radicalization is very convincing, and the examples brought forward are equally so. Repression acts in various ways to foster radicalization through discouragement of moderates, radicalization of moderates, spirals of violence or "reciprocal adaptation of tactics" (2013, 68), the incidence of transformative and emotionally charged events, cognitive effects confirming the propaganda, or the perception that there is no other way out. The idea of threat, particularly in relation to one's own community, is a constant motivation for radicalization and was in fact identified as one of the few factors always present in individual radicalization pathways (Jensen, Atwell Seate, and James 2018). Yet, the specific relation and interaction with the state—so central in social movement scholarship—has been somewhat neglected in the radicalization one, possibly because both jihadi and right-wing radicalization in Europe, both paramount in contemporary times, have directly engaged the state to a lesser extent than left-wing terrorism in the past. Only some authors have discussed the role of state actions in radicalization—see for example the concept of co-radicalization (Logvinov 2017; Hummel and Pisoiu 2014).

The second mechanism at the onset phase of clandestine political violence is *competitive escalation*. This mechanism is in effect similar in nature to the first one, as it refers to the increase and intensification of violence, yet it differs in terms of actors. It is not a confrontation between the movement and the state, but between the movement and opposing movements, and between parts of the same movement. In regard to the latter, della Porta (2013, 112) concludes in relation to her cases that "the radicalization of repertoires of action was, in some movements, a competitive asset in intermovement relations." As organizations competed for support of the same constituencies, imitation and outbidding took place. This mechanism clearly parallels the outbidding thesis in the terrorism literature (Bloom 2004).

With the *activation of militant networks*, della Porta addresses a central mechanism in radicalization: namely the continuity of social networks from earlier less radical stages through militancy and ultimately terrorism. In the conclusion of her case studies on this mechanism, della Porta notes first of all that networks of friends, relatives, and political peer groups are likely to highly influence political choices—radical or moderate. Thus, participation in groups with links to radical networks increases the chances of an individual being recruited into a radical movement. Specifically, in all four types of clandestine violence della Porta found that "peer groups to which individuals belonged played a very important role in determining their successive political choices (for instance, joining a more structured movement's organization), particularly in passages from low-risk to high-risk activism" (della Porta 2013, 143). Moreover, friendship often fortified the level of commitment and vice versa. These relational processes strengthened underground groups and also created new ones (143–44). The role of social networks in recruitment—through both friendship and kinship—is also broadly known (e.g., Sageman 2004). For jihadi radicalization, the peculiar reoccurrence of siblings in terror attacks has been noted. What the social movement literature and this work (as well as della Porta's 1995 research) adds is a deeper analysis of the significance of these relationships after joining, in particular the reciprocal relationship to commitment, as well as to socialization into the ideology.

A further mechanism is *organizational compartmentalization*, which refers to parts of the movement splitting, going underground, and becoming more violent. Della Porta (2013, 147) argues that splinter groups exploit environments favorable to militancy and "undergo further radicalization and eventually create new resources and occasions for violence. These radical groups, in other words, themselves become agents, or entrepreneurs, for the propagation of violence." In della Porta's analysis, organizational compartmentalization occurs as an adaptation to increasing repression and decreasing support. Aside from accounting for this dynamic, della Porta also takes the opportunity to position herself with regard to the logic of action in such organizations, namely between ideological determinism and instrumentalism, or the strategic approach. While rejecting the fact that organizational behavior might be determined by ideological content, she acknowledges the effect of internal norms on this behavior, as interests are cognitively constructed and strategic choices are both normatively constrained and dependent on the ways opportunities and resources are perceived (della Porta 2013, 148). In recognizing restricted strategic choices, della Porta draws on the broader neoinstitutionalist scholarship and considers organizations as "socializing agents and as producers of norms" (149). This approach parallels in its eventual conclusion the devoted actor model, according to which "sacred values and identity fusion interact to produce willingness to make costly sacrifices for a primary reference group even unto death, that is, sacrificing the totality of self-interests" (Atran 2016).

Della Porta also offers here a preview of the following mechanisms: *action militarization* and *ideological encapsulation*. Violence increases and evolves from discriminate to indiscriminate violence—again under the effects of repression, but also as a consequence of internal competition for leadership—while ideology becomes increasingly obscure and an instrument for internal consumption. In describing action militarization, della Porta formulates this evolution as a transition from propaganda-oriented actions to actions that are inner-oriented and simply aimed at organizational survival (against the state)—in other words, the logic of propaganda vs. the logic of survival. Specifically, della Porta (2013, 178) argues that "in all of the four types of clandestine violence . . . the more isolated the groups and the stronger the repression, the more they gave up propaganda aims and focused on organizational survival." This mechanism manifests itself through increasing lethality and brutality, with attacks becoming (more) indiscriminate; this is again traced back to decreasing support and increasing repression: "although action tended initially to propagate the aims of the clandestine organizations in the broader population, with the passing of time—and rising and more focused repression—all the groups concentrated their attention on the internal war with the state" (della Porta 2013, 202). Ideological encapsulation designates a thinking characterized by Manichean worldviews, overly simplified generalizations, fear of contamination, essentialization of violence as valuable per se, and so on. The importance of dichotomous views for radicalization cannot be overstated (see, e.g., Weis and Zick 2007), and social movement literature has made an important contribution in explaining how these emerged within groups in the first place.

Relational Approaches to Radicalization

Relational approaches to radicalization build on relational approaches to social movements, which in turn are part of the "contentious" research program. The latter was initiated by Douglas McAdam, Sidney Tarrow, and Charles Tilly (2001) as a reaction to the lack of nuance within the classic social movement research program. Tilly (2003) took this further with particular application to violence. Contentious politics refers to "episodic, public, collective interaction among makers of claims and their objects when (a) at least one government is a claimant, an object of claims, or a party to the claims and (b) the claims would, if realized, affect the interests of at least one of the claimants" (McAdam, Tarrow, and Tilly 2001, 5). The idea of the book was to show that various forms of contention, such as social movements, revolutions, strike waves, nationalism, and democratization, involve similar mechanisms and processes (2001, 4).

The authors involved in this research program had previously contributed to the "political process" program. Originating from a structuralist tradition and having focused on a range of "contentious politics" in Europe and North America, the authors describe their subsequent evolution as one where they "discovered the necessity of taking strategic interaction, consciousness, and historically accumulated culture into account" (McAdam, Tarrow, and Tilly 2001, 22). They go on to explain that social communication, social ties, and dialogue should be perceived "as active sites of creation and change" rather than simply through structural, rational, and cultural explanations (22). As such, they shifted their focus of research from the more typical social movement variables (i.e., opportunities, threats, framing, and structures) toward *explanatory* mechanisms and processes—mobilization, actors, and trajectories (32–34). This means that authors working on radicalization in this theoretical tradition have seen as their paramount mission the discovery and further development of "mechanisms."

Tilly (2003, 19–20) defined causal mechanisms originally as:

> Mechanisms are causes on the small scale: similar events that produce essentially the same immediate effects across a wide range of circumstances. Analysts often refer to large-scale causes (poverty, widespread frustration, extremism, resource competition, and so on), proposing them as necessary of sufficient conditions for whole episodes of collective violence. Here, in contrast, we search for recurrent small-scale mechanisms that produce identical immediate effects in many different circumstances yet combine variously to generate very different outcomes on the large scale.

Mechanisms are less than laws aiming at "selective explanation of salient features by means of partial causal analogies" (Goodin and Tilly 2006). Moreover, they are neither exclusive nor sufficient, but can be central and "robust" if despite different situations and settings they materialize in similar forms with the same effects (Goodin and Tilly 2006, 14). Mechanisms have also been classified in three categories—environmental, cognitive, and relational—whereby this scholarship clearly predominantly talks about relational mechanisms. Environmental mechanisms "alter relations between the social circumstances in question and their external environment, as for example when drought depletes the agriculture on which guerillas depend for their day-to-day survival." Cognitive mechanisms "operate through alterations of individual and collective perceptions, as when members of a fighting group decide collectively that they have mistaken an enemy for a friend." Finally, relational mechanisms "change connections among social units, as when a gang leader makes a deal with a cocaine wholesaler and thus converts petty protection rackets into high-risk drug merchandizing" (Tilly 2003, 20). Robert Goodin and Charles Tilly (2006) elaborate again on these three types of mechanisms. In terms of environmental mechanisms, they point to external conditions and settings that may have an impact on social life. Namely, words such as "disappear," "enrich," "expand," and "disintegrate" that relate to individuals' environments can manipulate social interactions. Moreover, cognitive mechanisms are depicted through words such as "recognize," "understand," "reinter-pret," and "classify," as they indicate how individuals and groups perceive changes. Finally, relational mechanisms are described through words like "ally," "attack," "subordinate," and "appease" (Goodin and Tilly 2006, 16).

An example of a relational mechanism would be boundary activation, which refers to a shift in social interactions so that they organize increas-ingly around an "us vs. them" boundary and differentiate between within-boundary and cross-boundary interactions (Tilly 2003, 20). In the earlier book on dynamics of contention, McAdam, Tarrow, and Tilly (2001) men-tion a series of mechanisms, such as competition for power, diffusion, and repression. Diffusion is the shift of similar forms and "claims of contention" across different boundaries and ideologies. Repression refers to attempts to quell contentious acts by individuals or groups (68–9). The authors argue that repression has predictable consequences on threatened groups such as: strengthening their resistance; fostering a shift in tactics to avoid detec-tion; and deterring other groups from mobilizing and acting. Moreover, repression could be "selective" and isolate the more militant groups, or repression could be "generalized" whereby more moderates start to turn toward the extremists (69). These mechanisms reflect especially in della Porta's work. Another relevant mechanism for our discussion is radicaliza-tion, or, as McAdam, Tarrow, and Tilly put it, "the expansion of collective action frames to more extreme agendas and the adoption of more trans-gressive forms of contention" (2001, 69, emphasis removed).

Following the precepts of the contentious politics school, younger scholars have set to apply and develop these concepts further. Possibly under the influence of the new radicalization paradigm, they have effec-tively conceptualized the entire spectrum of mechanisms toward political violence as radicalization; the latter is thus no longer just a mechanism. Eitan Alimi, Lorenzo Bosi, and Chares Demetriou (2015), for example, list 30 sub-mechanisms, among which are the ones mentioned above. They look at the emergence of Al-Qaeda, the Red Brigades, and Ethniki Organosis Kyprion Agoniston (EOKA) from the respective broader move-ments and create a model based on a combination of identified mecha-nisms. In an earlier article, they introduced their theoretical framework as "Relational Dynamics and Processes of Radicalization: A Comparative Framework" (2012). In addition to the existing "mechanisms," they also present the concept of "arenas of interaction" where the actual exchanges between the actors take place. These arenas of interaction correspond to four general relational mechanisms, which however do not cover all drivers of radicalization.

The first arena lies between the movement and the political environment. The political environment has an influence on the actions of social movements and is considered by movements when they develop their strategy. This arena is comprised of relations with the state and inter-state institutions like international organizations, non-state elite centers of power (e.g., parties, the media), and symbolic configurations (e.g., public opinion). The crucial general mechanism active in this arena is that of *opportunity and threat spirals*. These are actions, decisions, events, and developments that positively or negatively change the political conditions for a movement and influence its strategy of contention. What matters here is the change of the strategic positions of the movement vis-à-vis its political environment and the influence on its political leverage. As an example, the authors mention court legislation that might change the space of action of the group by repositioning it in the political environment. The second arena is the intra-movement interactive arena with opposition movements as field of actors. Such opposition movements have common beliefs and interests, interact informally with each other, and affect each other's strategy. Movements can vary on goals, modes of action, and ideology. Internal dynamics, power relations, or division of labor may induce tensions among movement actors. Here the central mechanism is *competition for power* among the actors that may undercut or complement each other's strategies in the battle for power and support of adherents. This mechanism is not limited to external actors but also comprises internal political competitors. The third arena is the interaction between movement activists and security forces. This is different from the arena between movements and the political environment insofar as the security forces actually engage with movement activists on the ground. The central mechanism here is *outbidding*. This refers to action-counteraction dynamics that reciprocally raise the stakes of the actors in response to each other. This may be limited to negotiated management but might also shift to violence. This mechanism affects the prevailing tactics (e.g., disruptive, conventional, or violent). The last arena is the interaction of a movement with a rival movement or a countermovement. This often occurs in times of ethnic contentions where social boundaries are subject to activation and mobilization. The central mechanism for radicalization here is *object shift* and occurs when new claims of a movement pertain to a countermovement complementing existing claims aimed at authorities. A countermovement that has a clear agenda of inflicting damage on the other movement opens up a new front of contention that heavily influences the process of radicalization.

Social Movements and Culture

The general tendency in contemporary social movement research, following the developments of the past decades, has been to reject determinism and strain as (simple) explanations of protest and political violence. Rational choice has also been criticized for the extent to which it requires an objective perception of reality and calculation of gain vs. cost (see, e.g., Alimi, Bosi, and Demetriou 2015). Some other scholars, however, have taken this further to argue that a strategic approach to political violence—that is, as something aiming to achieve political objectives—would rather not (always) be suitable, as it ignores the compelling force of culture. In reference to the Chechen separatist-Islamist movement, Hank Johnston (2008, 322) for example argues that: "the emphasis on strategy in cultural analysis of social movements often misses the compelling quality of a cultural text, especially those elements of a deep cultural grammar that give rise to ritual aspects of social action. In addition to strategic decisions, I propose that movements sometimes reflect in their trajectories qualities that are strongly—almost ritualistically—culturally determined." He shows how cultural and religious scripts matched to give a particular form of separatist resistance; at the same time, the author himself admits and outlines how these elements of "deep cultural structure" have in fact been strategically manipulated by movement leaders. Similarly, Farhad Khosrokhavar (2016, 14–15) criticizes the rationality of suicide bombing, arguing that jihadism has "its own rationality" and the "manifestation of a subculture of death within it is based on a deep alienation, manipulation, and perverted sense of life that are difficult to entirely explicate using rational choice theory." Another element characterizing the culture of jihad, in his view, is humiliation in three manifestations: The first is direct humiliation through oppression. The second is vicarious humiliation, or "humiliation by proxy"—namely occurring to individuals who are not directly affected by this oppression, but who to some extent also undergo stigmatization and as a result experience a "sub-culture of self-estrangement and indignity" (Khosrokhavar 2016, 198). Finally, a third type of humiliation is of a different nature, going back to the beginnings of Islam and referring to the Qur'anic invective to humiliate the other two religions, in the sense of showing and implementing the superiority of Islam (199). Such manifestations of humiliation, the author goes on to argue, are furthermore reinforced by the media reporting of Muslim humiliation worldwide. Other authors have implicitly or explicitly contested this type of account (see, e.g., Pisoiu 2012; Wiktorowicz 2005). For the most part, while perhaps acknowledging the existence and subsequent manipulation of grievances, most authors understand jihadi violence as primarily strategic. Robert J. Brym and Bader Araj (2006), for example, show through a sophisticated quantitative analysis in an overall interactive model that most Palestinian suicide bombing can be explained as retaliation against Israeli killings and vice versa.

Outlook on Social Movement Research at the Crossroad

Social movement research on radicalization has made important contributions in particular by showing the complexities and interrelationships between the various actors involved in the scene of political violence. These contributions have been acknowledged and especially praised by critical terrorism studies scholars, who have even tended to declare this the ideal approach to studying terrorism (Jackson 2011). Their preference for this strand of research is logical, given their common points of showing continuity with other forms of political violence, as well as their interest in context and critical stance toward the state. That said, there are a series of avenues left to explore from this perspective. In the following section, I outline a series of shortcomings, which are at the same time the bridges toward other fields of study and disciplines whose input is necessary to complete the picture. In particular, I point to the dire need to involve *psychology* and *social psychology* more than has hitherto been done. I also point out some *empirical* and *theoretical irregularities* which require additional empirical investigation, especially into contemporary European forms of terrorism and political violence.

Looking beyond Social Movements

The first shortcoming is related to the nature of the social movement paradigm, which *focuses first and foremost* on organizations, movements, and very often also the state or state institutions—essentially on *groups of individuals, rather than individuals.* This focus is logical, given the sociological and political science origin of the literature. Some authors, notably della Porta, have claimed to also integrate the individual level in their models, as the "micro-level of analysis." In so doing, they have provided interesting insights into how and why individuals "go underground." Faithful to the approach, these mechanisms always involve an interaction between the individual and the social environment. As a consequence, obvious *par-*

allels with social psychology arise, without however these being outlined or exploited to a greater extent in the social movement literature. In keeping with the social movement emphasis on continuity and evolution of political involvement, della Porta (1992) emphasizes how members of the terrorist groups she examined were previously active in various left-wing organizations and were more broadly embedded in these political countercultures. Joining these organizations occurred as a matter of friendship and kinship relations. Counterculture involved similar music, lifestyle, and language, as well as the formation of affective ties, but also the formation of political attitudes. The next step, joining of the underground group—or for some, going underground together—also occurs on the basis of existing social networks. Recruitment through existing *social networks* or "affective networks" works due to both the low social cost imposed by the transition and the existence of strong affective ties. As a specificity here, it appears that for recruitment in the underground, the ties need to be stronger than for recruitment in non-militant groups, as there needs to be trust among the members, given the situation of illegality and risk. Apart from social networks, going underground occurred also as a reaction to an event, such as the victimization of a friend or the risk of arrest. The transition is however also marked by a series of elements of continuity: In the previous political countercultures, there was already contact with violence, martial skills, and structures of violence as small groups were formed from which recruitment to underground then took place.

The importance of social networks is also something that marked the initial contributions of Marc Sageman to the field of radicalization literature. In *Understanding Terror Networks*, Sageman (2004, vii) analyzed data based on the biographies of 172 terrorists and found that while no single profile fitted members of the global Salafi jihad movement, overall they tended to be young men from middle-class, educated, and religious backgrounds (96). With regard to joining the jihad, Sageman rejected the "common notions of recruitment and brainwashing" and instead argued that joining occurs along a "three-prong process: social affiliation with the jihad accomplished through friendship, kinship, and discipleship; progressive intensification of beliefs and faith leading to acceptance of the global jihad ideology; and formal acceptance to the jihad through the encounter of a link to the jihad" (135). Sageman stressed the importance of *social bonds* and contended that whilst factors such as relative deprivation, religion, and ideology were also important, it was more likely that social and emotional support as well as a common identity are instrumental in the process of joining jihadi groups (135). This conclusion was supported by the fact that

78% of the sample were found to be cut off from their social and cultural origins at the time of joining the movement (92–3). Working or studying abroad as expatriates, these individuals sought like-minded companions with similar backgrounds. For many of these Muslims in Western countries, despite the fact that many were not particularly devout believers beforehand, the mosque was a natural place to look for companionship. Friendships were based on a shared sense of loneliness, alienation, and resentment toward their host societies, and they developed a common collective identity based on religious ties (97). As the relationships intensified, their religious beliefs became increasingly extreme along with the resolve to connect with a group that shared their sentiments. In other words, they were a "bunch of guys" who sought out jihad together (97–8).

In elaborating on the role of social networks, Sageman does not make explicit reference to the literature on social movements. What additionally both he and della Porta fail to account for are the psychological processes at play when joining such networks. Two psychological mechanisms have been otherwise proposed in the socio-psychological literature to account for this transition: cognitive dissonance and "love." Clark McCauley and Sophia Moskalenko (2008, 420) translate the gradual nature of joining in socio-psychological terms as the "power of step-by-step self-persuasion through one's own behavior." They furthermore note that "hundreds of experiments have shown a strong tendency for self-justification after an individual does something stupid or sleazy" (420). In other words, people would generally tend to confirm, repeat, and find justifications for immoral or otherwise "bad" behavior. McCauley and Moskalenko (2008) also offer an explanation for why social network ties with close individuals are relevant in joining groups, namely the necessity of trusting the people who join new: "No terrorist wants to try to recruit someone who might betray the terrorists to the authorities. In practice, this means recruiting from the network of friends, lovers, and family" (421).

A second shortcoming relates to the lacking use of *psychological* concepts and theories to enlighten and enrich the account of individual radicalization. Individual psychology is clearly indispensable in this area; yet, instead of consulting major and emerging psychological theories and concepts on individual radicalization, authors use layman's concepts such as "cognitive opening" and "affective ties," if they use them at all. In part drawing on social movement research, Quintan Wiktorowicz (2005) identifies four processes that increase the probability of an individual joining a terrorist organization. The first is a "cognitive opening" born out of certain preconditions such as identity or personal crisis. A cognitive opening can then encourage individuals to look toward alternative ideas and worldviews, which may include religious seeking. Radical groups target these potential recruits within preexisting social environments or during public events by framing their ideology as one that "makes sense" and is attractive to the seeker. In della Porta's work, affective ties are important for joining, as discussed, but also for socialization into the ideology. In her account, there is a reinforcing dynamic between emotions and ideology. Affectively, solidarity among members increases, first of all due to the situation of danger with which they are all confronted, but also due to the developing sense of responsibility for the others. Strong affective ties are needed for the adoption of new values, the new reality, and the new identity, similar to primary socialization. On the reverse, the increasingly selective and absolute perception of reality increases the feeling of danger and thus solidarity among the members of the underground group. In the broader terrorism literature, some work has been pursued to investigate emotions (Baele 2017; Cottee and Hayward 2011), yet this topic is far from sufficiently addressed to date.

Finally, again on the background of lacking psychological concepts, the effect of ideology on individual behavior is operationalized in a rather deterministic way. Pursuant to socialization in the radical ideology, individual actions are conceptualized as direct implementations of radical norms and ideas. According to della Porta (1995), individual *engagement in acts of violence* occurs primarily as derived from the acquired norms, values, and ideology, which includes the depersonalization of the enemy, a self-perception as hero, and a perception of the situation as war. A more nuanced take on this can be observed in the work of Wiktorowicz (2005) and Daniela Pisoiu (2012), who introduce elements of rational choice in order to maintain individual agency shaped but not determined by its discursive environment. Wiktorowicz (2005) also emphasizes the socialization factor but explains individual motivations not as a reflection of a particular type of identity, but as a rational choice pursuant to a change in the definition of self-interest, which becomes spiritual salvation. Furthermore, the adoption of alternative norms and values does not occur as a result of processes and features inherent to underground organizations (isolation and absolutist ideology) but through the mobilizing rhetoric of movement entrepreneurs. Framing Theory has outlined a series of framing and resonance mechanisms. Out of these, Wiktorowicz emphasizes the resonance element of "authority of the frame articulator," in this case, that of the religious scholar and ideologue Omar Bakri, whose credibility draws on reputation, charisma, character, and personality (2005, 26). Having internalized these alternative norms and values, individuals orient their choices accordingly. They are not guided by the pursuit of some common good, but by mere self-interest, which, however, has been redefined as a consequence of this indoctrination. For Wiktorowicz, rationality is shaped by ideology and, moreover, limited to the pursuit of one goal only—spiritual salvation.

> Rather than seeing their own interest as material or political, individuals come to see their dominant self-interest in "spiritual terms"—saving their souls on Judgment Day. It is not simply that activists are socialized to believe in the inherent goodness of civic virtue; instead, they are socialized to believe that social activism and civil obligations are necessary vehicles to ensure salvation. Socialization redefines self-interest, and helping produce the collective good is a means, not an end, toward fulfilling individual spiritual goals . . . Activists engage in actions for the collective good because that is what is necessary to protect spiritual self-interest. In this sense, even seemingly altruistic behavior can be understood as the rational pursuit of self-interest. (2005, 28)

Importantly, rational choice in this case is not a matter of anticipated reward but of cognitive restructuring. That is, individuals effectively function in an alternative system, which alters the very nature of preferences. Furthermore, and also different from the intentional rational choice approaches, individual agency is reduced to one choice only—salvation or damnation.

> . . . the ideology provides a heuristic device for those interested in the hereafter. Socialization, or what activists term *tarbyia* ("culturing" Muslims in proposer Islamic beliefs and practices), is intended to inculcate both interest in salvation as well as ideologically sanctioned strategies for reaching Paradise. In the case of radical Islamic groups, audiences are "cultured" to believe that true believers must engage in (or at least support) violence because this kind of activism is divine order: particular forms of activism are proscribed as fulfilling God's will. Just as importantly, the ideology posits things like arrest and death as benefits rather than risks, glorified sources of honor and pride. (2005, 29)

The model developed by Daniela Pisoiu (2012) to explain Islamist radicalization in Europe combines rational choice in the psychology of terrorism with elements from Social Movement Theory: Framing Theory. The main motivational categories are standing, recognition, and reward. Furthermore, the concept of "interpretative frameworks" is key, as these worldviews shape the nature of these motivational categories. They are "components of the overall motivation or criteria according to which decisions to engage, stay and act orientate, and concretize in specific selective incentives at specific times along the process" (Pisoiu 2012, 85). Standing refers to "a position of prestige and superiority relative to, and as a reflection of, the social surrounding, based on commonly shared values as to what standing should constitute . . . these values are: *courage, altruism, power* and *specialized knowledge*" (86). Recognition is "the perceived *approval* and *support* of actions and activities by the social surrounding, again based on a commonly shared apprehension of what is valuable and acceptable" (94). Finally, reward "refers to the idea of making a difference, doing something valuable to impact and change a given situation seen as unfair." In this case, perceived oppression and injustice affects Muslims worldwide (87). These categories are not specific to Islamist terrorism, or terrorism in general. As she explains: "The fact that standing might be associated with being a mujahid is traced to the fact that, within a certain worldview, heroism is a value, and one associated with the activities involved in being a mujahid, such as defending the global community of Muslims or a particular Muslim community against 'occupation.' In other groups, standing will concretise into something completely different" (85). From this emerges the relevance of "radical interpretative frameworks"—a concept similar to that of "frames."

Although in essence a rational choice approach, Pisoiu's (2012) model also involves a redefinition of essentially rational choice incentives by their "situation" within interpretative frameworks. They are similar but in a number of ways different to "frames" and "collective beliefs":

As opposed to collective action frames, interpretative frameworks are more inclusive; they are not limited to the prognostic, diagnostic and motivational functions in relation to an issue, but include general and specific meanings, norms and values. In this sense, they are more similar to collective beliefs, with the difference being that interpretative frameworks are not stable and limited to any "social environment," but are in continuous evolution, relative to individuals and groups and therefore with numerous overlapping levels. (109–10)

She elaborates on how these frameworks emerge, are learned, and become legitimized, as well as which role social contacts play. Furthermore, she analyzes mechanisms through which these frameworks become exclusivist and absolute and how that leads to violent activities by individuals. Radical interpretative frameworks emerge in her study as a layer of interpretation with a certain degree of absolutism. They draw on the concepts conflict, oppression, aggression, injustice, and self-defense, and include a concrete enemy and war reality (e.g., the United States or the West and the war in Iraq). Pisoiu argues that grievances are strategically constructed in order to motivate action like retaliation or resistance conceptualized as self-defense. The establishment of an Islamic state with regulations based on the Qur'an and divine law would stop injustice and suffering.

Pisoiu suggests two ways through which radical interpretative frameworks can be adopted. These are learning ways of doing and thinking and forming ways of doing and thinking (i.e., within a group). The first draws on Framing Theory and occurs through various mechanisms such as the authority of the frame articulator or empirical credibility. The study shows that this is often facilitated by religious nescience of some individuals that renders religious speeches even more credible and convincing. The more credible these sources are, the more legitimization is attached to them and the more likely the framework will be accepted. Forming as the second way of doing and thinking occurs through discussions on current events and the cementation of attitudes toward these issues. Arguably, such discussions take place nowadays more and more online. With relation to framework exclusivizing and how that interacts with social isolation, there are clear parallels with the work of della Porta. Personal and ideational reference points for alternative views vanish and with it the tolerance for these alternative views and perspectives. The outside world is then more and more rejected socially and politically because of a parallel moral system and an incompatibility with these values and worldviews. Importantly, an implication of such a radical parallel moral system is the legitimization of jihad as armed battle against occupiers, as self-defense, or as resistance.

Moving Forward

Thinking about the contribution of social movement research to radicalization research and what can be done in the future, it is obvious to point out the vast dimensions of this literature and how paradigms other than the one on contentious politics could also be applied. Beyond that, it is imperative to test and possibly adapt existing social movement models of radicalization in the context of more atypical patterns of group radicalization, such as the ones connected to contemporary jihadi and right-wing radicalization in Europe. In the typical social movement radicalization models, terrorist groups would arise out of broader protest movements as a consequence of an interaction with state repression and other movements, typically involving a spiral of violence among these actors. In the case of jihadi radicalization in Europe, and arguably different to jihadi radicalization in Muslim countries, terrorism occurred before the radicalization of a movement, and before a movement—namely the Salafi movement—was even there. In simplistic terms, there were first the terror groups and terror attacks, and then the emergence and growth of a Salafi movement as such. In the right-wing extremist spectrum, and specifically Germany, the emergence of the National Socialist Underground (NSU) group and their terror activities occurred on the background of a rather lenient state policy toward right-wing extremist groups. Clearly, a number of organizations were banned—which led to the spread and nuclearizing of right-wing extremist structures—yet we do not see in this case an actual confrontation, certainly not of the dimensions and intensity of those having occurred in the 1970s between the state and left-wing movements. The observations of French sociologist Olivier Roy (2015) also tend to confirm these suspicions about the adequacy of the classical social movement paradigm for contemporary jihadi radicalization in Europe. Though still using the word "movement," he notices that individuals do not radicalize as a spearhead of a broader movement, but rather as a matter of "peer radicalization," in separation from and to the dismay of their parents. What we are dealing with, he argues, is a youth movement, but more in the form of a youth subculture which has very much to do with delinquent subcultures—something confirmed by the petty criminal pasts of many. More important and perhaps unsettling, they do not follow the pattern of a radicalization of a movement, as assumed in the classical model, but: "In a word, their radicalization is not the consequence of a long-term 'maturation' either in a political movement (Palestine, extreme left, extreme right) or in an Islamic environment. It is on the contrary a relatively sudden individual jump into violence, often after trying something else (Merah tried to enlist into the French army)" (Roy 2015, 8). Finally, it appears essential to consider again the definition of radicalization. In the social movement take, violence is a necessary ingredient, while debates in terrorism and extremism studies make a point out of whether or not violence should be included in the definition. Indeed, the argument that not all radicalism is, or has been historically, bad is an important one to remember. Social movement research insists on a natural development of terrorism from social movement protest and violence. Based on these last two considerations, however, it appears plausible that the spheres of social movement radicalization, radicalization, and terrorism overlap, but not completely.

REFERENCES

Alimi, Eitan Y., Lorenzo Bosi, and Chares Demetriou. 2012. "Relational Dynamics and Processes of Radicalization: A Comparative Framework." *Mobilization: An International Quarterly* 17 (1): 7–26. https://doi.org/10.17813/maiq.17.1.u7rw3 48t8200174h

Alimi, Eitan Y., Lorenzo Bosi, and Chares Demetriou. 2015. *The Dynamics of Radicalization: A Relational and Comparative Perspective*. Oxford: Oxford University Press.

Atran, Scott. 2016. "The Devoted Actor: Unconditional Commitment and Intractable Conflict across Cultures." *Current Anthropology* 57 (S13): S192–203. https://doi.org/10.1086/685495

Baele, Stephane J. 2017. "Lone-Actor Terrorists' Emotions and Cognition: An Evaluation Beyond Stereotypes." *Political Psychology* 38 (3): 449–68. https://doi.org/10.1111/pops.12365

Bloom, Mia M. 2004. "Palestinian Suicide Bombing: Public Support, Market Share, and Outbidding." *Political Science Quarterly* 119 (1): 61–88. https://doi.org/10.23 07/20202305

BMI (Bundesministerium des Innern), ed. 1981. *Analysen Zum Terrorismus*. Opladen: Westdeutscher Verlag.

Brym, Robert J., and Bader Araj. 2006. "Suicide Bombing as Strategy and Interaction: The Case of the Second Intifada." *Social Forces* 84 (4): 1969–86. https://doi.org/10.1353/sof.2006.0081

Coolsaet, Rik, ed. 2013. *Jihadi Terrorism and the Radicalisation Challenge: European and American Experiences*. London: Routledge.

Cottee, Simon, and Keith Hayward. 2011. "Terrorist (E)Motives: The Existential Attractions of Terrorism." *Studies in Conflict & Terrorism* 34 (12): 963–86. https://doi.org/10.1080/1057610X.2011.621116

della Porta, Donatella. 1992. "Institutional Responses to Terrorism: The Italian Case." *Terrorism and Political Violence* 4 (4): 151–70. https://doi.org/10.1080/09 546559208427179

della Porta, Donatella. 1995. *Social Movements, Political Violence, and the State: A Comparative Analysis of Italy and Germany*. Cambridge: Cambridge University Press.

della Porta, Donatella. 2013. *Clandestine Political Violence*. Cambridge: Cambridge University Press. https://doi.org/10.1017/CBO9781139043144

Goodin, Robert E., and Charles Tilly. 2006. "It Depends." In *The Oxford Handbook of Contextual Political Analysis*, edited by Robert E. Goodin and Charles Tilly, 3–32. Oxford: Oxford University Press. https://doi.org/10.1093/oxfordhb/978 0199270439.003.0001

Horgan, John G. 2004. *The Psychology of Terrorism*. London: Routledge. https://doi
.org/10.4324/9780203496961

Hummel, Klaus, and Daniela Pisoiu. 2014. "Das Konzept Der 'Co-Radikalisierung'
Am Beispiel Des Salafismus in Deutschland." In *Gefährliche Nähe: Salafismus
Und Dschihadismus in Deutschland*, edited by Klaus Hummel and Michail Log-
vinov, 183–98. Stuttgart: Ibidem-Verlag.

Jackson, Richard, ed. 2011. *Terrorism: A Critical Introduction*. Basingstoke: Palgrave
Macmillan.

Jensen, Michael A., Anita Atwell Seate, and Patrick A. James. 2018. "Radicalization
to Violence: A Pathway Approach to Studying Extremism." *Terrorism and Political Violence* 32 (5): 1067–90. https://doi.org/10.1080/09546553.2018.1442330

Johnston, Hank. 2008. "Ritual, Strategy, and Deep Culture in the Chechen National
Movement." *Critical Studies on Terrorism* 1 (3): 321–42. https://doi.org/10.1080
/17539150802514981

Khosrokhavar, Farhad. 2016. *Inside Jihadism: Understanding Jihadi Movements
Worldwide*. London: Routledge.

Logvinov, Michail. 2017. "Ko-Radikalisierung: 'Do Not Overreact—You'll Just
Create Worse Problems.'" In *Salafismus, Radikalisierung und terroristische Gewalt:
Erklärungsansätze—Befunde—Kritik*, edited by Michail Logvinov, 89–95. Wies-
baden: Springer Fachmedien. https://doi.org/10.1007/978-3-658-17658-7_9

Malthaner, Stefan. 2017. "Radicalization: The Evolution of an Analytical Paradigm." *European Journal of Sociology/Archives Européennes de Sociologie* 58 (3):
369–401. https://doi.org/10.1017/S0003975617000182

McAdam, Douglas, Sidney Tarrow, and Charles Tilly. 2001. *Dynamics of Contention*.
Cambridge: Cambridge University Press.

McCauley, Clark, and Sophia Moskalenko. 2008. "Mechanisms of Political Radicalization: Pathways Toward Terrorism." *Terrorism and Political Violence* 20 (3):
415–33. https://doi.org/10.1080/09546550802073367

Oberschall, Anthony. 2004. "Explaining Terrorism: The Contribution of Collective
Action Theory." *Sociological Theory* 22 (1): 26–37. https://doi.org/10.1111/j.14
67-9558.2004.00202.x

Pisoiu, Daniela. 2012. *Islamist Radicalisation in Europe: An Occupational Change Process*. London: Routledge. https://doi.org/10.4324/9780203805800

Post, Jerrold, Ehud Sprinzak, and Laurita Denny. 2003. "The Terrorists in Their
Own Words: Interviews with 35 Incarcerated Middle Eastern Terrorists." *Terrorism and Political Violence* 15 (1): 171–84. https://doi.org/10.1080/095465503
12331293007

Ranstorp, Magnus. 2010. *Understanding Violent Radicalisation: Terrorist and Jihadist
Movements in Europe*. London: Routledge. https://doi.org/10.4324/978020386
5743

Roy, Olivier. 2015. "What Is the Driving Force behind Jihadist Terrorism?—A Scientific Perspective on the Causes/Circumstances of Joining the Scene." Presented at the BKA Autumn Conference, *International Terrorism: How Can Prevention and Repression Keep Pace?* Mainz, November 18. https://life.eui.eu/wp-co
ntent/uploads/sites/7/2015/11/OLIVIER-ROY-what-is-a-radical-islamist.pdf .

Sageman, Marc. 2004. *Understanding Terror Networks*. Philadelphia: University of Pennsylvania Press.

Silke, Andrew. 2001. "The Devil You Know: Continuing Problems with Research on Terrorism." *Terrorism and Political Violence* 13 (4): 1–14. https://doi.org/10.10 80/09546550109609697

Tilly, Charles. 2003. *The Politics of Collective Violence*. Cambridge Studies in Contentious Politics. Cambridge: Cambridge University Press. https://doi.org/10.10 17/CBO9780511819131

Weis, Karin, and Andreas Zick. 2007. "Annäherungen an eine Sozialpsychologie des Terrorismus." *Wissenschaft und Frieden* 25 (1): 13–18.

Wiktorowicz, Quintan. 2005. *Radical Islam Rising: Muslim Extremism in the West*. London: Rowman & Littlefield.

THREE

Islamic Doctrines

Theorizing Radicalization through the Concept of "The New Spaces of Jihadism"

Mohamed-Ali Adraoui

This study is devoted to analyzing the doctrinal aspects of the mechanisms involved in "radicalization with reference to Islam" and to introduce a notion that can potentially help us better understand the current tendencies of jihadist political violence. Indeed, by putting forward the concept of "the new social spaces of jihadism," this chapter will shed light upon the key dimensions through which the type of violence that we now call "radicalization" has emerged and evolved in the last several decades. According to Farhad Khosrokhavar (2014, 21), radicalization refers to "the articulation between a radical ideological vision and the relentless desire to implement it." This definition makes it possible to investigate the foundations and evolution of religious and political thought that are the basis of the development of jihadist movements, to which radicalization refers as emphasized by public opinion and decision-makers. I aim to explore what I refer to as "spaces of jihadism" in order to recontextualize the rationales of radicalization with reference to Islam. I will particularly explore these rationales with regard to the emergence of a new conception of legitimacy based on armed combat. By focusing on the contours of this contemporary jihadist mold on which the actors of this "struggle for Islam" promote discourse, representations, and movements, I hope to shed light on the numerous ways in which reference to Islam is used in an uncompromising, revolutionary, and insurrectionary manner.

Thanks to the concept of "spaces of jihadism," I aim to evoke the scope, responsibility, activity, and implementation of the armed effort called on to fulfill a specific religious aim. This includes justifications of violence on the one hand, and tactical and strategic implications on the other, all of which find legitimacy in a political and religious dispute. I will focus on this dispute, exploring how it has undergone certain evolutions from one generation to the next. This chapter focuses on one of the numerous dimensions of the analysis of jihad-inspired radicalization. Alongside the essential psychological, sociological, economic, and anthropological approaches to the issue, this analysis touches on the ideological side of the rationales for radical, extremist, and violent engagement. I also hereby use the approach of spaces of jihadism as it makes it possible to capture the evolutions leading up to the breaking point marked by the emergence of the Islamic State organization.

Studies on contemporary Islam-inspired terrorism and political violence have become numerous, as jihadist radicalization seems to have spread to a global scale in the last several years, increasingly affecting diverse social profiles. Doing so, academic debates on the explanations and analyses of these types of radicalism have been flourishing. As brilliantly demonstrated by Arun Kundnani (2012),[1] studies related to Islam-inspired violent activism since 9/11 have principally given rise to two kinds of explanations: the theological and the psychological-theological, thus avoiding focus on political considerations and leading to address the issue of a "new" generation of terrorism (jihadist) that would need to be opposed to the "old" one mainly incarnated by leftist activists. However, in addition to being challenged by other established scholars in the field of terrorism and political violence—such as Martha Crenshaw, according to whom "new" versus "old" paradigms reflect similar phenomena that are "grounded in an evolving historical context" (2011, 25), illustrating a change in degree, not in kind—theological and psychological-theological never exist ex nihilo. Most important, religious justifications to the contemporary jihadist forms of violence represent a social, political, and ideological construction, constantly implying a huge level of agency, even of ideological innovation. The nowadays jihadist rationale and the way they have made a certain use of violence by some people evolving in certain contexts legitimately did

---

1. On the benefits and shortcomings in the use of the concept of "radicalization," see: Coolsaet (2019).

not emerge out of nowhere, and the notion of "theology" appears to be less relevant than ever when one decides to go in-depth with the issue of "violence in Islam." By recontextualizing the ideological factors of its emergence within an almost century-long history of Islamist movements as well as the more recent birth of jihadist branches through this notion, it becomes possible to understand why we currently face such phenomena within Islamically-motivated global political violence. It is thus useful to isolate three spaces through which we can clarify the nature of jihadist movements, and in reference to these, it is possible to understand the underpinnings of the contemporary phenomenon of radicalization.

These three spaces cannot be understood without keeping in mind that what has constituted the ideological basis of jihadist movements for several decades is the fact that their actors do not draw on a religious construction during normal times. Precisely because they are convinced that Islam is in danger, the reaction that the current leaders and activists of this armed jihad initiate must be global, insurrectional, and exceptional. The understanding of jihad (*Fiqh al-Jihad*) that is valued in these movements puts a form of martial law at the heart of its reasoning. This is because it concerns a conflict against enemies, which needs to be carefully defined in such a way as to mobilize certain categories of Muslims into action in given territories. The aim of this is to promote a certain methodology of violence to create a new political and religious entity (an expansionist entity in the case of the Islamic State). As a war is supposedly being waged against the *umma*[2] and the principles of Islam, jihadists come to theorize a state of exception. Their definition of jihad in merely spiritual or charitable terms seems, from their point of view, outdated. It is in this sense that these new spaces of jihadism provide ideological structures for phenomena of radicalization, which are today increasingly visible. Significantly, becoming radicalized comes down to embracing a specific grammar of violence.[3] Put a different way, this chapter will address how

---

2. From the root *u-m*, which is the same as that for maternity. This term designates the motherland of believers, namely the chosen means of belonging, of identifying, and, for Islamists and jihadists, of organizing Muslims throughout the world. The aim of the latter is to reunite this on all historically Islamic territories under a sole and unique religious and political authority (the caliphate).

3. I do not mean to ignore that the sociology of engagement generally follows a number of factors and is part of an interaction between different cognitive frames. I propose here to shed light on one of them (the "jihadist doctrine"), which is the common denominator of all current phenomena of radicalization. If it is almost impossible to take the exact measure of the determinants (social, economic, political, psychological, etc.) of violent engagement with reference to Islam, the doctrinal motivation is, at least theoretically, that which is affirmed with the greatest force.

the radicalization, as contested as it may academically be, highly benefits from a reflection built upon the notion of the spaces of jihadism. As this contribution does not focus on the drivers of radicalization, it will not deal with the motivations and factors generally highlighted by the people who legitimize and use the tools of political violence in order to achieve their religious purposes. In this chapter, radicalization refers, at a conceptual level, to jihadism as a moral representation and a political practice. More specifically, it does relate to one of the three spaces identified and explained next. Indeed, getting through a radicalization process means that one is a person undertaking to harm an enemy through a certain methodology that is violent. In this regard, this chapter does concern non-physically and physically violent actions. Radicalization, thus, has to do with any of these three dimensions and activities: being part of the scope of jihadism; defining enemies of Islam; and adopting and putting some methodologies/strategies into practice. Besides, on a longer historical run, thinking in the terms of the spaces of jihadism allows us to describe and analyze the similarities and differences between Al-Qaeda and the Islamic State at a closer level. In this respect, as shown in this chapter, the new generation of jihadists worldwide embodies "a radicalization of radicalization." Each space of jihadism simultaneously becomes intensified, deepened, enlarged, and oriented toward the highest level of terror achievable. The Islamic State has, indeed, acted as it sought to maximize the level of fear and harming through the fulfillment of the most important amount of radicalism (scope, enemies, and strategy), which is probably why the current generation of jihadists may be the most violent but also the last one with such a level and legitimization of indiscriminate violence. With "jihad" (at least in their understanding) having to encompass the whole of the contemporary Islamicness, the logics become to either join the Islamic State's design or to reject it. For all these reasons, thinking in terms of the spaces of jihadism turns out to be one of the most relevant and fecund grids to promote when it comes to examining the current phenomena we are to face.

From Jihad to Jihadism (Roy 2017)

Systematizing the Law of Exception

Based on the Arab root *j-h-d*, the concept of *al-Jihad* in the Muslim religion refers to the effort undertaken to change the state of a person or a group toward a greater degree of moral, spiritual, social, and even legal allegiance to Islam. It designates a positive action whose aim is to achieve compliance with the spirit and the text (widely debated) of this tradition. This notion, central in the different historical forms adopted by Islam, is thus deeply tied to the aims of believers, who are a part of various social configurations by virtue of which they assess specific priorities. It is therefore not only a concept with multiple meanings, but also importantly one that can be stretched and extended, in that the aspiration toward a more Islamic existence can potentially concern all spheres of human life. The scope, activity, methodology, and aims of jihad thus form what I call the social spaces of jihadism. Through these dimensions, it becomes possible to grasp the image actors have of radicalization in various contexts where it has been observed for a number of years.

Unlike radical integralist movements (Donegani 1993), which aim to transform their societies without using strategies of physical violence and without forgetting the majority of believers who favor a pacifist conception of this effort for God, for several decades jihadist movements have been updating religious debates with the aim of legitimizing contemporary antagonisms with regard to a series of various enemies. All of these efforts are united, in this perspective, by their animosity toward "authentic" Islam. In this way, the current phenomena of radicalization using reference to Islam claim to be part of a specific religious concept, that of armed jihad (Turner 2014) as it has been understood for several centuries in Sunnite tradition.

The first space related to this ideological mold is that of the enemy and thus refers to the ideological perimeter of adversity, the past and present definition of which makes it possible to speak of a switch from jihad to jihadism. Unlike historically dominant interpretations within the *Fiqh al-Jihad* that are not based on the figure of the enemy in the modern sense of the word,[4] contemporary jihadist movements put this at the heart of their engagement. Their transformation of religion is thus primarily carried out by constructing an ideology that is grounded in ontological enmity. It is because certain groups are presented as extreme toward Muslims that the latter consider themselves justified to declare a form of martial law against them. Historically, this responsibility of defending "Islam in danger" mainly fell on political powers claiming, in a wide range of regimes (e.g.,

---

4. It is indeed primarily a question of the short-term adversary. If the defense of the *umma* is a constant in all theories regarding the right to use force, there is no specific and constant definition of the antagonistic figure. It is the responsibility of the clergy to define the enemy within a specific context, how to fight them, and for what exact purposes.

caliphates, sultanates, emirates, kingdoms, and, more recently, presidential systems, etc.), to represent all or part of the *umma*. It is thus primarily a question of a defensive jihad whose mission is to reestablish a power that draws its legitimacy from religious belonging and respect of Islamic orders, be these legal, moral, jurisdictional, or otherwise, in the absence of which the practice of the Muslim religion would be threatened. In other words, because it ensures the continuation of the practice of Islam as a religion, armed combat is legitimate (Cook 2005).[5]

Since the nature of the opposition that is supposed to unite, from this perspective, Muslims against otherness is no longer purely metaphysical or religious but also political and conflictual, the principles declared in normal times become suspended, as authorized by Islamic clergy who have proposed to conceptualize the *Fiqh al-Jihad* for centuries (Bonney 2004). These clerics have rendered violence and even killing lawful and feasible because the *umma* is in a situation of war, meaning that what is usually professed must give way to a logic of exception. If, for instance, peace is the norm, the advent of an exceptional situation authorizing all or some Muslims to reason in terms of necessity (*al-Darura*) renders the use of force not only advisable but necessary in order to combat adversity (Peters 1996). This martial construction of politics raises essential questions for researchers, who must consider jihadism as the systematizing of martial law from which specific issues emerge.

The Contemporary Origins of Jihadism

At the crossroads of jihadism, we have two schools of thought that have interacted to produce the conception of armed combat that leads us to talk about jihadism today. The evolution of militant, political, and radicalized Islam in the 20th century gave birth to a new vision, one that certainly inherits the traits of previous centuries, but which also projects itself in a new symbolic and military space.

The evolution of the Egyptian Muslim Brotherhood is a first key factor. This movement was first concerned with preaching at the time of its

---

5. This work is one of the most successful summaries of the history of different categorizations of jihad, of which armed combat is one of the indisputably accepted occurrences. Its definition, however, has been for centuries part of a defensive and non-extensive understanding of the right to use military violence against an enemy, which most often had the characteristic of being circumstantial and non-ontological. For an even more detailed study of the rules governing the use of violence in the aim of killing in classic Medieval texts, see: Abou El Fadl (2001, 1999).

founder, Hassan al-Banna (assassinated in 1949) (Lia 1999). However, the movement's ideology gave birth to, via the radical(ized) thinker Sayyid Qutb (executed in 1966) (Calvert 2010), a vision that adopts the early fundamentalist heritage but disqualifies, once pushed to its extreme, the military regime at the head of the Egyptian state since the 1952 *coup d'état* that brought Colonel Nasser to power. The radicalization of the Brotherhood's thought was first carried out against an authority that was guilty, in the eyes of a number of increasingly violent activists from the 1970s onward, of usurping identification with Islam even though its actions were supposed to show the contrary (the hunting down of Islamists being in their eyes a sign of disloyalty). This is why the notion of jihad was reactivated by the first "Islamic groups" (*al-Jama'at al-Islamiyya*) that began to theorize the right to violence (against a regime that "betrays" Islam). Armed jihad against "the deviant prince," and by extension against its allies, was thus integrated into the customs of Islamic movements, subsequently forming part of the contemporary conception of jihadism (Kepel 2003a).

The second source of influence comes from the Arabian Peninsula by virtue of the strengthening and globalization of Salafi theses (as mainly expressed in the Wahhabi movement). Indeed, the understanding of the dogma and social relations taught in Saudi Arabia (benefiting from its energetic centrality following the second half of the 20th century) also participates in the emergence of a jihadist field. While contemporary Salafism (Cavatorta and Merone 2017; Meijer 2009) is marked by intense debates, which aim to revive original Islam (that of the *Salaf Salih*[6]), it cannot be denied that the schools of thought that are prone toward a systematized armed jihad were influenced by the fundamentalism taught within the oil monarchies. Reflecting the image of the religious and military struggle borne in the 18th century following the alliance between the imam Muhammad Ibn Abdul-Wahhab and the tribal leader Muhammad Ibn Al-Sa'ud (al-Rasheed 2012), some jihadist movements perpetuated this armed jihad for authentic Islam. The war in Afghanistan during the 1980s thus enabled generations of fighters from the Muslim world (and beyond) to come to the country in order to lead the first armed jihad at a global level.

---

6. From the root *s-l-f*, referring to that which precedes and forms the name *Salaf* that designates the first generations of Muslims, following which being Salafi means trying to produce the model of faith, practice, and even of society of the early times of Islam. Jihadism was for a long time called "Salafism-jihadism" due to the desire to reform Muslim societies in a fundamentalist way (i.e., return to the origins of Islam) and to fight their enemies by a vehement, revolutionary, and military understanding of jihad. The root *s-l-h* is that of virtue, which is why the first Muslims are generally called "Virtuous Predecessors" or "Old Sages" (*Salaf Salih*). See: Brachman (2008).

A breaking point is observed after this period as several generations of armed jihad actors started affirming that the liberation of the Islamic Afghan territory was only one step in the struggle for the reestablishment of *umma* rights that have been "scorned." The ambition, no longer only circumstantial but, from then on, pan-Islamic and unspecified at a geographic and temporal level (i.e., any situation turning to the disadvantage of Muslims could be targeted by armed jihad), turned the first movements of defense of Muslim communities into a model to follow during broader conflicts to come. The convergence of different generations of radicalized actors who began to redirect their engagement toward an aim detached from any specific territories to the benefit of an "opportunistic" struggle is a central phenomenon. The theater of action will now depend on conflicts occurring in Muslim societies, even if the fuse was not lit by any initial religious representation (e.g., Chechnya, Bosnia, Iraq, etc.). This led to the a posteriori justification of armed jihad in order to mobilize coreligionists in the name of a sacred reference against authorities who were blamed for usurping Islamic belonging (e.g., the Saudi monarchy after the Gulf War, the Egyptian regime, etc.) and against which is pronounced the anathema (*al-Takfir*). This subsequently makes it legal to overthrow a power that is no longer Muslim, while leading the fight against the powers accused of weaving a conspiracy against the *umma*. It is through this imprecise opposition strategy that armed jihad became the regulating factor of Islamic identity and the norm in times of societal organization. The relation to otherness thus constitutes the trademark of the jihadist experience (Cook 2005).

Defining and Naming the Enemy: The First Space of Jihadism

Jihadism distinguishes itself by ignoring customary laws that correspond to periods of peace (thus justifying the use of force and more generally the suspension of all or part of daily customs and practices, e.g., the right to no longer pray in defense of the city if the enemy is at its walls). It also stands apart from the vision that is generally described as "classic" armed jihad (*al-Jihad bil-Sayf*) by its global stance. The latter no longer consists of restricting the military effort to a given territory or political configuration, but in igniting a world revolution with the aim of producing a sole and exclusive sovereignty commanding the entire *umma*. If the theme of defending coreligionists remains central, as illustrated by the conflict in Afghanistan, it is through a form of global insurrection, not bound to a

---

7. "Jihad through the Sword."

specific territory (at least until the emergence of the Islamic State) and no longer a geographically situated struggle, that the jihadist avant-garde aims to unite the *umma*.[8]

Thus the first space of jihadism concerns the perimeter of adversity and, by extending the ideological and military target, the first imperative becomes naming the enemy (Schmitt 1997). The enemy is the one opposed to the promotion of "authentic" Islam, the defense of which is ensured by believers who are lucid and determined enough to handle this responsibility. This means, therefore, that since the "unimpaired" Islam for which jihadists fight is subsequently faith and nation, dogma and territory, law and sovereignty; the figure of the enemy is extendable and able to evolve. Here resides the first impetus of the phenomena of radicalization, since it consists in the triggering of violence with the aim of achieving a specific strategic objective and/or generating psychological terror aimed to weaken the enemy.

If, until the 1990s, jihadist radicalization was carried out in reaction to two main figures of injustice, the last decade of the 20th century witnessed some major changes that now structure the landscape of violence, more dynamic and disparate than ever before. Until this period, jihadist targets were essentially states that "betrayed" Islam, the Egyptian regime being a primary example as evidenced by the wave of attacks against military bases in the country and charges against leading political dignitaries, namely President Sadat, who was killed in 1981. Non-Muslim states were also targeted by armed jihad with a view to liberating conquered Muslim territory. Current jihadism stands apart by its broader and deeper space of adversity.

The 1990s largely signaled the current evolutions influencing phenomena of radicalization. Since this time, the extensiveness of the space of adversity has produced, under the notable influence of the Algerian conflict and the first globalized wave of Al-Qaeda jihadism (Kepel 2003b), an increasingly demilitarized conceptualization of the enemy. If the actors of contemporary armed jihad see themselves as soldiers, their targets must theoretically be part of a martial relationship, which means that the enemy represents an alter ego and must be the paradigmatic target within this perspective. Yet this space of jihadism has subsequently undergone an important break, as the religious construction that presides over this engagement starts to include civilians as part of an ideological and opportunistic gradation involving both military personnel of targeted states, as well as people

---

8. For an explicit presentation of jihadist aims and strategies by two historical figures (Osama Bin Laden and Ayman al-Zawahiri) see: Holbrook (2014).

removed from the military apparatus but regarded as statutorily or morally united with these states.

If the conflict in Afghanistan evidenced a relatively classic military opposition between two camps (the Soviet army and its local allies on the one hand and anti-regime forces assisted in particular by the first trans-national jihadist communities on the other[9]), Russian civilians were never targeted. The martial law of the period confined the use of violence to a bilateral antagonism in which the enemies were clearly identified. The extensiveness of armed jihad was weak, but it substantially evolved a decade later when the identification of an Algerian "usurping state" influenced a domestic battle, which was no longer against an "invader of the land of Islam" but rather against a "treacherous" power. The considerations that followed concerned the definition of hostility that Algerian jihadist groups confronted. Primarily, this included the Islamic Salvation Army (a direct emanation of the political movement Islamic Salvation Front) and the Armed Islamic Group (more radical and at odds with the "minimalist" strategy of the former since it targeted, beyond the military, any individual or group accused of coming to its aid or defending its actions). Are people who do not serve in the military but who work for the state, such as police officers, legitimate targets? What about the families of these individuals? Is it right to expand the space of jihadism even if it means throwing society into a full insurrection? The Algerian conflict is even more important as it heralds, in its French component, the junction between a national and international agenda that has become central in today's jihadist movements. If much still needs to be clarified about the interconnected ties and instrumentations between certain jihadist groups and the Algerian regime of the period (Martinez 2000), France, as a country accused of supporting the government of the time, became a legitimate target. French civilians were at risk of a violent attack at any moment by, for instance, inside fighters like Khaled Kelkal,[10] whose story has common elements with a number of current traits of terrorist radicalization phenomena (prior involvement in "classic" crime, a history of weak religious practice, and the weight of familial and social deculturation) (Roy 2017).

The same debates can be observed within Al-Qaeda during this time. It was at this time that the first de-territorialized attacks were organized by the true first global jihadist movement, fueled by a consideration of the enemy as encompassing not only opposing armies but all persons linked

---

9. Even if in reality they practically did not fight.

10. The perpetrator of the attacks in the Saint-Michel train station on July 25, 1995, was linked to the Armed Islamic Group and killed by the French police while at large.

with a group identified as hostile toward Muslims, to the point of integrating the geographic territory of non-Muslim power into the scope of violent action. Thus, after having proclaimed the Soviet Union defeated by its attacks, the first generations of armed combat for Islam turn against the United States. The United States was accused not only of sponsoring the Israeli state for decades, but also of supporting incumbent regimes in the Muslim world that were actually "renegade" for being politically and strategically involved in alliances that harmed the Islamic nation, as for instance illustrated by the proximity maintained for several decades between Saudi Arabia and the United States. With the aim to expel the American ally from Islamic territory and more specifically from the Arabian Peninsula, Al-Qaeda,[11] through the intermediary of Osama Bin Laden, designated military targets as a priority (in the context of an identified conflict to which was added a jihadist force or a terrorist enterprise aimed to influence the morale or political orientation of the enemy). The attacks of September 11, 2001, on U.S. territory (foreshadowed by a first attack in 1993, the targeting of American embassies in Kenya as well as in Tanzania in 1998, and the offensive against the USS *Cole* in the Gulf of Aden on October 12, 2000), as well as military and terrorist jihad movements in Iraq after 2003 against the American invasion, but also the Shia presence (strengthened by the fall of Saddam Hussein), form part of a war built ideologically from the identification of a double enemy. This enemy is imagined in the two images of the invader and the traitor (or the usurper). In this respect, faithful to a martial conception of the legal foundations on which the *Fiqh al-Jihad* is based, if civilians are killed during a conflict or act of terrorism, they are considered—even if they are "good Muslims"—collateral victims whose death is unavoidable. This is because the good resulting from the death (the defense of the *umma*) is seen as greater than the distress caused to individuals and their families.

The political and religious configuration of this period, despite notable changes, breaks with the current generation, which is not only involved in a phenomenon of re-territorialization of the jihadist project, but maybe above all in an explosion of the space of adversity. A jihadist paradigm shift has been initiated by the Islamic State by virtue of which the *umma* is now supposed to have its own state (Gerges 2017). The relationship with the rest of the world conditions a permanent state of war[12] in the aim of

---

11. Whose emergence is directly linked to the Soviet invasion of Afghanistan and its aftermath; see: Gerges (2011).

12. Built from the void produced by the vacancies of the Syrian and Iraqi Baath power, accentuated in the Iraqi case by the illegitimacy of U.S. presence. See: Hashim (2017).

encompassing by force over the long term all of Muslim territory, and even potentially more. Thus, the caliphate-immediate building principle (Wasserstein 2017) led to a central ideological reformation within jihadist movements. With geographic expansionism clearly at the core of the ambition, a constant state of conflict is created with an incessantly growing number of enemies, the number of which but also the nature of which is subject to constant fluctuation in order to justify the constant movement on which the Islamic State[13] was founded. All of the states which ended up intervening in the Syrian (or Iraqi-Syrian) conflict, taking into account the involvement of the Islamic State, are likely to be identified as enemies of Islam, and no longer just because they are found guilty of being allies of "corrupt" regimes or nations at war against Muslims (Israel for instance). Stepping in front of the path of the "state of the caliphate" means war, and hostility toward powers like France, the United States, and Russia are no longer motivated by their having assisted discredited regimes in the Muslim world, but rather by their direct military intervention against which modern jihadist movements intend to react.[14]

Such a change has clear repercussions on phenomena of radicalization within predominately Muslim societies but also beyond, as radicalization now has two main faces, unlike movements linked to Al-Qaeda (Staffel and Awan 2016). First, joining a conflict zone where the Islamic State is involved no longer has the sole objective of bringing down a specific enemy but of gaining an expanding embryonic state. In other words, jihad and *hijra*[15] are now combined. Second, the permanent state of war for people who identify themselves in this project but remain in their country produces an imported type of conflict. This conflict corresponds to a low-intensity struggle that feeds on ideological allegiances that are now transnational, but especially on a quest for savagery[16] whereby moral weakening becomes

---

13. The slogan of which is in this sense is explicit: "Stay and spread!" (*Baqiyya wa-Tatamadad.*)

14. This is illustrated by a famous text from the 1990s by Ayman Al-Zawahiri aimed against the Egyptian Muslim Brotherhood. Unlike the texts of the 1980s that emphasized the voice of electoral participation, there is no longer any way to solve the huge problems of the Muslim world except through violence and armed jihad with a view to reestablishing the caliphate in the long term, legal Islamist engagement having only sparked a "bitter harvest." See: Hatina (2012).

15. From the root *h-j-r* which refers to the departure, abandonment, or exile, in the image of the one undertaken in the year 622 by Muslims of Mecca toward Medina in order to protect their faith. The obligation of leaving a land where the practice Islam is presented as threatened is found in a number of contemporary Salafi schools of thought.

16. As shown by the text of the theorist (whose identity is in doubt) Abu Bakr Al-Naji, *The Administration of Savagery: The Most Critical Stage through which the Islamic National Will Pass,*

at least as important as human and material destruction. The effect of stupefaction and omnipotence, particularly in a primarily non-Muslim context, leads to diversifying the figure of the enemy, even to totalizing it, by seeking to target the security of an entire social body, no longer with a specific objective. As such, the enemy is not only the state but also the society that is supposed to produce the anti-Islamic movements against which jihadists intend to react.

Since, unlike Al-Qaeda, the targets are indiscriminate, the sociological profile of the attacks of the last several years has been characterized by a different kind of violent opportunism. A form of inventiveness is left to the actor, who is no longer in this context a fighter of armed jihad but rather a "soldier of the Caliphate" (Manne 2017), meaning that their actions must serve the propaganda and strategy of a state seeking permanent war. The two main categories of enemies have thus become holders or representatives of a sovereign function or authority. This is illustrated by the murder of two French police officers committed by Larossi Abballa in the city of Magny-en-Vexin in 2016, the attack against British soldiers in London in 2017, or the killing of a regular individual that is mainly motivated by inflicting psychological terror (even if the strategic agenda is never absent). In this latter case, the question no longer involves collateral victims but rather primary targets, and these attacks are not the result of an initial combat between military forces or institutional security services (e.g., army, police, etc.), but are conceived of to impose the idea of a cross-cutting conflict led against any person or group deemed worthy of being killed. Armed jihad is in this sense an individualized process where a person or a small network first conceives of their radicalization before theorizing about a target, unlike previous generations that became radicalized because they already had an enemy in mind (e.g., the United States, Arab regimes, etc.). The definition of the target is thus more individualized and in a certain way part of the "biography" of the fighter-soldier who will find people to violently attack. If the overall cognitive frame is provided by the ideology promoted by the Islamic State, the individual aspect is essential. The latter enables a psychologically rooted jihadism, to the extent that

---

published online in 2004. This book discusses the need to provoke military interventions in enemy states in order to widen recruitment opportunities among coreligionists living in these countries. According to this text, the Islamic State could influence with its propaganda by structuring in an enduring way a divide within societies that have remained for a long time aside from conflicts involving jihadist forces. This text grants central importance to extreme brutality with the aim of making an impression, but also of putting the enemy at fault by pushing it in turn toward the worst systematic violence against Muslims.

the target is only rarely specified in an ideological supra-discourse, to the benefit of individual creativity bearing on both the mode of action and the potential victim.

Moreover, the IS generation, which developed outside of the Muslim world, distinguishes itself by the search for a homology between its targets and the groups fought by the caliphate in the Middle East. The opposition henceforth concerns any representative of a group against which the state of the caliphate is built, such as Christian minorities in Syria and Iraq, with fighters of the jihadist movement called to target Europe as well. This explains, for example, the beheading of Father Jacques Hamel in Saint-Étienne-du-Rouvray on July 26, 2016, in the same way as the enemies of the Islamic State in the Middle East. In this respect, unlike the process of defining the enemy within Al-Qaeda–affiliated groups, there does not seem to be a separation between the "close" target (fake Muslim regimes) and the "far" target (non-Muslim states coming to their aid, primarily the United States) (Gerges 2009). This is because the jihadist state construction that characterizes the Islamic State, as well as its expansionist aim, generates a field of adversity that is all over the place. Soldiers, civilians, and religious individuals are all metaphysical, political, and strategic enemies that justify a shift in the fighting paradigm used by actors in the wake of the Islamic State.

Conducting Jihadism: Subjects of Armed Jihad between Historical Heritage and Identity Reconstruction

The Subject of Jihad and Jihadism

The space for conducting armed jihad follows a similar rationale of expansion and diversification. Indeed, it seems today that the de-territorialization that has been advocated for several decades by Al-Qaeda, as well as the attempt to build an Islamic state in the Middle East before envisioning its geographic expansion, generated a globalized identification with the jihadist agenda. It is no longer only a question of rushing to defend a threatened religion, but also of taking part in a utopic plan, even of seeking death rather than defending coreligionists. Therein lies a kind of reversal of the historical logic present in works dealing with armed jihad, since coming to the help of fellow Muslims remains important but gives rise to a desire for omnipotence specific to contemporary jihadism. We can clearly see it in the experience led by the "State of the Caliphate" (i.e., the Islamic State). The gain previously expected was moral, measured by the yardstick of divine approval. It is today palpable because it is indexed on the success of a new type of state construction. It is no longer only a question of coming to aid but of radically changing the terms of the political and religious authority in Muslim territory. The meaning of defending the interests of the *umma* has thus dramatically changed. The individualism of the approach and the motivation is seen in the way that victims are secondary. A number of fighters have nonetheless demanded to take part in the Syrian conflict or to carry out attacks in their countries against enemies that are targeted according to a rationale that is increasingly diluted and extensive. It is thus no longer a question of leading a religious and military effort with the aim of reestablishing all or part of the *umma* with well-understood rights (e.g., security, dignity, etc.). Instead, it involves fulfilling oneself through military jihad as well as through the participation in a project that is not only defensive but that also seeks to overthrow all previously observed states and social structures. Thus, the jihadist engagement evokes a profound change in the way the armed fight for Islam is conducted.

The two main categories of believers are historically in charge of the theorization as well as the implementation of armed jihad. Between these two categories, only one is indisputably involved in this military effort, notwithstanding the time and place. The second is interpreted by the first in regard to the depth and nature of its involvement.

The first group is the Islamic clergy, who for a number of centuries were distinguishable by their function of managing the goods of salvation intended for their coreligionists. Most often, they interact with a political authority, which they offer to guide toward greater compliance with religious principles (which is in this sense a method also thought of as jihad through good counsel, *al-Nasiha*). The orthodox position defended by the majority of clerics (mainly Sunnis for centuries) is consented obedience. In other words, society, understood as a political sphere, is made up of three types of actors, only two of which have the freedom to hold power in theory. Due to a fear of anarchy and revolt (*al-Fitna*), which is constitutive of the political order in this perspective, the people must focus on spiritual and worldly affairs in such a way as to reserve the responsibility of power to clerics and princes. Clerics, drawing their legitimacy from their mastery of the sacred texts, legitimize the princes, who are in turn forced in their exercise of power to comply with religious orders (absence of moral perversion, defense of the *umma*, respect of prescriptions contained in Islamic law called *al-Chari'a*, etc.) (Amanat and Griffel 2007). Thus, clerics hold a bipolar position within Muslim society, in the interaction between the people and the princes, while ensuring to provide the latter with the demands of the former (e.g., justice, protection, morality, etc.) in exchange for the people's obedience to the prince. Yet, this religious construction contains in itself the possible reason for a dispute. What is the status of deviation from or even of an apparent or proven betrayal by the prince with regard to Islam such as it is defended by the clergy, who have nonetheless legitimized the incumbent power? Do the people, who have been asked to obey in order to bring about the conditions of religious and political stability, now have the right to break the agreed constraint of allegiance?[17]

It is now possible to understand why the role of conducting armed jihad falls into two categories of actors within this vision. When the enemy is in this way internal, clerics who have not betrayed the *umma*, as well as the segments of people who follow them, are authorized to declare armed jihad against the deviant prince, whose self-declared belonging to Islam does not suffice to justify the allegiance because their actions are interpreted as antagonistic to the religious order. The reform for exercising power no longer happens through the intervention of the clergy cooperating on good terms with the prince toward greater compliance with religious norms and values. Instead, it is exercised by a violent military movement undertaken with the aim of pushing the holder of political authority back to greater Islamic reason, or even more radically, of removing the power in favor of a new authority that is supposedly faithful to the Islamic order. When the enemy is external, the ordinary clergy-believer duo must act in order to protect the political and social body that the *umma* represents from a non-Muslim authority that would produce a sort of anomie of identity, law, and morality in which there would no longer be a "true" Islam.

The Identity Dimension of Radicalization

There is a common element to the jihadist visions embodied by Al-Qaeda and the Islamic State. The need to defend Islam behooves no longer just a part of the *umma* (*Fard al-Kifaya*) that is responsible for armed combat, but as many Muslims as possible, even all of them. It is therefore a question of an individual duty (*Fard al-'Ayn*), and all believers can grasp the necessity of joining the war effort through armed combat, financial donations, prayer, or intellectual combat. This kind of approach largely explains why any Muslim is likely to join a jihadist organization according to the theorists

---

17. These debates form part of the question of allegiance and renouncement (*al-Wala wal-Bara*) in Islam, interpreted by the clergy in such a way as to both produce the religious conditions of obedience to a power as well as the conditions of its dispute. See: Wagemakers (2012).

concerned. The radicalization of certain Muslims today echoes a process of enrollment more than a process of recruitment in that radicalization precedes the relationship to jihad. The space of conducting armed jihad thus now involves believers whose motivation relates to the desire to defend the *umma* under threat and the desire to take part in a violent project that implies permanent war. Taking part in armed jihad is at the crossroads of considerations that are no longer only of a religious motivation but also of a "de-secularized" reason for violent action. Indeed, the analysis of trajectories of radicalized individuals leads one to question the significance of religious socialization and, in so doing, the anchoring in an institutionally Islamic ideology. Even if radicalized individuals, including proclaimed leaders of contemporary armed jihad, refer to ambitions of embodying an avant-garde (*al-Tali'a*) that is strong enough to put all principles of Islam into practice (starting with the combat "on the path of God," *al-Jihad fi as-Sabil li-Lah*), one wonders whether this space of jihadism is not at the intersection of other motivational dynamics. These dynamics could include a preexisting appetite for violence. In this respect, given the repetition of the same sociological profiles of radicalized individuals over the past several years (e.g., young, weak religious education, belonging to the most socioeconomically disadvantaged social groups, prior involvement in "classic" criminal circles), one wonders about the use of jihadism as a grammar of dispute in broad terms. In this respect, religious intensification is the consequence of social and political radicalization.

On the other hand, contemporary jihadism is differentiated from other historical forms of armed jihad by a radical reworking of the construction that has prevailed for several centuries. In terms of religious theorists (clerics), the figure of the enemy now takes on multiple forms and justifies in this respect a permanent state of war. This is because the lack of adhesion to the caliphate plan (in the case of the Islamic State) is equivalent to a declaration of war. Thus, there is potential or real martial action among the sole "true" believers who have understood that the Muslim faith involves not only spiritual, cultural, and social ethics but also a state allegiance to an entity in constant search of expansion. Armed jihad is thus no longer directed against the outside or inside enemy but potentially against any coreligionist whose refusal to swear allegiance to the Islamic State jihad movement is seen as an act of disloyalty against Islam. From this emerges a large gap between jihadism as conceptualized by Al-Qaeda theorists and that imagined by the Islamic State, in that the former never considered Muslims who did not join the group as directly at fault, viewing them instead as a mass that needs to be convinced and mobilized through victories against the enemies of Islam. On the contrary, in the vision of the Islamic State, the field of adversity potentially reaches any person refusing to reinforce the jihadist project. The main consequence of this is to divorce, morally, politically, and in terms of identity, the self-proclaimed avant-garde from the rest of the believers, through a bond of both solidarity and disqualification. Indeed, since the responsibility of armed jihad is in this perspective supposed to be ensured by all Muslims, the fact that only one part of the *umma* decides, in the case of jihadism as theorized by the Islamic State, to gain lands of the caliphate ends up dividing the mother country. The conception of armed jihad as a collective responsibility results in separating Muslims almost ontologically between those who accept responsibility and the others who are disqualified for refusing to consider that the service of religion is accompanied by a military component. As such, the avant-garde, put at the center of the reflection within jihadism as conceived by Al-Qaeda, takes on a more radical definition, to the point of being confused in certain types of discourse as the one legitimate perimeter of the *umma*. The participation in armed jihad thus symbolizes, in the final analysis, the criteria of Islamic belonging. In this regard, this conception participates in a new definition of the Muslim condition since participation in the armed effort (such as it is understood by the Islamic State) determines affiliation to the religion. From this perspective, radicalization is no longer a violent engagement but an exclusive adherence to a religious community that is erecting itself in a relationship of exclusivity and exclusion with coreligionists who refuse to migrate toward IS territories or fight in their country of origin to reinforce the permanent state of war. The category of "Muslim civilian" is thus disappearing and losing relevance. Radicalization is interpreted as the victory of the continuous martial state, contrary to the exceptional nature that characterized it in past definitions of armed jihad (Corne 2004; Hashmi 2002; Khadduri 1955).

Strategic Space: The Means of Jihadism: Between Squad Formations and Viral Paradigm

The jihadist mold has raised new questions regarding ways of producing, spreading, and organizing waves of violence against people who are targeted in response to their animosity toward and/or betrayal of Islam. Radicalization is thus observed not only in intellectual debates regarding the definition of categories of actors involved in armed jihad, but also in the appropriation of new forms of violence. It is a political act because it is part of a vision of war as a phenomenon that pits good against evil from a meta-physical point of view, while following a specific agenda that intends to change political structures (e.g., borders, sovereignty, etc.) and overthrow power relations (e.g., foreign influences, structures of alliances). Radical-ization must therefore be understood as part of a broader political struggle, where the local or national theater of operation obeys the same rationales of military and political antagonism that involve coreligionists in other regions of the world. The actor of jihadism, living as a soldier of Islam, is seen as global and thus must act as globally. All means of waging war are allowed, as long as the theorists of jihadism accept these methods. The lack of a Muslim army (here obviously jihadist) in a non-Muslim society capable of leading the fight in the name of God makes underground action necessary. On the contrary, when the theater of operation involves an army understood in the classic sense of the term, radicalization is understood as an engagement of a group of fighters involved in one or several conflicts.

Joining a Foreign Jihadist Movement: The Phenomenon of Squad Formation

It is estimated that around 35,000 people are currently in jihadist orga-nizations implanted in the Levant (Lister 2016). International jihadists illustrate a dynamic of squad formation of modern armed jihad, whose implementation is at once disparate and international. Al-Qaeda's strategy was to take part in all conflicts in which Muslim populations were impli-cated in order to redirect the ideological meaning of their struggle toward a jihadist vision (strategy of the "jihadization" of conflicts). In reality, how-ever, the main armies were not made up of international fighters. This territorial and social paradigm shift initiated by Al-Qaeda experienced a radical change over the last few years with the emergence of the caliph-ate plan. Here, squad formation means participating in the construction of a national religious army. The use of a military resource that straddles different continents represents one of the two faces of contemporary radi-calization. Becoming radicalized can resemble engagement in a military structure with a statist ambition just as much as it can be committing vio-lence in one's country of origin. The former illustrates a change of scale compared to the past phenomenon of building an army under the author-ity of an identified Muslim power in the aim of reestablishing all or part of the *umma* in its rights. This is indeed a question of structuring not only a military movement whose action is no longer bounded in time but also of moving toward a meticulous destruction of the international order. Squad formation (referring to a globalized military vanguard) is thus part of a global geopolitical project that illustrates the specificity of modern jihadism, namely that the only real way to defend Islam and Muslims is no longer in the search for an ex-ante order but the toppling down of all current political forms that are portrayed as contradictory to the religious norm. The process of enrollment that characterizes this part of radicalization does not fit the mold of a temporary draft, but rather an almost definitive mass rising, since the aim is indeed geopolitical upheaval. The relationship to time is also radically different since the victory of the *umma* is seen as consubstantial to the destruction of any real adversity. Being seen as hostile toward Islam only once can justify becoming a target. Since the conflict is now global, squad formation embodies the embryo of a transnational army. This aspect of radicalization thus evokes a form of normalization over time, since the formation of an enduring army brought to fight against an increasing number of enemies is the accepted purpose. This squad formation is radical in that it involves integration into an extremist movement, but the process in itself is classic since it is comparable to the formation of groups of fighters from a transnational base. This once more reinforces the hypothesis of a specificity in modern jihadism compared to the history of armed jihad in past centuries, to the extent that the globalization of recruitment is much more a case of globalization of contemporary forms of violence than the reproduction of a multi-secular religious ideology.

Terrorist Radicalization:
From a Sponsor's Paradigm to a Viral Paradigm

Another substantial development in the way the jihadist offer is available in the strategic space is the legitimation and use of terrorism, even though the latter is not theorized as such by the clergy and activists concerned. The understanding of violence in modern jihadism is thus part of a political conception, since it serves specific strategic goals. The war that is waged against enemies as diverse as some Arab regimes or certain non-Muslim powers (Western or otherwise) is a matter of perpetuating politics and religion by other means. Ordaining, conceiving, and leading a martial situation, through which jihadist groups aim to carry out a religious plan, consequently involves resolving the question of how to wage war, and in their case expanding its meaning to include the use of terrorism (the secular term interpreted in this vision as the continuation of the sacred war by other means). More specifically, thinking of themselves as those who initiate a response to violence committed against Islam and Muslims, the use of terrorism is justified because the impression that their enemies are waging a total war reinforces its legitimacy. Notably, in the jihadist literature, suffering from civilian losses during conflicts and/or military interventions determines the targeting of other civilians in jihadist violence. Major differences between the vision of Al-Qaeda and the Islamic State in the engagement of non-military individuals include the impossibility of avoiding collateral victims and the inclusion of civilians in the field of adversaries. In these two understandings of armed jihad, it is justified to carry out actions dedicated to spreading terror within primarily non-fighting populations.

As seen previously, the Islamic State has extended the field of injustice, and alongside an expansionist strategy that changes the parameters of engagement of certain Muslims worldwide in modern jihadism, terrorist radicalization has undergone important developments. The sociology of targets, as well as the modes of action used, have substantially transformed. From the Al-Qaeda generation to that of the Islamic State, the goals have switched from institutional to cultural. While this does not mean that each group is not interested in the other category, their two core targets are no less distinguished by a different ambition. In the first case, the use of terrorism, as illustrated by the targeting of the Pentagon, the White House, and the World Trade Center in September 2001, is explained by the desire to attack symbols of U.S. power. The United States is indeed a far-off enemy, but it is present enough in Arab countries to influence a number of states against which Osama Bin Laden was rebelling (Kepel and Milelli 2010). The shift in political orientation thus seems to be the main objective of the terrorist project. Even the attacks of March 11, 2004, against civilians in Madrid in the Atocha, El Pozo del Tio Raimundo, and Santa Eugenia train stations, arose from a violent reaction to Spain's participation in a military coalition in Iraq in the spring of 2003. One of the main reasons why these actions were undertaken was to punish a belligerent state and discourage any possible actor from invading a Muslim country. Referring to another type of persons but equally targeted for being an enemy of Islam and Muslims, the killing of several members of the newspaper *Charlie Hebdo* was part of a similar rationale since the foe, represented by artists and journalists making fun of the prophet of Islam on behalf of freedom of speech and creation, was sentenced to death. This, of course, aimed to send a message of terror, but also to react to what is interpreted as an intentional provocation (i.e., *Charlie Hebdo* outraging Muslims to humiliate them, thus pursuing a long-started war against Islam as argued in the jihadist literature). Moreover, the method of organization of such attacks is characterized by the involvement of an organization responsible for, at the very least, targeting legitimate enemies, but also of financing and even almost entirely preparing the terrorist attack in question (Hoffman and Reinares 2014). This sponsor's paradigm is the trademark of the Al-Qaeda generation.

On the other hand, terrorism seems to be part of a viral paradigm. Traditionally, jihadist terrorism was characterized by a classic relationship that unites three parties. In this three-party scheme, two are linked by both a common ideological and organizational affiliation in the aim of damaging a third category of people (two against one). However, this situation seems to be increasingly replaced with a new one that I call "viral terrorism." I use the term "viral" to the extent that, aside from the attacks of November 13, 2015, in Paris and those of March 22, 2016, in Brussels, there exists now a phenomenon of diffuse cultural influence. Indeed, a sort of moral preparation precedes taking action. New generations of jihadists using terrorist methods adopt a modus operandi through which the act is committed and the figure of the enemy is specified. Armed combat is a form of acculturation before being the fruit of military action. The shift to violence functions in a viral model in that a relation of hostility is introduced or reinforced among certain people who will implement it with violence that they themselves design. Indeed, there is a substantial amount of individual creativity, given that the ideological aspects are known (e.g., permanent state of war, identification of the enemy, etc.) while the practical details of the terrorist act are left up to the perpetrator. It is thus not so much a question of an act that is ordered as it is of terrorist careers being triggered. Hostility toward others is implemented using jihadist methods even though it could have been undertaken using symbolic, verbal, or (more classically) physical violence. Terrorist radicalization seems here to be joining the jihadist agenda as used by the Islamic State but is determined in reality based on motivations that are more complex. Historical armed jihad operates according to a clear and circumstantial definition of the enemy and of the action to be set in motion. Yet, since contemporary jihadism is a systemization of martial law, it leads, primarily in its most current form, to a dilution of the relationship to jihad. Any hostile phenomenon (even a non-religious one) thus finds itself being included in an ideology that was structured in another region of the world. The Islamic State offers the conditions for converting existing social or interpersonal tensions into a sacred battle. In this respect, the opportunities for armed jihad are even more substantial since they are atomized and part of an individual biography. The trajectory of a Muslim can push them to convert frustrations and unease into a jihadist ideology, leading them to consider their environment through a radical religious prism. The homology between personal psychological tensions and the desire to defend coreligionists in other regions of the world substantially explains terrorist radicalization. As they are steeped in a transnational ideological combat, local interactions involving certain Muslims become "jihadized." The suicidal drive, the desire to hurt a despised group, or even the feeling of solidarity with coreligionists pushes the jihadist ideology to be considered from a certain degree of opportunism. Thus, the ideological supply does not necessarily generate the demand. Instead, certain social profiles seize an opportunity to express in religious words their preexisting radicalism by identifying with the doctrinal system provided by the Islamic State. The current jihadist generation thus no longer only functions based on the jihadization of a tangible conflict in a given world region. Instead, it functions on a jihadization of social relations and tensions within a given society, which are often not even predominately Muslim (Neumann 2016; Rabasa and Benard 2014).

The sponsor's paradigm has not necessarily been abandoned, as it seems to be privileged when the Islamic State wishes to intervene in the phase of military withdrawal in the Middle East, for instance. However, the simultaneous emergence of a viral model in which the relationship seems inverse (i.e., mental radicalization precedes violent engagement) undeniably reinforces the psychological effect of these new forms of terrorism. This leads us to question whether it is possible to speak of a revolution of the Islamic State since, despite a probable end as an aspiring state, its ideology will still be able to influence or even spark a number of missions to come. In this sense, the terrorist radicalization that has emerged in the past few years illustrates a form of revolution since it is based on a new grammar. Jihadism has become a mass counterculture (Atran 2016). This is marked by a strong combination of seeking to cause terror with individualization. It then needs to pervade, for a number of years to come, the ideology of actors whose personal profiles and motivations are as diversified as ever. In this sense, it seems justified to evoke a new generation of jihadism that embodies a real break with what we have seen up until now.

REFERENCES

Abou El Fadl, Khaled. 1999. "The Rules of Killing at War: An Inquiry into Classical Sources." *The Muslim World* 89 (2): 155–57.

Abou El Fadl, Khaled. 2001. *Rebellion and Violence in Islamic Law*. Cambridge: Cambridge University Press.

al-Rasheed, Madawi. 2012. *A History of Saudi Arabia*. Cambridge: Cambridge University Press.

Amanat, Abbas, and Frank Griffel, eds. 2007. *Shari'a: Islamic Law in the Contemporary Context*. Stanford: Stanford University Press.

Atran, Scott. 2016. *L'État Islamique Est Une Révolution*. Paris: Les Liens Qui Libèrent.

Bonney, Richard. 2004. *Jihad: From Qur'an to Bin Laden*. Basingstoke: Palgrave Macmillan.

Brachman, Jarret M. 2008. *Global Jihadism: Theory and Practice*. London: Routledge.

Calvert, John. 2010. *Sayyid Qutb and the Origins of Radical Islamism*. New York: Columbia University Press.

Cavatorta, Francesco, and Fabio Merone, eds. 2017. *Salafism after the Arab Awakening: Contending with People's Power*. New York: Oxford University Press.

Cook, David. 2005. *Understanding Jihad*. Berkeley: University of California Press.

Coolsaet, Rik. 2019. "Radicalization: The Origins and Limits of a Contested Concept." In *Radicalization in Belgium and the Neatherlands: Critical Perspectives on Violence and Security*, edited by Nadia Fadil, Francesco Ragazzi, and Martijn de Koning, 29–51. London: I.B. Tauris.

Corne, Patricia. 2004. *God's Rule: Government and Islam*. New York: Columbia University Press.

Crenshaw, Martha. 2011. "New v. Old Terrorism: A Critical Appraisal." In *Jihadi Terrorism and the Radicalisation Challenge in Europe*, edited by Rik Coolsact, 25–36. London: Ashgate.

Donegani, Jean-Marie. 1993. *La Liberté de Choisir: Pluralisme Religieux et Pluralisme Politique Dans le Catholicisme Français Contemporain*. Paris: Presses de la FNSP.

Gerges, Fawaz. 2009. *The Far Enemy: Why Jihad Went Global*. Cambridge: Cambridge University Press.

Gerges, Fawaz. 2011. *The Rise and Fall of Al-Qaeda*. Oxford: Oxford University Press.

Gerges, Fawaz. 2017. *ISIS: A History*. Princeton: Princeton University Press.

Hashim, Ahmed S. 2017. *The Caliphate at War: The Ideological, Organizational and Military Innovations of Islamic State*. Oxford: Oxford University Press.

Hashmi, Sohail H., ed. 2002. *Islamic Political Ethics: Civil Society, Pluralism, and Conflict*. Princeton: Princeton University Press.

Hatina, Meir. 2012. "Redeeming Sunni Islam: al-Qaida's Polemic against the Muslim Brothers." *British Journal of Middle East Studies* 39 (1): 101–13.

Hoffman, Bruce, and Fernando Reinares, eds. 2014. *The Evolution of the Global Terrorist Threat: From 9/11 to Osama Bin Laden's Death*. New York: Columbia University Press.

Holbrook, Donald. 2014. *The Al-Qaeda Doctrine: The Framing and Evolution of the Leadership's Public Discourse*. London: Bloomsbury Academic.

Kepel, Gilles. 2003a. *Muslim Extremism in Egypt: The Prophet and Pharaoh*. Berkeley: University of California Press.

Kepel, Gilles. 2003b. *Jihad: The Trail of Political Islam*. Cambridge, MA: Harvard University Press.

Kepel, Gilles, and Jean-Pierre Milelli, eds. 2010. *Al-Qaeda in its Own Words*. Cambridge, MA: Harvard University Press.

Khadduri, Majid. 1955. *War and Peace in the Law of Islam*. Baltimore: Johns Hopkins University Press.

Khosrokhavar, Farhad. 2014. *Radicalization*. Paris: FMSH, Interventions.

Kundnani, Arun. 2012. "Radicalisation: The Journey of a Concept." *Race & Class* 54 (2): 3–25.

Lia, Brynjar. 1999. *The Society of the Muslim Brothers in Egypt: The Rise of an Islamic Mass Movement*. Cornell: Ithaca Press.

Lister, Charles. 2016. *The Syrian Jihad: Al-Qaeda, the Islamic State and the Evolution of an Insurgency*. New York: Oxford University Press.

Manne, Robert. 2017. *The Mind of the Islamic State: ISIS and the Ideology of the Caliphate*. New York: Prometheus Books.

Martinez, Luis. 2000. *The Algerian Civil War: 1990–1998*. New York: Columbia University Press.

Meijer, Roel, ed. 2009. *Global Salafism: Islam's New Religious Movement*. New York: Oxford University Press.

Neumann, Peter R. 2016. *Radicalized: New Jihadists and the Threat to the West*. London: I.B. Tauris.

Peters, Rudolph. 1996. *Jihad in Classical and Modern Islam: A Reader*. Princeton, NJ: Marcus Wiener.

Rabasa, Angel, and Cheryl Benard. 2014. *Eurojihad: Patterns of Islamist Radicalization and Terrorism in Europe*. Cambridge: Cambridge University Press.

Roy, Olivier. 2017. *Jihad and Death: The Global Appeal to Islamic State*. New York: Oxford University Press.

Schmitt, Carl. 1997. *The Concept of the Political*. Chicago: University of Chicago Press.

Staffel, Simon, and Akil N. Awan, eds. 2016. *Jihadism Transformed: Al-Qaeda and Islamic State's Global Battle of Ideas*. New York: Oxford University Press.

Turner, John A. 2014. *Religious Ideology and the Roots of the Global Jihad*. Basingstoke: Palgrave McMillan.

Wagemakers, Joas. 2012. "The Enduring Legacy of the Second Saudi State: Quietist and Radical Wahhabi Contestations of *Al-Wala' wal-Bara*.'" *International Journal of Middle East Studies* 44 (1): 93–110.

Wasserstein, David J. 2017. *Black Banners of ISIS: The Roots of the New Caliphate*. New Haven: Yale University Press.

FOUR

Conversion Models

Juliette Galonnier

The past two decades have witnessed a swift propagation of the notion of "radicalization." Its meaning, however, remains contested. Scholars have referred to radicalization as "a source of confusion" (Sedgwick 2010), a "buzzword" that is used by "political elites and so-called specialists" (Marchal and Salem 2018) but proves "a total nightmare to operationalize as a topic for research" (Githens-Mazer 2012). It is often said to lack scientific rigor (Neumann and Kleinmann 2013) and to be "plagued by assumption, intuition and conventional wisdom" (Githens-Mazer and Lambert 2010). Critiques of the radicalization concept as it is used in commonsense discourse contend that it overtly focuses on individual and psychological processes and places too much emphasis on ideological and theological interpretations, at the expense of social and political considerations. They argue that radicalization is often portrayed as a "virus" of extremist beliefs spreading across individuals, which precludes any explanation of the actual passage from beliefs to violence (Malthaner 2017; Kundnani 2012). The recent *critical turn* in radicalization studies also highlights the negative effects of radicalization discourses in terms of securitization, depoliticization, and the construction of suspect communities through the racialization of a stereotypical "Muslim figure" (Fadil, Ragazzi, and de Koning 2019; Baker-Beall, Heath-Kelly, and Jarvis 2015). In sum, radicalization as a concept has proven unsatisfactory and needs reframing. This chapter argues that the conversion literature can be of some help in that endeavor.

Like radicalization, *conversion* is also a very contentious word: scholarship on conversion is enormous and characterized by numerous debates (for a complete overview, see Gooren 2007; Richardson and Kilbourne 1989). For instance, scholars disagree as to how much change is necessary to identify a religious shift as conversion (Le Pape 2009). In addition, people whom we call "converts" do not necessarily use this term to self-identify. Alternative terms have been suggested, such as "transition" (Wadud 2007, 5), "reversion" (Van Nieuwkerk 2006), "alternation" (Travisano 1970), or "adhesion" (Nock 1933) (for an overview, see Barylo 2018). There are also distinctions between what some authors call "external" and "internal" conversions (Hervieu-Léger 1999, 120–25), the former referring to religious change across traditions and denominations (shifting from one religion, or none, to another) and the latter to reconnection and intensification of practice within a religious tradition (the so-called "born-again" phenomenon). Finally, narrow understandings of conversion have also been criticized for placing too much emphasis on individual and theological factors. For the sake of clarity, we can start by defining conversion with Mercedes García-Arenal (2001, 7) as "the range of processes through which individuals or groups engage in beliefs, rituals and social practices that are different from those into which they were born." This simple definition has the merit of encompassing a broad range of religious and social transformations, from gradual to sudden, from dramatic to subtle.

This chapter investigates the relationship between radicalization and conversion. There are two main ways of envisioning the conceptual links between these notions. The first one, informed by some recent statistical evidence, argues that conversion provides fertile ground for radicalization and that converts are more likely than other believers to engage in the path of politico-religious violence. The second one, motivated by theoretical concerns, suggests that radicalization is best defined as *a subtype of conversion* (one that involves violent ideology and action), and that scholars working on radicalization have much to learn from the conversion and new religious movements (NRMs) literature. This chapter alternately explores these two options: It concludes that the first option tends to reproduce the shortcomings underlined by critiques of the radicalization concept and that the second one is most promising in terms of theoretical and empirical prospects.

Conversion as Fertile Ground for Radicalization?

A growing number of studies in the scholarly and gray literature investigate the elective affinities between conversion to Islam and contemporary radicalization (Rushchenko 2017; Mullins 2015; Van San 2015; Bartoszewicz 2013; Flower 2013; Simcox and Dyer 2013; Karagiannis 2012; Kleinmann 2012; Uhlmann 2008; for an overview, see Schuurman, Grol, and Flower 2016). They argue that Muslim converts are more likely than non-converts (so-called "born Muslims") to partake in violent forms of politico-religious militancy, although we still need to understand why. Scott Flower and Scott Kleinmann (2013) underline that "how the mechanisms of conversion correlate and intersect with the mechanisms of radicalization is not well understood." In this strand of scholarship, the word "convert" usually refers to "external converts," or people who did not grow up in a religious or cultural Muslim environment. A "convert" is therefore mostly identified by the fact that they do not belong to any of the ethnic and racial categories commonly associated with Islam in Western collective representations (e.g., Middle Eastern, North African, South Asian, to name only a few).

Counting Converts in Violent Politico-Religious Movements

Security concerns over converts first emerged with the advent of Al-Qaeda in the 1990s, which featured significant numbers of so-called "converts" in its midst (Roy 2011). These concerns have heightened with the rise from 2014 onward of Daesh, which displayed an even larger percentage of converts. Studies have found that the share of converts involved in radical movements is disproportionately high compared to their actual share in the Muslim population. A number of figures have been circulating, although caution must be exerted as to their methodologies and reliability. For instance, Lorenzo Vidino and Seamus Hughes (2005) have established that out of 71 people charged with various Daesh-related activities in the United States in 2015, 40% could be defined as converts, or people who were not raised in Muslim families. Given that the share of converts in the American Muslim population at large is around 21% (Pew Research Center 2017, 119), this indicates a clear overrepresentation. Such disproportion is even more striking in Western Europe, where the percentage of converts among Muslims generally does not exceed 5% (Schuurman, Grol, and Flower 2016). In 2015, the French Home Ministry established that out of the 1,923 French citizens enrolled in Daesh, 23% (roughly 440 people) could be characterized as "converts" (Mathiot 2015). In the UK, Sam Mullins (2015) has argued that among the 427 individuals who supported Al-Qaeda–related activities between 1980 and 2013, 47 (11%) were converts. In Belgium, Marion Van San (2015) has estimated that among the 329 young people who joined Daesh in Syria, 10% were converts. Such figures suggesting that converts are overrepresented in violent movements have produced bewilderment and concern.

The "Radical Convert" as Contemporary Boogeyman

The spectacular and shocking trajectories of a small number of violent converts have made the headlines in North America and Western Europe, producing both fascination and moral panic among the public. Indicative of such fascination is the fact that, in comparison to their non-convert counterparts, radical converts are more frequently given nicknames, such as the "White Widow" (Samantha Lewthwaite, UK), "Jihad Jane" (Colleen LaRose, United States), "Lady Jihad" (Maria Giulia Sergio, Italy), the "Blue-Eyed Emir" (Richard Robert, France), the "Shoe Bomber" (Richard Reid, UK), the "Dirty Bomber" (Jose Padilla, United States), or the "American Taliban" (John Walker Lindh, United States). The "radical convert" has in fact become a highly telegenic character in popular culture. Suffice it to look at recent TV shows to appreciate this centrality. To take only one example, *Homeland* (2011) features a white American Marine, Nick Brody, who was held hostage by Al-Qaeda for eight years and was eventually turned by the organization. While coming back to the United States as a war hero, he is actually planning a suicide attack against the vice president. The tropes of treason, duplicity, and brainwashing have considerably skewed the representations of Muslim converts in the contemporary period. While they had historically been portrayed as pirates, adventurers, Orientalists, or Sufi mystics, the figure of the "fanatic religious warrior" has now outshined all others. The highly visual and Hollywood-style mise-en-scènes of Daesh have also contributed to durably ingrain the archetypal image of "the convert": a light-skinned, blue-eyed, bearded man wearing camouflage clothing and sporting an AK-47 in its male version; and a determined woman dressed in a *niqab* covering her entire body, except for the eyes (also blue), in its female incarnation. As a result, conversions to Islam are increasingly apprehended through the univocal lens of threat and securitization, with converts being presented as more radical than non-converts. "Converts are often the most dangerous," once declared French anti-terrorist judge Jean-Louis Bruguière (Leclerc 2012). Scholar Esra Özyürek (2009) has referred to such a complex set of fears about violence, proselytism, and Islamic invasion as "convert alert": converts have deepened moral panics over the pervasive threat of Islam because they are seen as a more insidious menace.

Liminality and "Convertitis"

In contrast, scholars have sought to provide a dispassionate analysis of why converts seem more likely than non-converts to join the ranks of radical movements. Several explanations have been put forward. Radical Islam being one of the most dramatic causes currently available in the political landscape, a first explanation suggests that young people holding apocalyptic ideals can embrace it without necessarily entertaining a close connection to the religion of Islam itself. This is what Olivier Roy (2016) calls "the Islamization of radicalism," whereby extreme interpretations of Islam simply provide the ideological coating for violent aspirations, without constituting the cause of radicalization itself. Thus, non-Muslims can readily appropriate distorted Islamic references to satisfy their destructive leanings and legitimate their actions. In that case, the conversion to violent modes of action precedes the conversion to specific Islamic beliefs, which is purely instrumental and contingent.

A second explanation reverses the direction of causality and indicates that people who convert to Islam—for a variety of reasons: spiritual or moral quest, marriage, friendly relations, travels, political commitment, identity search, etc.—are subsequently more "vulnerable" to radicalization. British convert and Islamic scholar Timothy Winter (Abdal Hakim Murad) has for instance argued that some converts can be afflicted by what he sarcastically calls *"convertitis."* As he puts it, "The initial and quite understandable response of many newcomers is to become an absolutist. This mindset is sometimes called 'convertitis.' It is a common *illness*, which can make those who have caught it rather difficult to deal with. Fortunately, it almost always wears off" (Murad 2014 [1997], emphasis mine). In a nutshell, the amusing neologism of convertitis has been coined to designate the oftentimes absolutist behavior adopted by some overzealous converts at the beginning of their entry into Islam, as they strive to incorporate all new religious norms at once and become "perfect Muslims" overnight (see also Jensen 2006). The literature on conversion to Islam proffers a substantial body of research that can account for converts' greater propensity to embracing stringent and univocal interpretations of the religion. A central finding of this literature is that conversion to Islam is an experience of "liminality." In his study of rites of passage in Central Africa, anthropologist Victor Turner (1969, 95) defined liminality as the intermediary state between the phase of separation and the phase of reincorporation that characterize those rituals (*limen* is a Latin word meaning "boundary" or "threshold"). He wrote that "the attributes of liminality or liminal personae are necessarily ambiguous. . . . Liminal entities are neither here nor there; they are betwixt and between the positions assigned and arrayed by law, convention and ceremonial" (95). Liminality, therefore, is to be understood as "an area of ambiguity, a sort of social limbo." Likewise, conversion can sometimes alienate individuals from their milieu of origin and put them into a liminal phase: Not only are they shunned by their family and eschewed by their friends, they can also encounter obstacles in their efforts to thrive in Muslim community spaces (Galonnier 2017; Moosavi 2012; Woodlock 2010): issues of cultural, generational, class, or ethnic/racial difference frequently come in the way of successful religious integration. Converts often report having trouble asserting their Islamic legitimacy. Imperfectly belonging to neither world, they are often depicted as "edge men," "transitional beings," or "threshold people" (Finn 1990).

In her study of female converts in Australia, anthropologist Karen Turner (2019, 73, 79) has aptly argued that convertitis "is not just a fanaticism or fervor in the early stages," but "an embodied resistance to the experience of liminality and ambiguity that new converts experience when becoming Muslim." She convincingly shows how some converts enshrine their religious transformation into rigid and conspicuous practice to prove their Muslimness to others and adopt literalist black-and-white interpretations of their religion in order to mitigate the uncertainties inherent to their liminal position. Thus, some converts undergo radical life changes overnight, which often implies brutally getting rid of former habits and hobbies or severing ties with friends and family. Others incorporate all at once a series of demanding religious practices at the risk of severe "religious burn out." By overperforming their religiosity, they intend to shrink the liminal phase and accelerate the completion of their rite of passage. "Fortunately, [this disease] almost always wears off," says Timothy Winter. Indeed, the majority of converts who suffer from convertitis early on in their journey progressively soften their practice over time. Yet, it has been argued that convertitis provides fertile ground for radicalization in the case of converts who do not find a stable community network to fall on their feet. This resonates with the uncertainty–identity theory outlined by John F. Morrison (see chapter 5, this volume) to account for an individual's move toward extremism.

Echoing these analyses, research conducted in Europe has shown that radical Islamic movements tend to attract second-generation immigrants of Muslim descent characterized by disenfranchisement, social anomie, and family dissolution, that is, not immersed in a solid Muslim culture (Khosrokhavar 2014). Such lack of grounding opens avenues for their entry into groups that offer a strong social identity and promote a worldview drastically different from mainstream society. The same applies to converts. Scholars have demonstrated that converts are for instance particularly interested in the rationalist, deculturalized, and univocal textual approach promoted by Islamic currents such as Salafism, because they posit that religious authority derives exclusively from the mastery of scripture rather than cultural competency or the practice of Islam for generations. By Salafi standards, a "good" Muslim is not necessarily someone immersed in majority-Muslim culture, but someone who lives their life by the book. Salafism is conceived by its supporters as independent from tradition: universal, democratic, and meritocratic. As such, Salafism exerts great attractiveness upon new Muslims in search of religious authenticity. Mohamed-Ali Adraoui (2013), who conducted long-term qualitative studies on Salafism in France, highlights that between a fourth and a third of his Salafi respondents are converts. Adraoui (2019) further notes that although various Islamic movements, such as Sufis or Tablighis, feature large numbers of converts in their midst, Salafism is the only one having elevated the convert to such a central position. Salafi-oriented rhetoric is refreshing for converts who often struggle to assert their religious legitimacy in Muslim spaces. Within Salafism, their "lack" of Muslim culture is precisely considered an asset and a source of symbolic capital, for it allegedly enables them to decipher with greater ease what is cultural *bid'ah* (harmful innovation) from what is "truly" Islam. While Salafism alone does not lead to violence (Crettiez et al. 2017; Githens-Mazer 2012), and while studies have demonstrated that many Salafis strictly oppose jihadism (Inge 2017), its rhetorical tropes can be successfully enlisted by violent movements to specifically attract converts.

Limits

Overall, in spite of interesting findings related to liminality and the quest for religious legitimacy, the idea that conversion provides fertile ground for radicalization remains limited in its prospects. First, an inverted look at available statistics shows that radicalization "remains an ultra-minority attitude" among converts (Roy 2004, 318). If we consider that the general French convert population oscillates around 100,000 people, the actual number of those who joined fighting groups (roughly 440 in 2015) represents less than 1%. Hence, the spectacular trajectories of a few converts should not obscure the daily reality of the remaining 99%. Conversions to Islam in their overwhelming majority are mundane and banal and do not fit into dominant framings of threat and menace. Most converts positively embrace their state of "liminality": They enjoy their roles as cultural "passers," "bridges," or "ambassadors" (Bartoszewicz 2013) and promote a rhetoric of "syncretism" between their culture of origin and their newly embraced religion, rather than an attitude of symbolic battle, radical differentiation, or conflict (Wohlrab-Sahr 1999). The focus on converts as "more dangerous" is therefore misleading, for conversion alone is not a determining factor of radicalization.

Second, this strand of scholarship tends to reify the boundaries between converts and non-converts in a way that is artificial and unwarranted. The internal convert/external convert divide often turns out to be a false dichotomy, which is actually based on racialized assumptions about who is Muslim and who is not. Research has demonstrated that many second-generation Muslims closely resemble converts, for they understand religion very differently from their parents (Arslan 2010; Duderija 2007; Roy 2004): In fact, born-again Muslims typically insist on reciting the *shahada* at the mosque to mark their renewed interest in the religion and interpret their reconnection with diligent practice as a form of conversion. The boundaries between so-called converts and so-called born Muslims are therefore particularly blurry and can hardly be considered as a relevant explanation. More important, people who join radical movements, even when they were born in Muslim families, profess an understanding of religion that is so drastically different from the one in which they were raised that it is safe to characterize their trajectory as a form of conversion.

Third, this perspective tends to reproduce the tropes of "contagion" and "vulnerability," which have proven detrimental to radicalization research. The idea that converts are more "malleable" and vulnerable to the viruses of brainwashing and indoctrination, in part because of the so-called illness of "convertitis," leads to pathologizing accounts of radicalization. The use of medical metaphors has been criticized by many scholars because it entails a framing of Muslim communities in terms of "risk" (converts being at once more "risky" and "at risk"). Such conceptions obscure social and political considerations in the development of radical trajectories (Heath-Kelly 2013). According to Anthony Richards (2011), they "deflect us from what has generally been agreed in terrorism studies—that terrorism involves the perpetration of rational and calculated acts of violence."

In sum, such approaches to conversion and radicalization reproduce some of the flaws identified by critiques of the radicalization concept (e.g., pathologization, racialization of Muslim identities, lack of conceptual rigor in distinguishing so-called converts from non-converts, heavy reliance on mainstream media representations, etc.). Therefore, rather than considering conversion as a factor of radicalization, a more sustainable and integrated approach is to conceptualize radicalization as a subtype of conversion and to enlist conversion models as a means to understanding radicalization processes. Indeed, as put by Roland Marchal and Zekeria Ould Ahmed Salem (2018, 5), radicalization can be understood as "the *conversion* or recruitment of groups or individuals to violent ideologies and actions" (emphasis mine). In what follows, I suggest going back to conversion scholarship to explore what radicalization means.

Radicalization as a Form of Conversion

As mentioned in the introduction to this chapter, conversion, like radicalization, is a contested concept. Interestingly, part of the debates in the conversion literature closely mirror those surrounding radicalization. Controversies around conversion models can therefore help illuminate the radicalization concept and provide solid ground for its theoretical refoundation. The literature on conversion emerged at the end of the 1960s in the United States when the rapid development of "new religious movements" (NRMs) such as the Unification Church, The Family, Aum Shinrikyo, or the People's Temple prompted questions about religious change and re-affiliation (Barker 1989). Hundreds of studies on conversion have been published since then. While NRMs do not necessarily promote violence, they share with contemporary radical groups a number of characteristics: small group size, atypical demographics (predominance of young people), first-generation membership, charismatic leaders, unequivocal belief systems, emphasis on us/them divides, and antagonistic relations with society (Barker 1995). While we lack solid empirical (and especially ethnographic) studies on radical groups and movements (partly because of access and safety issues), we do have a long tradition of immersive and interview-based qualitative research on conversion, whose insights can be productively enlisted to shed light on some aspects of radicalization. As a result, an increasing number of studies, initiated by Marc Sageman (2004), have envisioned parallels between radicalization and NRMs/conversion research (see also Ferguson and Binks 2015; Borum 2011; Shterin and Yarlykapov 2011; Dawson 2009; Sedgwick 2007; Langone 2006). This is a much welcome trend since the literature on conversion is rich with findings that can illuminate the process of radicalization itself. In the remainder of this chapter, I highlight four main debates of conversion scholarship that can be relevant to students of radicalization: the issue of agency; the question of time and processual change; the centrality of collective life; and the matter of embodied practice.

Agency

Two paradigms have historically characterized conversion research. The "old" paradigm saw conversion in passive terms, as something irrational that suddenly "happened" to the individual. Studies of religious conversion have long been dominated by such a deterministic understanding, which influenced most of the models until the 1970s. In the passivist paradigm, the individual is at the mercy of external forces that make them convert: for instance, a set of social predispositions that renders them "vulnerable" and a brainwashing cult that takes advantage of this vulnerability. They have no agency over their own religious decisions and passively receive a new belief and ideology. According to James Richardson (1985), "this view of forced conversion implies that if enough information is available about a person's psychological and social background; then one can predict whether or not that person will be converted." The old paradigm has been criticized on the ground that it neglects the agency of individuals and strives to identify high-risk "profiles," an endeavor which has turned out to be vain, as emphasized by Daniela Pisoiu (chapter 2) and John F. Morrison (chapter 5) in this volume. The overwhelming majority of researchers have progressively moved away from such pathologizing interpretations of conversion and have distanced themselves from brainwashing models. It is considered that "coercive conversions" (Lofland and Skonovd 1981) are extremely rare, and so are cases of coercive radicalization. In fact, according to specialist of terror networks Marc Sageman (2004, 125), "five decades of research have failed to provide any empirical support for the brainwashing thesis."

Instead, a new understanding of conversion emerged at the end of the 1970s, focusing on converts as autonomous actors engaged in activities of meaning-seeking. As put by Bryan Taylor (1976), the focus shifted from "someone who is converted" to "someone who converts." The "new" paradigm portrays conversion as the result of an active quest for truth by a subject. Roger Straus's research (1976) on how individuals "change themselves" was one of the first explicitly active treatments of religious conversion. This is not to suggest that individuals are purely autonomous agents strategically trying out different options and exercising their absolute free will, as some rational choice theories would have it. To be sure, these choices remain constrained by social conditions of existence and interpersonal relations (see the following sections). Yet, the new paradigm helps us depart from pathologizing accounts of conversion and radicalization by considering how certain sets of beliefs and practices might actually make sense for some individuals at certain points in their lives. This approach can be productively enlisted to understand how and why individuals deliberately adopt radical beliefs and behaviors.

Time and Change

Another dividing line in conversion research has to do with the relationship to time and change. Early works on conversion conceptualized it as a marked rupture between a before and an after. In line with the genealogy of conversion as a predominantly Christian term (Asad 1993), these accounts were heavily influenced by Paul's conversion story as related in the Bible (Mossière 2007): On the road to Damascus, Paul, a young and ambitious Jewish man who acquired fame by persecuting the first Christians, is blinded by the light and saved by God. Sudden and dramatic, his conversion is also a single terminal event, inaugurating a dichotomous relationship to time: Paul was Jewish; he is now Christian.

Contrasting with this narrative of discontinuity, sociological and anthropological literature on conversion has tended to emphasize the continuous nature of religious change. Several scholars have proposed to conceptualize conversion as a *process* with various stages (Rambo 1993; Greil and Rudy 1983; Straus 1979; Lofland and Stark 1965) or even as a *career* (Richardson 1978; Gooren 2005). In a seminal article, Straus (1979) wrote that "the act of conversion is not a terminal act." In his study of conversion across the Mediterranean world during antiquity, Thomas Finn (1997, 30) added that conversion "meant a transforming change of religion, but *not something over and done with*" (emphasis mine). These considerations have been applied to the study of conversion to Islam specifically. Tina Gudrun Jensen (2006) explores how converts learn to become Muslim, emphasizing that conversion to Islam is "a *gradual process* of change and transformation" (emphasis mine). As for Anna Mansson McGinty (2006, 188), she writes that "the process of becoming Muslim is *neither final nor predictable*; there are no sudden breaks or absolute changes; it is gradual" (emphasis mine). Juliette Galonnier (2018) has also argued that becoming Muslim is not about "moving into" Islam but rather a process of "moving toward" it.

This gradual approach to conversion is actually in line with findings from the sociology of deviance (Parrucci 1968), especially Howard Becker's work on marijuana users. In *Outsiders* (1991 [1963], 30), Becker writes: "We are not so much interested in the person who commits a deviant act once as in the person who sustains a pattern of deviance over a long period of time, who makes of deviance a way of life, who organizes his identity around a pattern of deviant behavior." Likewise, sociological scholarship on conversion is not so much interested in the person who simply converts as in the convert who maintains a pattern of religiosity in the long run. Thus, Straus (1979, 161) has argued that the "reasons why a person might seek conversion become of secondary interest to the question of *how does a person manage to maintain across time* any form of strict social, behavioral and/or phenomenological organization" (emphasis mine). Straus suggests that instead of focusing on the *why* of conversion and endlessly looking for static conversion causes or motives, it is more fruitful to study *how* religious commitment is built and maintained over time. In the case of new religious movements or radical groups, such commitment can be secured by the development of a plausibility structure (Berger 1967), the emphasis on discipline—strict churches are strong (Iannaccone 1994), the enforcement of a sense of religious exclusivism (being the only saved sect), the threat of exclusion from the group, and the ability to offer a straightforward economy of salvation.[1]

In short, what matters for these scholars is not so much the decision to convert but rather how conversion is secured and stabilized and how converts progressively solidify religious dispositions and learn to persevere in their beliefs and actions in spite of challenges and contradictions. Contrary to the Pauline assumption, complete religious change is not acquired through the mere act of conversion. It must be *achieved* a posteriori. Hence, while it is often presented as a single event pinpointed in time, conversion is rather made of a multiplicity of events that stretch over time: It is a drawn-out process of accomplishment, rather than a fait accompli. It seems more appropriate, therefore, to talk of "converting persons" rather than "converts," and we might as well start talking about "radicalizing individuals" instead of "radicals," for radicalization is, like conversion, a protracted process (Crettiez 2016). An attention to time also implies taking into account what individuals convert *from*, in addition to what they convert *to*. What is it that converts and radicals leave behind? What type of self and life do they withdraw from? What social role do they exit (Ebaugh 1988)? Answers to these questions must be a central part of our investigations.

---

1. The centrality of the economy of salvation in the radicalization process is particularly evident in the German case study provided by Robert Pelzer and Mika Moeller in chapter 8 of this volume.

Micro, Macro, and Meso Approaches: The Centrality of Collective Life

One additional cleavage separates scholars who see conversion as a purely individual act from those who view it as the result of macro-sociological changes. In the first approach, characteristic of early academic models, religious change is described as a personal and intimate gesture. Here again, the influence of the Pauline metaphor seems preponderant. In the Bible, Paul, alone, suddenly embraces a new worldview and rejects his former social identity. His experience is ineffable, incommunicable to other human beings: Conversion is portrayed as individual and individuating, a subversive gesture that asserts the importance of private faith over group identity.

Such understanding of conversion as an eminently individual act has been severely criticized. Danièle Hervieu-Léger notices that "conversion, which is presented by those concerned with it as the most intimate and private experience they ever went through, is in fact a social and socially determined act" (1999, 120, my translation). The individualistic approach to conversion, it is argued, misses the larger processes at play (Yang 1998). It is unable to understand for instance why whole societies or communities massively convert to a religion at a particular point in time. According to Orlando Woods (2012), "changes in the structure of society, perhaps unknown to converts themselves, play a key role in determining religious choice." Hence, scholars have advocated for a more macro understanding of religious conversion by linking it to larger social processes and by taking into account the structures of societies, specifically in terms of socioeconomic equality and political regimes as well as precipitating historical events.

Yet, the cleavage between the individualist and macro perspectives leaves unaddressed the intermediary role of collective life. On the one hand, the individualist conception misses the fact that in order to corroborate personal convictions, individuals cannot rely on their own subjectivity. They need to share their experience with others to obtain an external proof that their beliefs are relevant (Hervieu-Léger 1999, 180; Richardson and Kilbourne 1989). Thus, even in the realm of religious individualism, believing implies belonging, if not to an institutionalized religion, at least to a small group with whom one can share one's beliefs. This is as true about conversion as it is about radicalization, since recent research shows that lone-wolf radicalization is mostly a myth (Crettiez et al. 2017). On the other hand, the macro sociological perspective explains conversion by a series of societal changes (e.g., invasions, commercial exchanges, economic incentives), but never gets to explain how, practically, individuals get to learn about the new beliefs, practices, rules of sociability, speech manners, food habits, and clothing requirements of their new religion. While phenomena of massive conversions certainly stem from large historical changes, they need to be operationalized at the micro-sociological level.

Certainly, small groups have a role to play in this endeavor. Accordingly, a number of studies now focus on the meso role of religious groups in structuring conversion and radicalization paths. Indeed, research on small groups has demonstrated that it is through them that "individuals find arenas to enact their autonomous selves and to demonstrate allegiance to communities and institutions" (Fine and Harrington 2004, 344). Small groups help converts operationalize religious dogmas that would otherwise remain very abstract. Conversion, therefore, is not only an individual or macro-sociological event, but also a meso sociological process involving interaction between converts and group members. Writing about the learning process of smoking marijuana, Howard Becker (1953, 242) explained that: "an individual will be able to use marijuana for pleasure only . . . [after] a *series of communicative acts in which others point out new aspects of his experience to him*, present him with new interpretations of events, and help him achieve a new conceptual organization of his world, without which the new behavior is not possible" (emphasis mine). Hence, interaction with others appears crucial in the formation of a new self. This analysis applies word for word to the experience of converts, who stabilize their religious practice and progressively build loyalty toward the group through exchanges with their peers.

Accordingly, several sociological studies on conversion have devoted substantial attention to the role of small groups and collective life (Balch 1980; Snow and Phillips 1980). Straus (1979) was the first to conceptualize conversion as a "*collective accomplishment*." Theodore Long and Jeffrey Hadden (1983), in their study of the Unification Church, propose to understand conversion as a *process of socialization*. They suggest that we pay closer attention to the ways religious groups *create* and *incorporate* new members. According to them, recruitment precedes belief and commitment. In her study of conversion to Mormonism, Sophie-Hélène Trigeaud (2013) also convincingly describes how Mormons "manufacture" (*fabriquer*) members through an all-encompassing education that durably shapes their subjectivity. Yannick Fer (2010), in his ethnography of conversion to Pentecostalism, highlights the central role of Pentecostal institutions in shaping conversion trajectories while maintaining the illusion that converts reconnect with their "true selves." In an interview study with American converts to Russian Orthodoxy, H. B. Cavalcanti and H. Paul Chalfant (1944, 452) argue that collective life should be given a central place in scholarship on conversion: It "should be seen as more than the wallpaper that forms the background of your beliefs," but rather as "the creative energy which forms individuals' norms and values."

A significant part of the conversion literature also insists on "role playing," "trying out," and "experimenting" as central to religious change. Thus, David Bromley and Anson Shupe (1979) reverse the conventional sequence of conversion explanations (pre-dispositioning needs → new beliefs → practice and inclusion into a group) and consider on the contrary that novices first meet a group, then start experimenting with their new role as potential believers, and subsequently embrace the corresponding set of beliefs (if the situation suits them). For David Snow and Richard Machalek (1983), conversion is characterized by an ability to "embrace the convert role." In his study of a UFO cult, Robert Balch (1980) has aptly shown that participants convert by adopting the roles of converts, even though they do not necessarily believe in all the precepts of the cult. In his interpretation, conversion results first and foremost from participation: It is by actively engaging in a conversion role that seekers develop dispositions that might eventually convince them to adhere to a new set of beliefs. This is in line with the comments made by John F. Morrison in chapter 5 of this volume, according to which social involvement with a group tends to precede ideological commitment.

In sum, individuals cannot convert alone: They need the support of religious groups to give them guidelines, set the modalities of their worship, accompany them throughout their transformation and grant them recognition as authentic members of the group. Carolyn Chen (2008, 61), in her study of Taiwanese immigrants converting to Christianity, therefore explains that converts *belong before believing*. Conversion processes are therefore eminently *relational*. This is also in line with past research on terrorism showing that social networks tend to matter more than ideological convictions in the commitment to action (Sageman 2004, 113). In this perspective, radicalization "stems from complex and contingent sets of interactions among individuals, groups, and institutional actors" (della Porta 2018, 463).

Beliefs and Practices: The Role of Embodiment

A last debate focuses on whether conversion happens at the cognitive or behavioral level. In a seminal yet contested article, John Lofland and Rodney Stark (1965) had defined conversion as a "change in worldview or perspective." In this view, conversion was said to happen at the level of consciousness. It was akin to a "change of heart" (Heirich 1977), a "reorientation of the soul" (Nock 1933). It occurred when new beliefs were adopted and professed. Even if most sociological works also recognize the importance of a change in behavior and practices for conversion to be complete, these new behaviors and practices are generally described as *resulting from* the adoption of new beliefs (Snow and Machalek 1984).

Yet, recent anthropological research on religion has demonstrated that religious practices are much more than a mere reflection of beliefs. Rather, they can also be the *means* through which beliefs are cultivated. The idea that bodily practices are meant to create moral dispositions has first been put forward by Marcel Mauss (1973, 87), who wrote that "at the bottom of all our mystical states, there are body techniques." This idea has been further explored by Talal Asad (1993) and Saba Mahmood (2012), who each talk about the role of prayer as a means to cultivate pious selves and reinforce the desire for worship.

These considerations have recently been applied to the study of conversion (Van Nieuwkerk 2014; Yang and Abel 2014). In a valuable ethnographic study on Muslim converts in Missouri, Daniel Winchester (2008, 1754–55) has written extensively about the primary role of embodied religious practices in converts' attempts to develop their moral Muslim selves and embrace a new Muslim habitus. He found that "converts did not see their practices as derivative of an already fully-formed moral reason, but rather understood practices such as prayer and fasting as central to the ongoing development of their new moral selves." Karin Van Nieuwkerk (2014) also writes that "conversion is not solely a mental activity of accepting a new belief. It requires the embodiment of new social and religious practices." In her study of female converts to Islam in France and Quebec, Géraldine Mossière (2011) also suggests that her interviewees become Muslim by "disciplining their bodies" to "transform their spirit." This scholarship invites us to acknowledge the central role of the *body* in processes of conversion, an "absolutely crucial" factor, which according to Manni Crone (2016) has been largely ignored in radicalization research. The incorporation of a new set of religious beliefs and practices involves a number of body techniques that must be studied. This is particularly necessary when examining the development of violent dispositions. As put by Crone (2016, 601), "Young aspiring extremists do not become radicalized by taking part in highbrow discussions about the concept of jihad. Rather, they pick up specific ways of behaving, fighting, shooting and dressing." There is therefore no clear-cut separation between "cognitive" (mind) or "behavioral" (body) transformation, and if anything, it seems that the latter predates the former. This must be taken into account in current research, which often tends to differentiate between cognitive and behavioral radicalization—or radicalization of opinion and radicalization of action (McCauley and Moskalenko 2014)—while the two are in fact inextricably linked: It is not about "either or," as Peter Neumann (2013) reminds us.

Conclusion

In this chapter, I have argued that conversion models can play their part in solving the puzzle of radicalization. Indeed, conversion scholarship has been exposed to the same debates and controversies that now engulf the concept of radicalization: It has been criticized for pathologizing religious transformations, for overemphasizing individual factors, for prioritizing ideology and beliefs over practice, and for neglecting the processual nature of change. Scholars have taken into account such criticisms to craft more rigorous conversion research. This literature can therefore be productively enrolled to overcome the shortcomings of current radicalization research. Several takeaway points can be drawn from this chapter.

First, the concept of "liminality" is useful in thinking about the tipping conditions that can foster radicalization. A central characteristic of conversion trajectories, liminality constitutes a state of indeterminacy and uncertainty. While it is generally happily embraced, it can also push some individuals to adopt rigid, intransigent, and possibly violent behavior.

Second, recent conversion studies encourage us to break away from pathologizing explanations of radicalization, in which individuals are portrayed as passive, contaminated, or brainwashed. Such approaches have now been rejected in conversion scholarship, which rather advocates taking seriously individuals' agency, worldviews, and repertoires of justification.

Third, in understanding radicalization and conversion, it appears more productive to focus on the *how* rather than the *why*, that is, to trace *routes* rather than *roots* (Horgan 2008). The literature on conversion has demonstrated that we should move away from an analysis of static causes and motives to an analysis of dynamic processes and trajectories. Interpretations in terms of predispositions, "profiles," or sociological determinisms have proven limited, and it is more fruitful to focus on the contingent assemblages of conditions and circumstances that potentially lead to radicalization.

Fourth, in describing how people reorder and reorient their lives, we must break away from a dichotomous approach to time and change, characterized by a marked rupture between a before and an after. Conversion is rather a continuous, gradual, and protracted process. Furthermore, such a process is not linear, but made of forward and backward moves, doubts and hesitations that unfold in a chronologically irregular manner. This indeterminacy must be further considered in radicalization research.

Fifth, it is necessary to pay acute attention to the role of social networks, affective ties, and interaction. Radicalization must be framed as a collective accomplishment rather than an isolated individual gesture. Greater attention must be paid to how movements attract, incorporate, and manufacture new members by durably shaping their sense of self through interaction.

Sixth, the literature on conversion teaches us that beliefs are not the only locus of religious transformation and that it is through embodied practice, participation in collective life, and role learning that genuine conviction is ultimately produced. Thus, it becomes necessary to move from an exclusive focus on "ideas" to a more pragmatic approach about how radical commitment is secured: In particular, it is important to understand how new radical beliefs and modes of action become incorporated into one's body.

In sum, paying attention to the debates in the conversion literature helps us break away with conventional wisdom about radicalization and enables us to refound the concept on a more rigorous basis. Yet, conversion models are not a panacea, and several caveats must be borne in mind when applying them to the study of radicalization.

One limit of the conversion literature is its strong religious connotation. Even though conversion models have been used to study enrollment in different types of groups and careers, such as Alcoholics Anonymous (Greil and Rudy 1983) or anorexia (Darmon 2008), they remain firmly associated with studies on religion and religious phenomena. Although religion and ideology do play a role in radicalization processes, this should not deflect us from the fact that these processes are not *only* religious and ideological but also social and political.

Another limit of conversion models is that they do not sufficiently cover the organizational dynamics and relational positionalities of various converting groups. An encompassing view of the larger ecosystem of these groups is missing, which prevents us from explaining why some of them start viewing violence as a legitimate mode of action and others do not. Stefan Malthaner (2017, 375) has highlighted the need to embed the analysis of "radical movements and militant groups within a broader relational field of actors involved in political conflict." Conversion models are not necessarily equipped to do that: As such, they are only one entry point into the study of radicalization and must be complemented with other approaches, such as social movement theories (see Pisoiu, chapter 2 of this volume).

Finally, one of the remaining questions of the conversion literature is the issue of deconversion, disaffiliation, and disengagement (Fillieule 2015), whereby converts "move out" after having "moved in" (Van Nieuwkerk 2018). Given the high turnover rates of NRMs—research suggests that the overwhelming majority of joiners end up leaving (Dawson 2009, 7)—one can wonder about the sustainability of conversion. Solving this puzzle requires extensive longitudinal research. In addition, we must also explore what has been called the "challenge of the second-generation" (Barker 1995). In other words, what happens to converts' children? Can commitment be secured across generations? Do the "born-intos" behave like the "born-agains"? Likewise, in the coming years students of radicalization will have to face the challenge of determining whether radical beliefs and behaviors are transmitted across generations or fade away.

REFERENCES

Adraoui, Mohamed-Ali. 2013. *Du Golfe Aux Banlieues: Le Salafisme Mondialisé.* Proche Orient. Paris: Presses Universitaires de France.

Adraoui, Mohamed-Ali. 2019. "Trajectoires de Convertis au Salafisme en France: Marginalisation, Socialisation, Conversion." *Archives de Sciences Sociales des Religions* 186 (2): 53–70.

Arslan, Leyla. 2010. *Enfants d'Islam et de Marianne.* Paris: Presses Universitaires de France. https://doi.org/10.3917/puf.arsla.2010.01

Asad, Talal. 1993. *Genealogies of Religion: Discipline and Reasons of Power in Christianity and Islam.* Baltimore, MD: Johns Hopkins University Press.

Baker-Beall, Christopher, Charlotte Heath-Kelly, and Lee Jarvis, eds. 2015. *Counter-Radicalisation: Critical Perspectives.* London: Routledge.

Balch, Robert W. 1980. "Looking Behind the Scenes in a Religious Cult: Implications for the Study of Conversion." *Sociology of Religion* 41 (2): 137–43. https://doi.org/10.2307/3709905

Barker, Eileen. 1989. *New Religious Movements: A Practical Introduction.* London: HMSO.

Barker, Eileen. 1995. "Plus Ça Change . . ." *Social Compass* 42 (2): 165–80. https://doi.org/10.1177/003776895042002002

Bartoszewicz, Monika G. 2013. "Controversies of Conversions: The Potential Terrorist Threat of European Converts to Islam." *Perspectives on Terrorism* 7 (3): 17–29. https://www.jstor.org/stable/26296937

Barylo, William. 2018. "People Do Not Convert but Change: Critical Analysis of Concepts of Spiritual Transitions." In *Moving In and Out of Islam*, edited by Karin van Nieuwkerk, 27–43. Austin: University of Texas Press.

Becker, Howard S. 1953. "Becoming a Marihuana User." *American Journal of Sociology* 59 (3): 235–42.

Becker, Howard S. 1991 [1963]. *Outsiders: Studies in the Sociology of Deviance.* New York: The Free Press.

Berger, Peter L. 1967. *The Sacred Canopy: Elements of a Sociological Theory of Religion.* New York: Doubleday & Company.

Borum, Randy. 2011. "Radicalization into Violent Extremism I: A Review of Social Science Theories." *Journal of Strategic Security* 4 (4): 7–36. https://doi.org/10.50 38/1944-0472.4.4.1

Bromley, David G., and Anson D. Shupe. 1979. "Just a Few Years Seem like a Lifetime: A Role Theory Approach to Participation in Religious Movements." In *Research in Social Movements, Conflicts and Change, Vol. 2*, edited by Louis Kriesberg, 159–85. Greenwich: JAI Press.

Cavalcanti, H. B., and H. Paul Chalfant. 1994. "Collective Life as the Ground of Implicit Religion: The Case of American Converts to Russian Orthodoxy." *Sociology of Religion* 55 (4): 441–54. https://doi.org/10.2307/3711981

Chen, Carolyn. 2008. *Getting Saved in America: Taiwanese Immigration and Religious Experience*. Princeton: Princeton University Press.

Crettiez, Xavier. 2016. "Penser la Radicalisation: Une Sociologie Processuelle des Variables de l'Engagement Violent." *Revue Française de Science Politique* 66 (5): 709–27. https://doi.org/10.3917/rfsp.665.0709

Crettiez, Xavier, Sèze Romain, Bilel Ainine, and Thomas Lindemann. 2017. "Saisir les Mécanismes de la Radicalisation Violente: Pour une Analyse Processuelle et Biographique des Engagements Violents." Paris: Rapport de Recherche Pour la Mission de Recherche Droit et Justice. https://halshs.archives-ouvertes.fr/hals hs-01592825

Crone, Manni. 2016. "Radicalization Revisited: Violence, Politics and the Skills of the Body." *International Affairs* 92 (3): 587–604. https://doi.org/10.1111/1468 -2346.12604

Darmon, Muriel. 2008. *Devenir Anorexique: Une Approche Sociologique*. Paris: La Découverte.

Dawson, Lorne L. 2009. "The Study of New Religious Movements and the Radicalization of Home-Grown Terrorists: Opening a Dialogue." *Terrorism and Political Violence* 22 (1): 1–21. https://doi.org/10.1080/09546550903409163

della Porta, Donatella. 2018. "Radicalization: A Relational Perspective." *Annual Review of Political Science* 21 (1): 461–74. https://doi.org/10.1146/annurev-pol isci-042716-102314

Duderija, Adis. 2007. "Literature Review: Identity Construction in the Context of Being a Minority Immigrant Religion: The Case of Western-Born Muslims." *Immigrants & Minorities* 25 (2): 141–62. https://doi.org/10.1080/02619280802 018132

Ebaugh, Helen Rose Fuchs. 1988. *Becoming an Ex: The Process of Role Exit*. Chicago: University of Chicago Press. http://site.ebrary.com/id/10814949

Fadil, Nadia, Francesco Ragazzi, and Martijn de Koning, eds. 2019. *Radicalization in Belgium and the Netherlands: Critical Perspectives on Violence and Security*. London: I.B. Tauris.

Fer, Yannick. 2010. "The Holy Spirit and the Pentecostal Habitus. Elements for a Sociology of Institution in Classical Religion Pentecostalism." *Nordic Journal of Religion and Society* 23 (2): 157–76.

Ferguson, Neil, and Eve Binks. 2015. "Understanding Radicalization and Engagement in Terrorism through Religious Conversion Motifs." *Journal of Strategic Security* 8 (1–2): 16–26. https://doi.org/10.5038/1944-0472.8.1.1430

Fillieule, Olivier. 2015. "Disengagement from Radical Organizations: A Process and Multi-Level Model of Analysis." In *Movements in Times of Transition*, edited by Bert Klandermans and Cornelis van Stralen, 34–63. Philadelphia: Temple University Press.

Fine, Gary Alan, and Brooke Harrington. 2004. "Tiny Publics: Small Groups and Civil Society." *Sociological Theory* 22 (3): 341–56.

Finn, Thomas M. 1990. "It Happened One Saturday Night: Ritual and Conversion in Augustine's North Africa." *Journal of the American Academy of Religion* LVIII (4): 589–616. https://doi.org/10.1093/jaarel/LVIII.4.589

Finn, Thomas M. 1997. *From Death to Rebirth: Ritual and Conversion in Antiquity*. Mahwah, NJ: Paulist Press.

Flower, Scott. 2013. "Muslim Converts and Terrorism." *Counter Terrorist Trends and Analyses* 5 (11): 6–9.

Flower, Scott, and Scott Kleinmann. 2013. "From Convert to Extremist: New Muslims and Terrorism." *The Conversation*, May 24, 2013. http://theconversati on.com/from-convert-to-extremist-new-muslims-and-terrorism-14643

Galonnier, Juliette. 2017. "Choosing Faith and Facing Race: Converting to Islam in France and the United States." Sociology, Paris and Evanston: Sciences Po and Northwestern University.

Galonnier, Juliette. 2018. "Moving In or Moving Toward. Reconceptualizing Conversion to Islam as a Liminal Process." In *Moving In and Out of Islam*, edited by Karin van Nieuwkerk, 44–66. Austin: University of Texas Press.

García-Arenal, Mercedes. 2001. *Conversions Islamiques: Identités Religieuses en Islam Méditerranéen*. Maisonneuve et Larose.

Githens-Mazer, Jonathan. 2012. "The Rhetoric and Reality: Radicalization and Political Discourse." *International Political Science Review* 33 (5): 556–67. https://doi.org/10.1177/0192512112454416

Githens-Mazer, Jonathan, and Robert Lambert. 2010. "Why Conventional Wisdom on Radicalization Fails: The Persistence of a Failed Discourse." *International Affairs* 86 (4): 889–901. https://doi.org/10.1111/j.1468-2346.2010.00918 .x

Gooren, Henri. 2005. "The Conversion Career Approach: Why People Become and Remain Religiously Active." Rochester, NY: Society for the Scientific Study of Religion (SSSR).

Gooren, Henri. 2007. "Reassessing Conventional Approaches to Conversion: Toward a New Synthesis." *Journal for the Scientific Study of Religion* 46 (3): 337–53. https://doi.org/10.1111/j.1468-5906.2007.00362.x

Greil, Arthur L., and David R. Rudy. 1983. "Conversion to the World View of Alcoholics Anonymous: A Refinement of Conversion Theory." *Qualitative Sociology* 6 (1): 5–28. https://doi.org/10.1007/BF0098719

Heath-Kelly, Charlotte. 2013. "Counter-Terrorism and the Counterfactual: Producing the "Radicalisation" Discourse and the UK PREVENT Strategy." *The British Journal of Politics and International Relations* 15 (3): 349–415.

Heirich, Max. 1977. "Change of Heart: A Test of Some Widely Held Theories About Religious Conversion." *American Journal of Sociology* 83 (3): 653–80. https://doi.org/10.1086/226598

Hervieu-Léger, Danièle. 1999. *La Religion en Mouvement: le Pélerin et le Converti*. Flammarion.

Horgan, John. 2008. "From Profiles to Pathways and Roots to Routes: Perspectives from Psychology on Radicalization into Terrorism." *The ANNALS of the American Academy of Political and Social Science* 618 (1): 80–94. https://doi.org/10.1177/0002716208317539

Iannaccone, Laurence R. 1994. "Why Strict Churches Are Strong." *American Journal of Sociology* 99 (5): 1180–1211. https://doi.org/10.1086/230409

Inge, Anabel. 2017. *The Making of a Salafi Muslim Woman: Paths to Conversion.* Oxford: Oxford University Press.

Jensen, Tina Gudrun. 2006. "Religious Authority and Autonomy Intertwined: The Case of Converts to Islam in Denmark." *The Muslim World* 96 (4): 643–60. https://doi.org/10.1111/j.1478-1913.2006.00151.x

Karagiannis, Emmanuel. 2012. "European Converts to Islam: Mechanisms of Radicalization." *Politics, Religion & Ideology* 13 (1): 99–113. https://doi.org/10.1080/21567689.2012.659495

Khosrokhavar, Farhad. 2014. *Radicalisation.* Paris: Éditions de la Maison des sciences de l'homme. http://books.openedition.org/editionsmsh/10882

Kleinmann, Scott Matthew. 2012. "Radicalization of Homegrown Sunni Militants in the United States: Comparing Converts and Non-Converts." *Studies in Conflict & Terrorism* 35 (4): 278–97. https://doi.org/10.1080/1057610X.2012.656299

Kundnani, Arun. 2012. "Radicalisation: The Journey of a Concept." *Race & Class* 54 (2): 3–25. https://doi.org/10.1177/0306396812454984

Langone, Michael D. 2006. "Responding to Jihadism: A Cultic Studies Perspective." *Cultic Studies Review* 5 (2): 268–306.

Le Pape, Loïc. 2009. "Tout Change, Mais Rien ne Change: Les Conversions Religieuses Sont-elles des Bifurcations?" In *Bifurcations*, edited by Michel Grossetti, 212–23. Paris: La Découverte.

Leclerc, Jean-Marc. 2012. "Bruguière: Les Convertis à l'Islam Sont les Plus Dangereux." *Le Figaro*, October 7, 2012. https://www.lefigaro.fr/actualite-france/2012/10/07/01016-20121007ARTFIG00163-terrorisme-les-proselytes-musulmanssont-dangereux.php

Lofland, John, and Norman Skonovd. 1981. "Conversion Motifs." *Journal for the Scientific Study of Religion* 20 (4): 373–85. https://doi.org/10.2307/1386185

Lofland, John, and Rodney Stark. 1965. "Becoming a World-Saver: A Theory of Conversion to a Deviant Perspective." *American Sociological Review* 30 (6): 862–75. https://doi.org/10.2307/2090965

Long, Theodore E., and Jeffrey K. Hadden. 1983. "Religious Conversion and the Concept of Socialization: Integrating the Brainwashing and Drift Models." *Journal for the Scientific Study of Religion* 22 (1): 1–14. https://doi.org/10.2307/1385588

Mahmood, Saba. 2012. *Politics of Piety: The Islamic Revival and the Feminist Subject.* Princeton: Princeton University Press.

Malthaner, Stefan. 2017. "Radicalization: The Evolution of an Analytical Paradigm." *European Journal of Sociology / Archives Européennes de Sociologie* 58 (3): 369–401. https://doi.org/10.1017/S0003975617000182

Marchal, Roland, and Zekeria Ould Ahmed Salem. 2018. "What Is the Concept of 'Radicalization' Good For?" *Politique Africaine* 149 (1): 5–20. https://doi.org/10.3917/polaf.149.0005

Mathiot, Cédric. 2015. "Profil des Jihadistes Français: La Ratatouille de France 2." *Libération*, December 1, 2015. https://www.liberation.fr/desintox/2015/12/01/profil-des-jihadistes-francais-la-ratatouille-de-france-2_1417423

Mauss, Marcel. 1973. "Techniques of the Body." *Economy and Society* 2 (1): 70–88. https://doi.org/10.1080/03085147300000003

McCauley, Clark, and Sophia Moskalenko. 2014. "Toward a Profile of Lone Wolf Terrorists: What Moves an Individual from Radical Opinion to Radical Action." *Terrorism and Political Violence* 26 (1): 69–85. https://doi.org/10.1080/09546553.2014.849916

McGinty, Anna Mansson. 2006. *Becoming Muslim: Western Women's Conversions to Islam*. Basingstoke: Palgrave Macmillan.

Moosavi, Leon. 2012. "British Muslim Converts Performing 'Authentic Muslimness.'" *Performing Islam* 1 (1): 103–28. https://doi.org/10.1386/pi.1.1.103_1

Mossière, Géraldine. 2007. "La Conversion Religieuse: Approches Épistémologiques et Polysémie d'un Concept." Montréal: Centre d'Études Ethniques des Universités Montréalaises: Groupe de Recherche Diversité Urbaine.

Mossière, Géraldine. 2011. "Devenir Musulmane pour Discipliner le Corps et Transformer l'Esprit: L'Herméneutique du Sujet Pieux Comme Voie de Restauration du Soi." *Ethnologies* 33 (1): 117–42. https://doi.org/10.7202/1007799ar

Mullins, Sam. 2015. "Re-Examining the Involvement of Converts in Islamist Terrorism: A Comparison of the U.S. and U.K." *Perspectives on Terrorism* 9 (6): 72–84. https://www.universiteitleiden.nl/binaries/content/assets/customsites/perspectives-on-terrorism/2015/volume-6/6-re-examining-the-involvement-of-converts-in-islamist-terrorism.-a-comparison-of-the-u.s.-and-u.k.-by-sam-mullins.pdf

Murad, Sh. Abdal Hakim. 2014 [1997]. "British and Muslim?" Masud.Co.Uk. http://masud.co.uk/british-and-muslim

Neumann, Peter. 2013. "The Trouble with Radicalization." *International Affairs* 89 (4): 873–93.

Neumann, Peter, and Scott Kleinmann. 2013. "How Rigorous Is Radicalization Research?" *Democracy and Security* 9 (4): 360–82. https://doi.org/10.1080/17419166.2013.802984

Nock, Arthur Darby. 1933. *Conversion*. New York: New York University Press.

Özyürek, Esra. 2009. "Convert Alert: German Muslims and Turkish Christians as Threats to Security in the New Europe." *Comparative Studies in Society and History* 51 (1): 91–116. https://doi.org/10.1017/S001041750900005X

Parrucci, Dennis J. 1968. "Religious Conversion: A Theory of Deviant Behavior." *Sociology of Religion* 29 (3): 144–54. https://doi.org/10.2307/3710147

Pew Research Center. 2017. "U.S. Muslims Concerned About Their Place in Society, but Continue to Believe in the American Dream: Findings from Pew Research Center's 2017 Survey of U.S. Muslims." July 26, 2017. https://www.pewforum.org/2017/07/26/findings-from-pew-research-centers-2017-survey-of-us-muslims

Rambo, Lewis. 1993. *Understanding Religious Conversion*. New Haven: Yale University Press.

Richards, Anthony. 2011. "The Problem with 'Radicalization': The Remit of 'Prevent' and the Need to Refocus on Terrorism in the UK." *International Affairs* 87 (1): 143–52. https://doi.org/10.1111/j.1468-2346.2011.00964.x

Richardson, James T. 1978. *Conversion Careers: In and Out of the New Religions*. Beverly Hills, CA: Sage.

Richardson, James T. 1985. "The Active vs. Passive Convert: Paradigm Conflict in Conversion/Recruitment Research." *Journal for the Scientific Study of Religion* 24 (2): 163–79. https://doi.org/10.2307/1386340

Richardson, James T., and Brock Kilbourne. 1989. "Paradigm Conflict, Types of Conversion, and Conversion Theories." *Sociological Analysis* 50 (1): 1–21. https://doi.org/10.2307/3710915

Roy, Olivier. 2004. *Globalised Islam: The Search for a New Ummah*. London: Hurst and Co.

Roy, Olivier. 2011. "Al-Qaeda: A True Global Movement." In *Jihadi Terrorism and the Radicalisation Challenge: European and American Experiences*, edited by Rik Coolsaet. Surrey: Ashgate.

Roy, Olivier. 2016. *Le Djihad et La Mort*. Paris: Seuil.

Rushchenko, Julia. 2017. "Converts to Islam and Home Grown Jihadism." London: The Henry Jackson Society. http://henryjacksonsociety.org/wp-content/uploads/2017/10/HJS-Converts-to-Islam-Report-web.pdf

Sageman, Marc. 2004. *Understanding Terror Networks*. Philadelphia: University of Pennsylvania Press.

Schuurman, Bart, Peter Grol, and Scott Flower. 2016. "Converts and Islamist Terrorism: An Introduction." The Hague: International Centre for Counter-Terrorism (ICCT). http://icct.nl/publication/converts-and-islamist-terrorism-an-introduction

Sedgwick, Mark. 2007. "Jihad, Modernity, and Sectarianism." *Nova Religio: The Journal of Alternative and Emergent Religions* 11 (2): 6–27. https://doi.org/10.1525/nr.2007.11.2.6

Sedgwick, Mark. 2010. "The Concept of Radicalization as a Source of Confusion." *Terrorism and Political Violence* 22 (4): 479–94. https://doi.org/10.1080/09546553.2010.491009

Shterin, Marat, and Akhmet Yarlykapov. 2011. "Reconsidering Radicalisation and Terrorism: The New Muslims Movement in Kabardino-Balkaria and Its Path to Violence." *Religion, State and Society* 39 (2–3): 303–25. https://doi.org/10.1080/09637494.2011.604512

Simcox, Robin, and Emily Dyer. 2013. "The Role of Converts in Al-Qa`ida-Related Terrorism Offenses in the United States." *CTC Sentinel* 6 (3): 20–24.

Snow, David A., and Richard Machalek. 1983. "The Convert as a Social Type." *Sociological Theory* 1: 259–89. https://doi.org/10.2307/202053

Snow, David A., and Richard Machalek. 1984. "The Sociology of Conversion." *Annual Review of Sociology* 10 (1): 167–90. https://doi.org/10.1146/annurev.so.10.080184.001123

Snow, David A., and Cynthia L. Phillips. 1980. "The Lofland-Stark Conversion Model: A Critical Reassessment." *Social Problems* 27 (4): 430–47. https://doi.org/10.2307/800171

Straus, Roger A. 1976. "Changing Oneself: Seekers and the Creative Transformation of Life Experience." In *Doing Social Life: The Qualitative Study of Human*

Interaction in Natural Settings, edited by John Lofland, 252–72. New York: Wiley Interscience.

Straus, Roger A. 1979. "Religious Conversion as a Personal and Collective Accomplishment." *Sociology of Religion* 40 (2): 158–65. https://doi.org/10.2307/370 9786

Taylor, Bryan. 1976. "Conversion and Cognition: An Area for Empirical Study in the Microsociology of Religious Knowledge." *Social Compass* 23 (1): 5–22. https://doi.org/10.1177/003776867602300101

Travisano, Richard. 1970. "Alternation and Conversion as Qualitatively Different Transformations." In *Social Psychology Through Symbolic Interaction*, edited by Gregory P. Stone and Harold Faberman, 594–606. Waltham, MA: Ginn-Blaisdell.

Trigeaud, Sophie-Hélène. 2013. *Devenir Mormon: La Fabrication Communautaire de l'Individu*. Rennes: Presses Universitaires de Rennes.

Turner, Karen. 2019. "Convertitis and the Struggle with Liminality for Female Converts to Islam in Australia." *Archives de Sciences Sociales des Religions* 186 (2): 71–91.

Turner, Victor W. 1969. *The Ritual Process: Structure and Anti-Structure*. Chicago: Aldine.

Uhlmann, Milena. 2008. "European Converts to Terrorism." *Middle East Quarterly* 15 (3): 31–7.

Van Nieuwkerk, Karin. 2006. "'Islam Is Your Birthright.' Conversion, Reversion and Alternation. The Case of New Muslimas in the West." In *Cultures of Conversion*, edited by Jan N. Bremmer, Wout J. Van Bekkum, and Arie L. Molendijk, 151–64. Leuven: Peeters. https://repository.ubn.ru.nl/handle/2066/41409

Van Nieuwkerk, Karin. 2014. "'Conversion' to Islam and the Construction of a Pious Self." In *The Oxford Handbook of Religious Conversion*, edited by Lewis R. Rambo and Charles E. Farhadian, 667–86. Oxford: Oxford University Press. https://doi.org/10.1093/oxfordhb/9780195338522.013.028

Van Nieuwkerk, Karin, ed. 2018. *Moving In and Out of Islam*. Austin: University of Texas Press.

Van San, Marion. 2015. "Lost Souls Searching for Answers? Belgian and Dutch Converts Joining the Islamic State." *Perspectives on Terrorism* 9 (5).

Vidino, Lorenzo, and Seamus Hughes. 2005. "ISIS in America, From Retweets to Raqqa." Washington DC: Program on Extremism, George Washington University. https://extremism.gwu.edu/sites/g/files/zaxdzs2191/f/downloads/ISIS %20in%20America%20-%20Full%20Report.pdf

Wadud, Amina. 2007. *Inside the Gender Jihad: Women's Reform in Islam*. Oxford: Oneworld.

Winchester, Daniel. 2008. "Embodying the Faith: Religious Practice and the Making of a Muslim Moral Habitus." *Social Forces* 86 (4): 1753–80. https://doi.org /10.1353/sof.0.0038

Wohlrab-Sahr, Monika. 1999. "Conversion to Islam: Between Syncretism and Symbolic Battle." *Social Compass* 46 (3): 351–62. https://doi.org/10.1177/0037 76899046003010

Woodlock, Rachel. 2010. "Praying Where They Don't Belong: Female Muslim Converts and Access to Mosques in Melbourne, Australia." *Journal of Muslim*

Minority Affairs 30 (2): 265–78. https://doi.org/10.1080/13602004.2010.4940 76

Woods, Orlando. 2012. "The Geographies of Religious Conversion." *Progress in Human Geography* 36 (4): 440–56. https://doi.org/10.1177/0309132511427951

Yang, Fenggang. 1998. "Chinese Conversion to Evangelical Christianity: The Importance of Social and Cultural Contexts." *Sociology of Religion* 59 (3): 237–57. https://doi.org/10.2307/3711910

Yang, Fenggang, and Andrew Stuart Abel. 2014. "Sociology of Religious Conversion." In *The Oxford Handbook of Religious Conversion*, edited by Lewis R. Rambo and Charles E. Farhadian, 140–62. Oxford: Oxford University Press. https://doi .org/10.1093/oxfordhb/9780195338522.013.006

FIVE

Social Psychology

John F. Morrison

> Perhaps a useful starting point for what follows is the assumption
> that terrorists are ordinary people to the extent that they are not dis-
> tinguishable from other "ordinary" people who make choices in the
> contexts in which they find themselves. (Taylor and Horgan 2006,
> 588)

It may seem logical to believe that any person involved in terrorism must be
"different," "crazy," or even a "psychopath." Why else, and how else, could
they become involved in such acts, and threats, of violence, often targeting
innocent civilians? However, the research into the psychology of terrorism
does not back up this "logical" assumption. Characterizing involvement in
terrorism as the result, and an expression of, "psychological disturbance"
ostensibly ignores the role that an individual's social and political world
can play in their trajectory toward terrorism (Horgan 2017). It, resultantly,
can mislead those aiming to counter terrorism by focusing purely on a psychological disorder rather than the holistic rationale for terrorist engagement. Such an approach ignores the heterogeneity of terrorist actors, their
roles, and the rationales for becoming involved (Gill and Corner 2017).
By crudely treating psychological disorders as a dichotomous variable, it
ignores their complexity and variety. Recent nuanced research has highlighted that by respecting these complexities we can gain a greater understanding of the role, if any, which mental disorders can play in terrorism.

It has been found that the prevalence rates of specific psychological disorders can differ significantly within terrorist subsamples, most specifically when comparing lone actor and group offenders (Gill and Corner 2017; Corner and Gill 2015; Gill 2015). However, this does not denote that any psychological disorder is in fact the *cause* of engagement in terrorism. For the purposes of this chapter the focus is purely on the social psychology of radicalization within group-based terrorists.

In the quote that opened this chapter, Max Taylor and John Horgan articulated that assuming that terrorist actors are "ordinary people" is a "useful starting point" to gaining an understanding of their involvement in terrorism, at each stage of the terrorist process, from initial involvement to disengagement (2006, 588). If we are to assume this, then when we look to psychology to explain terrorist behavior it is incumbent on us not only to look at psychological disorders, but also to respect the knowledge that we have gained from the analysis of other "ordinary" people across a range of psychological subdisciplines. This chapter focuses on one such subdiscipline, social psychology, which looks at understanding the "relationships, influences, and transactions among people, and particularly group behaviour" (Borum 2011a, 20). The chapter is specifically looking at what social psychology can tell us about radicalization. For the purposes of this chapter, radicalization is defined as "the social and psychological process of incrementally experienced commitment to extremist political or religious ideology" (Horgan 2009, 152). For many researchers, this is seen as a prerequisite to engagement in terrorism or involvement with a terrorist group (Schmid 2013). However, radicalization should not be considered as a proxy for, or a necessary precursor to, terrorism (Borum 2011a). An individual's radicalization can, and does, continue after their initial engagement with a terrorist group and/or terrorist activity. Their involvement may be a result of, and/or justified by, a rationale independent of any ideological radicalization. Radicalization is but one of a variety of trajectories into terrorism (Borum 2011a).

When analyzing radicalization from a psychological, criminological, or sociological standpoint one of the most promising theoretical approaches has been *rational choice theory* (RCT). This theory sees terrorist involvement as the result of a series of cost-benefit analyses. Whether you are looking at an individual's decision to join a terrorist group; a group's decision of who to recruit; an attacker's choice of time, location, or weapon; or a recruit's decision to disengage from the group, one can apply the rational choice theory to understand the decision-making process. Each of these behaviors can be assessed by considering how the actors perceived the nature and outcomes of their decisions, and from that how they assessed the costs and benefits of their decision-making processes. For some even suicide terrorism can be seen as a rational act (Wintrobe 2003). By applying this cost-benefit analysis we are not interested in psychological traits. Rather we wish to consider the normality of the decision-making process leading to what many would consider to be "abnormal" behavior. This approach has been applied successfully by Daniela Pisoiu (2011) in her analysis of Islamist radicalization in Europe. Through the application of RCT she sees radicalization being tantamount to an "occupational change process." Alongside the obvious downsides of membership come rewards, recognition, status, and emotional satisfaction (Pisoiu 2011). By applying theories such as RCT we can meet the challenge of Horgan and Taylor (2006, 588) to consider ordinary people "who make choices in the contexts they find themselves." Each of the factors discussed throughout this chapter can, and do, influence the cost-benefit decision-making processes theorized within rational choice theory.

As is indicated by the chapters in this volume, to gain as comprehensive an understanding as possible of radicalization, and all other concepts relating to involvement in terrorism, we must look at it through an interdisciplinary lens. This will allow us to understand the various facets influencing both individual and group radicalization. As we strive to gain this comprehensive understanding we must not look only at research that has analyzed radicalization and terrorism specifically. In doing so we blinker our vision of what a wider understanding of a variety of fields of research can give us. Therefore the present chapter focuses not only on social psychology research that has analyzed radicalization but also on the broader relevant social-psychological literature. This is because there is a range of concepts and research not directly concentrating on radicalization that can assist in the development of our understanding. In doing so, this dissipates the all too regular urge in terrorism studies to "reinvent the wheel" in order to understand a specific behavior.

By focusing on the contribution that social psychology can make, and has already made, to our understanding of radicalization, the aim is not to put forward a psychological profile of a radicalized actor. In fact, the goal is the complete opposite. It is acknowledged here that there is no psychological profile of a radicalized individual, and/or terrorist actor, and nor will there ever be. This is due to the heterogeneity of terrorism, terrorists, contexts, roles, and rationales. If we were to focus on the quest for a profile, assuming psychologically static qualities, then we run the risk of ignoring the external dynamics, and their qualities, that contribute to the radicalization process. It is this very absence of a psychological profile that necessitates employing a social-psychological approach to radicalization and terrorism. Within this chapter a variety of social-psychological concepts are assessed, including uncertainty (Hogg 2012), trust (Morrison 2016), and the individual quest for significance (Kruglanski et al. 2014). These are within an analysis of two dominant sub-themes, namely *social ties* and *personal identity*.

The terrorism literature is hung up on a variety of methodological issues and difficulties in researching this complex phenomenon. Repetitively, terrorism researchers lament about an inability to gain access to valid and reliable data, be this from primary source interviews or otherwise (Silke 2008). This has led some to, in my opinion wrongly, declare that there has been stagnation in terrorism research (Sageman 2014). For the social-psychological understanding of radicalization to thrive and advance, researchers must be able to meet with and interview radicalized individuals and groups to assess what, if any, social-psychological factors played a role in their radicalization. While difficult, this is not impossible (Horgan 2012). However, primary interview research, while important, should not be considered the only available means we have to gain a social-psychological understanding of radicalization and/or involvement in terrorism.

What follows is the analysis of how social psychology can help us understand radicalization in general. This is designed to give the reader a broad understanding of the psychological processes linked with radicalization. These processes can be associated with a variety of ideological forms of radicalization, unless otherwise stated. It is this general understanding which is first required before we can specify forms of radicalization (e.g., Islamist or right-wing radicalization). We also need to be sure that we are not differentiating if and when there is no clear empirical evidence for this distinction. In terrorism studies there has traditionally been a tendency to differentiate motivations to engage in terrorism as distinctly different from non-political criminality. However, there is much that we can learn from the wider criminological, sociological, and psychological literature. Similarly, within terrorism studies there is at times a tendency to demarcate Islamist terrorism as significantly different, and potentially more problematic, than all other forms of terrorism. Yet there is also much that can be learned about these processes and motivations by analyzing engagement in other forms of terrorism, while still acknowledging if and when there are objectively different processes and mechanisms in play.

The Importance of Context

Throughout this chapter there will be a discussion of some key contributions social psychology can make, and has already made, to our understanding of radicalization. Radicalization is clearly a complex social-psychological process. The discussions of uncertainty, deindividuation, influential individuals, and quests for significance will enlighten us to an extent. However, throughout there must be an appreciation for the parallel role of context, otherwise these insights become worthless. There is a growing acknowledgment of the appreciation for the heterogeneity of terrorist actors. Members of terrorist groups can have different roles, different ranks, different backgrounds, different educational attainment, and different rationales for initially engaging with, and ultimately maintaining membership with, a terrorist group (Horgan, Shortland, and Abbasciano 2018). Alongside these factors is the heterogeneity of contexts in which an individual becomes radicalized. The process of radicalization does not occur in a vacuum (Ravn, Coolsaet, and Sauer 2019). While the social group, and self-perception, can play a key role in an individual's radicalization, the influence of the context in which this radicalization occurs is equally vital to understand. This respect for personal and contextual heterogeneity does not only help us understand the variety of reasons and avenues taken to radicalize. It also helps us develop effective counterterrorism and counter-radicalization strategies.

Just because a group of individuals all radicalize to adhere to a specific extremist ideology, and ultimately join the same group, does not necessarily mean that their radicalization took place for the same reasons. If we take the example of ISIS, it is clear that the individual radicalized in war-torn Syria has a different rationale for radicalization when compared to the individual radicalizing within the relatively peaceful context of Western Europe, North America, Australia, or elsewhere. The direct experience of conflict and in-group discrimination or violent activity versus the distant consumption of propaganda and depictions of perceived injustices provide extremely different contexts in which the radicalization process can and does take place. These contexts can also, at times, differentiate between those who require ideological radicalization as a prerequisite for engagement with a terrorist group and those whose engagement with a terrorist group is purely driven by the context in which they find themselves and their loved ones.

The importance of context is exemplified in the application of the Situational Action Theory (SAT) by Noémie Bouhana and Per-Olof Wikström

(Bouhana 2019; Bouhana and Wikström 2010). Through their research they aim to understand what people, in what contexts, and at what times can be considered as "at risk" of radicalization (Bouhana 2019, 11). They outline that some individuals may be more susceptible to radicalization and the attraction to "extremist moral systems." However, it is not enough for practitioners to concentrate on changing individuals; it will be more beneficial to change the context in which this radicalization takes place. This is due to the understanding that vulnerability to extremism is "inherently context dependent" (Bouhana 2019, 23). It is therefore vital that throughout the reading of this chapter, and others in the volume, the centrality of context is always considered, even if and when the authors do not allude to it.

In Search of a Model

Radicalization researchers are currently consumed with the apparent need to develop an individual model, which can enable us to track and predict a variety of individuals' radicalization trajectories. These models, regularly presented via metaphor (Horgan 2017), too often ignore the complexity and heterogeneity of terrorist actors, their roles, and their rationales in the quest for neatness. However, radicalization, and in turn terrorism, processes are not neat and often do not conform to these models. There should be a realization amongst analysts and researchers alike that there is no one model that explains everyone's radicalization. As is alluded to above, what is more important, and more useful, is an understanding of the context surrounding radicalization (Borum 2011b). Despite the drawbacks of these multiple models, they do provide us with an insight into radicalization, which can direct us toward specific areas of social psychology to give us a deeper understanding. The majority of these models acknowledge that the ideological transformation taking place during radicalization is a social-psychological process, influenced by emotions, cognitions, and social influences (King and Taylor 2011).

As Michael King and Donald Taylor (2011) have observed, both Randy Borum (2003) and Fathali Moghaddam (2005) noted in their models of radicalization that in the process of radicalizing, individuals experience feelings of relative deprivation. This occurs when individuals compare their material conditions to those of others, especially others within an out-group. They in turn view their own group's perceived disadvantage as an injustice. When this is deemed to be a significant injustice or discrimination it may be used as a justification for engagement in violent action. Within relative deprivation, the perceived deprivation is subjective rather than objective in nature. Within social psychology, personal relative deprivation has been found to connect to inward-oriented emotions, including a reduction in self-esteem, heightened depression, and engagement in delinquency. However, group-based relative deprivation, whereby you perceive your group rather than you personally to be deprived in comparison to specific out-groups, has been seen as a strong predictor of collective action and prejudice directed against the relevant out-groups (King and Taylor 2011). It is vital to note when considering relative deprivation that this relates not to actual deprivation but to the perception of deprivation. The perceived deprivation need not be socioeconomic but can relate to a range of issues, from status, to opportunity, to security. It has been observed that while relative deprivation may establish the pool of those who could be potentially radicalized, it is the social networks a person holds that determine whom from this pool is likely to be recruited. However, this relative deprivation can be manipulated and accentuated by recruiters and ideologues wanting to solidify a justification for adherence to radical beliefs. This key role of the social network is analyzed in detail in this chapter's section on social ties.

Borum (2011b, 26) posits that each of the existing models of radicalization have components relating to three central factors:

1. The development of antipathy toward a target group,
2. The creation of a justification for violent action, and
3. The elimination of social and psychological barriers that could inhibit action.

Throughout the chapter is an analysis of the social-psychological processes that can enable these components. In their own analysis of radicalization, Clark McCauley and Sophia Moskalenko (2011) utilize social-psychological principles to explain the radicalization of individuals, groups, and mass populations. This chapter will focus primarily on individual radicalization. Within their analysis these three central factors identified by Borum are once again present. The mechanisms they identify as influencing individual radicalization are: personal grievance, group grievance, slippery slope, love, risk and status, and unfreezing. These mechanisms should not be considered mutually exclusive. An individual may have multiple mechanisms take place leading to their radicalization. While McCauley and Moskalenko refer to these as mechanisms, Borum points out they may actually be better described as "different precipitants or contributing factors" (2011b, 28).

When the authors refer to an individual radicalizing as a result of a personal grievance, this refers to either them or a loved one being the victim of a perceived harm or injustice. This perceived grievance is oftentimes a result of a significant out-group's (or a representative of that out-group's) position, policy, or actions. When someone is radicalized because of a group grievance, the perceived harm or injustice targets a group: their in-group. In their analysis of these mechanisms, McCauley and Moskalenko (2011) propose that personal and group grievances are rarely far apart for those who have been radicalized. The slippery slope phenomenon involves the individual becoming incrementally radicalized through small involvements with a group participating in a political conflict. In turn, they radicalize through a progression of behaviors. Much of the radicalization literature focuses on negative personal relationships and social-psychological phenomena. However, by labeling love as one of the mechanisms of individual radicalization, McCauley and Moskalenko (2011) highlight the role of the most positive emotion of all. Within this they propose that individuals can become radicalized as a result of their positive social emotional bond with an individual or individuals belonging to a radicalized group. This love can draw them into action on behalf of the group. They outline that while trust may determine which radicals or terrorists are recruited, it is love that will determine who will join (see also Morrison 2018, 2016). In espousing the role of risk and status as part of the radicalization process, McCauley and Moskalenko (2011) further distance the radicalization process from being ideologically centered. They state that the risk-taking and status acquired through engagement in terrorism, and with a terrorist group, can especially attract young males. Their final mechanism of "unfreezing" refers to an individual who, after experiencing a destabilizing life event, opens themselves up to new ideas and an identity that may include the possibility of political radicalization (McCauley and Moskalenko 2011).

McCauley and Moskalenko (2008, 417) hypothesize that the radicalization process can be modeled as a pyramid: As the pyramid goes from its base to its apex, "higher levels are associated with decreased numbers but increased radicalization of beliefs, feelings and behaviors." Therefore, radicalization can be assessed along a gradient that distinguishes between terrorists at the tip of the pyramid and their sympathizers at the base. In their 2014 analysis, Kruglanksi and colleagues similarly proposed that there are degrees of radicalization. They illustrate that these degrees of radicalization can be observed by witnessing what an individual "does with" their radicalization. They propose that a person who is a non-combatant member of a terrorist group is less radicalized than a suicide bomber. Across their spectrum, a person who merely supports the terrorist group and their ideology is less idolized than either of these actors (Kruglanski et al. 2014). The notion of degrees of radicalization or the pyramid model proposed by McCauley and Moskalenko (2008) are worthwhile threads to follow. However, dictating that levels of radicalization are in some way analogous to the roles that a person does or does not occupy within a terrorist movement proposes that radicalization is synonymous with involvement in terrorism. This misses the whole point of what radicalization actually is, as dealt with earlier. It proposes that a person's role within the organization is solely the result of their level of adherence to and belief in a specific ideology. This is similar to declaring that a frontline soldier is the most committed to the ideological rationale for their army engaging in combat, a proposal which does not stand up to scrutiny.

Social Ties

Key to the decisions we make in life and the trajectory that life takes are the social ties we hold and discard. The beliefs and actions of individuals with whom we share a personal relationship can shape our own beliefs and actions. This is true for all of us, including those who are radicalized or going through the process of radicalization. Throughout the radicalization literature it has been consistently found that the social ties and network an individual maintains play a significant role in the radicalization process.

In his seminal work analyzing the political socialization of the German Red Army Faction, Klaus Wasmund (1986) demonstrated through data triangulation a more comprehensive understanding of the key social-psychological factors influencing "radicalization" and engagement in terrorism. By combining the analysis of individual terrorist biographies; statements by family members, friends, colleagues, and other acquaintances; materials written by the terrorists; statements and confessions; and the political environment of the time, Wasmund achieved one of the most comprehensive social-psychological analyses of any terrorist group. If one is to assess Wasmund's research findings through a modern-day radicalization lens, the key message is that social involvement with the group actually preceded any ideological commitment. This goes against many modern-day researchers' ascertainment that any involvement in terrorism or with a terrorist group is preceded by ideological radicalization. Wasmund concluded that for many the reasoning behind their engagement with the terrorist group was not because of any ideological commitment but because of their social and personal connections. At the early phase of commitment to and involvement with the group, the members went through a process of dissociation from existing social ties. This involved calling into question existing social and emotional ties, followed by loosening these ties, and ultimately denying everything from their previous lives. In joining what Wasmund (1986) referred to as "total groups," the terrorists were entering an intense, tightly knit community, further segregating them from their previous social existence.

Similar to Wasmund, Donatella della Porta (1988), in her analysis of the Italian Red Brigades, points to the importance of social bonds preceding any ideological commitment or radicalization. In her analysis of 1,214 members of the Red Brigades, she found that it was the social ties and strengthening friendships gained from within the movement that maintained individual involvement in the terrorist group. Like Wasmund, she found that as these ties strengthened, external social ties became weaker and in turn powerless to offset the effect of the group. Yet again, it was the social bonds rather than ideology that were shaping individuals' actions, beliefs, and life trajectories. Through the processes observed by Wasmund, della Porta, and others, terrorists form social connections with a close-knit, influential social group. In turn they adopt the ideology of the group, thus strengthening their social bonds. These research findings should not be seen as completely discounting radicalization preceding terrorist involvement. However, they do highlight the heterogeneity of processes.

When we are looking specifically at the radicalization of Islamist terrorism, the power of social ties has been most notably emphasized in the research of Marc Sageman and his "bunch of guys" theory of radicalization, a theory originally developed by the Canadian police. In this theory, Sageman (2004) proposed that jihadist membership and violence was, in his observation, preceded by alienation from previous social ties, followed by the dominance of social associations with those similar to themselves. They then became a closed society where individuals would adopt the beliefs of the group, which in turn would become more extreme, often resulting from individual members within the group looking to "outdo" the others. This ultimately resulted in the adoption of extremist ideologies, which acted as a justification for the planning of and engagement in terrorism. Through this intense social isolation from any external individuals, groups, or influences, the members of the group gained a heightened level of trust and support for their in-group. However, this was parallel to intensified hate for designated out-groups, who they deemed to have wronged their in-group's ideology and its followers in some way. When this ultimately led to engagement in terrorist violence, they used the perceived victimization of their in-group as justification of their actions.

Already in this chapter we have seen the role that love is hypothesized to play within the radicalization process (McCauley and Moskalenko 2011). Love comes into play due to the interpersonal relationships, or the desire for an interpersonal relationship, between the radicalizing individual and an existing member of the group. The loved one could be classed as an influential individual within the radicalization process. The role of the influential individual can, and does, spread beyond loved ones. One of the most significant forms of influential individual is the role model. This can be someone within the group, a relative, a former organization member, or a noted ideologue. Within the process of radicalization, the role model can be utilized as a "source of authoritative legitimacy" (Horgan 2014). This can be to legitimize an ideological viewpoint and can ultimately play a significant role in the justification of engagement in violent activity. Therefore the perception of the authority that the radicalizing individual holds plays a significant role not only during their process of radicalization, but also in their sustained commitment to the group once a member (Horgan 2014).

Influential individuals play a significant role across a variety of forms of extremism, radicalization, and initial engagement with terrorist groups. In 2011 the present author wrote about why people become violent dissident republicans (Morrison 2011). In this research, based on interviews with close to 50 leadership and rank-and-file members, it was found that influential individuals played a significant role in a person's trajectory toward engagement in violent dissident Irish republicanism. Many of the individuals joining the dissident groups had choices to make between which strain of Irish republican ideology to follow and which group to ultimately join. While the ideological and strategic debates were taking place around them, one of the key factors that consistently played a vital role in their affiliation and decision-making process was the position and views of those they trusted (Morrison 2016) and were influenced by (Morrison 2011).

While the influence of Irish republican ideology was present, it was not the dominant catalyst. In the discussion of influential individuals, it is understandable to focus on the role of positive influencers. These can be organization members, peers, comrades, relatives, or leadership figures. However, it was found that while positive influencers can pull individuals toward an ideology or organization, there could be negative influencers, who can push them toward it. These can be influential members of the perceived out-group, an individual responsible for personal or group griev-ance, an unloved relative, or a peer.

Throughout the history of terrorism there have been numerous exam-ples of influential individuals playing key roles within the radicalization process. These may be high profile individuals within the terrorist orga-nization or support group. Alternatively they may be inconspicuous peo-ple unheard of outside of the terrorists' and sympathizers' circles. Within modern-day French Islamist terrorism, one of the key high-profile influen-tial individuals has been Omar Diaby. Diaby, also known as Omar Omsen, is the self-proclaimed emir of a group of French jihadists in Syria. Many of those he inspired were from the southern French city of Nice, the site of the horrific truck attack in the summer of 2016 as well as Diaby's own home city. Diaby rose to prominence in 2012 through his production of a series of videos entitled *19HH*, named after the 19 hijackers responsible for the September 11, 2001, atrocities in the United States (Malsin 2016). After reportedly joining and fighting for Al-Nusra Front in Syria in 2013, he was falsely declared dead in 2015. He claims that he faked his own death in order to seek medical attention in Turkey (Kennedy 2016). His period of combat within Syria gave further legitimacy and influence to his online recruitment videos. They are seen by many as being one of the key reasons for French recruits of jihadist groups in Iraq and Syria. They have led to Diaby being declared "France's number one recruiter of jihadists" (Ken-nedy 2016). The example of Diaby shows that one does not to have direct face-to-face social interactions with an individual for them to be influential. This can happen, as in the case of Diaby, via their online presence. How-ever, Diaby's influence has not just been present online. Many accounts demonstrate his direct influence on those around him in his locality. To sum up the role of an influential individual, we can look at a quote from a resident of Nice's Saint-Roch neighborhood, where Diaby spent many of his formative years: "Omar, he was a legend here. . . . Everyone, especially little kids, looked up to him. He was a big guy, very charismatic. Everyone knew him. He had a lot of power among the people here" (Kennedy 2016).

Justification for Violence

As Randy Borum has acknowledged (2011b, 26), each existing model of radicalization focuses on creating justification for violence. It is therefore imperative for us to try and understand, from a social-psychological point of view, how and why radicalized or radicalizing individuals justify the utility of terrorist violence.

In *The Terrorist*, Max Taylor (1988) proposed that those who engage in terrorism and with a terrorist group develop what in social psychology is known as deindividuation. This refers to when a person, as part of the process of actively associating with a particular group, loses their own personal identity and replaces it with the group's identity. This in turn can lessen any constraints that would have previously held them back from certain impulsive or unusual behavior (Taylor 1988). In normal day-to-day life, we regulate our interactions with others as a result of our self-awareness. However, in certain situations, due to engagement with or membership in a group, this self-awareness can be blocked. It has been proposed that the conditions that block self-awareness are anonymity, high levels of arousal, feelings of group unity, and a focus on external events and goals (Taylor 1988). The process of radicalization and involvement with a terrorist group oftentimes involve some measure of secrecy and, resultantly, anonymity. The illegal nature of some of the acts associated with these processes can also produce high levels of psychological stress and arousal. The combination of secrecy and illegality can in turn produce significant group unity. And, finally, all terrorist groups and actors are almost always concentrating on external events, which can justify their existence or their continued radicalization. With all of these combined there is a reduction in an individual's self-awareness, and a significant shift in how they perceive their experiences takes place. This deindividuation results in a person having a decreased ability to either monitor or regulate their activity, and therefore their concern for how others perceive them and their behavior is significantly reduced (Taylor 1988). While an ideology and organizational goals may be used as justification for violence and a terrorist group's existence, this process of deindividuation may be one factor that helps individuals detach themselves from the long-term consequences of their radicalization. Taylor proposes that the results of this deindividuation can help us understand the relative "normality" of terrorist actors operating in parallel to their capacity to engage in acts of extreme violence (1988).

When assessing the justification of violence, one is often drawn to the question of why an individual may be able to justify their own violence while simultaneously condemning the parallel violence of those within a designated out-group. Max Taylor and Ethel Quayle (1994), in *Terrorist Lives*, account for this—the justification of violence through blaming external actors—by drawing on the psychological concept of attribution, specifically fundamental attribution error and the actor-observer effect.

They propose that we are more likely to explain others' behavior in terms of "disposition." This is especially true when we look at pejorative explanations. Therefore if someone does something where we and/or our in-group perceive any form of injustice, we are likely to blame them personally (e.g., they are bad, they deliberately victimized and targeted us). However, if we are to focus on our own behavior, for example engagement in terrorist activity, we no longer focus on the dispositional explanations for actions. Instead, the actor-observer effect states that we explain these behaviors in light of the situation we find ourselves in. Terrorists therefore explain their engagement in political violence by blaming others and the perceived victimization or injustice toward their in-group, while in the same instance ignoring any situational factors that may have led to the out-group engaging in this perceived victimization. This therefore assists them in evading any responsibility for their violence by blaming this on the actions, behaviors, and dispositions of others (Taylor and Quayle 1994).

Personal Identity and Self-Concept

When we are trying to understand the radicalization of individuals, we are asking a range of questions (see Borum 2011b, 26). How does the individual develop antipathy toward the target group? How do they justify their use of violence? How are the social and psychological barriers to actions eliminated? And why are others in similar situations not also radicalized? As has been repeated throughout this chapter, there are a range of answers to these questions that seem simple at first glance, but which upon further analysis are inherently complex. One of the greatest contributions that the social psychology literature can make (and has made) comes from the understanding of personal identity. This refers to the concept that people have about themselves and how this evolves throughout the course of their life. Alongside the idea of personal identity, we must also consider a person's self-concept: their beliefs about themselves and how they perceive their own personal attributes (Baumeister 1999). Recent research into the social psychology of radicalization has addressed this by focusing on the radicalizing individual's involvement in a quest for significance (Kruglanski et al. 2014) and/or uncertainty in their own personal identity and self-concept.

While Arie Kruglanski and colleagues (2014) may have questionable observations relating to the degrees of radicalization, their research does propose an interesting component to the models of radicalization. They posit one of the key components of an individual's radicalization is a "quest for personal significance." They state that underlying the variety of motives people may have for joining a terrorist group, there is this desire to matter, an urge to be someone and to have respect (Kruglanski et al. 2014). Even when one considers the role that love plays in individual radicalization, as McCauley and Moskalenko (2011) have, the resultant radicalization may be the quest for that loved one's approval and one's own resultant personal significance. If someone radicalizes inspired by the desire for vengeance, this can be seen as an attempt to restore the balance of power lost at the point of initial personal grievance. Kruglanski and colleagues (2014) propose that this significance quest can be activated in three ways: through humiliation and loss of significance, leading to psychological deprivation; through the anticipation of significance loss, leading to psychological avoidance; or through the opportunity for significance gain, which enables the psychological construct of incentive.

As with each of the concepts discussed here, the quest for personal significance is not something exclusive to the radicalizing individual. This has been identified as a fundamental human motivation by a range of psychological theorists outside of the analysis of terrorism and radicalization (Frankl 2000; Maslow 1967; Becker 1962). This quest for significance, or self-actualization, sees the individual seeking to serve a cause of higher worth and value than the self, therefore making their life significant. This can be achieved through membership in or support for a specific social group or movement (Kruglanski and Orehek 2011). Some seek to achieve this through charity work, membership in a political party, or pursuing a vocation. However, others seek to achieve significance in their life through their membership in a terrorist group or movement. In their pursuit of significance in their life individuals may find themselves becoming violently radicalized.

The concept of quest for significance shares some similarities with the proposal that individual radicalization can be seen as the result of individual uncertainty. Michael Hogg (2012) and others (see, e.g., Doosje, Loseman, and van den Bos 2013; Hogg, Kruglanski, and van den Bos 2013) propose the uncertainty–identity theory as the foundation of an individual's movement toward extremism. This theory posits that when an individual is uncertain about their own beliefs, attitudes, and perceptions, they seek out others similar to themselves in order to make self-comparisons that will confirm the legitimacy and appropriateness of their attitudes and perceptions (Hogg 2012). There is an urge during times of personal uncertainty to go on a quest for confirmation: to seek out those who will verify and confirm aspects of oneself, including one's beliefs and attitudes, rather than gaining an accurate reflection (Hogg 2012).

However, when finding relevant opinions is unachievable, the need for certainty is stimulated, and the individual may become more susceptible to social influence. This desire for certainty can leave individuals vulnerable to extremist individuals and groups who promise certainty in the form of simplistic, binary, good/bad ideologies and the accompanying fundamentalist practices and belief systems. This provides the individual with the ability to combat their uncertainty by grounding their existence in a world of consensus, where everyone in the in-group is "right/good" and those in the designated out-groups are "wrong/bad." Therefore membership in a terrorist group such as ISIS can and does give individuals a greater degree of certainty in their beliefs. There is a certainty that those who do not abide by the Islamic practices from the time of the Prophet Muhammad are not considered true Muslims (*takfiri*) and those who do are true Muslims. It outlines in clear binary terms one's enemies and one's comrades and allies.

This in turn prevents individuals from encountering a diversity of viewpoints and beliefs. This is part of the desire to have one's own personal beliefs vindicated, to make the world they live in more predictable and their own behavior more successful (Hogg 2012): predictability achieved through certainty. People have all sorts of reactions to uncertainty, and there are different forms of uncertainty a person can face. Some see uncertainty as a challenge to embrace. This can in turn result in promotion and approach behaviors. However, if uncertainty is perceived as a threat, we are more likely to become protective and avoidant. It is this latter perception of and reaction to uncertainty that may be more likely to lead one toward extremism (Hogg 2012).

The role that group membership and ideological adherence plays in reducing uncertainty is a complex one. By committing to become a member of a specific group we resultantly assign the prototypical attributes of the group to ourselves. In doing so we conform to the organizational norms, in turn changing our own identity and self-concept and reducing the uncertainty. This also removes the uncertainty relating to how others may behave and what social interactions we may have with them (Hogg 2012). For those who are uncertain, the most attractive group to join is one that is said to have high entitativity. This is a group that has clear structural boundaries, a common purpose and fate, internal homogeneity (Campbell 1958), and clearly defined membership criteria (Hogg 2012). When one looks to extremist groups, they meet these criteria. They may seem unappealing to many based on their authoritarianism and control of one's life and identity. However, when an individual is facing high levels of uncertainty—be this societal uncertainty as a result of civil war, natural disasters, economic collapse, or terrorism, or personal uncertainty brought about by unemployment, adolescence, bereavement, or a marital separation—it is hypothesized that these groups can become more appealing. They reduce one's uncertainty by providing an unambiguous sense of self through the social validation of one's identity and worldview (Hogg 2012). These groups can provide cognitive closure for those with a high need for it (Kruglanski and Orehek 2012). Within the social psychology literature, closure relates to the wish for a firm answer to a question and the aversion to uncertainty (Kruglanski and Webster 1996). Arie Kruglanksi and Edward Orehek (2012) propose that an individual in search of closure has a tendency to seize those invoking a similar perspective to their own. This can result in a failure to consider other opinions and perspectives. In turn this can also lead to an inability to adjust worldviews as a result of social feedback, thus making the adoption of extreme views more likely.

From a point of uncertainty, membership in a group or movement (whether physical, virtual, ideological, or all three) can provide people with a great sense of pride (Tajfel and Turner 1979). To bolster their own self-image, members will at times look to both enhance the status of their in-group and hold and promote prejudicial beliefs against the designated out-groups (Harris, Gringart, and Drake 2014). This in turn can lead to an expansion of the perceived homogeneity of the in-group and the concurrent prejudice directed toward the out-groups. This aspect of social identity theory can lead to the development and escalation of an "us versus them" mentality. The combination of group identification and intergroup discrimination was seen to be most potent at the point where there was uncertainty about the social self (Hogg 2000). Recounting Max Taylor's proposal of the process of deindividuation (1988), the process of promoting the group's image to bolster one's own self-image fits. If the organizational identity is becoming synonymous with an individual's personal identity, the promotion of the group will have a positive effect on that person's self-image.

If what the group stands for is under threat, this can lead to a behavioral manifestation of the protection of the certainty that the group, its structures, ideology, and purpose provide. This behavioral manifestation may come in the form of political violence or terrorism. While Hogg, Kruglanski, and others have proposed the uncertainty–identity theory in relation to extremism in general, Bertjan Doosje, Annemarie Loseman, and Kees van den Bos (2013) applied the theory specifically to the radicalization of Islamic youths in the Netherlands. They proposed that alongside personal uncertainty, the process of radicalization was driven by perceived injustice and perceived group threat. They argued that at times of doubt people are more likely to seek to protect their worldview. This can and does include their religious worldview and can predict a perception of in-group superiority. The sample used in their research was 131 Dutch Muslim youth. This was a non-terrorist sample and therefore should not be considered as representative of a terrorist group. The authors found that within this sample, personal uncertainty, perceived injustice, and group-threat factors were determinants of a radical belief system. This radical belief system included a belief in the superiority of Muslims, the perceived illegitimacy of Dutch authorities, disconnection from society, and distance from others.

Those promoting the uncertainty–identity theory acknowledge the role that influential individuals (discussed earlier) can play within the radicalization process. For those who are focused on their identity and are seeking certainty in a group, the most influential individuals can be the prototypical members occupying leadership positions. During the process of radicalization, they can be seen as trustworthy sources for normative information and may be perceived as constantly acting in the best interests of the group, its ideology, and its goals (Hogg 2012). These influential individuals, and specifically their consistency, can assist in the process of uncertainty reduction. However, if and when these leaders violate this trust, either through their actions or sentiments, this can play a significant role in resurrecting previous uncertainty (Hogg 2012). If one of the individuals upon whom you base your newfound certainty forfeits your trust and goes against the prototypical behavior of the group, this can have a significantly destabilizing effect.

Conclusion

To be able to prevent the radicalization of individuals irrespective of ideology, we must first understand why and how they radicalize. It will only get us so far to adopt an ideology-focused analysis. This should not be construed as a statement that ideology plays no role. On the contrary, it clearly has a substantial part to play. However, many of the most significant aspects of radicalization take place independent and irrespective of ideology. This is a social-psychological process, hence the need for an insight from relevant social-psychological research both past and present.

This chapter has served as a critical introduction to the significant contributions of social psychology to developing our understanding of radicalization. While radicalization can take place at the personal, group, and mass levels (McCauley and Moskalenko 2011), the focus here has primarily been on personal radicalization. There are various reasons and mechanisms leading to personal radicalization. These range from personal and group grievances (McCauley and Moskalenko 2011) to the quests for significance (Kruglanski et al. 2014), certainty, and beyond (Hogg, Kruglanski, and van den Bos 2013). These and other factors and mechanisms are each influenced in some way by the social and psychological circumstances in which people find themselves. This includes their interactions with and perceptions of members of their in-group and designated out-groups.

For us to develop our understanding of the social psychology of radicalization and terrorist involvement, it is imperative that we make a concerted effort to achieve a greater empirically based understanding of the processes involved. This must include not just looking at the social-psychological processes leading to radicalization, but also assessing if and when these processes are applicable in non-radicalized populations, as well as those who cognitively radicalize but never engage in violent activity. It is only when we have this comparative understanding that we can fully grasp exactly what takes place in the radicalization of would-be terrorists. This empirical analysis must assess the roles of social ties, personal identity, deindividuation, relative deprivation, and self-concept, as well as a range of other social-psychological concepts. This must not take place in a disciplinary silo. This and all analyses of radicalization and terrorist involvement must be approached from an interdisciplinary perspective. Within this perspective, we must assess at which stages of the radicalization process are certain social-psychological concepts dominant, and if and when there is a stage at which their effect may be weakened. It is with this understanding that a strategy may be implemented with the aim of preventing, redirecting, and dissipating the effect of radicalization.

REFERENCES

Baumeister, Roy F., ed. 1999. *The Self in Social Psychology*. Philadelphia: Psychology Press Taylor & Francis.

Becker, Wesley C. 1962. "Developmental Psychology." *Annual Review of Psychology* 13: 1–34.

Borum, Randy. 2011a. "Radicalization into Violent Extremism I: A Review of Social Science Theories." *Journal of Strategic Security* 44: 7–36.

Borum, Randy. 2011b. "Radicalization into Violent Extremism II: A Review of Conceptual Models and Empirical Research." *Journal of Strategic Security* 44: 37–62.

Borum, Randy. 2003. "Understanding the Terrorist Mindset." *FBI Law Enforcement Bulletin*: 7–10.

Bouhana, Noémie. 2019. *The Moral Ecology of Extremism: A Systematic Perspective*. UK Commission for Countering Extremism.

Bouhana, Noémie, and Per-Olof Wikström. 2010. "Theorizing Terrorism: Terrorism as Moral Action: A Scoping Study." *Contemporary Readings in Law and Social Justice* 2(2): 9.

Campbell, Donald T. 1958. "Common Fate, Similarity, and Other Indices of the Status of Aggregates of Persons and Social Entities." *Behavioral Science* 3: 14–25.

Coolsaet, Rik. 2010. "EU Counterterrorism Strategy: Value Added or Chimera?" *International Affairs* 86 (4): 857–73.

Corner, Emily, and Paul Gill. 2015. "A False Dichotomy? Mental Illness and Lone Actor Terrorism." *Law and Human Behavior* 39: 23–34.

della Porta, Donatella. 1988. "Recruitment Processes in Clandestine Political Organizations: Italian Left-Wing Terrorism." *International Social Movement Research* 1: 155–69.

Doosje, Bertjan, Annemarie Loseman, and Kees van den Bos. 2013. "Determinants of Radicalization of Islamic Youth in the Netherlands: Personal Uncertainty, Perceived Injustice and Perceived Group Threat." *Journal of Social Issues* 693: 586–604.

Frankl, Viktor E. 2000. *Man's Search for Ultimate Meaning*. New York: Basic Books.

Gill, Paul. 2015. *Lone Actor Terrorists: A Behavioural Analysis*. Oxford: Routledge.

Gill, Paul, and Emily Corner. 2017. "There and Back Again: The Study of Mental Disorder and Terrorist Involvement." *American Psychologist* 723: 231–41.

Harris, Kira, Eyal Gringart, and Deirdre Drake. 2014. "Understanding the Role of Social Groups in Radicalization." *7th Australian Security and Intelligence Conference*. Perth: Australia.

Hogg, Michael A. 2000. "Subjective Uncertainty Reduction Through Self-Categorization: A Motivational Theory of Social Identity Processes." *European Review of Social Psychology* 11: 223–55.

Hogg, Michael A. 2012. "Self-Uncertainty, Social Identity, and the Solace of Extremism." In *Extremism and the Psychology of Uncertainty*, edited by Michael A. Hogg and Danielle L. Blaylock, 19–35. Oxford: Wiley-Blackwell.

Hogg, Michael A., Arie Kruglanski, and Kees van den Bos. 2013. "Uncertainty and the Roots of Extremism." *Journal of Social Issues* 693: 407–18.

Horgan, John. 2017. "Psychology of Terrorism: Introduction to the Special Issue." *American Psychologist* 723: 199–204.

Horgan, John. 2014 *The Psychology of Terrorism: Second Edition*. London: Routledge.

Horgan, John. 2012. "Interviewing the Terrorists: Reflections on Fieldwork and Implications for Psychological Research." *Behavioral Sciences of Terrorism and Political Aggression* 4 (3): 195–211.

Horgan, John. 2009. *Walking Away From Terrorism: Accounts of Disengagement from Radical and Extremist Movements*. London: Routledge.

Horgan, John. 2008. "From Profiles to Pathways and Roots to Routes: Perspectives from Psychology on Radicalization into Terrorism." *ANNALS of the American Academy of Political and Social Science* 618 (1): 80–94.

Horgan, John, Neil Shortland, and Suzette Abbasciano. 2018. "Towards a Typology of Terrorism Involvement: A Behavioral Differentiation of Violent Extremist Offenders." *Journal of Threat Assessment and Management* 5 (2): 84.

Kennedy, Dana. 2016. "France's Infamous Undead Jihadist Recruiter." *Daily Beast.* June 6. http://www.thedailybeast.com/frances-infamous-undead-jihadist-recruiter

King, Michael, and Donald M. Taylor. 2011. "The Radicalization of Homegrown Jihadists: A Review of Theoretical Models and Social Psychological Evidence." *Terrorism and Political Violence* 234: 602–22.

Kruglanski, Arie. W., and Donna M. Webster. 1996. "Motivated Closing of the Mind: 'Seizing' and 'Freezing.'" *Psychological Review* 103: 263–83.

Kruglanksi, Arie W., and Edward Orehek. 2012. "The Need for Certainty as a Psychological Nexus for Individuals and Society." In *Extremism and the Psychology of Uncertainty*, edited by Michael A. Hogg, and Danielle L. Blaylock, 3–18. Oxford: Wiley-Blackwell.

Kruglanksi, Arie W., and Edward Orehek. 2011. "The Role of the Quest for Personal Significance in Motivating Terrorism." In *The Psychology of Social Conflict and Aggression*, edited by Joseph Forgas, Arie W. Kruglanski, and Kipling Williams, 153–66. New York: Psychology Press.

Kruglanski, Arie W., Michele J. Gelfand, Jocelyn J. Belanger, Anna Sheveland, Malkanthi Hetiarachchi, and Rohan Gunaratna. 2014. "The Psychology of Radicalization and Deradicalization: How Significance Quest Impacts Violent Extremism." *Advances in Political Psychology* 351: 69–93.

Malsin, Jared. 2016. "Meet the Man from Nice Who Rose to Become a Major Jihadist Recruiter." *Time.* July 15, 2016. http://time.com/4408537/nice-attack-omar-diaby-jihadist

Maslow, Abraham H. 1967. "A Theory of Metamotivations: The Biological Rooting of Value-life." *Journal of Humanistic Psychology* 7: 93–127.

McCauley, Clark, and Sophia Moskalenko. 2008. "Mechanisms of Political Radicalization: Pathways Toward Terrorism." *Terrorism and Political Violence* 20 (3): 415–33.

McCauley, Clark, and Sophia Moskalenko. 2011. *Friction: How Radicalization Happens to Them and Us.* New York: Oxford University Press.

McCauley, Clark R., and Mary E. Segal. 1987. "Social Psychology of Terrorist Groups." In *Groups Processes and Intergroup Relations*, edited by Clyde A. Hendrick, 231–26. Newbury Park, CA: Sage.

Moghaddam, Fathali M. 2005. "The Staircase to Terrorism: A Psychological Exploration." *American Psychologist* 60 (2): 161–69.

Morrison, John F. 2018. "The Trustworthy Terrorist: The Role of Trust in the Psychology of Terrorism." In *Victims and Perpetrators-Understanding the Complexity of Terrorism*, edited by Orla Lynch and Javier Argomaniz, 133–48. London: Routledge.

Morrison, John F. 2016. "Trust in Me: Allegiance Choices in a Post-Split Terrorist Movement." *Aggression and Violent Behavior* 28: 47–56.

Morrison, John F. 2011. "Why Do People Become Dissident Irish Republicans?" In *Dissident Irish Republicanism*, edited by P.M. Currie and Max Taylor, 17–41. London: Continuum.

Pisoiu, Daniela. 2011. *Islamist Radicalisation in Europe: An Occupational Change Process.* London: Routledge.

Ravn, Steine, Rik Coolsaet, and Tom Sauer. 2019. "Rethinking Radicalisation:

Addressing the Lack of a Contextual Perspective in the Dominant Narratives on Radicalisation." In *Radicalisation: A Marginal Phenomenon or a Mirror of Society*, edited by Noel Clycq, Christiane Timmerman, Dirk Vanheule, Rut Van Claudenberg, and Stiene Ravn, 21–46. Leuven: Leuven University Press.

Sageman, Marc. 2014. "The Stagnation in Terrorism Research." *Terrorism and Political Violence* 26 (4): 565–80.

Sageman, Marc. 2004. *Understanding Terror Networks*. Philadelphia: University of Pennsylvania Press.

Schmid, Alex P. 2013. *Radicalization, De-Radicalization, Counter-Radicalization: A Conceptual Discussion and Literature Review*. The Hague: International Centre for Counter-Terrorism.

Silke, Andrew. 2008. "Research on Terrorism: A Review of the Impact of 9/11 and the Global war on Terrorism." In *Terrorism Informatics: Knowledge Management and Data Mining for Homeland Security*, edited by Hsinchun Chen, Edna Reid, Joshua Sinai, Andrew Silke, and Boaz Ganor, 27–50. New York: Springer.

Tajfel, Henri, and John C. Turner. 1979. "The Social Identity Theory of Intergroup Behavior." In *The Social Psychology of Intergroup Relations*, 2nd ed., edited by Stephen Worchel and William G. Austin, 7–24. Chicago: Nelson Hall.

Taylor, Max. 1988. *The Terrorist*. London: Brassey's.

Taylor, Max, and Ethel Quayle. 1994. *Terrorist Lives*. London: Brassey's.

Taylor, Max, and John Horgan. 2006. "A Conceptual Framework for Addressing Psychological Process in the Development of the Terrorist, Terrorism and Political Violence." *Terrorism and Political Violence* 184: 585–601.

Wasmund, Klaus. 1986. "The Political Socialisation of West German Terrorists." In *Political Violence and Terror: Motifs and Motivations*, edited by Peter Merkl, 191–228. Berkeley: University of California Press.

Wintrobe, Ronald. 2003. "Can Suicide Bombers Be Rational?" Unpublished: University of Western Ontario.

PART II

Patterns of Radicalization in Western Europe

SIX

Belgium

Sarah Teich

Belgium has been a major hotbed for radicalization in Europe. At least 498 Belgians traveled to Syria and Iraq as foreign fighters, signifying one of the highest per capita figures in Western Europe (Van Ostaeyen and Van Vlierden 2018). Belgians have been highly involved in terrorist attacks throughout Europe, with the Zerkani network in particular playing a central role in both the 2015 Paris attacks and the 2016 Brussels attacks. This chapter points to both push and pull factors in an attempt to explain, specifically, Islamic radicalization in Belgium.[1] Poor demographic realities of the Belgian Muslim community—including low levels of employment, low educational achievement, poor integration, high levels of discrimination and intolerance, and inconsistent governmental funding—might be factors that push this community toward radicalism and provide a fertile ground for radical parties, organizations, and networks to then emerge, influence, and recruit. This chapter examines these dynamics through the dual lens of both Social Movement Theory and Clark McCauley and Sophia Moskalenko's (2008) framework for radicalization. These particular theoretical frameworks are utilized because there is some evidence that these socio-

---

1. This chapter is adapted from a 2016 publication by the author, titled "Islamic Radicalization in Belgium" and published by the International Institute for Counter-Terrorism. As such, this chapter focuses solely on Islamic radicalization in Belgium around those years. There may be other forms of radicalization present in Belgium, including right-wing radicalization, that merit additional research. This chapter was written in 2016 and last updated in 2019.

logical models are particularly well-suited to the analysis of radicalization. Beyond that, by examining radicalization through the lens of sociology and refusing to place undue emphasis on religiosity or ideology, the discourse becomes less divisive and counter-radicalization strategies become more productive.

The Demographics: Providing a Fertile Ground

Belgium hosts a large, and growing, Muslim population. According to the most recent Pew Research Center statistics, roughly 6% of the Belgian population is Muslim, making Islam the country's largest minority religion, and giving Belgium the second highest Muslim population per capita within the European Union (Liu 2012). The Muslim population of Belgium has also been growing rapidly, nearly doubling over the past decade. In 2005, Muslims numbered 364,000, comprising roughly 3.5% of the Belgian population. In 2014, Muslim numbers increased to 650,000, comprising roughly 6% of the Belgian population (Kern 2014). Part of this growth can be attributed to Muslim immigration into Belgium.

Muslim immigration into Belgium has recently been characterized by asylum seekers from unstable countries (Petrovic 2012). However, the first wave of Muslim immigration into Belgium was economic; it began in the 1960s with an increase in demand for foreign labor from Morocco, Turkey, Tunisia, and Algeria (Petrovic 2012). Muslim populations in Belgium continue to reflect this first immigration wave: The largest Muslim groups in the country are still Moroccans, Turks, Algerians, and Tunisians, and they are still largely concentrated in Brussels and Antwerp. Antwerp is roughly 17% Muslim, Brussels is roughly 26% Muslim, and both cities are home to a growing number of Muslim converts (Kern 2014).

Low Education and Low Employment

Muslims in Belgium achieve disproportionately low education levels (Fadil, El Asri, and Bracke 2014). Using the International Standard Classification of Education, outlined in figure 6.1, only 12% of Muslims hold high educational achievement, while a staggering 65% hold low educational achievement. In contrast, 23% of non-Muslims hold high educational achievement, and only 47% of non-Muslims hold low educational achievement (*Euro-Islam* n.d.).

Regarding employment, there is no data specifically on Muslim employ-

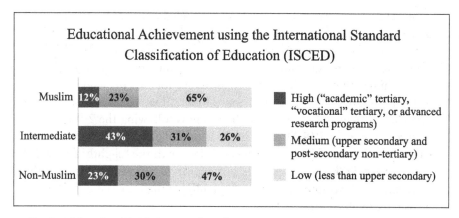

Fig. 6.1. Educational Achievement of Muslims in Belgium

ment levels in Belgium. However, employment discrimination is rampant. Studies have shown that both job and housing applications are more likely to be rejected when the name of the candidate is Muslim (*Euro-Islam* n.d.).

Poor Integration

Until 2012, Belgium lacked formal integration conditions, and Wallonia and Flanders held separate integration policies (Kern 2014). The original lack of integration legislation at the federal level may have been due to the belief among Belgian authorities that foreign workers would eventually return to their home countries. There is compelling evidence that this laissez-faire mindset was ineffective, especially for Muslim immigrants (Petrovic 2012). One 2007 study found that Muslim immigrants to Belgium identified more strongly with their origin country than with Belgium, and these sentiments were significantly stronger than those of non-Muslim immigrants (Saroglou and Mathijsen 2007). Another survey found that only 30% of Muslim males ages 15 to 25 (and only 25% of Muslim females in that age group) reported feeling accepted by Flemish society (Kern 2014). The same survey also found that over 50% of Muslim youths in Belgium felt they were victims of racism; 60% of Muslim youths in Belgium believed they would never be integrated into Belgian society; and although 93% of all respondents held Belgian citizenship, 42% considered themselves foreigners in Belgium (Kern 2014).

Beginning in 2012, integration legislation became a national priority. New legislation, implemented in 2013, stipulated formal integration requirements for naturalization. These included a minimum residence of five years, proof of economic participation, knowledge of at least one of the national languages, and proof of social integration (Hope 2015). These legislative changes drastically shifted Belgian integration policy—among other things, they broadened the possibilities for loss of Belgian citizenship and limited family reunification (Hope 2015). There was some preliminary evidence of integration effectiveness following the 2013 legislative reforms. The 2014 Migrant Integration Policy Index ranked Belgium at number 7 (out of 38 European countries), with the "slightly favorable" score of 67. Still, this index does not appear to adequately measure the perceptions of Muslim youth, which highlights the importance of further research (Teich 2016).

Following the March 2016 Brussels attacks, Belgium introduced new integration requirements. First, third-country nationals and their dependent family members were required to sign a newcomers' statement confirming that they understand and agree to act in accordance with the fundamental values and norms of Belgian society. Refusal to sign such a statement would result in an inadmissible application. Second, third-country nationals and their dependents were required to provide evidence of their integration efforts, which would be assessed according to criteria listed in the legislation. If authorities decided that a newcomer had not made a reasonable effort to integrate, they might terminate that individual's right to reside. Certain categories of third-country nationals were exempt from the new requirements, including refugees and students. Nevertheless, these new requirements drew criticism. Some argued that the newcomers' statement requirement risked deepening prejudice against Muslim immigrants. Others argued that the failure of immigrants to integrate was in part due to the discrimination against them—and that requiring proof of integration efforts could lead to wrongfully blaming the immigrants (Morelli 2016).

High Levels of Discrimination and Intolerance

The reality of widespread intolerance and discrimination in Belgium likely impedes successful integration. In fact, 25% of Belgians show intolerant attitudes (above the EU average of 14%), and studies point to systemic employment and housing discrimination against Muslims (Fadil, El Asri, and Bracke 2014). Further, intolerance and discrimination have increased. In the months following the Brussels attacks in 2016, the Belgian Counter-Islamophobia Collective reported a spike in violence against Muslims and found that Muslim women disproportionately faced discrimination (Bayrakli and Hafez 2017).

Discrimination and Islamophobia have been cited by Fouad Belkacem, the leader of Sharia4Belgium, as the reasons why he began his radical activity. While in prison, Belkacem wrote on Facebook that the "arrogance and deeply rooted Islamophobia of the Belgian state" was his main motivation for establishing Sharia4Belgium (Van Ostaeyen 2014). He elaborated as follows:

> For more than 50 years now, Muslims are humiliated and forced to beg for simple rights, such as places to pray and locations for ritual slaughter. Any Belgian Muslim with foreign roots is still considered an asylum seeker by public opinion, and even when he speaks both official languages fluently, he constantly risks being treated like his grandfather back in the seventies. (Van Ostaeyen 2014)

Guy Van Vlierden (2016) repeatedly points out an interesting possibility that the early success of the Vlaams Blok (later rebranded to "Vlaams Belang" or VB) political party may have contributed to the problem. As a far-right political party with a strong anti-Islam and anti-immigrant platform, it used slogans such as "our own people first," "fit in or leave," and "freedom or Islam: dare to choose" (Van Vlierden 2016a, 58). VB leader Filip Dewinter once asserted that a Muslim girl in a headscarf is not Flemish, even if she speaks Dutch and was born in Flanders, because "a cat born in a fish-shop is still a cat and not a fish" (Van Vlierden 2016a, 58). VB's breakthrough happened in 1991, when it tripled its vote and presence in the federal parliament from three to seventeen seats (Federale Overheidsdienst Binnenlandse Zaken 2008). In the 2004 regional elections in Flanders, it reached a peak of almost 25% of the vote (Federale Overheidsdienst Binnenlandse Zaken 2008). Thanks to an agreement between the other parties, VB has been unable to find a coalition partner (Van Vlierden 2016a). Nevertheless, its heavy presence may have had an impact on the treatment of Muslims in Belgium and contributed to low levels of integration among the Muslim population. Compared to other countries in Europe, where analogous parties remained marginal until more recently, there is an entire generation of Muslims in Belgium who have faced the message—spread across billboards, flyers, and television commercials—that they should "fit in or leave" (Van Vlierden 2016a).

Inconsistent Governmental Funding of Islam

As one of Belgium's "recognized" religious communities, the Muslim community is legally entitled to governmental funding. However, their actual receipt of funds has been inconsistent (*Berkley Center* n.d.). At first, the Muslim community's lack of representative institution prevented them from obtaining government funds (*Euro-Islam* n.d.). Then, it was the rocky relationship between the Belgian government and the Muslim Executive of Belgium (EMB) that hindered the community's receipt of funds. The relationship deteriorated following accusations of fundamentalist ties within the EMB. Despite its unstable past, the EMB is still operational, advocating on behalf of the Muslim community (Birnbaum 2015). Meanwhile, the extent of the EMB's fundamentalist ties remains unclear.

Two additional legalities prevent the Muslim community from consistently receiving funding. First, formal recognition of a mosque is a precondition for it to receive funding, and obtaining recognition is a long and bureaucratic process (Fadil, El Asri, and Bracke 2014). Consequently, although there are approximately 328 mosques in Belgium, less than one quarter of these are officially recognized (Fadil, El Asri, and Bracke 2014). Second, mosques in Flanders are required to use the Dutch language, tolerate women and homosexuals, and cease preaching of extremist ideas— requirements that apply only to Islam (Fadil, El Asri, and Bracke 2014).

The Three Major Recruitment Networks in Belgium

Of course, poor demographic realities are not the end of the story. These realities simply provide the context in which to examine radicalization in Belgium. In the Belgian context, three major organizations have played a part in recruiting individuals to terrorist activity. These networks are: Sharia4Belgium, Resto du Tawhid, and the Zerkani network. The Zerkani network is the most infamous, as it claims responsibility for both the 2015 Paris attacks and the 2016 Brussels attacks. There is considerable overlap between the three networks.

Sharia4Belgium

Sharia4Belgium was the first main hub of radicalization in Belgium. They were a Salafist group with a pro-sharia ideology, working to move foreign fighters from Belgium to Syria (Bouchaud 2015). Although Sharia4Belgium is now a designated terrorist organization, they operated in Belgium for many years as a legitimate Muslim organization. Sharia4Belgium was established in 2010, following the model of Islam4UK, an Islamist organization formed by Omar Bakri and Anjem Choudary in 2008 (Bouchaud 2015). Almost immediately after its creation, Sharia4Belgium rose to distinction through its protests of a proposed public headscarf ban. Sharia4Belgium had the clearly articulated aim of implementing Sharia law throughout Belgium, and the organization tried to appeal strongly to Belgian Muslims to overthrow the national democracy (Kern 2011). Sharia4Belgium promoted a political vision of religion, openly affirming the supremacy of Islam and rejecting both democracy and the separation of church and state (Bouchaud 2015). Sharia4Belgium's anti-democratic stance continued to deepen throughout the years and, as a result, the organization was banned in 2013 (Eeckhaut 2013).

Although officially disbanded in 2013, Sharia4Belgium appeared to continue operations unofficially. They operated mainly in Flanders but had branches throughout the country (Eeckhaut 2013). After the group's disbandment, the extent of Sharia4Belgium's terrorism links began to be discovered. The organization played a major role in recruiting Belgians to travel to Syria as foreign fighters, with an estimated 10% of Belgian foreign fighters being linked to Sharia4Belgium (Crawford 2015). By March 2013, at least 70 former members and sympathizers of Sharia4Belgium were actively fighting in Syria against the Assad regime (Crawford 2015). To date, approximately 80 foreign fighters in Syria and Iraq are directly linked to Sharia4Belgium. Most of these foreign fighters are believed to be fighting alongside Al-Qaeda's Al-Nusra Front in Syria (Bouchaud 2015). Evidence emerged throughout the Sharia4Belgium trial that Fouad Belkacem, spiritual leader of the organization, indoctrinated dozens of young Belgians through lectures designed to recruit and radicalize (Crawford 2015). Belkacem was considered highly effective in radicalizing young Belgians through powerful street sermons and videos on social media.

It was in February 2015 that the criminal court judge presiding over the Sharia4Belgium trial ruled the group a terrorist organization. Subsequently, Belkacem, along with other organization members, was sentenced to 12 years in prison. Despite these actions, a wide Sharia4 network continues to exist throughout the world (Vidino 2015). As one of the largest and most well-known Sharia4 franchises, Sharia4Belgium had contacts and influence with many other organizations (Vidino 2015). Therefore, it is likely that the Belgium-based organization's ideology, tactics, and strategy continue to influence the global Sharia4 network.

Resto Du Tawhid

Resto du Tawhid was a smaller network led by 41-year-old Muslim convert Jean-Louis Denis (Van Ostaeyen 2016). The group operated around the Gare du Nord Brussels railway station, distributing food to the poor and recruiting those marginalized individuals to terrorism activities (Van Ostaeyen 2016). Their aim "consisted primarily in offering a platform, via charitable actions . . . for attracting candidates for jihad, most often young men" (Brunsden 2016). Denis used social media and online chat rooms to promote his ideology, which included a complete rejection of Belgian law and democracy (Brunsden 2016). He pushed for his volunteers and followers to travel to join terrorist groups abroad, and by one estimate, Denis is linked to at least 50 Belgian foreign fighters (Van Ostaeyen 2016). Denis was arrested in 2013 and sentenced to 10 years in prison in a trial that concluded in 2016. There was significant overlap between Resto du Tawhid and Sharia4Belgium, as Denis was both leader of Resto du Tawhid and leader of Sharia4Belgium's Brussels branch (Van Ostaeyen 2016). Denis also provided a key connection between Sharia4Belgium and the Zerkani network (Van Ostaeyen 2016).

The Zerkani Network

Considered the most dangerous of the three, the Zerkani network—headed by 43-year-old Moroccan-born Khalid Zerkani—was directly linked to both the 2015 Paris attacks and 2016 Brussels attacks. Khalid Zerkani moved to Belgium in 2002 (Soufan and Schoenfeld 2016). Otherwise known as "Papa Noel," he operated in and around Molenbeek, the Brussels borough now infamous as a breeding ground for terrorism (Van Ostaeyen 2016). The network operated clandestinely, more like a gang than an organization (Van Ostaeyen 2016). Zerkani's network has been recognized as "one of the largest and most successful Islamic State recruitment networks in Europe" (Soufan and Schoenfeld 2016). Zerkani indoctrinated young Belgians and encouraged them to commit petty crimes along the way—justified as taking *ghanima* (the spoils of war) (Van Vlierden 2016b). Unlike Sharia4Belgium and Resto du Tawhid, the Zerkani network recruited many criminals with little or no Islamic background (Van Ostaeyen 2016). Zerkani's radical Islamist ideologies provided a justification for these individuals to continue their criminal behavior—which might explain the attraction of radicalism for these young petty criminals (Soufan and Schoenfeld 2016). Instead of lecturing disaffected youth on Islamic theology, Zerkani managed to convince these individuals that their criminal behavior was in service of a larger Islamic purpose (Soufan and Schoenfeld 2016). Recruiting petty criminals was extremely beneficial for Zerkani, as the increased criminality of this network enabled the group to more effectively travel to Syria and plan attacks (Van Ostaeyen 2016). Drawing on their criminal connections, new recruits were able to acquire weapons, chemicals, cars, and safe houses with greater ease (Van Ostaeyen 2016). The network also used the proceeds of petty criminal activity to finance travel of foreign fighters to Syria (Soufan and Schoenfeld 2016). The Zerkani network was linked to at least 59 Belgian foreign fighters in Syria and Iraq, and evidence revealed that they also facilitated the travel of Denis's recruits (Van Vlierden 2016b). Although Zerkani played a lead role in the recruitment of young people, evidence revealed that the recruits encouraged each other to travel to join terrorist groups abroad (Van Ostaeyen 2016). This is consistent with the fact that the Zerkani network remained active after Zerkani's arrest in 2014. Zerkani is currently serving a 15-year prison sentence in Belgium.

One of the most well-known members of the Zerkani network was Abdelhamid Abaaoud, architect of the 2015 Paris attacks (Van Ostaeyen 2016). A dual Belgian-Moroccan national, Abaaoud was involved in gang activities and petty criminality before falling in with the Zerkani network (Martinez et al. 2015). After joining, Abaaoud also allegedly played a key role in the Islamic State's external operations branch (Soufan and Schoenfeld 2016). He was allegedly involved in several European plots over the past few years: the attack on the Jewish Museum of Belgium in 2014; the attempted attack that was thwarted in Verviers, Belgium, in January 2015; and the 2015 Paris attacks (Van Ostaeyen 2016). He was also suspected of involvement in the plot by Sid Ahmed Ghlam to attack a Paris church in 2014 and the attempt by Moroccan extremist Ayoub el-Khazzani to attack a Thalys train in 2015 (Van Ostaeyen 2016). Following the 2015 Paris attacks, Abaaoud was killed during a raid of the Saint-Denis neighborhood outside Paris. Although Abaaoud coordinated the Paris attacks, investigators believe Algerian Islamic State operative Mohamed Belkaid, killed by police in March 2016, was the overall leader of the cell (Soufan and Schoenfeld 2016). Molenbeek residents Salah and Ibrahim Abdeslam were other notable members of the cell involved in the 2015 Paris attacks. Ibrahim detonated a suicide vest in the attacks on the Boulevard Voltaire, and Salah was arrested a few months later after an extensive manhunt. His trial proceeded in 2018, and he is currently incarcerated after being sentenced to the maximum possible, 20 years. Born in Belgium, the brothers were allegedly radicalized under the influence of Abaaoud. After Salah was arrested, the remaining cell members involved in the Paris attacks—Najim Laachraoui, Khalid El Bakraoui, and Ibrahim El Bakraoui—accelerated their attack on the Brussels metro and airport (Van Ostaeyen 2016). The suspected bomb-maker of the cell was Najim Laachraoui. All three Brussels bombers died in the explosions on March 22, 2016.

It is notable that the Zerkani network included multiple brothers and many members who knew each other beforehand. Ibrahim and Khalid El Bakraoui were brothers, as were Salah and Ibrahim Abdeslam. Abdelhamid Abaaoud and Ibrahim Abdeslam were in prison together. This demonstrates that radicalization in Belgium, at least in this case, is community-centric and tightly knit (Soufan and Schoenfeld 2016). More generally, the majority of individuals in the Zerkani network had criminal backgrounds. At least 11 had a Moroccan background. At least 14 had ties to Brussels, and many of those were tied specifically to the Molenbeek district (Soufan and Schoenfeld 2016). These commonalities and preexisting relationships between the members are consistent with research suggesting that radicalization is a group process—radicalized individuals recruit their close family and friends, and the network continually expands through these community circles.

Radicalization Locations: Role of Mosques, Prisons Remains Unclear

Mosques

The majority of Belgian Muslims are Sunni in orientation, and the Grand Mosque of Brussels is funded by Saudi Arabia. The influence of Saudi Arabia became concerning several years ago, as their promotion of Wahhabism came under fire for effectively promoting intolerance and violence. However, academics have begun to express serious concerns that the increasing focus on Saudi Arabia is not only baseless but counterproductive. For one thing, it remains impossible to prove. Moreover, the "anti-Salafism campaign" risks counterproductive effects (Fadil, Ragazzi, and de Koning 2019, 48). Making distinctions with respect to which types of Islam are welcome in Western societies risks further alienating large portions of the Belgian Muslim populations and unintentionally reinforcing the warped narrative, spouted by terrorist networks and recruiters, that there is no space for Islam in Western Europe (Fadil, Ragazzi, and de Koning 2019).

Similarly, neither the Rida Mosque (the largest Shia mosque in Brussels) nor the Masjid Annasr (the only mosque in the city of Vilvoorde) has been conclusively linked to terrorism. Even in Molenbeek, an area well-known as a radicalization hotbed, its deputy mayor asserts that although there are at least 22 mosques in the borough, extremists and recruiters tend to meet in clandestine meeting places and prayer sites, usually in private homes (Traynor 2015). There is some indication that this is thanks to the cooperation of Belgian Muslim communities, in particular the vigilance of the mosques' trustees (Coolsaet 2016).

In Belgian Prisons, Overcrowding Might Be a Factor

Across the European continent, there have been numerous examples of individuals radicalized in prisons. In Belgium, both Ibrahim al-Bakraoui and Abdelhamid Abaaoud were allegedly radicalized in prison. Additionally, Abaaoud and Ibrahim Abdeslam spent time in prison together, which possibly led to the radicalization of the latter (as well as the subsequent radicalization of Salah Abdeslam). As the Zerkani network specifically targeted individuals with criminal backgrounds for recruitment, that this pattern is prevalent in Belgium is hardly surprising. Moreover, incarcerated individuals in general are often described as those most vulnerable to recruitment efforts—due to their perceived oppression, limited religious knowledge, and penchant for violence.

Interestingly, one U.S. study found that radicalization is more prevalent in overcrowded prisons (Hamm 2008). Belgium is among the countries with the most overcrowded prisons in Europe, with over 100 inmates per 100 available places to house them. Some believe that lower density prison systems have increased capacity to monitor their inmates and therefore are more attuned to the signs of prison radicalization. Nevertheless, it is important to note that there is a dearth of systematic studies investigating the rates of prison radicalization or how it occurs.

Belgian Terrorists: Some Commonalities

By now, it is a well-established fact that there is no one "terrorist profile." Nevertheless, in the Belgian case, and particularly when analyzing Islamic radicalization in Belgium, there are certain commonalities, notably regarding location, age, employment, education, and criminality.

Most are from the Brussels-Antwerp axis. This includes Antwerp, Brussels, and several towns in between such as Mechelen and Vilvoorde (Kern 2014). This is not surprising, given the limited dispersion of Muslims in Belgium. This is also not surprising considering that both the Zerkani network and Resto du Tawhid were based in Brussels, while Sharia4Belgium was based in Antwerp. Approximately 75% of Belgian foreign fighters currently in Syria are from the Brussels-Antwerp axis, and the majority of those from Brussels grew up, or at least spent time, in the infamous Molenbeek district of the city (Soufan and Schoenfeld 2016). It is worth noting, however, that radicalization occurs throughout the entire country. To illustrate this point: Out of 589 municipalities in Belgium, 87 have had at least one individual leave to fight in Syria (Van Vlierden 2016a).

Most fall between the ages of 17 and 25 years old (Kern 2014). However, it is interesting to consider differences between the recruits and the leaders—because while "most" might be under 25 years of age, both Denis (leader of Resto du Tawhid) and Zerkani (leader of the Zerkani network) are in their forties.

Most are lacking conventional "qualifications" (Kern 2014). Again, this is not surprising given the low educational achievement and low employment rates of Muslims in Belgium. Low education and employment might serve as grievances that recruiters may use, and low education in particular might make individuals more susceptible to radicalization, if their critical thinking skills are less developed by formal education.

Many hold a criminal record (Stellini 2015). Given the high rate of radicalization that appears to occur in Belgian prisons, and the fact that the Zerkani network seems to specifically target criminals for recruitment, this is not surprising. Considering the frequent use of radical Islam to justify criminality and violence, it would be an interesting future avenue of study to more deeply investigate the susceptibility of criminals to radicalization.

Select Cases

Many of the following names have been referenced in the above discussion of the recruitment networks, but for purposes of clarity and to summarize, table 6.1 shows a list of select cases of radicalized Belgians.

Application of Social Movement Theory and McCauley and Moskalenko's Framework to the Situation in Belgium

There are a wide variety of theoretical frameworks that can be utilized to analyze radicalization. Islamic radicalization in the Belgium context can benefit from the use of all of the theories discussed in part I of this volume. Unfortunately, such an endeavor is beyond the scope of this chapter. While further studies can and should examine radicalization in Belgium through the lens of additional frameworks, this chapter will limit itself to

TABLE 6.1. Select Cases of Radicalized Belgians

Radical	Network(s)	Status	Key Points
Khalid Zerkani	The Zerkani Network	Incarcerated—serving a 15-year prison sentence	43-year-old, Moroccan-born; Otherwise known as "Papa Noel"; Recruited in and around Molenbeek; Leader of the Zerkani Network; Arrested in 2014.
Abdelhamid Abaaoud	The Zerkani Network	Deceased—killed in police raid	Architect of the 2015 Paris attacks; Dual Belgian-Moroccan national; Previous criminality; Involved in several European plots; Following Paris attacks, killed during a raid of the Saint-Denis neighborhood outside Paris.
Ibrahim Abdeslam	The Zerkani Network	Deceased—suicide bomb, Paris attacks	Lived in Molenbeek; Spent time in prison with Abaaoud; Allegedly radicalized by Abaaoud; Detonated a suicide vest in the Paris attacks on the Boulevard Voltaire.
Salah Abdeslam	The Zerkani Network	Incarcerated—serving a 20-year prison sentence	Lived in Molenbeek; Brother of Ibrahim Abdeslam; Allegedly radicalized by Abaaoud; Previous criminality; Involved in the Paris attacks; Arrested following an extensive manhunt.
Najim Laachraoui	The Zerkani Network	Deceased—suicide bomb, Brussels attacks	The suspected bomb-maker; Involved in the Paris attacks; Involved in Brussels attacks; Accelerated attacks on Brussels metro/airport.
Khalid Bakraoui	The Zerkani Network	Deceased—suicide bomb, Brussels attacks	Involved in the Paris attacks; Involved in Brussels attacks; Moroccan descent; Previous criminality; Accelerated attacks on Brussels metro/airport.
Ibrahim Bakraoui	The Zerkani Network	Deceased—suicide bomb, Brussels attacks	Involved in the Paris attacks; Involved in Brussels attacks; Brother of Khalid Bakraoui; Moroccan descent; Previous criminality; Accelerated attacks on Brussels metro/airport.
Jean-Louis Denis	Resto du Tawhid and Sharia4Belgium	Incarcerated—serving a 10-year prison sentence	41-year-old, Muslim convert; Operated in Brussels; Led Resto du Tawhid; Led Sharia4Belgium Brussels; Arrested in 2013.
Fouad Belkacem	Sharia4Belgium	Incarcerated—serving a 12-year prison sentence	Sharia4Belgium leader; Spiritual leader; Famous for his online videos and powerful street sermons; Sentenced to 12 years in prison after Sharia4Belgium was ruled a terrorist organization in 2015.

Social Movement Theory and McCauley and Moskalenko's framework. The rationale behind this choice is twofold. First, there is an emerging appreciation for the applicability of sociological and group-level frameworks to the study of radicalization. Second, by focusing on the group level and avoiding an undue emphasis on religiosity or ideology, the discourse becomes less alienating and consequent counter-radicalization strategies are more productive.

Social Movement Theory

Social Movement Theory in general, and Framing Theory in particular, can help explain radicalization in Belgium. Social Movement Theory is discussed in depth in chapter 2 of this volume, but a brief refresher here might be useful. Developed by Mayer Zald and John McCarthy, Social Movement Theory first defined social movements as "a set of opinions and beliefs in a population, which represents preferences for changing some elements of the social structure and/or reward distribution of a society" (Zald and McCarthy 1987, 2). Traditional Social Movement Theory, formed in the 1940s, asserted "movements arose from irrational processes of collective behavior occurring under strained environmental conditions (what sociologists would call 'Strain Theory'), producing a mass sentiment of discontent" (Borum 2011, 17).

There are a few variants of contemporary Social Movement Theory: New Social Movement Theory focuses on macro structural processes; Resource Mobilization Theory focuses on group dynamics; and Framing Theory discusses how social movements frame messages in a certain way in order to construct and propagate meaning (Borum 2011, 18). Anja Dalgaard-Nielsen of the Danish Institute for International Studies explains how Framing Theory in particular, and Social Movement Theory in general, might be particularly useful in understanding radicalization:

> Movements diagnose problems and attribute responsibility, offer solutions, strategies, and tactics (prognostic framing), and provide motivational frames to convince potential participants to become active. Key to mobilization, according to this perspective, is whether the movement's version of the "reality" resonates or can be brought to resonate with the movement's potential constituency. (2008, 6)

In other words, the strained environmental conditions and mass discontent are framed in particular ways to facilitate recruitment. Social movements are primarily concerned with keeping themselves alive; they use and redirect large-scale discontent to mobilize the masses.

Putting all this together, Social Movement Theory in general, and Framing Theory in particular, can help explain radicalization: these social movements, in an effort to keep their organizations alive, recruit new members from strained populations by framing their personal grievances as political ones. In this way, their organizations begin to resonate with the people they are trying to recruit, and they keep their organization alive by continuing to radicalize European youth. This is consistent with the importance that McCauley and Moskalenko place on small groups. They emphasize that personal grievance is unlikely to cause group sacrifice unless framed and interpreted as a group grievance (McCauley and Moskalenko 2008, 419).

The applicability of Social Movement Theory to radicalization is only beginning to be appreciated. Donatella della Porta was one of the first to connect Social Movement Theory to radicalization in a study of Italian and German militants (Borum 2011, 18). Quintan Wiktorowicz also used Social Movement Theory principles to develop a four-step developmental framework for radicalization in Western democracies (Borum 2011, 18). This chapter will continue this trend and attempt to demonstrate that radicalization in Belgium is consistent with Social Movement Theory principles and, in particular, Framing Theory.

Push Factors as Strained Environmental Conditions

As articulated by Social Movement Theory, movements arise out of strained environmental conditions producing a mass sentiment of discontent (Borum 2011). The "push factors" described above—namely, the poor demographic realities of Muslims in Belgium—can be conceptualized as strained environmental conditions consistent with Social Movement Theory principles.

First, poor socioeconomic realities of Muslims in Belgium can be considered a grievance, or a "strained environmental condition." Muslims in Belgium experience low levels of educational achievement and employment. Many Muslims with professional degrees remain unemployed for years, partly as a result of rampant employment discrimination (*Euro-Islam* n.d.). In terms of education, only 12% of Muslims (compared to 23% of non-Muslims) hold high educational achievement, while 65% of Muslims (compared to 47% of non-Muslims) hold low educational achievement (*Euro-Islam* n.d.). Social Movement Theory emphasizes grievances at the community level, so regardless of the socioeconomic conditions of individual recruits, the situation in Belgium is consistent with these principles. Nevertheless, it is interesting to note that many of the recruits do not come from impoverished backgrounds. Abdelhamid Abaaoud's grandfather was a coal miner, but his father climbed the socioeconomic ladder by running a successful clothing store and turning it into a family business—he was even able to send his eldest son to an elite school (Van Vlierden 2016a). Saïd El Morabit, a Sharia4Belgium recruit and foreign fighter, held a leading role in an insurance firm before leaving for Syria and dying in combat (Van Vlierden 2016a). Soufiane and Adel Mezroui, two brothers recruited by Sharia4Belgium, lived in a 2,500-square-meter villa with a fitness room, sauna, and indoor pool. Their father had a successful business trading tropical woods and importing Moroccan furniture (Van Vlierden 2016a).

Belgian Muslims' poor integration into Belgian society can be considered another grievance, or a "strained environmental condition." Belgian Muslim immigrants have been found to identify with their origin country over Belgium (Saroglou and Mathijsen 2007), and 70% of Muslim males aged 15 to 25 (a primary demographic for radicalization) feel unaccepted by Flemish society (Kern 2014). Especially noteworthy is the clear lack of confidence among Muslim youth that they will be able to integrate in the future: Of the Muslim youths surveyed, 60% believed they would never be integrated into Belgian society, and although 93% of all respondents held Belgian citizenship, 42% considered themselves foreigners in Belgium (Kern 2014).

The high levels of discrimination and intolerance against Belgian Muslims can be considered yet another grievance, or a "strained environmental condition." One study revealed 25% of Belgians show intolerant attitudes, above the EU average of 14% (*Euro-Islam* n.d.). Another study revealed that over 50% of Belgian Muslim youths had personally experienced racism (Kern 2014), and this only worsened following the 2016 Brussels attacks (Bayrakli and Hafez 2017). Widespread employment and housing discrimination also falls under this category. The high levels of discrimination in Belgian society might be related to the early successes of an outspokenly anti-Islam and anti-immigrant political party (Van Vlierden 2016a). Belkacem himself even cited high levels of discrimination as the reason he began his radical activity with Sharia4Belgium (Van Ostaeyen 2014).

Lastly, the inconsistent governmental funding of the Muslim religious community can be considered another grievance, or a "strained environmental condition." In addition to the accusations of fundamentalism within the community's representative institution and the tumultuous relationship between the EMB and the government, there are the extra requirements for recognition imposed on mosques compared to other places of worship—which might cause the Muslim community to feel personally targeted for its religious beliefs.

This combination of factors may create a strained environment for Belgium's Muslims, as per the principles of Social Movement Theory. Nonetheless, as this framework articulates, a strained environment is not enough for mobilization or radicalization. It is important to consider the organizations and recruitment networks responsible for framing those personal grievances as political or ideological ones.

Organizations Responsible for Framing the Grievances

Sharia4Belgium, Resto du Tawhid, and the Zerkani network are clear cases of organizations that have successfully recruited dissatisfied youth by framing their grievances in a certain manner.

The now-disbanded Sharia4Belgium claimed responsibility for at least 10% of Belgian foreign fighters (Crawford 2015). Fouad Belkacem, the spiritual leader of the organization, was highly effective in radicalizing young Belgians and was famous for his online videos and powerful street sermons.

Resto du Tawhid used charitable actions, social media, and online chat rooms to radicalize vulnerable individuals (Brunsden 2016). The leader of the organization, Jean-Louis Denis, pushed for his recruits to travel to Syria and Iraq, and he facilitated connections with both Sharia4Belgium and the Zerkani network (Van Ostaeyen 2016).

The most dangerous and clandestine of the three, the Zerkani network was directly linked to the 2015 Paris attacks and 2016 Brussels attacks (Van Ostaeyen 2016). Khalid Zerkani, the creator of the network, was known as "Papa Noel" for his cash handouts (Van Ostaeyen 2016). Until his arrest in 2014, he indoctrinated young Belgians while encouraging them to commit petty crimes along the way—justified as taking *ghanima* (the spoils of war) (Van Vlierden 2016b). Unlike Sharia4Belgium and Resto du Tawhid, the Zerkani network recruited many individuals with criminal backgrounds and little to no knowledge of Islam (Van Ostaeyen 2016).

In addition to the three major recruitment networks, the Islam Party may also have participated in the reframing of Belgian Muslim grievances by approaching grieved Muslim youth and seeking political support. Redouane Ahrouch, creator and head of the Islam Party, worked to convince citizens of the importance of Islamic people and Islamic laws, with the end goal of establishing an Islamic state (Riaño 2014). The Islam Party positioned itself as a party to represent all Muslims who have felt excluded from Belgian society (Riaño 2014). As an advocate of Sharia law, the Islam Party may have played some role in radicalizing Belgian youth, or at least in contributing to the social isolation of Muslim communities in Belgium (Kern 2014).

McCauley and Moskalenko's Framework

McCauley and Moskalenko's framework for radicalization is also useful for examining radicalization in Belgium. This framework is discussed in depth earlier in this volume (see chapter 5), but here is a brief refresher.

McCauley and Moskalenko conceptualize radicalization as a pyramid structure, with the terrorists (who are few in number) at the apex of the pyramid and their sympathizers and supporters (who are many in number) at the base (2008, 417). From base to apex, higher levels of the pyramid are associated with increased radicalization but decreased numbers, as increased radicalization means more resources and time invested, as well as more risks taken, which many individuals are not willing to do. To explain how and why radicalization occurs, McCauley and Moskalenko point to 12 mechanisms of radicalization, which can act individually or in concert to radicalize at the individual, group, or mass-public level (2008, 417–18). The mechanisms, or pathways to violence, are delineated in table 6.2.

McCauley and Moskalenko point to the importance of groups in the mechanisms and process of radicalization (2008, 417). Without the presence of small groups to pressure members to participate, individuals will rationally choose to free-ride off the concessions achieved by the radical group. For instance, although personal victimization is cited as a pathway to individual radicalization, social psychologists find that personal grievance is unlikely to cause group sacrifice unless framed and interpreted as a group grievance (2008, 419).

Consistency with the Belgian Case

While it is impossible to ascertain the specific pathways used by Belgians, the dynamics evident in Belgium support the importance placed on small groups by McCauley and Moskalenko's framework.

For example, although Zerkani played a lead role in the recruitment of young people in the Zerkani network, evidence revealed that the recruits encouraged each other to travel to join terrorist groups (Van Ostaeyen 2016). This is consistent with the fact that the Zerkani network remained active after Zerkani's arrest in 2014, and with the allegation that Salah and

TABLE 6.2. McCauley and Moskalenko's Radicalization Mechanisms

Level	Mechanism
Individual	1. Personal victimization
	2. Political grievance
	3. Joining a radical group—the slippery slope
	Individuals slowly increasing their radical behavior.
	4. Joining a radical group—the power of love
	Individuals join because their loved ones are members.
Group	5. Extremity shift in like-minded peers
	It is a noted phenomenon that groups of like-minded people grow more extreme in their thinking over time.
	6. Extreme cohesion under isolation and threat
	7. Competition for the same base of support
	Increasing radical action helps recruitment when there is competition.
	8. Competition with state power—condensation
	When a radical group attracts state countermeasures, the risks increase and only the most radical members stay.
	9. Within-group competition—fissioning
	Within-group competition can cause fissioning, or splitting, of the terrorist group into cells that target one another.
Mass	10. Jujitsu politics
	Terrorist leaders provoke the state into attacking them, to mass radicalize their group.
	11. Hate
	12. Martyrdom

Ibrahim Abdeslam were radicalized under the influence of another network member, Abdelhamid Abaaoud. Further, the most significant Belgian terrorist plots in recent years appear to be largely connected to networks rather than the work of lone operators—with even the Thalys train attacker allegedly connected to Abaaoud (Van Ostaeyen 2016).

Moreover, the Zerkani network included multiple sets of brothers and individuals who knew each other before they became radicalized. Ibrahim and Khalid El Bakraoui were brothers; Salah and Ibrahim Abdeslam were brothers; Abdelhamid Abaaoud and Ibrahim Abdeslam were in prison together. Other commonalities—such as Moroccan background and ties to Molenbeek—suggest a community-centric radicalization (Soufan and Schoenfeld 2016).

Even beyond the Zerkani network were multiple individuals with connections to each other. Denis was both the head of Resto du Tawhid and the head of Sharia4Belgium's Brussels branch. He was also connected to the Zerkani network, which helped his recruits travel to Syria. These are just some examples of the interconnections that demonstrate a community-centric approach to radicalization, consistent with McCauley and Moskalenko's emphasis on the importance of small groups to the radicalization process.

Conclusion

Several years ago, Belgium emerged as a notorious capital of radicalization in Europe, and particularly of Islamic radicalization in Europe. Belgium had the largest foreign fighter population (per capita in Western Europe) travel to Iraq and Syria, and Belgian terrorists played a central role in two of the highest-profile attacks of the last decade: the 2015 attacks in Paris and the 2016 attacks in Brussels. Since the extent of radicalization in Belgium came to light, scholars and journalists alike have investigated what makes Belgium unique in Europe. This chapter attempts to shed further light on this puzzle by looking to the poor demographic realities of the Belgian Muslim population; the successful activities of three major recruitment networks; commonalities among Belgian terrorists; select cases of individuals radicalized; and consistency with two select theoretical frameworks. This chapter additionally looks to radicalization in prisons and mosques and highlights the need for further study.

Radicalization in Belgium may be best explained by looking to push and pull factors through the lens of sociological and group-level theoretical frameworks. Muslims in Belgium had real grievances, or "strained environmental conditions": low levels of educational achievement; low employment; rampant employment and housing discrimination; high levels of intolerance; poor integration; and inconsistent governmental funding. These poor demographic realities provided a fertile ground for radical networks to emerge, influence, and recruit. As Social Movement Theory postulates, strained environmental conditions are utilized and framed by recruiters to facilitate their efforts and keep their organizations alive. This is consistent with the situation in Belgium, which was characterized by the successful recruitment and radicalization activities of three major networks: Sharia4Belgium, Resto du Tawhid, and the Zerkani network. Radicalization in Belgium is also consistent with McCauley and Moskalenko's framework, specifically their emphasis on the importance of small groups to the process of radicalization.

Although counter-radicalization is beyond the scope of this chapter, this analysis of radicalization in Belgium might help shed some light on possible counter-radicalization and de-radicalization strategies. For instance, it might be useful to focus on the poor demographic conditions of Muslims in Belgium—specifically, the low integration, the low levels of education and employment, and the discrimination that makes the population susceptible to radical influencers. Focusing on these factors might result in a long-term preventative solution, as compared to solely increasing investment in policing. The implementation of affirmative action, tolerance educational programs, and community outreach might be ideas worth pursuing. At the same time, counternarrative initiatives might be useful in tackling the framing step of the process. In general, viewing radicalization in Belgium as a context-specific social problem, and tackling it accordingly, might be the best alternative for a safer Belgium in the future.

REFERENCES

Arutz Sheva Staff. 2015. "Radical Belgian Jihadist Group Gets Jail Time." *Arutz Sheva*. November 2. http://www.israelnationalnews.com/News/News.aspx/191 209#.VdUQTVNViko

Bayrakli, Enes, and Farid Hafez. 2017. "European Islamophobia Report 2016." Ankara, Turkey: Foundation for Political, Economic and Social Research.

Berkley Center for Religion, Peace & World Affairs. n.d. "Religious Freedom in Belgium." http://berkleycenter.georgetown.edu/essays/religious-freedom-in-bel gium (no longer available).

Birnbaum, Michael. 2015. "Why Is Tiny Belgium Europe's Jihad-recruiting Hub?" *Chicago Tribune*. January 17. http://www.chicagotribune.com/news/nationworld /chi-belgium-jihadist-20150117-story.html

Borum, Randy. 2011. "Radicalization into Violent Extremism I: A Review of Social Science Theories." *Journal of Strategic Security* 4: 7–36.

Bouchaud, Melodie. 2015. "Sharia4Belgium Leader and Dozens of Other Militants Are Sentenced to Jail Time." *VICE News*. February 12. https://news.vice.com /article/sharia4belgium-leader-and-dozens-of-other-militants-are-sentenced -to-jail-time

Brunsden, Jim. 2016. "Belgium: Journeys to Jihad." *Financial Times*. https://www.ft .com/content/ec698aca-2745-11e6-8ba3-cdd781d02d89

Coolsaet, Rik. 2016. *Jihadi Terrorism and the Radicalisation Challenge: European and American Experiences*. New York: Routledge.

Crawford, Duncan. 2015. "Sharia4Belgium Trial: Belgian Court Jails Members." *BBC News*. February 11, 2015. http://www.bbc.com/news/world-europe-3137 8724

Dalgaard-Nielsen, Anja. 2008. *Studying Violent Radicalization in Europe I: The Potential Contribution of Social Movement Theory*. Copenhagen: Danish Institute for International Studies.

Eeckhaut, Mark. 2013. "Sharia 4 Belgium—Militanten Naar Syrië." *De Standaard*. March 11. http://www.standaard.be/cnt/dmf20130310_00499216?word=sharia 4belgium

Euro-Islam. n.d. "Islam in Belgium." http://www.euro-islam.info/country-profiles /belgium

Fadil, Nadia, Farid El Asri, and Sarah Bracke. 2014. "Belgium." In *The Oxford Handbook of European Islam*, edited by Jocelyne Cesari. Oxford: Oxford University Press. https://doi.org/10.1093/oxfordhb/9780199607976.013.18

Fadil, Nadia, Francesco Ragazzi, and Martijn de Koning. 2019. *Radicalization in Belgium and The Netherlands: Critical Perspectives on Violence and Security.* London: I.B. Tauris.

Federale Overheidsdienst Binnenlandse Zaken. 2008. "Belgische Verkiezingsuitslagen." http://www.ibzdgip.fgov.be

Hamm, Mark S. 2008. "Prisoner Radicalization: Assessing the Threat in U.S. Correctional Institutions." *NIJ Journal* 261: 14–19.

Hope, Alan. 2015. "Who Wants to Be a Belgian Citizen?" *Flanders Today.* http://www.flanderstoday.eu/current-affairs/who-wants-be-belgian-citizen

Kern, Soeren. 2011. "Let's Turn Belgium into an Islamist State." *Gatestone Institute.* December 19. http://www.gatestoneinstitute.org/2682/belgium-islamist-state

Kern, Soeren. 2014. "The Islamization of Belgium and the Netherlands in 2013." *Gatestone Institute.* January 13. http://www.gatestoneinstitute.org/4129/islamization-belgium-netherlands

Liu, Joseph. 2012. "Table: Religious Composition by Country, in Percentages." Pew Research Center. December 18, 2012. http://www.pewforum.org/2012/12/18/table-religious-composition-by-country-in-percentages

Martinez, Michael, Ed Payne, Catherine E. Shoichet, and Margot Haddad. 2015. "Belgium Warns of Serious and Imminent Threat to Brussels." *CNN.* November 20. http://www.cnn.com/2015/11/20/world/paris-attacks

McCauley, Clark, and Sophia Moskalenko. 2008. "Mechanisms of Political Radicalization: Pathways Toward Terrorism." *Terrorism and Political Violence* 20: 415–33.

Morelli, David. 2016. "1, 2, 3, Integrate! Belgium Will Try to Force Migrant Integration." *Civil Liberties Union for Europe.* November 29. http://www.liberties.eu/en/news/bill-mandatory-integration-beligum-red-light-green-light

Petrovic, Milica. 2012. "Belgium: A Country of Permanent Immigration." *Migration Policy Institute.* November 15. http://www.migrationpolicy.org/article/belgium-country-permanent-immigration

Riaño, Sergio Castaño. 2014. "The Political Influence of Islam in Belgium." *Partecipazione e Conflitto* 7 (1): 133–51.

Saroglou, Vassilis, and François Mathijsen. 2007. "Religion, Multiple Identities, and Acculturation: A Study of Muslim Immigrants in Belgium." *Archive for the Psychology of Religion* 29: 177–98.

Soufan, Ali, and Daniel Schoenfeld. 2016. "Regional Hotbeds as Drivers of Radicalization." In *Jihadist Hotbeds: Understanding Local Radicalization Processes*, edited by Arturo Varvelli, 15–36. Milano: The Italian Institute for International Political Studies.

Stellini, David. 2015. "The European Jihadist: A Profile." *EPP Group.* http://www.eppgroup.eu/news/The-European-Jihadist%3A-a-profile

Teich, Sarah. 2016. "Islamic Radicalization in Belgium." *International Institute for Counter-Terrorism (ICT).* https://www.ict.org.il/UserFiles/ICT-IRI-Belgium-Teich-Feb-16.pdf

Traynor, Ian. 2015. "Molenbeek: The Brussels Borough Becoming Known as Europe's Jihadi Central." *The Guardian.* November 15. https://www.theguard

ian.com/world/2015/nov/15/molenbeek-the-brussels-borough-in-the-spotlig
ht-after-paris-attacks

Van Ostaeyen, Pieter. 2014. "Statement by Fouad Belkacem Sharia4Belgium." *Pieter Van Ostaeyen*. https://pietervanostaeyen.wordpress.com/2014/09/20/stat ement-by-fouad-belkacem-sharia4belgium

Van Ostaeyen, Pieter. 2016. "Belgian Radical Networks and the Road to the Brussels Attacks." *CTC Sentinel*. https://www.ctc.usma.edu/posts/belgian-radical-ne tworks-and-the-road-to-the-brussels-attacks

Van Ostaeyen, Pieter, and Guy Van Vlierden. 2018. "Citizenship and Ancestry of Belgian Foreign Fighters." *International Centre for Counter-Terrorism*. https:// icct.nl/wp-content/uploads/2018/06/ICCT-Van-Ostaeyen-Van-Vlierden-Belg ian-Foreign-Fighters-June2018.pdf

Van Vlierden, Guy. 2016a. "Molenbeek and Beyond: The Brussels-Antwerp Axis as Hotbed of Belgian Jihad." In *Jihadist Hotbeds: Understanding Local Radicalization Processes*, edited by Arturo Varvelli, 49–61. Milano: The Italian Institute for International Political Studies.

Van Vlierden, Guy. 2016b. "The Zerkani Network: Belgium's Most Dangerous Jihadist Group." *The Jamestown Foundation*. April 12. https://jamestown.org /program/hot-issue-the-zerkani-network-belgiums-most-dangerous-jihadist -group

Vidino, Lorenzo. 2015. "Sharia4: From Confrontational Activism to Militancy." *Perspectives on Terrorism* 9 (2).

Zald, Mayer N., and John D. McCarthy. 1987. *Social Movements in an Organizational Society*. New Brunswick, NJ: Transaction Books.

SEVEN

France

Joining Jihad and Joining the Army—A Comparison

Elyamine Settoul

The series of attacks that occurred on French soil in 2015, along with the growing numbers of foreign fighters on their way to Syria, have made jihadist radicalization a top priority in the hierarchy of threats. With roughly 1,500 to 2,000 of its nationals involved, France is arguably the first supplier of foreign fighters in the West, and the fifth worldwide. While it remains mostly male in its composition, the phenomenon also encompasses women and families with children. Far from being restricted to socially marginalized immigrant youth, it also comprises a significant share of converts and individuals hailing from a wide range of social backgrounds (Kepel 2017; O. Roy 2017; Bakker 2006; Sageman 2004). Although a substantial portion originates from disadvantaged suburban areas, the social and geographic repartition of fighters actually points to a great diversity of origins. Daesh can boast of having recruited 25,000 to 30,000 fighters hailing from more than 90 different countries over the span of a few years (Lister 2015). The mass increase in the number of fighters has been greatly enabled by the geographical proximity of the Syrian military theater, which is easily reached by European nationals, but also by the sharp increase in communication abilities afforded by new digital tools and social networks. Grasping the scope of the phenomenon requires a thorough investigation into the strategies launched by the Islamic State organization. This chapter intends to provide insights on radicalization processes as they unfold within the French context. In this regard, it should be noted that the French debate became quickly polarized on the issue of whether there was or was not a religious dimension to jihadism. For instance, Gilles Kepel argues that the phenomenon results first and foremost from the "radicalization of Islam." He claims that the dynamics of jihadism fall in line with rigorist Islamic practices, such as Salafism (Kepel 2017). In this perspective, Salafism acts as the antechamber for jihadism, and the difference between the two is one of degree rather than kind. Conversely, the analysis provided by Olivier Roy refers to the "Islamization of radicalism." He argues that jihadism is the only ideology of global protest against Western hegemony that is currently available. More than religion itself, it is nihilism and fascination with death that structure young jihadists' sense of identity (O. Roy 2017). Moving beyond this debate, my investigation into the French case indicates that these dynamics actually coexist.

In this chapter, I start by providing a typology highlighting the diversity of jihadist actors' profiles. Far from being a monolithic phenomenon, commitment to jihadism resembles a mosaic aggregating a wide range of actors whose motives and expectations vary significantly (Thomson 2014). The originality of my analysis lies in the comparison I draw between the rationales of jihadist commitment and those of military commitment in conventional armies. Perhaps counterintuitively, I hypothesize that the deeper motives underlying these two types of commitment are comparable on multiple levels. Both can be interpreted as attempts to (re)construct identity and overcome affective and/or narcissistic deficiencies. The comparison mostly relies upon data I collected during doctoral research on second-generation immigrant youth joining the army in France (Settoul 2012); interviews I conducted with jihadists' families; and the literature on commitment to jihadism. The discussion is also informed by insights from military sociology. This enables me to address both the operational modes and the communication and recruitment strategies of these two social spaces, which are usually deemed to be worlds apart.

The Mosaic of "Made in France" Jihadism

France is the West's largest supplier of Daesh fighters (Soufan Group 2015, 12). Many attempts have been made to account for what appears to be a "French exception." William McCants and Christopher Meserole argue, for instance, that the French *laïcité* (secularism) and the francophone political culture in general are factors conducive to radicalization. The authors contend that the conjunction of an "aggressive" version of secularism (regulations on conspicuous religious symbols) along with widespread urbanization and mass unemployment provides highly fertile ground for such phenomena to emerge (McCants and Meserole 2016). While stimulating, their research presents a number of biases. First, it encompasses countries whose levels of Francophonie, political cultures, and public management of religion greatly differ. Second, upon taking a closer look at statistics, it appears that the ratio of the number of fighters over the total population is smaller in France than in other countries such as Sweden, Switzerland, and Denmark. The assertion that there is a "French exception" or a "Francophone exception" is therefore highly questionable.

The high number of French jihadists can probably best be explained by other factors. First, it should be emphasized that France is host to Europe's largest Muslim population (Pew Research Center 2011). Whilst the share of converts engaged in radical militancy can at times be substantial, it is established that the majority of fighters who joined the Islamic State were raised in Muslim cultural heritage families (practicing or not). Consequently, the potential pool of French candidates to jihad is structurally larger than in most European countries. Another socio-political explanation pertains to what is commonly called "the *banlieues* [suburbs] predicament." Although French jihadists display a great diversity of sociological and geographical origins, the bulk of the recruiting ground hails from disadvantaged urban areas (Beckouche 2015). Located at the periphery of most large cities in France, the *banlieues* are places of social marginalization, where inhabitants are the primary victims of discrimination in access to housing, employment, and in their relations to the police (Valfort 2015; Dubet 1987). Socially mixed when they were first built in the 1960s, French *banlieues* have progressively become ethnicized and ghettoized from the 1980s onward. In spite of numerous announcements made by political officials, who declare on a regular basis that they want to launch a "Marshall Plan for the *banlieues*," public investment has never really met the challenges at hand. In these deprived neighborhoods, low voter turnouts also contribute to worsening inhabitants' political marginalization. Such a lasting state of affairs has led to a rigidification of identities and a deepening rift between French people and "*banlieue* French people." The situation is further aggravated by the depoliticized interpretation of the urban riots that periodically engulf these areas. Rioters' demands are often discredited, and the state response tends to focus on security issues (Kokoreff 2008; Marlière 2008; Mauger 2006). The objective is to end violence rather than identify its deeper roots.

As a result, feelings of marginalization have become deeply internalized by social actors, who in turn develop a binary worldview. Such a Manichean outlook does not only manifest itself in the religious dichotomy between Muslims and non-Muslims/infidels. It also unfolds in a multitude of binary oppositions that oversimplify the reality: whites/visible minorities (Mansouri 2013; Blanchard, Bancel, and Lemaire 2005); policemen/*banlieue* youth (Fassin 2011; Jobard 2002); rich/poor; Israelis/Palestinians (Hussey 2015). Such otherization of "them" against "us" creates an environment conducive to breakaway and radical attitudes.

The variety of the Islamic State French fighters' sociological profiles is a striking fact. Quite evidently, and as illustrated by several studies, such as John Horgan's (2008), the terms "pathways," "itineraries," and "social trajectories" are best suited to account for the dynamics of commitment (McCauley and Moskalenko 2008; Moghaddam 2005). The Islamic State has developed well-proven communication strategies to attract a broad spectrum of individuals, be they male or female, hailing from various social backgrounds, and converted or not. In a way, Daesh communication experts have appropriated McDonald's famous motto: "come as you are" and the organization will take care of the rest. While identifying definite profiles remains a difficult endeavor, it is nonetheless possible to make an inventory of their general sociological features and clusters of motives. Sociological analyses performed on 265 French jihadists who died in Syria and Iraq (2013–16) reveal that 52% hailed from immigration backgrounds and 56% came from priority neighborhoods. Their average age was 28, and 48% were unfavorably known to the police (e.g., for delinquency, etc.). The French Coordination Unit of the Fight against Terrorism (*Unité de Coordination de la Lutte Antiterroriste*, UCLAT) notes that a large share is made up of youth combining several kinds of difficulties (educational failures, economic hardship, etc.).[1] The interviews I conducted between 2015 and 2016 with 15 families who were directly affected by a relative's commitment to jihadism have enabled me to distinguish six main types of motives. These include humanitarian, religious, political, romantic/marital motives as well as regressive post-feminism and identity quest. It should be emphasized that these various motives are not mutually exclusive and can intersect in a variety of ways. Thus, one candidate can simultaneously be willing to engage in humanitarian work and rescue his "Muslim brothers from Syria" in the name of a Salafi-like religious ideal. Another candidate

---

1. See the article "Portrait-robot des 265 Djihadistes Français Tués en Irak et en Syrie," *L'Express*, September 1, 2017. https://www.lexpress.fr/actualite/societe/portrait-robot-des -265-djihadistes-francais-tues-en-irak-et-en-syrie_1939559.html

can define his commitment in highly political terms (anti-imperialist struggle) while being at the same time fascinated by violent action. Beyond such specific motives, as will be demonstrated, the dynamics of enrollment tend to be embedded in precarious social and family backgrounds. The media-friendly word "jihadist," therefore, encompasses widely disparate realities and refers to actors whose motivations can be very remote from the official project of restoring the caliphate. Research on this issue has demonstrated that, as soon as 2011, a number of youth went to Syria for humanitarian purposes (Bozarslan 2015; Burgat and Paoli 2013). Their aim was to rescue Syrian populations who were being bombarded by Bashar al-Assad's regime in the wake of the Arab Spring's popular uprisings. The proliferation of online videos displaying civilian casualties at the hands of the Syrian army prompted many young Westerners to converge to the area.

The second issue that plays a central role in fostering this type of commitment relates to politico-religious motives. Many young people traveled to that region to perform jihad (i.e., the holy war against the enemies of Islam) and restore the caliphate. Here, the objective is to bring justice for those Muslim populations who have fallen prey to "crusaders" throughout the world. Such gathering of international combatants willing to fight in the name of their coreligionists is not unprecedented. Afghanistan, Bosnia, Chechnya, and even Iraq have all been the theater of jihad operations in the past. Yet, Daesh stands out because of its fierce determination to reestablish a caliphate by means of weapons. The project of rebuilding a Muslim empire has a powerful appeal to the youth. The idea is to return to the early days of the Muslim empire, a mythical golden age, which is in fact utopian. Scott Atran stresses this point by recalling that the Islamic State's current success can only be grasped by acknowledging that it is first and foremost an ambitious collective endeavor (Atran 2016). Such an endeavor contrasts with the inertia of so-called unholy and corrupted Muslim states, which have proven unable, since the collapse of Arab nationalism, to offer a true political vision. Religious motives are also apparent in the desire to perform *hijra*, migrating to a Muslim land. Whilst *hijra* originally refers to the Prophet Muhammad's migration from Mecca to Medina in order to gain protection from the physical threat posed by wealthy polytheist Arab tribes, the concept has since then been enlarged in some currents of Islam to become a religious duty for all Muslims settled in the West. It should also be underlined that *hijra* to Syrian-Iraqi lands takes on a specific meaning, for those lands correspond to the Sham, which is a blessed territory from a Qur'anic standpoint. In some interpretations, living and dying in the Sham opens the doors to paradise, not merely for the believer but also for all his loved ones. This motive is clearly expressed by a number of Nice inhabitants who left for jihad after being exposed to the religious indoctrination of ideologue Omar Omsen: "When I met Omar, I realized that as a Muslim, it was my duty to go to this part of the world as an act of solidarity with my Muslim brothers and sisters. I am still in contact with my family in France but I do not wish to return. It is my duty as a Muslim to stay here" (Lina, 29 years, Nice).

While their profiles tend to be neglected, some young people also went to Syria with a highly sophisticated geopolitical outlook and firm convictions. These actors are able to articulate a critical reflection on Western powers' foreign policies in the Middle East (Crettiez et al. 2017). Like other generations before them, they denounce Western imperialism, the "double standards" of managing the Israeli-Palestinian conflict by the international community, as well as the cynicism that shows through the diplomatic relations that Western democracies continue to cultivate with some of the region's authoritarian regimes (e.g., Saudi Arabia, Qatar, etc.). Such massive volunteering is not new in itself and has many historical precedents. From 1936 to 1939, the International Brigades recruited about 35,000 volunteers hailing from 53 different countries to fight in the Spanish civil war (Prezioso, Rapin, and Batou 2008). Between 1980 and 1992, roughly 20,000 Muslim combatants (mostly Arabs) entered Afghanistan to counter the Soviet invasion (Hegghammer 2010). In the more recent period, it is estimated that between 1991 and 1995, 500 to 1,000 French nationals joined the various factions involved in the ex-Yugoslavia war.[2] Driven by political and ideological factors, such commitment can also fulfill a sense of adventure. In France, these aspects are often left unaddressed, and the government response to radicalization has tended to favor a depoliticized approach. Radical individuals are more often than not apprehended from a pathological standpoint. They are seldom considered political actors but are rather perceived as extremists or victims of brainwashing and cultish manipulation who require medical treatment. The fact that the issue is framed in terms of mind control has resulted in an inadequate response. Despite millions of euros invested in the first deradicalization center, its doors closed permanently after only a few months[3] (Benbassa and Troendlé 2017).

The few studies devoted to "female jihad" put forward two types of

---

2. Figures quoted by Pascal Madonna in "Les Volontaires Français dans les Guerres de Yougoslavie, 1991 à 1995," working paper, research seminar, IRSEM, March 4, 2016.

3. The paradigm of the mental manipulation was mainly developed by the French anthropologist Dounia Bouzar, who was a privileged interlocutor for the French government.

motives. The first one mostly concerns teenagers and young women and involves a quest for romance. Indeed, the Islamic State's cyber recruitment strategies are not restricted to bloody videos. Much less is known about the various media (pictures or videos) showcasing good-looking and well-built male jihadists, whose purpose is to appeal to young Western women so that they perform their *hijra*. Most of these women encountered personal or family traumas throughout their lives. Such is for instance the case of Julie, a 22-year-old French woman of Asian descent. Her mother, who comes from a Parisian *banlieue*, recounted her journey to me: "My daughter was raped at a very young age and it remained a family secret. . . . Towards the end of her teenage years, she fell in love with a man she had met on social networks, and she went to Syria along with her brother. There, she got married. Her husband died very quickly, and they offered her to remarry. There was nothing religious about her; she did not know Islam." Female jihadism also takes on more complex meanings. According to Farhad Khosrokhavar, some women's commitment relates to what he calls regressive post-feminism. He equates this controversial notion with a disenchanting portrayal of the feminist struggle that was led by previous generations. Promoted by often-converted middle-class women, this post-feminism "glorifies the virile manhood of those who expose themselves to death and who, through that confrontation, prove to be manly, serious and sincere" (Khosrokhavar 2015). By carrying their jihadist project forward, these women seek to recover what contemporary societies do not or no longer offer (i.e., a social world in which male and female roles are strictly codified). In some ways, they willingly swap their autonomy and independence for a clearly delineated and regulated world that provides them with a sense of psychological security against the anxiety of freedom (Benslama and Khosrokhavar 2017). Regardless of their actual motives, women hold a doubly strategic role for the Islamic State. Not only do they provide comfort to male fighters but, more important, they also ensure the sustainability of the caliphal project by giving birth to a future generation of combatants, the "caliphate's lion cubs."

Finally, a significant share of jihadists are looking for a sense of identity and self-worth. I now turn to this segment of combatants. Khosrokhavar has already highlighted the strong recurrence among candidates to jihad of fatherless family backgrounds—which are "beheaded," as he puts it (Khosrokhavar 2015). The search for meaning certainly relates to identity and affective issues (oftentimes both) but does not exclude fascination with action and violence. A recent documentary film depicting young French jihadists enlisted by Omar Omsen is particularly illuminating in that respect (Boutilly, Husser, and Prigent 2016). The interactions between the propagandist and his young draftees closely resemble those that are commonly taking place in educational centers. Among this youth, the lack of identity or family markers is often combined with narcissistic tendencies. The jihadist commitment project is precisely designed to fill those affective and egotist shortcomings. Enrolling in the jihadist struggle on Syrian-Iraqi lands provides young Westerners with an opportunity for both positive identification and collective exaltation. By bringing them together under the cosmopolitan "foreign fighters" battle flag, it lifts them out of their condition as "Western *banlieues* losers" and grants them the much more gratifying status of "God's fighters in the East." The caliphal project fully transforms the individual by instantly turning passive bystanders located at the periphery of the system into actors who actively built a system, in this case the caliphate. Such a project is all the more exciting because it also satisfies a desire for action and adrenaline. The war capital and virile manhood highlighted in Daesh's propaganda videos are significant pull factors for some young people. Such was the case of Antoine, a former student in the city of Toulouse who eventually left for Syria. His mother stated in her interview that "he could spend entire nights on the internet playing combat games and looking at propaganda videos by the Islamic State. His life was driven by fighting sports and appetite for action. He didn't know much about Middle Eastern geopolitics. He fought and died there." Lying behind the homogenizing word of "jihadist" is therefore a multiplicity of highly heterogeneous realities. The term conflates a range of actors whose motivations vary greatly but who all believe that the Islamic State project can meet their desires, needs, and identity and affective flaws.

It should be noted, however, that the literature on jihadists' motives tends to rely on synchronic frameworks of interpretation. Yet, the effects of jihadist socialization on individuals' worldviews should also be taken into account. My own research on the military demonstrates that a number of young draftees were mostly motivated by material considerations (e.g., pay, housing, opportunity for travel, etc.) upon joining the army. It is only through their military experiences (e.g., external operations, daily regiment life) that they progressively reoriented their discourses and resorted to vocational arguments (e.g., patriotism, nation, flag, etc.) that were initially completely absent. I argue that the same can be said of jihadists. The motives they express after having experienced jihad in Syria and Iraq are not necessarily the same as those that triggered their commitment in the first place. Some may join Daesh because they are looking for thrill and adventure but may eventually soak up Salafi-jihadi beliefs. As they acquire a military or jihadist *ethos*, young people's discourses evolve. This points to the need to use a diachronic and longitudinal perspective in order to identify the changing dynamics and narrative evolutions that are most likely to occur. In the armies, the youth themselves are not necessarily aware of these discursive shifts. Such forms of biographical illusion must therefore be carefully considered in order to avoid any bias in scholarly work (Bourdieu 1986).

The following section draws a parallel between jihadist commitment and military commitment. It highlights the many similarities between these two fields in terms of the resources and opportunities afforded to their members, as well as from a more formal standpoint (communication, marketing). The comparison takes as a starting point the many commonalities between the social trajectories of jihadists and young servicemen enlisted in French armies.

Jihadist Commitment and Military Commitment: Beyond Symbolic Antagonisms

In the collective imagination, the figure of the jihadist is most probably seen as the absolute antonym of the Western army man. Such perception is especially warranted in light of the importation, over the last few years, of international conflicts onto Western soil, which is manifest in the increasing number of physical attacks against Western soldiers. For instance, during the tragedy that occurred in February 2012 in Toulouse and Montauban, Mohammed Merah slayed three French soldiers and injured another because of their alleged involvement in the Afghan military theater. In May 2013, French soldier Cédric Cordiez from Gap's 4th cavalry regiment and British soldier Lee Rigby from the Royal Regiment of Fusiliers were respectively assaulted in Paris and killed in London. In October 2014, Michael Zehaf-Bibeau shot a caporal down in front of Ottawa's National War Memorial. Two days before that, in Saint-Jean-sur-Richelieu, two soldiers had been knocked over and one of them succumbed to his injuries. In March 2016, Ayanle Hassan Ali assaulted Toronto's army recruiting center and wounded two soldiers with a knife. In February 2017, Egyptian national Abdallah El-Hamahmy attacked a French military patrol next to the Louvre Museum. Ziyed Ben Belgacem assaulted a female French soldier in the Orly Airport in March 2017 before being eliminated. In August 2017, in the city of Levallois-Perret, another Parisian suburb, one man injured six soldiers with his vehicle. Committed by Muslims willing to avenge their coreligionists suffering at the hands of "crusaders' armies" throughout the world, this series of attacks exemplifies the emergence and normalization of a threat that is both unpredictable and anxiety-provoking. It also gives credence to the idea that there is an inexorable alterity between two segments of the youth that are opposed in every way, namely those who chose to integrate socially through a profession that stresses patriotism as a cardinal value, and those who are disaffiliated and fall prey to nihilism and serious identity troubles.

Yet, social reality does confine itself to such a binary framework. Specifically, the detailed analysis of some jihadists' biographical trajectories yields interesting results and exhorts us to be more nuanced in our conclusions, or at least to depart from a Manichean understanding of commitment logics. In fact, the many parallels and porosities between trajectories of jihadist and military commitment are apparent in a number of cases. Thus, Lionel Dumont, a former member of the Roubaix gang (1996), had completed his military service at the 4th Marine Infantry Regiment of Fréjus. He then went to Djibouti with the 5th Overseas Interarms Regiment, where he took part in the UN multinational intervention in Somalia under the French humanitarian operation named Oryx (1992–1993). In July 2010, before conducting his attacks in the Toulouse area, Mohammed Merah had attempted to enroll in the French Foreign Legion. Similarly, a number of testimonies concerning Hasna Ait Boulahcen, who was related to the Bataclan theater attacks' perpetrators (November 13, 2015), reveal that she was strongly willing to enlist in the French army. Jihadist Quentin Roy, who hailed from the Parisian suburb of Sevran, had also thought about joining the army (V. Roy 2017, 50). Other examples taken from abroad can also be mentioned. For instance, convert Abdul Shakur (born Steven Vikash Chand) was enrolled during four years in Canada's Royal regiment (2000–2004) before engaging in terrorist activities, such as the thwarted Toronto attack of June 2006 (Bramadat and Dawson 2014). These examples feature among the most notorious, but other less-known cases can also instantiate this phenomenon.[4] The ambivalent character of these jihadists' social trajectories is rather unsettling, for the values commonly associated with jihadist and military commitment are deemed diametrically opposed in collective representations.

The research I conducted on the military commitment of second-generation immigrants in France provides insights on the various areas

---

4. According to the data I collected from various professionals (prison guards, army men, policemen, intelligence services), several dozen jihadis currently in Syria had attempted to enroll in the French army or the national police force.

of convergence that are likely to bring closer two realms that are, on the face of things, highly antagonistic. Throughout this study, I developed a typology of commitment logics for this segment of the population. One of the categories, called "rupture commitment," encompasses actors whose social trajectories share many commonalities with those who are attracted by radical religious projects, especially in their extremist or Salafi version. Specifically, these included many youths hailing from unstable, if not precarious, social and family backgrounds. Upbringing in dismantled families and lack of a father figure were especially recurring characteristics. Without necessarily articulating it in an explicit manner, many embraced the arms profession because of the affective, familial environment it provided. While they appear very different at first sight, the military and religious fields are therefore characterized by a number of similarities that are worth delving into. In both cases, there is a search for a positive identity in a socially structuring environment, or at least a rewarding normative framework. Danièle Hervieu-Léger, among others, has highlighted various common features between the religious and military experiences. Besides subordination to a transcendental power, be it God for the former and the mission (militarily speaking) for the latter, both appeal to notions of obedience, asceticism (especially through physical training in the military case), and starkness. More specifically, the congruence between the two is most apparent in their use of the notion of "sacredness." Hervieu-Léger stresses that the experience of the sacred is to be found in the "feelings of depth" that occur when societies produce a specific type of collective experience, the "us experience," which characterizes those moments where individuals realize they form an entity that is greater than the sum of their single atoms (2009). Like religious commitment, military careers provide an opportunity for young draftees to exit a negative cycle, recover a form of life balance, and *in fine* escape the downward spiral of failure and self-deprecation.

Beyond their apparent divergence, religious and military commitments share one additional attribute: that of fostering positive identities and alleviating protean affective deficiencies by providing a sense of brotherhood, which can take the form of a community of believers (*umma*) or that of the arms profession (brothers in arms). This quest for an environment that is both affective and authoritarian is also a feature of born-agains' social experiences. Being included in a religious or military group provides a sense of both safety and collective power that is particularly looked for by youth in search of identity. Psychologists would use the notion of "containing" to describe this quest for guidance and boundary-seeking. Both types of commitment can therefore appeal to youth with similar socio-psychological profiles, some of whom wander in a kind of "identity no man's land." Such weak identity anchoring is also tied to generational and cultural factors. The overwhelming majority of jihadists are between 18 and 26 years old, a time in their lives when they are leaving behind their childhood ideals to look for those that will structure their adult life. According to Fethi Benslama, the strength of the jihadist offer lies in its ability to connect the global to the intimate. For these young people, the harm caused to the Muslim world (domination, colonization) resonates with individual and narcissistic wounds (Benslama 2016).

Their identity quest is also made more complex by a series of secondary factors. Deep anthropological shifts in contemporary families (e.g., single-parent households, stepfamilies, etc.) along with the disappearance of those rites of passage that used to provide symbolic landmarks (national service) and the increasingly precarious conditions of entry into working life have undeniably affected young people's identity formation. This process is further aggravated by intergenerational ruptures. Young people's socialization, particularly those who hail from postcolonial immigrant backgrounds, is punctuated by traumas, whose traces are particularly enduring for they have never been put into words nor cathartically released by the parental generation. The symbolic, linguistic, and cultural gap stemming from parents' cultural uprooting produces great identity uncertainty, the consequences of which have been carefully studied by sociologists such as Abdelmalek Sayad (1999). Generally hailing from poor rural areas in the former colonies, parents have been socialized in cultural environments in which the oral tradition prevails and where the Muslim religion is relatively permeable to syncretism and cultural borrowing (e.g., North African Malikism, African marabout practices). They speak dialectal Arabic, whose symbolic prestige is considerably lesser than classical Arabic and Qur'anic Arabic. By contrast, most of their children grew up at the periphery of large Western industrial cities and have been educated in French schools. Enlisted in the 1960s and '70s as a conveniently cheap and docile labor force, many fathers have experienced a sharp drop in social status following the massive waves of industrial relocation in the 1990s and 2000s. Unable to support their families after experiencing this social downgrade, fatherly figures have symbolically collapsed in the domestic realm, for the identity of the father is often inextricably tied to his professional standing. The ensuing (cultural and symbolic) duality between parents and children provides fertile ground for alienation. Hence, young people start looking for symmetrical counter-models in order to offset degrading feelings. Parents' oral and "folkloric" Islam is cast aside in favor of a "pure" Islam and an orthopraxy that feeds on texts and videos released by international Muslim scholars (Amghar 2011, 162–63). The invisibility of the working-class father who used to hug the walls has now made way for the conspicuousness of traditional Islamic clothes (*qamis*). The derogatory designation of "beur"[5] as a category of second-class citizenship has now made room for the figure of the Muslim, which allows for identification with a transnational community. Such an identification process is also fueled by the hyperpoliticization of Islam-related debates (e.g., headscarf, minarets, halal, etc.) and the negative media coverage of Islam (Hajjat and Mohammed 2016; Deltombe 2007).

The fact that individuals engaging in extremist behavior are often looking for meaning has been theorized by social psychology scholars working on radicalization (see Morrison, chapter 5 of this volume). Thus, according to Arie W. Kruglanski (Kruglanski et al. 2014), the desire to "get respect by becoming someone" is a central driving force in radicals' trajectories. As for Michael Hogg (2011), he relies on uncertainty–identity theory to characterize the experiences of actors whose identity construction is faltering. In a way, extremist movements provide certainty and composure to individuals who are looking for them. Small radical groupings also tend to foster homogeneity among their members by suppressing individual distinctive features. This process, which Max Taylor (1988) calls "deindividuation," is also found in military socialization. Both types of socialization (military and jihadist) aim at creating a self-reinforcing identity and cultivating a binary worldview that clearly demarcates the inside from the outside. These homogenization and cohesion techniques are also apparent in the use of songs and recitations. As in Western military cultures, jihadists resort to chanting to strengthen the fervor and internal cohesiveness of the group. For instance, *anashid* are chanted Islamic poems that are particularly valued among these groups (Hegghammer 2015). The role and significance of such activities in reinforcing group identity has been extensively documented by military sociologists. Investigating military cadences, Marie-Anne Paveau demonstrates for instance how they are meant to strengthen group bonds by picturing the relation between what is "inside" and what is "outside" as deeply antagonistic (1998). Akin to the black flag under which Daesh fighters unite and with which they self-identify, chants enable combatant groups to cement their internal identity and galvanize one another in times of adversity.

_____

5. Stemming from the word "Arab" written in backward slang, the term "beur" refers to French nationals of North African descent. Widely used in the 1980s, it has now fallen into abeyance and has negative, if not derogatory, overtones.

In addition, jihadist and military commitments both closely relate to the body. The literature in military sociology highlights young people's strong willingness to use their bodily capital (i.e., their physical dispositions) as a resource to succeed professionally (Teboul 2017; Settoul 2015; Sauvadet 2006; Wacquant 2002). The same holds true for Daesh's foreign fighters. Investigations into jihadists' biographical trajectories reveal the central significance of manly and war capital. Many aspirants to jihad practice combat sports and take great care in attending to and increasing their physical capital (Crettiez et al. 2017, 44). Furthermore, both jihadist and military commitments have the specificity of valuing and transforming the body. They offer the opportunity to incorporate a new *hexis* as well as specific body techniques. In the army, such bodily work involves daily physical training (e.g., attention, muscular development, etc.), while socialization into jihadist groups favors a greater observance of religious rituals and even the embodiment of diligent religious orthopraxy (e.g., daily prayers, fasting, etc.).

The parallel can be further extended to decision-making processes, which often entail significant biographical shifts. The concept of biographical bifurcation I use in my research to account for the commitment process of some of my military interviewees is equally illuminating to grasp and describe the social trajectories of jihad volunteers (Settoul 2012; Bidart 2006). The decision to enlist rarely stems from a lengthy reflection, time-wise. Some choose to join the army to put a halt to a downward spiral of social marginalization (e.g., economic hardship, crime, etc.). Others do it out of boredom with their socio-professional or family environment. And still others enroll after a friendly or romantic encounter. Their decision often takes the shape of a biographical bifurcation, for it is both rapid in its process and heavy in its consequences for one's subsequent pathways. The various testimonies gathered from jihadists' friends and relatives frequently point to the oftentimes abrupt and almost unpredictable nature of their decision to leave. Media stories tracing combatants' trajectories always insist on the surprise and even the stupefaction that invariably struck their social circles. Furthermore, a number of youth left for Syrian-Iraqi lands only a few weeks after their conversion to Islam.

Recruiting at All Costs! A Comparison of Recruitment Systems

Comprehending commitment logics, whether in the military or jihadist realm, requires shifting the attention upstream to what may be called the recruitment offer. Most Western armies are now facing massive recruitment imperatives. Indeed, the armies' professionalization process resulted in huge quantitative needs in terms of personnel, of about several thousand people per year. The analysis of military institutions' enrollment strategies shows a wide use of the emotional range. Contrary to popular misconception, the patriotic or nationalist fiber remains scantly mobilized in this communication aiming at attracting youth toward these professions. To enlarge the recruitment pool, the Ministry of Defense increasingly uses emotional fiber, as explained by this colonel, a senior official in charge of the French Army recruitment: "When we want to recruit a young guy, our first objective is to create an emotion by impressing him: we need to show something extraordinary. For instance, we present tanks or helicopters on recruitment booth in order to durably mark his mind."[6] To achieve the enrollment of tens of thousands of young people coming from around a hundred different nations, the Islamic State has also relied on an extremely thorough communication grounded in the creation of emotions among young people. In order to optimize its seduction strategy, Daesh has invested greatly in the internet and social networks. As demonstrated by a large number of studies, this strategy is not new; other jihadist movements, such as the Tunisian group Ansar Al-Sharia, already used such highly efficient media channels to circulate their propaganda. Engaged in jihad 3.0, the Islamic State has progressively mastered the science of internet virality, thereby increasing tenfold the digital impact of its messages. Jihadist propaganda scholar Javier Lesaca has examined more than 800 Daesh-produced videos. His conclusion is that they are far from exclusively based upon traditional religious appeals. In fact, from a formal standpoint, a significant portion of Daesh productions, such as *Flames of War* or *19HH*, are directly inspired from Western pop culture and Hollywood blockbusters, such as *American Sniper*, *V for Vendetta*, or even *The Matrix* (Lesaca 2017).

Video games have also become a chief source of inspiration for the organization's communication strategy. Well-aware of young people's fascination with heroic figures, Daesh public relations officers stretch their imagination and appeal to the youth by passing on footage featuring highly aestheticized combatants. Images frequently display groups of very masculine, heavily armed hooded soldiers striking poses that are highly reminiscent of those commonly conveyed in the most popular war video games, such as *Call of Duty* or *Battlefield*. Interestingly, these ever-more-realistic

---

6. Interview conducted with a French colonel responsible for military recruitment strategies.

video games also constitute a strategic medium for human resources managers in the army. Thus, in the United States, partnerships have been established between video games developers, researchers, and the military. Attached to the University of Southern California, the Institute for Creative Technologies is a research center that directly collaborates with the army in order to improve soldiers' training via simulators and maximize the military's recruitment capacities. Distributing free video games is also common practice. In France, such methods are less prevalent and less formalized, yet they are being experimented with. For instance, marketing ads for military trades and occupations have been embedded into video games. National defense actors' growing interest for young people's cultural practices is also apparent in a number of other instances. In 1999, the French Ministry of Defense released a 40-second video clip that was directly inspired by *Matrix*'s latest technological processes (Merchet 1999). The virtualization of reality therefore appears as a top-notch marketing technique for recruitment professionals. Having great impact upon teenagers and post-teenagers, such increasingly used marketing strategies have also raised concerns among scholars. Many academics, like Isabelle Gusse, speak out against the blurring of boundaries between, on the one hand, a virtual world that constantly beautifies and glamorizes fighters' heroism, and on the other hand, the cruel, brutal, and bloody reality of any war activity (Gusse 2013).

The French context is characterized by the great numerical significance of French nationals enrolled as jihadists on the Syrian-Iraqi theater. The growing literature on this topic has identified with certainty some of this phenomenon's distinctive features. Far from being a monolithic group, French (and foreign) jihadists make up a heterogeneous batch of actors whose motivations are clearly split. Daesh appears as a kind of supermarket, able to provide a wide range of goods and items to anyone looking for something. The organization has managed to craft an efficient propaganda that simultaneously promises religion, humanitarian work, politics, brotherhood, adrenaline, and even love. French debates have tended to revolve around jihadism's religious dimension (or lack thereof). For some, jihadism stems from the radicalization of Islam. In that perspective, religious interpretations and practices are to be considered crucial explanatory factors. By contrast, according to others, radical Islam amounts to nothing more than a superficial coating that gives meaning to underlying social radicalism. According to this interpretation, the grievances held by some segments of the youth find a semantic expression in the jihadist ideology, which is the only true transnational utopia currently existing in the landscape of protest.

Yet, the great diversity of jihadists' sociological profiles indicates that the two explanations coexist. They are complementary rather than exclusive.

Nonetheless, the conclusions that emerge from drawing a parallel between military commitment and jihadist commitment tend to downplay religious interpretations in favor of an explanation based upon integration and identity issues. Such identity issues stem from a triple predicament, which is simultaneously socioeconomic (difficulties to integrate socially), generational (transitioning into adult life), and migratory (parents' cultural uprooting, feelings of humiliation). The comparison between the military and jihadist fields points to many commonalities. Beyond symbolic antagonisms, the two provide their members with very similar resources. These include access to a gratifying identity and to an affective environment for young people with family problems, along with a sense of brotherhood (brothers in arms/*umma*) and the opportunity to quench their thirst for heroism and adrenaline. These jihadists' trajectories strikingly echo the social psychology literature on radicalization. They are fueled by a quest for self-esteem, and in some cases they are driven by an attempt at identity (re)construction within a particularly precarious social and family environment.

REFERENCES

Adraoui, Mohamed-Ali. 2020. *Salafism goes Global: From the Gulf to the French Banlieues*. Oxford: Oxford University Press.

Amghar, Samir. 2011. *Le Salafisme d'Aujourd'hui: Mouvements Sectaires en Occident*. Paris: Michalon.

Atran, Scott. 2016. *L'Etat Islamique Est Une Révolution*. Paris: Les Liens.

Baker-Beall, Christopher, Charlotte Heath-Kelly, and Lee Jarvis. 2014. *Counter-Radicalisation: Critical Perspectives*. New York: Routledge.

Bakker, Edwin. 2006. "Jihadi Terrorists in Europe, Their Characteristics and the Circumstances in Which They Joined the Jihad: An Exploratory Study." The Hague: Clingendael Institute.

Beckouche, Pierre. 2015. "Terroristes Français: Une Géographie Sociale Accablante." *Libération*, December 28.

Benbassa, Esther, and Catherine Troendlé. 2017. "Les Politiques de 'Déradicalisation' en France: Changer de Paradigme." *Sénat* 633 (2016–17).

Benslama, Fethi. 2016. *Un Furieux Désir de Sacrifice. Le Surmusulman*. Paris: Seuil.

Benslama, Fethi, and Farhad Khosrokhavar. 2017. *Le Jihadisme des Femmes: Pourquoi Ont-elles Choisi Daech?* Paris: Seuil.

Bidart, Claire. 2006. "Crises, Décisions et Temporalités: Autour des Bifurcations Biographiques." *Cahiers Internationaux de Sociologie* 120: 29–57.

Blanchard, Pascal, Nicolas Bancel, and Sandrine Lemaire. 2005. *La Fracture Coloniale. La Société Française au Prisme de l'Héritage Colonial*. Paris: La Découverte.

Bourdieu, Pierre. 1986. "L'Illusion Biographique." *Actes de la Recherche en Sciences Sociales* 62/63: 69–72.

Boutilly, Romain, Antoine Husser, and Frederique Prigent. 2016. "Jihad: Les Recruteurs, Complément d'Enquête." Video Documentary. https://www.yout ube.com/watch?v=GtIDBTkthbo&t=116s

Bozarslan, Hamit. 2015. *Révolution et Etat de Violence: Moyen-Orient 2011–2015*. Paris: CNRS Éditions.

Bramadat, Paul, and Lorne Dawson. 2014. *Religious Radicalization and Securitization in Canada and Beyond*. Toronto: University of Toronto Press.

Burgat, François, and Bruno Paoli. 2013. *Pas de Printemps pour la Syrie: Les Clés pour Comprendre les Acteurs et les Défis de la Crise (2011–2013)*. Paris: La Découverte.

Coolsaet, Rik. 2019. "Terrorismes et Radicalisations à l'ère Post-Daech." *Revue Internationale de Criminologie et de Police Technique et Scientifique* 3: 322–46.

Coolsaet, Rik. 2013. *Jihadi Terrorism and the Radicalisation Challenge: European and American Experiences*. London: Ashgate.

Crettiez, Xavier, Romain Sèze, Bilel Ainine, and Thomas Lindemann. 2017. "Saisir les Mécanismes de la Radicalisation Violente: Pour une Analyse Processuelle et Biographique des Engagements Violents." *Rapport de Recherche pour la Mission de Recherche Droit et Justice*. http://www.gip-recherche-justice.fr/wp-content/up loads/2017/08/Rapport-radicalisation_INHESJ_CESDIP_GIP-Justice_2017 .pdf

Deltombe, Thomas. 2007. *L'Islam Imaginaire: La Construction Médiatique de l'Islamophobie en France, 1975–2005*. Paris: La Découverte.

Dubet, François. 1987. *La Galère: Jeunes en Survie*. Paris: Fayard.

Fadil, Nadia, Francesco Ragazzi, and Martijn de Koning, eds. 2019. *Radicalization in Belgium and the Netherlands: Critical Perspectives on Violence and Security*. London: I.B. Tauris.

Fassin, Didier. 2011. *La Force de l'Ordre: Une Anthropologie de la Police des Quartiers*. Paris: Seuil.

Geisser, Vincent. 2003. *La Nouvelle Islamophobie*. Paris: La Découverte.

Gusse, Isabelle. 2013. *L'armée Canadienne Vous Parle: Communication et Propagande Gouvernementale*. Montréal: Presses de l'Université de Montréal.

Hajjat, Abdellali, and Marwan Mohammed. 2016. *Islamophobie: Comment les élites Françaises Fabriquent le "Problème Musulman."* Paris: La Découverte.

Hecker, Marc. 2018. "137 Nuances de Terrorisme. Les Djihadistes Français?" *Focus Stratégique*, 79: IFRI.

Hegghammer, Thomas. 2010/2011. "The Rise of Muslim Foreign Fighters: Islam and the Globalization of Jihad." *International Security* 35: 53–94.

Hegghammer, Thomas. 2015. "The Soft Power of Militant Jihad." *New York Times*. December 18.

Hervieu-Léger, Danièle. 2009. "Fait Religieux et Métier des Armes." *Inflexions* 10: La Documentation Française.

Hogg, Michael. 2011. "Self-Uncertainty, Social Identity, and the Solace of Extremism." In *Extremism and the Psychology of Uncertainty*, edited by Michael Hogg and Danielle L. Blaylock, 19–35. Oxford: Wiley-Blackwell.

Horgan, John. 2008. "From Profiles to Pathways and Roots to Routes: Perspectives from Psychology on Radicalization into Terrorism." *Annals of the American Academy of Political and Social Science* 618 (1): 80–94.

Hussein, Hasna. 2016. "La Propagande de Daech." *Esprit* 10: 16–19.

Hussey, Andrews. 2015. *The French Intifada Review. The Long War between France and Its Arabs*. London: Granta Books.

Jobard, Fabien. 2002. *Bavures Policières? La Force Publique et ses Usages*. Paris: La Découverte.

Kepel, Gilles. 2017. *Terror in France: The Rise of Jihad in the West*. Princeton: Princeton University Press.

Khosrokhavar, Farhad. 2015. *Radicalisation*. Paris: Maison des Sciences de l'Homme.

Kokoreff, Michel. 2008. *Sociologie des émeutes*. Paris: Payot.

Kruglanski, Arie W., Michele J. Gelfand, Jocelyn Bélanger, Anna Sheveland, Malkanthi Hetiarachchi, and Rohan Gunaratna. 2014. "The Psychology of Radicalization and Deradicalization: How Significance Quest Impacts Violent Extremism." *Advances in Social Psychology* 35 (1): 69–93.

Ledésert, Soline. 2010. "Pour Recruter l'Armée s'Incruste dans les Jeux Video en Ligne." *Rue 89*. February 9.

Lesaca, Javier. 2017. *Armas de Seducción Masiva: La Factoría Audiovisual con la que Estado Islámico ha Fascinado a la Generación Millennial*. Ediciones Península.

Lister, Charles. 2015. "Returning Foreign Fighters: Criminalization or Reintegration?" *Policy Briefing*. Brookings Doha Center.

Mansouri, Malika. 2013. *Révoltes Postcoloniales au Cœur de l'Hexagone*. Paris: Presses Universitaires de France.

Marliere, Eric. 2008. *La France Nous a Lâchés! Le Sentiment d'Injustice Chez les Jeunes des Cités*. Paris: Fayard.

Mauger, Gérard. 2006. *L'émeute de Novembre 2005. Une Révolte Protopolitique*. Broissieux: Éditions du Croquant.

McCants, William, and Christopher Meserole. 2016. "The French Connection: Explaining Sunni Militancy around the World." *Foreign Affairs*. March 24. https://www.foreignaffairs.com/articles/2016-03-24/french-connection

McCauley, Clark, and Sophia Moskalenko. 2008. "Mechanisms of Political Radicalization: Pathways to Terrorism." *Terrorism and Political Violence* 20 (3): 415–33.

Merchet, Jean-Dominique. 1999. "L'Armée Recrute en 3D, Un Clip de 5,2 Millions pour Attirer les Soldats." *Libération*. September 15.

Moghaddam, Fathali M. 2005. "The Staircase to Terrorism: A Psychological Exploration." *American Psychologist* 60 (2): 161–69.

Neumann, Peter, and Scott Kleinmann. 2013. "How Rigorous Is Radicalization Research?" *Democracy and Security* 9 (4): 360–82.

Paveau, Marie-Anne (dir.). 1998. "Le Langage des Militaires: Les Militaires et l'Ordre du Discours: Doctrine, Lexique et Representations." *Les Champs de Mars* 3: 47–67.

Pew Research Center. 2011. "The Future of the Global Muslim Population." January 27.

Prezioso, Stefanie, Ami-Jacques Rapin, and Jean Batou. 2008. *Tant Pis Si la Lutte est Cruelle, Volontaires Internationaux Contre Franco*. Paris: Editions Syllepse.

Ragazzi, Francesco. 2014. "Vers un "Multiculturalisme Policier"? La Lutte Contre la Radicalisation en France, aux Pays-Bas et au Royaume-Uni." *SciencesPo: Centre de Recherches Internationales*. September 1, 2014. https://www.sciencespo.fr/ceri/fr/content/vers-un-multiculturalisme-policier-la-lutte-contre-la-radicalisation-en-france-aux-pays-bas-

Roy, Olivier. 2017. *Jihad and Death: The Global Appeal of Islamic State*. New York: Oxford University Press.

Roy, Véronique. 2017. *Quentin, Qu'ont-ils Fait de Toi?* Paris: Robert Laffont.

Sageman, Marc. 2004. *Understanding Terror Networks*. Philadelphia: University of Pennsylvania Press.

Sauvadet, Thomas. 2006. *Le Capital Guerrier: Concurrence et Solidarité entre Jeunes de Cité*. Paris: Armand Colin.

Sayad, Abdelmalek. 1999. *La Double Absence: Des Illusions de l'Émigré aux Souffrances de l'Immigré*. Paris: Seuil.

Sedgwick, Mark. 2010. "The Concept of Radicalization as a Source of Confusion." *Terrorism and Political Violence* 22 (4): 479–94.

Settoul, Elyamine. 2012. *Contribution à la Sociologie des armées: Analyse des Trajectories d'Engagement des Militaries Issus de l'Immigration*. Paris: PhD Institute of Political Studies of Paris.

Settoul, Elyamine. 2015. "Classes Populaires et Engagement Militaire: Des Affinités électives aux Stratégies d'Intégration Professionnelle." *Lien Social et Politiques* 74: 95–112.

Soufan Group. 2015. "Foreign Fighters: An Updated Assessment of Flow of Foreign Fighters into Syria and Iraq." *Soufan Group*. December 1, 2015.

Sourbier-Pinter, Line. 2001. *Au-delà des Armes: Le Sens de la Tradition Militaire*. Paris: Actes Sud.

Taylor, Max. 1988. *The Terrorist*. London: Brassey's Defence Publishers.

Teboul, Jeanne. 2017. *Corps Combattant: La Production du Soldat*. Paris: Maison des Sciences de l'Homme.

Thomson, David. 2014. *Les Jihadistes. Qui Sont ces Citoyens en Rupture de la République? Pour la Première Fois ils Témoignent*. Paris: Les Arènes.

Valfort, Marie-Anne. 2015. "Discriminations Religieuses à l'Embauche: Une Réalité." *Institut Montaigne*. October 2015. https://www.institutmontaigne.org /publications/discriminations-religieuses-lembauche-une-realite

Wacquant, Loïc. 2002. *Corps et âmes: Carnets Ethnographiques d'un Apprenti Boxeur*. Paris: Agone.

EIGHT

Germany

Individual Variations in Relational Mechanisms of Radicalization

Robert Pelzer and Mika Moeller

Over the past decade, convictions for offenses related to so-called Islamist terrorism have increased sharply in Germany. The main reason for this has been a wave of mobilizations recruiting jihadists for conflicts in Syria and Iraq. According to German security authorities, 1,050 individuals left Germany between 2013 and 2020 to join or support the so-called Islamic State (IS) as well as Al-Qaeda–affiliated or other Islamist groups in Syria and Iraq, of which about one third had already returned to Germany by 2019 (BfV 2019a). Furthermore, there have been nine jihadist terrorist plots executed in Germany since 2010 (BfV 2019b; BfV 2021). Between 2015 and 2018, the Federal Prosecutor General of the Federal Supreme Court initiated criminal investigations against 2,461 suspects related to so-called Islamist terrorism, resulting in the conviction of 61 individuals due to membership in or support of a (foreign) terrorist group and/or planning of serious subversive or other crimes (Deutscher Bundestag 2018). The average age of those recruited to Syria or Iraq at the moment of their first departure was 25.8 years,[1] with 79% being male. Even though 61% were

---

1. Statistics are available for 784 people who left for Syria or Iraq between 2014 and June 2016.

born in Germany, 81% had immigrant backgrounds,[2] and 18% were converts to Islam. There is information available for 189 individuals indicating their previous engagement in criminal activities before and throughout the process of their radicalization, particularly crimes involving property, violence, and drugs. The majority (80%) of those making such journeys are considered to belong to the Salafi movement, but only 268 (37%) had been active members of mosques or other Islamic associations prior to their departure for Syria or Iraq (BKA, BfV, and HKE 2016).

These profiles fit with the overall picture of European jihadism, where most jihadist foreign fighters are young men in their mid to late twenties, and between 6% and 23% are converted, but the majority are born Muslims (Boutin et al. 2016). In most cases, radicalization does not take place within mainstream Salafi environments but either individually or in small groups of like-minded individuals around militant Salafi groups or radical mosques (Vidino, Marone, and Entenmann 2017, 83). Many jihadists are "born-again" Muslims who have re-converted to a radical version of Islam after having lived a secular life previously (Roy 2017).

Involvement in terrorism is not a result of a single decision but, rather, the outcome of a developmental "pathway" that gradually unfolds (Borum 2011), without necessarily following a linear direction (McCauley and Moskalenko 2017; Hafez and Mullins 2015). There is a broad consensus among researchers in the field of radicalization research and terrorism studies that such pathways should be understood as forming a multifaceted and complex "psychosocial process" (Horgan 2008) that is affected by a variety of factors and mechanisms at the individual, group, and movement levels. Individual dimensions of a person's life are primarily considered to be starting points of their developmental pathway, which is open to different influences (see, e.g., Wiktorowicz 2005). To explain pathways of radicalization, numerous studies refer to relational and group dynamics, particularly emphasizing the role of personal relationships and social networks in connecting individuals to (more) radical groups or movements and socializing them into violent ideologies (for Salafi jihadism specifically, see empirical studies by Reynolds and Hafez 2017; Malthaner 2014; Sageman 2008; Wiktorowicz 2005). Previous research has also highlighted the potentially radicalizing effect of peer-group dynamics (see, e.g., McCauley and Moskalenko 2017; Lützinger 2010). Further, the importance of interactions between radical activism and the state and/or activists and coun-

---

2. According to the criteria for official statistics taken in Germany, a person is considered to have an immigrant background if they, or at least one parent, were not born as a German citizen (Statistisches Bundesamt 2017).

termovements has also been stressed (see Pisoiu, chapter 2 of this volume; della Porta 2013).

Although it is understood that conflictual interactions with the state and other movements play a crucial role in radicalization processes, the responses of individuals or groups are contingent upon recognition and interpretation of these interactions (Wiktorowicz 2002; McAdam, Tarrow, and Tilly 2001). This chapter aims to analyze varying responses of members of radical groups to such conflictual interactions via the empirical example of the German Salafi-jihadist group Millatu Ibrahim, which was involved in conflictual interactions with a right-wing movement in Germany as well as with German police, culminating in the criminalization of the group. We believe this case fits well with the explanatory framework offered by Social Movement Theory (see chapter 2 on social movements by Pisoiu, this volume), in particular Donatella della Porta's theory of clandestine violent groups emerging out of broader social movements. According to della Porta (2013), during the emergence phase of such groups three mechanisms need to be set in motion, namely escalating policing, competitive escalation, and the activation of militant networks. There is basic evidence for the existence of all three mechanisms in the case presented here. First, escalating policing led to criminalization of the group Millatu Ibrahim, which at least accelerated decisions of some group members to join the jihad in Syria or Iraq. Second, the mechanism of competitive escalation also played a role in the formation phase of Millatu Ibrahim, which founded itself in 2011 as a splinter group from the Salafi mainstream, claiming to represent "true Islam." Third, it is evident that some members of the group collectively decided to join jihad, emerging out of a previously existing network of like-minded "brothers" with a shared common experience of activism in propagating *da'wa* (i.e., "invitation to Islam," a form of proselytizing). However, it is noteworthy—and in need of explanation—that only some members of the group left Germany to join jihadist organizations in Syria/Iraq, making the case quite interesting, since this implies that the effects of relational dynamics on radicalization processes have obviously varied across different subgroups within Millatu Ibrahim or for different types of individuals. One question arising from this observation is how the respective activists understood and interpreted their own reactions to the situation of escalating state repression. Here, we investigate different patterns of interpretation regarding the group's situation in light of growing repression as well as two models for reaction to the situation which might explain varying responses among group members, culminating in the continuation of legal *da'wa* activism, on the one hand, and a transitioning into violent jihad on the other.

Converts only made up one part of Millatu Ibrahim, which at its height had approximately 50 members and was ultimately outlawed in Germany in 2012. However, as shall be shown in this chapter, the group laid down rigorous requirements for the transformation of member identity. Becoming a "true believer" was conceptualized as a process of desistance from the deviant state of unbelieving, with group members being requested to radically change their behavior and thinking, which can well be understood as a process of conversion. However, conversion to a Salafi jihadist worldview is only a starting point for the analysis conducted in this chapter, which primarily focuses on the dynamics taking place after the adoption of a radical worldview that strongly determines the individual's sense-making processes concerning interactions in the social world.

The case of the Millatu Ibrahim group can also be productively interpreted through the lenses offered by social-psychological theories. Although our empirical data does not provide any evidence clearly revealing the inner group dynamics of Millatu Ibrahim, we assume that the group confirmed and stabilized the commitment of its members, while also pressuring them to scale up their personal efforts. As will be shown in this chapter, one consequence of adopting Salafi-jihadist religious beliefs is great pressure within a given group to comply with religious rules in daily life and optimize one's level of self-purification. The believer is guided to constantly examine the authenticity of their intentions in order to be allowed to enter paradise, but this process cannot be achieved with complete certainty. Uncertainty–identity theory (Hogg, Kruglanski, and van den Bos 2013; see also chapter 5 on the social psychology of radicalization by Morrison, this volume) could be drawn upon here to help explain the believer's quest for confirmation in this situation of personal uncertainty.

This chapter is structured into three sections. First, it provides an overview of the Salafi movement in Germany, out of which the Millatu Ibrahim group emerged. Second, it describes the development of the Millatu Ibrahim group and analyzes the social process of interaction with the German police and countermovements. Third, in order to analyze how these interactions were interpreted by group members, it presents two contrastive case studies on the interpretations and reactions of two leading activists of the Millatu Ibrahim group: One activist, Denis Cuspert, finally participated in violent jihad in Syria/Iraq, whereas the other, Hasan Keskin, continued to promote nonviolent *da'wa* in Germany.

Salafism in Germany and the Genesis of a Salafi-Jihadist Tendency

In 2014, there were about 26 million people in Germany with no religious affiliation. The largest religious group was Christians, with approximately 23.9 million people estimated to be Catholics and about 22.6 million Protestants (REMID 2017a, 15). Meanwhile, in 2016 an estimate of 4.4 to 4.7 million people were Muslims (Stichs 2016), forming the largest non-Christian community in Germany, with the vast majority being Sunnis (REMID 2017b). Also in 2016, about 27.3% of the Muslims in Germany were recent immigrants, due to the massive influx of refugees in the previous few years, with roughly 1.2 million Muslims coming to Germany between 2011 and 2015 (Stichs 2016). No valid information about the number of converts to Islam is available, however.

In 2020, the German Federal Office for the Protection of the Constitution (Bundesamt für Verfassungsschutz) estimated that about 28,715 people belong to Islamist groups, with the largest being the expanded Salafi movement, which grew from about 3,800 adherents in 2011 to about 12,150 in 2020 (BMI 2017, 6; BMI 2020, 196–7), expanding strongly between 2013 and 2017. In the course of this rapid increase, various groups and associations formed representing different perspectives on Islamic teachings and concepts, though essentially the Salafi movement in Germany can be differentiated into a mainstream tendency and a radical Salafi scene. The majority of Salafi preachers in Germany can be attributed to the mainstream, which focuses on *da'wa*, purification of the self, religious education, and refraining from violence (Wiedl 2014, 14). In contrast, radical Salafis propagate elements of the Salafi-jihadist worldview, such as calling for (defensive) jihad; rejecting loyalty toward unbelievers, including their institutions and norms; as well as promoting antagonism toward "pseudo Muslims" (*takfirism*). Salafi activism only emerged in Germany in the early 2000s, later than it did in Great Britain, the Netherlands, or France (Malthaner and Hummel 2012, 249). But the scene has expanded since the mid-2000s, with the emergence of a younger generation of activists preaching in German. Making extensive use of the internet to spread their teachings and mobilize for seminars (Malthaner and Hummel 2012, 249), such preachers quickly gathered followers—mainly second-generation Muslim immigrants but also non-Muslim youth converting to Islam. Due to differing opinions on the questions of *takfir, taghut* (i.e., false gods or idols), and jihad, the movement split in 2008 into a larger mainstream, with the association *Einladung zum Paradies* (EZP, "Invitation to Paradise") as the most prominent representative, and a smaller radical tendency represented by *Die Wahre Religion* ("The True Religion"; Wiedl 2014, 41). The defining moment here was a statement by preacher Ibrahim Abou-Nagie from Die Wahre Religion that if you do not share the view that governors who do not rule via Allah's laws are unbelievers, you are an unbeliever yourself. Within this radical stream, a whole range of preachers started adopting the position that fighting against "apostate" rulers and Western military presence in the Muslim world is not only permitted but is even an obligation. Through the teachings of Abu Muhammad al-Maqdisi and other radical proselytizers, Muslims were called upon to dissociate themselves from unbelievers and their values, including loyalty to democratic institutions (Wiedl 2014, 73).

In 2010, the moderate Salafi stream came under pressure from the state and the media, as well as from right-wing countermovements. First, criminal investigations were launched against EZP activists on suspicion of "dissemination of publications harmful to young persons," and the Ministry of the Interior commenced an investigation against the EZP, aiming to eventually prohibit the association (Dantschke 2014, 182). Second, because of protests from residents, the group had to abandon a plan to establish a large *da'wa* center in the German city of Mönchengladbach. These and other conflicts in 2010 can be seen as leading toward a watershed moment in the development of the Salafi movement in Germany (Malthaner and Hummel 2012, 253), with moderate preachers retreating into the background, whereas preachers from the radical tendency began propagating their Salafi-jihadist positions even more openly than before. In the course of 2010, radical websites such as salafimedia.de were launched, where lectures by prominent international jihadi preachers, including the aforementioned al-Maqdisi, were published side by side with lectures by preachers from the radical tendency.

Apparently motivated by the ongoing stigmatization of the Salafi movement, both tendencies reunified in June 2011. A little later, the head of the EZP, Pierre Vogel, dissolved the association and moved to Egypt, while the more radical Die Wahre Religion moved to the foreground. In December 2011, Die Wahre Religion intensified their *da'wa* activities in the public sphere by launching a campaign called *LIES!*—which means "READ!" in German in the imperative grammatical mood—and copies of the Qur'an were distributed in more than 100 locations throughout Germany, mainly on shopping streets and market squares. The *LIES!* campaign and Abou-Nagie's Die Wahre Religion were finally banned in 2016, due to the high number of activists—more than 140—who had left Germany to join jihad in Syria and Iraq (de Maizère 2016).

To sum up these developments, it can be said that certain characteristics of the Salafi-jihadist tendency in Germany were the outcome of an internal differentiation process within the Salafi movement, which evolved in the context of social and political conflicts over the presence of *da'wa*-practicing Islamists proselytizing in the public sphere. An anti-Islamic countermovement began mobilizing against this public Salafi activism, and pressure to maintain social order by the state subsequently increased. Such social reactions challenged the radical tendency to assert its collective identity against external pressure. In these conflicts with adversaries of (radical) Islam, especially those group norms that lie at the center of collective identity came under pressure, such as for the radical Salifists the obligation to defend the religion of Islam against its enemies. Their split from the mainstream tendency can thus be understood as an act of identity assertion, making it necessary to clarify, redefine, and mark the boundaries between the inside and outside of their worldview.

The Millatu Ibrahim Group: Relational Factors of Radicalization

One outcome of this differentiation process was Millatu Ibrahim (MI), which emerged from the fringes of the radical Salafi tendency at the end of 2011 and marked a new dimension of Salafi-jihadist activism in both quantitative and qualitative terms. Nearly every day after its founding, a new lecture or sermon was held and published on one of the group's websites, openly propagating Salafi-jihadist positions. Members of the group continued and intensified their previous *da'wa*-stage engagement in conflictual interactions with adversaries, culminating in the criminalization and dissolution of Millatu Ibrahim only half a year after its formation. After the group was banned and its mosque closed, at least 15 of the approximately 50 presumed group members left Germany to support jihadi terrorist organizations in Syria/Iraq. They were between 18 and 36 years old (mean and mode: 25 years).[3]

---

3. This figure only includes cases of foreign fighters reported in the media, so it could be even more. Florian Flade (2012a, 2012b) estimates the number of Millatu Ibrahim members up to its banning in May 2012 to be approximately 50, with 30 to 40 regular visitors to its mosque (Flade 2012b), but there is at present no reliable information available.

Activities and Ideology: The Idea of Probation

The name of the group refers to al-Maqdisi's 1984 publication *Millat Ibrahim (The Religion of Ibrahim) and the Calling of the Prophets and Messengers*, and the group's logo was a black flag with white-lettered inscription of the *shahada*, the Islamic profession of faith. Although conceptualized as a transnational network with branches in Great Britain and Pakistan, the activities of the Millatu Ibrahim network had a clear national focus in Germany. First established as an internet project at the end of 2011, the network established a center in the city of Solingen, in North Rhine-Westphalia, at the beginning of 2012. The founder of Millatu Ibrahim, the Austrian jihadist Mohamed Mahmoud, took over the Ar-Rahmah mosque, which had been used before by the Die Wahre Religion and the group DawaFFM, and renamed it the Millatu Ibrahim Mosque (Wiedl 2012, 49). He also assumed primary leadership of the association, which had about 50 members. Within a very short time frame, the three heads of the group—Mohamed Mahmoud (Abu Usama al Gharib), the ex-rapper Denis Cuspert (Abu Maleeq, later Abu Talha al-Almani), and Hasan Keskin (Abu Ibrahim)—organized a large and frequently occurring number of activities.

Although also supporting revolutionary political activism in Muslim countries, the thematic and practical focus of Millatu Ibrahim was not on political activism per se but, rather, on organizing and mobilizing among its adherents a strict, purist form of translating fundamentalist doctrine into practice. The main components of Millatu Ibrahim praxis included:

a) extensive *da'wa* work, including participation in the *LIES!* campaign, but also organization of *da'wa* social events, such as playing soccer or hosting barbecues, and last but not least the defense of Islam in public against blasphemy;

b) practical and spiritual support of Muslim prisoners (e.g., on ansarul-aseer.com), Muslims in conflict zones (Al-Nusra project), and *mujahideen* with donations, propaganda, and *dua* (i.e., prayer);

c) everyday religious practices strictly complying with the Qur'an and *sunna*; and

d) fulfilment of the duty of *hijra* (i.e., emigration), including

e) fighting jihad until the Millatu Ibrahim member either achieves the "ultimate victory" against the "enemies of Islam" or dies as a martyr.[4]

---

4. Members of the group, or at least some of them, swore the following oath: "Either victory or *shahada*" (*shahada* in this case means martyrdom), sometimes followed by the words "until the head explodes."

In the literature, the ideology of MI is referred to as Takfir Salafism (Hummel 2014) or a mixture between purist Takfirism, radical political activism, and jihadism (Holtmann 2014, 273). During the period of activism in Germany, the Millatu Ibrahim preachers referred to various ideologues propounding Takfir Salafism/jihadism, such as Abu Muhammad al-Maqdisi, Khaled Ar-Rashed, Abul Fadl Umar Al-Haddushi, Hafiz Ibn Ajab Ad-Dusari, and Munthir Ash-Shinqitī. The group understood itself as an exclusive collective of true believers emancipating itself through their brotherliness from all competing forms of solidarity in society. As with other Salafis, Millatu Ibrahim adherents believed that belonging to the "sect of the saved"—those who will directly enter paradise—requires that the believer constantly prove their religious qualities (personal probation before God). This process includes not just following and enforcing the rules of God's law in the outer world but also purifying the self from all profane, need-oriented intentions and eliminating subjective reasoning. Most important, good deeds that are not performed with a "pure intention" are considered worthless, but the believer can never truly know whether the individual really has achieved an authentic purity of intent such that God will accept their deeds on the day of final judgment. Due to the high degree of uncertainty involved in personal probation before God, the individual is guided to continuously evaluate, prove, and improve their religious performance, including meticulous examination of the purity of their intentions.

Interaction with External Events and Adversaries

Apart from their *da'wa* activism on the streets, such as distribution of the Qur'an in urban areas, the group mainly became publicly visible through their extensive use of the internet and social media. From September 2011 to August 2012, Millatu Ibrahim published 420 videos on one of its core websites (Al-Ghurabaa), of which 270 were produced by the leading trio of the group: Hasan Keskin, Denis Cuspert, and Mohamed Mahmoud. Most of these videos were also posted on YouTube. Based on screenshots of the website at different points in time, we were able to quantify the group's posting activities. Each post was then assigned to a specific category, allowing us to analyze the frequency of a posted topic across time.[5] Figure 8.1

---

5. As the Al-Ghurabaa website has been offline since August 2012, the data gathered for this study is based on archived screenshots of parts of the website at different points in time. The time intervals between the screenshots are irregular, especially at the beginning of the

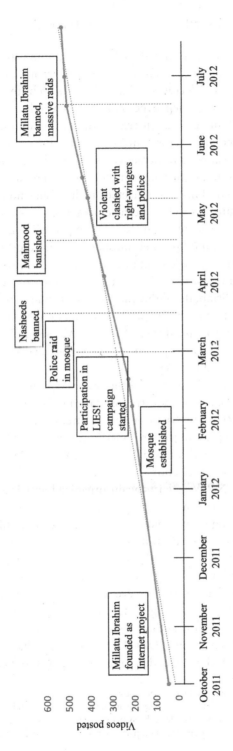

Fig. 8.1. Timeline of Events Related to Millatu Ibrahim and Total Number of Videos Posted on its Website, Al-Ghorabaa

shows a timeline of events related to Millatu Ibrahim's lifespan and the development of its online activism. The blue curve represents the number of video statements and lectures published on its website, Al-Ghurabaa, with blue dots indicating when screenshots for data collection were taken.

The group was founded as an internet project in November 2011. With the foundation of the Millatu Ibrahim mosque in Solingen and commencement of the *LIES!* campaign, the activities of the group and its interactions with local politics, right-wing countermovements as well as security authorities, increased. This was reflected in the rising number of video statements and lectures as well as in the emergence of two new topic categories: "news and statements" and "READ campaign." Both topic categories remained relevant until the website shut down in August 2012. At the end of February 2012, the police conducted its first raid on the MI mosque. Two weeks later, three *nasheeds* (i.e., religious chants) by Denis Cuspert were banned. In addition, the authorities launched an investigation against Cuspert for "incitement of the people." At the end of April, the Hesse Ministry of the Interior demanded that Mohamed Mahmoud leave Germany within four weeks. To avoid expulsion by the authorities, he left Germany in April and immigrated to Egypt.

On the first of May, Millatu Ibrahim activists led protests by Salafi activists against an anti-Islamic demonstration staged in Solingen by the right-wing party Pro NRW. The Salafi protesters attempted to break through the police barrier to prevent the Pro NRW protesters from showing caricatures of the Prophet Muhammad. Several members of MI were arrested by the police including the "emir" of the Salafi protests, Hasan Keskin. A few days later, Pro NRW activists again organized anti-Islamic protests, this time in front of the King Fahd Academy in Bonn, displaying cartoons critical of and mocking Islam. Among other organizations, Millatu Ibrahim mobilized for a counterdemonstration, which brought together between 500 and 600 participants. During the demonstration, the police were heavily attacked by Salafi activists, including a knife assault by one activist. In the aftermath of the demonstration, several video clips, including a *nasheed* by Denis Cuspert ("Labbayk"), glorified this violent militancy. Immediately following the riots, the authorities began investigating Millatu Ibrahim, Die Wahre Religion, and DawaFFM. Finally, Millatu Ibrahim was banned at the end of May 2012, due to its "acts against the constitutional

---

chosen time frame. Between the first screenshot in October 2011 and the second screenshot in February 2012, 124 days had passed, whereas in the subsequent period the time intervals vary between 9 and 46 days. Nevertheless, the available data has allowed us to identify periods of time where posting activities and focus on particular topics increased or stagnated.

order and ideas against understanding among nations" (BMI 2013) followed by nationwide raids against the group in mid-June. Subsequently, a couple of Millatu Ibrahim members initiated their departure to Syria/Iraq, most of them traveling through Egypt or Turkey. After the ban of MI, Cuspert called upon German Muslims to emigrate (*hijra*) or at least engage in jihad inside Germany. Some of his adherents followed him and Mahmoud, who had already emigrated in April 2012, to Egypt. Especially after the fall of Hosni Mubarak, Egypt had become a common destination for both political and Salafi jihadists. Meanwhile, Hasan Keskin stayed in Germany, leading the activities of the remaining MI members.

We measured the frequency of topics circulating in postings on Millatu Ibrahim's website to analyze the effects of external events on the group's public discourses.[6] We expected the intensifying interactions with adversaries beginning in February 2012 to lead to a rise of jihad-and repression-related topics. However, the results of the analysis seem inconsistent. Whereas postings related to jihadi ideologue Abu Muhammad al-Maqdisi significantly increased starting in April, the topics "Muslims in prison" and "Muslim sisters" (also related to repression) did not increase but, rather, had been dominant topics right from the beginning.[7] Aside from this, the situation in Syria became a more and more important topic. At the beginning of June 2012, a new platform, An-Nusrah.com, was founded to support Muslims in Syria and was advertised in several video clips on Al-Ghurabaa, calling for donations. But there does not seem to have been any link between the events in Syria and confrontations with police and right-wing movements in Germany. We conclude that the frequencies of topics posted on the group's main website over time indicate that repression and stigmatization were fundamental to the group right from the beginning, whereas the topic of jihad gained increasing importance in light of the situation in Syria/Iraq as well as conflictual interactions with the state and other socio-political forces.

---

6. Our quantitative analysis of topics displayed in Al-Ghurabaa posts (n = 420) is based on tags assigned to each post by users or administrators of the website.

7. Particular attention was paid to the case of Filiz Gelowicz, also known as Sayfillah al-Ansariyya, the wife of Fritz Gelowicz, the former Emir of the Sauerlandgruppe, which had planned bomb attacks against Americans in Germany in 2007. Filiz Gelowicz collected money for her husband and also publicly requested donations for jihadi fighters. In March 2011, she was sentenced to two and a half years in prison for spreading jihadist propaganda but was released early for good behavior in April 2012. Several videos as well as some *nasheeds* were published by Millatu Ibrahim requesting support for her.

Individual Sense-Making in the Face of Repressive Events:
Two Case Studies

Our analysis of topic frequencies on MI's main website has not provided any information about the sense-making processes guiding its members vis-à-vis changing conditions during the group's lifespan. For this purpose, we qualitatively analyzed the contrasting narratives of two leading figures of Millatu Ibrahim: Hasan Keskin and Denis Cuspert. We selected these activists for two reasons: First, as both were leading figures of Millatu Ibrahim, there are video statements and lectures from both of them available from different points in time, allowing us to analyze how interpretations of external events were evolving and possibly changing over time. Second, both activists not only projected and propagated a different role model regarding how to deal with the repressive events but also put this model into practice. After Millatu Ibrahim was banned by authorities, Keskin continued by carrying out nonviolent *da'wa* in Germany, whereas Cuspert left Germany to join violent militant jihad in Syria. Data would also have been available to analyze the case of the third leading figure, Mohamed Mahmoud, who like Cuspert also became a foreign fighter for the Islamic State. However, Mahmoud had become a jihadist long before the foundation of Millatu Ibrahim. Furthermore, he did not take part in the confrontations with police and right-wing protesters because he had already left Germany before they happened.

The case studies presented here focus on how the two leading Millatu Ibrahim activists, Keskin and Cuspert, interpreted the group's or movement's social situation at different points in time during the course of interactions they had with their social environment. Methodologically, this implies taking a reconstructive approach to qualitative analysis, interpretively piecing together the internal perspectives of the individuals under study (Bohnsack 2010; Glaser and Strauss 1967). We are interested in exploring the following questions: (1) How did these activists perceive and interpret their changing situation, caused by attacks from out-group socio-political forces? (2) What kinds of action did they see as being consistent with their beliefs in face of these changing conditions? and (3) Did these interpretations and the appropriate actions derived from them change over time? Prior to their public deletion, we were able to save 58 video statements from Cuspert that were uploaded to YouTube or other social media platforms (between April 2010 and April 2014) and 25 video statements from Keskin (between February 2012 and September 2013). We coded the videos into thematic categories, including references made to external events, and selected videos from each case for in-depth analysis. The selected videos represent different points in time during their shared (group) interactions with the social environment, while simultaneously reflecting different points in time along their differing (individual) pathways through radicalization.

Hasan Keskin: Continuity of Activism

Hasan Keskin was born in 1984 and grew up as a second-generation Turkish immigrant in North Rhine-Westphalia. After graduating from high school, he spent a year focusing on Islamic studies at university, among other subjects. After leaving university, he worked a variety of temporary jobs and later became self-employed as a restauranteur (Frigelj 2013). The media reports that Keskin had been engaged in the Turkish-Islamist Hilafet Devleti movement, which aimed at building a caliphate in Germany but was banned in 2001 (Flade and Frigelj 2012). In 2011, he became a founding member of Millatu Ibrahim.

The first analyzed video speech delivered by Keskin *before confrontations peaked*—titled "Allah Will Complete His Light"[8]—was recorded several days before the police carried out its first raid on the Millatu Ibrahim mosque at the end of February 2012. However, the group had already been confronted by massive attacks in the media during this phase. In the lecture, Keskin calls upon group members (and potential supporters viewing the video online) to trust in God's promise of the victory of Islam—a victory not independent from the actions of Islam's enemies but also independent of their own contributions: "Allah will complete His Light, even though the unbelievers may detest it. This religion, this Islam, will triumph, whether with us or without us. Allah 'Subhan-Allah' has promised victory" (Keskin 2012a). Consequently, the believer should only worry about whether Allah will accept their actions in the end and let them participate in his "light of victory." In this regard, according to Keskin, being the target of attacks from the enemy should not be seen as a negative sign but, rather, as a first necessary condition for being on the right track: "If they do not speak against us today, it means that this da'wa is rubbish. Simple as that. . . . Any other Muslims left alone should be afraid, Achi [i.e., brother]. No way that you are doing da'wa and are left

---

8. All video transcripts were translated from German into English by the authors of this chapter.

alone" (Keskin 2012a). The second condition is to remain steadfast and fearless, for which Keskin lays down two guidelines: (1) to have positive instead of negative feelings in situations of being harmed or attacked by enemies—"We must be cheerful when we are facing a hard trial" (Keskin 2012a)—and (2) to continue propagating the "truth" without worrying about the consequences.

According to Keskin, such trials should not be considered an obstacle that one needs to overcome but, instead, a chance to prove one's steadfastness. We interpret this as a proactive model for opposing repression, which at the same time offers a means for coping with the aforementioned problem of the uncertainty of probation. Compared to the views of Cuspert (presented in the next section), Keskin's model seems to promote a higher degree of tolerance toward the perceived pressures entailed by religious probation vis-à-vis Allah—including the pressure to adapt one's own patterns of action—via cultivating an ability to draw confirmation from the negative reactions evoked by authorities and the public. According to this interpretation, da'wa, including the resulting negative sanctioning by the surrounding "infidel" society, is a sufficient way of proving one's steadfastness. Thus, there is no need for the activist to produce stronger, more reassuring signs of their personal probation or change their way of practicing da'wa, as long as it is effective at provoking negative reactions from nonbelievers. Keskin seems to be projecting a role model of activism in which repression is interpreted as a motivating factor to continue or increase the believer's probation efforts rather than to escalate confrontation with adversaries even more.

With the police raids taking place a few days after this speech, pressure on the group increased. In another video lecture, titled "Wallah Until Death—Biidhnillah" and produced shortly after the police raid, *during the peak of these confrontations*, Keskin welcomes his brothers and sisters with a bright face, saying:

> Yes, I am cheerful, dear siblings. I also see some other brothers smiling. Alhamdulillah [i.e., praise be to God]. I am cheerful, dear siblings, because Alhamdulillah I may belong to those who are being tested by Allah "Subhan-Allah." And if Allah "Subhan-Allah" loves someone, dear siblings, He is testing them hard. Alhamdulillah, He is testing them hard, Alhamdulillah. And therefore, the harder we are tested, the more testing we get, the happier we are, inshallah. May Allah give us only steadfastness and give us sincerity. Alhamdulillah. (Keskin 2012c)

By saying this, Keskin portrays himself as being confident about gaining Allah's goodwill by undergoing severe tests in light of the unbearable uncertainty of Allah's acceptance of all his efforts. He does not interpret such hard trials as burdens but, rather, as opportunities "that Allah puts at our feet" (Keskin 2012b), which simply need to be accepted and taken with a positive spirit. As the aim is to maximize these trials and ways of dealing with them during one's lifetime, so as to collect as much credit toward being allowed into paradise as possible, repression is presented as a double-edged sword. In a lecture held after the violent clashes in Solingen and Bonn in May 2012, he points out: "So it may be that death finds you or that you are sent to jail. Then you do not have the possibility to complete the planned plans" (Keskin 2012b). Although prison apparently means a hard trial with much suffering, it also means losing control over further opportunities. Even worse, sudden death reduces the opportunities for further trials to zero. From this point of view, repression not only provides chances for proving the purity of one's intentions but also generates time pressure, as in the worst case it might become one's last chance to achieve salvation. Given this time pressure, Keskin calls upon his brothers and sisters to significantly intensify their efforts:

> Achi, we have to get somewhere here, as long as we don't perform hijra, and you know, hijra is a duty, each of us has to do it, each of us has to get away, but at least until then he has to step up [his efforts in Germany]. (Keskin 2012c)

After the banning of Millatu Ibrahim, which followed *the peak of the group's confrontations*, like many other Millatu Ibrahim members Keskin moved to Egypt (Flade 2012b) but came back to Germany soon after. At the end of August 2013, he was given a nine-month suspended sentence for taking part in violent clashes with the police. A little later, he was jailed in Turkey, apparently during a trip. In a video message to his followers from jail, he expresses feelings of insecurity and weakness due to not knowing the reason for his imprisonment. He asks his followers to pray for him: "Dear siblings, do not forget about me in your Dua. Please do not forget this ignorant, sinful, and weak servant of Allah in your invocations" (Keskin 2013). In this situation of "weakness," he presents a great need to reaffirm his steadfastness, as revealed when he says:

> If they, the Tawaghit [i.e., associated with a false god or idols], think they can intimidate me, then they are very much mistaken. I'll say it

again: Allah, I'll go on. Until the head explodes. And there's no turning back in this regard. Allah, there's either victory or Shahada [i.e., martyrdom]. We don't know anything else. And we won't complete life with anything else, inshallah. (Keskin 2013)

Being incarcerated, repression involves a clear restriction of opportunities for action and a challenge to one's steadfastness, which seems to have put Keskin under pressure to publicly affirm his willingness for self-sacrifice. However, according to our interpretation of this sequence, Keskin seeks to maintain his steadfastness by "going on" with *da'wa* activism. There still seems to be no need to strive for a higher level of trials of one's steadfastness by escalating his activism toward violent jihad. He is calling for a willingness to self-sacrifice, but death—the *shahada*—does not appear to be a tangible possibility but, rather, the last station of the believer's probation efforts, after all other plans have been successfully carried out.

After being released from jail, Keskin returned to Germany and founded Tauhid Germany, as the successor organization of Millatu Ibrahim. In March 2015, Tauhid Germany was also banned by the Federal Minister of the Interior, and Keskin was sentenced to two years and seven months for breaching the public peace, bodily injury, and threats. After his appeal against the sentence was dismissed, he emigrated with his wife to Turkey in the summer of 2015.

Denis Cuspert: Escalation of Activism

In contrast to Hasan Keskin, although Denis Cuspert also left Germany for Egypt in June 2012, he ended up finally joining the Islamic State in Syria. Cuspert was a born Muslim and former rapper from Berlin (aka "Deso Dogg") who went through a criminal career before coming into contact with Salafi Islam. He was born in 1975, the son of a German mother and a Ghanaian father, who left the family early. His relationship with his stepfather, a soldier from the United States, was problematic. According to Cuspert, his parents did not care much about him, and he started to adopt known gangster rappers as role models, acting as a kind of replacement for his family (Möglich 2011). Later, he went into the gangster rap business himself (SenInnSport 2014, 8), where he had strong street credibility due to numerous imprisonments for property and violent crime, as well as illegal possession of arms and narcotics. Although he had been a member of a violent gang in his youth, by 2007 he presented himself as a devout Muslim and began to distance himself from the music business (SenInnSport 2014, 9). A video interview conducted in 2010 by Pierre Vogel, a popular German Salafi preacher, became his first public connection to the Salafi scene, though he was still going by the name of Deso Dogg. Later in 2010, however, he finally quit his music career entirely (SenInnSport 2014, 10). After the founding of Millatu Ibrahim in 2011, he became its public relations representative and a leading figure of the group.

In 2010, before the foundation of Millatu Ibrahim, Cuspert presented himself as a reborn Muslim who had quit his previous insincere lifestyle and gotten (back) on the right track with Islam, finding happiness and self-fulfillment. In video footage taken on his journey to Mecca (*hajj*) in 2010, Cuspert shared his enthusiasm for Islam with others:

> Everyone gets what he is entitled to. And what Allah "Subhan-Allah" has written for you. And Allah "Subhan-Allah" wrote the hajj journey for me, alhamdulillah, and up until here I have had many obstacles and many hard trials. . . . I can only advise you, if you seek blessedness, if you seek peace, if you want to be happy, then follow this path, inshallah. (Cuspert 2010)

Here, Cuspert presents himself as proud to have left his former life behind and successfully overcome all obstacles on the way (back) to Allah. He sees himself as being able to meet the requirements for being a good Muslim and appears to be looking forward to completing his purification from the formerly insincere lifestyle he had led in the past.

Cuspert soon became an accepted member of the Salafi community in Germany and began giving lectures across the country. Due to his former career inside the rap-music subculture and the publicity he received, he was invited by several Salafi preachers to talk about his way out of the "darkness of unbelieving." His progressing adoption of the Salafi world-view proceeded with growing expectations that he should stand firm on the path to God and fulfill his duties as a "true believer." However, this adoption was still in a preliminary stage, as he was still considering alternative interpretations of the world that deviate from the Salafi worldview. At this point of his development, the main focus in his lectures was on staying firmly on a "straight path," deviations from which were seen as unacceptable. For example, in June 2011, Cuspert assessed his perceived decrease in efforts by those engaging in *da'wa* in response to emerging negative media coverage as a "downfall":

I have observed how the brothers and sisters are reacting to the media, how they are concentrating on the media, they are no longer with da'wa, and da'wa is about to go down. (Cuspert 2011)

While he had previously motivated members to oppose repressive media coverage by continuing with *da'wa* and opposing joint activities, such as barbecues or meetings in natural setting and on the streets (Cuspert 2011), his perception of the situation appears to have been constantly transforming. Here, he presents himself as becoming increasingly concerned over the *da'wa* in-group's deviating from the "straight path."

In light of increasing repression against Millatu Ibrahim by security authorities in 2012, Cuspert presented himself in another lecture as being totally unaffected by the government attacks while, at the same time, being ready to fight against the enemy, in order to "keep the word of Allah." In contrast with Keskin, at this point Cuspert implied a need to step up personal efforts in order to prove his steadfastness, which consequently would require a modification of his activism. In an argumentative manner, he now referred to his past criminal life, from which he had already distanced himself, as a source of motivation and inspiration for taking action against police repression:

And I don't care if I'm raided. I don't care. Because they also raided me in my time of dschāhilīya [i.e., time of ignorance] but because I did haram [i.e., unlawful or sinful things]. And I defended myself. I fought against policemen, I fought against the criminal police, I fought against masked, armored servants of Sheytan [i.e., Satan] and that was in my dschāhilīya. Do you think I'll let myself get put down now? I will keep the word of Allah as high as I can. (Cuspert 2012a)

After this point, he began presenting himself as seeking to reach a state of complete obedience to God by being fully detached from secular things, needs, and intentions, as can be seen in a lecture from April 2012: *"Am I willing to sacrifice for a life in the afterlife? Am I ready for it? Are you ready for it? I am ready for it: I am willing to give my sweat, my tears and my blood"* (Cuspert 2012b). By this phase of his development, Cuspert had fully adopted Salafi-jihadist religiosity and defined himself as a jihadist. After Millatu Ibrahim was banned in June 2012 and large-scale raids against the Salafi movement took place, he soon left Germany to join and fight for jihadist groups in Syria and Iraq, where he reportedly died in 2018. Before leaving, he produced video footage accusing German society of "slowly slaughtering Muslims" (Cuspert 2012b) and calling upon his brothers and sisters *"who are on the haqq* [i.e., truth] *to support jihad, to emigrate or to carry out jihad here* [in Germany]" (Cuspert 2012b). In a situation where Muslims are being increasingly repressed, he considered jihad to be a necessary consequence of action for all those on the "true path of Allah." In fact, jihad is not only framed here as a duty of faith but as a strong sign of being close to Allah. By this point, practicing *da'wa* was no longer an appropriate sign of probation for him. According to the role model exhibited by Cuspert, when confronted with escalating repression the activist should produce stronger signs of his steadfast faith than mere *da'wa*.

Discussion

The Millatu Ibrahim activists Keskin and Cuspert, whose public speeches we have just examined, were strongly confronted by hostile reactions from sectors of the public and increasing repression by security authorities due to their activism. By interpreting repression as a trial of their faith, they presented themselves as "perfect believers" who—in accord with the idea of probation—constantly sought to test and improve their own "true" faith amid the uncertainty of whether they had passed the tests well enough for God to accept their efforts. Yet they both proposed different ways of making sense of these trials, representing two contrasting models for coping with the requirements of keeping their faith under increasingly worsening circumstances. The model represented by Keskin implies little need to dramatically alter one's overall pattern of action, as long as it continues to produce appropriate (here, negative) reactions from out-groups, thereby confirming the believer's self-perception of being on the right track. This model is characterized by a high degree of self-confidence that, by adopting it, the believer is staying firmly on the "path of Allah" and standing steadfastly against external pressure. Given this confidence that religious probation is being achieved, there is no need to seek a higher level of trials to reassure oneself of meeting the religious requirements. Thus, there is no need for the activist to change their model of activism by adopting violent means of action, for example. In contrast to Keskin, Cuspert interprets repression as a higher-level test of steadfastness that challenges the believer to fight. According to Cuspert, the believer needs to increase their personal investment when facing repression, which goes along with a general emphasis on fear that the in-group might fail along the pathway to God. The stronger this threat of failing appears, the higher the degree of personal investment must become. This leads, in the case of Cuspert's worldview, to an increasing degradation of life and an evolving wish to become reunited with God in death.

Given these two models for pursuing religious activism, it can be assumed that the repressive events described had different effects on the members of Millatu Ibrahim. Those who adopted the model represented by Keskin might have become motivated to continue or increase their activism but would have seen no need to go beyond legal activism, as long as opportunities for *da'wa* activism were not closed. For those who adhered to the escalation model represented by Cuspert, the repressive events generated a need to increase personal investment on the path of God, along with a need to reassure themselves of being steadfast through even more conspicuous signs of their obedience to God's requirements, even to the point of crossing over into illegal and violent activities. In this case, repressive events appear to have had a catalyzing effect on radicalization processes, pushing them toward a more extreme level.

Our two role models seem to be compatible with the findings of Martijn de Koning (2019), who investigated reactions of militant Sunni activists to repression in the Netherlands. He found two contradictory types of reaction: on the one hand, a desire to resist by not allowing repression or surveillance to affect one's daily life, which he calls "routinization," and on the other hand a desire "to speak out," which means mobilizing against repression ("mobilization"). De Koning (2019, 207ff.) also proposes that escalation can be seen as a paradox effect of militant activism: Whereas being under surveillance positively influenced the self-understanding of a "true" Muslim as a committed, steadfast activist, it also resulted in an intensification of counter-radicalization policies in the Netherlands. However, as illustrated in the case studies on the Millatu Ibrahim group presented here, the effects of maintaining steadfastness under escalating repression appear to be quite rational from the point of view of Salafi religious activists, as they are interpreted as a positive sign of being on the right track toward religious probation.

Conclusion

Some of the characteristics of the Salafi-jihadist scene in Germany between 2008 and 2010 were generated by internal differentiation processes within the Salafi movement, which evolved in the context of interactions between the Salafi movement and other sectors of German society. One outcome of this differentiation process was Millatu Ibrahim, which emerged at the end of 2011 and engaged in increasingly conflictual interactions with its adversaries, culminating in the criminalization of the group only half a year after its official founding. In the wake of its banning and threats of deportation of one of its leaders, at least 15 group members left Germany to join jihadist groups in Syria and Iraq. Due to the escalating interactions with out-groups that were taking place before joining the jihad, the radicalization of about a third of the group's members seems to fit well into the explanatory framework of Social Movement Theory, in particular della Porta's theory of clandestine violent groups emerging out of broader social movements. According to della Porta (2013), escalation of policing is a core mechanism in the emergence phase of (clandestine) violent groups. At the organizational level, repression can result in the closing of other political options, which can lead to violence as a strategic decision. It can also lead to a reciprocal adaptation and radicalization of actions on both sides, leading self-dynamically to violence (della Porta 2013, 68). At the individual level, transformative repressive events can contribute to justifying violence and pushing militant groups toward clandestinity (33).

In order to investigate how contentious interactions with adversaries affected processes of radicalization of Millatu Ibrahim group members, we have analyzed two contrastive cases of activists who represent different ways of making sense of the repressive events and who themselves went along different pathways of development. The ex-rapper Denis Cuspert ended up joining violent jihad, whereas another leading figure of the group, Hasan Keskin, continued to practice *da'wa* in Germany. The results of our analysis suggest that the two activists represent different role models for dealing with the Salafi requirement of steadfastness when confronted by repression. Keskin represents a model that, by continuing to do what they had already been doing, allows Salafi activists to understand themselves as being steadfast against external pressure, which can be interpreted as a positive sign of becoming accepted by God. In contrast, Cuspert represents a model of escalation of activism, expressing a need to increase one's personal investment in the face of repression. With this model, activists need to be reassured of their steadfastness through increasingly conspicuous signs of their willingness to engage in self-sacrifice as a significant expression of their obedience to God. In the case of Cuspert, repressive events might have accelerated the dynamic toward joining violent jihad. On the other hand, in the case Keskin, repression might have had no radicalizing but only a motivating or stabilizing effect on individual activism, since repression did not close off but only restricted opportunities to engage in *da'wa*.

To conclude, in the Salafi-jihadist model of religious activism, the individual activist is requested to follow the path of God without being concerned about social or political consequences. However, repressive events are interpreted by such activists as a trial of one's faith and, thus, puts pressure on them to demonstrate or reaffirm their religious convictions. As illustrated in our two case studies, Salafi activists can follow different models for dealing with these requirements. As we have attempted to show here, repressive pressure can accelerate or slow down the dynamics of radicalization but does not seem to have an independent, direct effect. To sum up, "escalating policing" (della Porta 2013) can be seen as a social mechanism of increasing radicalization, as here in the case of Salafi-jihadism, but its effectiveness greatly depends on the model of religious activism followed by individual believers.

The findings presented here are based on one case study of Salafi-jihadism. Given this limitation, further research should study reactions of Salafi-jihadist activists to repressive events on a broader database, taking into account a larger contrastive sample of activists with different roles within Salafi-jihadist movements.

REFERENCES

Bohnsack, Ralf. 2010. "Documentary Method and Group Discussions." In *Qualitative Analysis and Documentary Method in International Educational Research*, edited by Ralf Bohnsack, Nicolle Pfaff, and Wivian Weller, 99–124. Opladen: B. Budrich.

Borum, Randy. 2011. "Radicalization into Violent Extremism I: A Review of Social Science Theories." *Journal of Strategic Security* 4 (4): 7–36.

Boutin, Bérénice, Grégory Chauzal, Jessica Dorsey, Marjolein Jegerings, Christophe Paulussen, Johanna Pohl, Alastair Reed, and Sofia Zavagli. 2016. "The Foreign Fighters Phenomenon in the European Union: Profiles, Threats & Policies." *The International Centre for Counter-Terrorism – The Hague* 7 (2). https://doi.org/10.19165/2016.1.02

Bundesamt für Verfassungsschutz (BfV). 2021. "Anschläge in Deutschland (seit 2015)." https://www.verfassungsschutz.de/DE/themen/islamismus-und-islami stischer-terrorismus/zahlen-und-fakten/zahlen-und-fakten_node.html

Bundesamt für Verfassungsschutz (BfV). 2019a. "Islamistisch motivierte Reisebewegungen in Richtung Syrien/Irak." Bundesamt für Verfassungsschutz. https://www.verfassungsschutz.de/de/arbeitsfelder/af-islamismus-und-islamistischer -terrorismus/zahlen-und-fakten-islamismus/zuf-is-reisebewegungen-in-richtu ng-syrien-irak

Bundesamt für Verfassungsschutz (BfV). 2019b. "Übersicht ausgewählter islamistisch-terroristischer Anschläge." https://www.verfassungsschutz.de/de /arbeitsfelder/af-islamismus-und-islamistischer-terrorismus/zahlen-und-fakt en-islamismus/zuf-is-uebersicht-ausgewaehlter-islamistisch-terroristischer-ans chlaege

Bundeskriminalamt (BKA), Bundesamt für Verfassungsschutz (BfV), and Hessisches Informations-und Kompetenzzentrum gegen Extremismus (HKE). 2016. "Analyse der den Deutschen Sicherheitsbehörden Vorliegenden Informationen über die Radikalisierungshintergründe Und-verläufe der Personen, die aus Islamistischer Motivation aus Deutschland in Richtung Syrien Ausgereist sind."

Bundesministerium des Innern, für Bau und Heimat (BMI). 2020. "Verfassungsschutzbericht 2019."

Bundesministerium des Innern, für Bau und Heimat (BMI). 2017. "Verfassungsschutzbericht 2016."

Bundesministerium des Innern, für Bau und Heimat (BMI). 2013. "Verfassungsschutzbericht 2012."

Cuspert, Denis. 2012a. "Ich Werde Allahs Wort so Hoch Halten Wie ich Nur Kann." YouTube video. Retrieved March 2017.

Cuspert, Denis. 2012b. "Mein Weg (01.02.2012)." YouTube video. Retrieved March 2017.

Cuspert, Denis. 2011. "Einige Worte zur Kommenden Da'wa (27.06.2011)." YouTube video. Retrieved March 2017.

Cuspert, Denis. 2010. "Ermahnung an Die Jugend in Deutschland (09.11.2010)." YouTube video. Retrieved March 2017.

Dantschke, Claudia. 2011. "'Lasst Euch Nicht Radikalisieren!'–Salafismus in Deutschland." In *Salafismus in Deutschland. Ursprünge und Gefahren einer Islamisch-Fundamentalistischen Bewegung*, edited by Thorsten Gerhard Schneider, 171–86. Bielefeld: Transcript.

de Koning, Martijn. 2019. "Routinization and Mobilization of Injustice: How to Live in a Regime of Surveillance." In *Radicalization in Belgium and the Netherlands: Critical Perspectives on Violence and Security*, edited by Nadia Fadil, Francesco Ragazzi, and Martjin de Koning, 197–216. London: I.B. Tauris.

de Maizère, Thomas. 2016. "Pressemitteilung zum Vereinsverbot der Vereinigung 'Die Wahre Religion (DWR)' alias 'Stiftung LIES.'" *Bundesministerium des Innern und fur Heimat*. November 15.

della Porta, Donatella. 2013. *Clandestine Political Violence*. Cambridge: Cambridge University Press.

Deutscher Bundestag. 2018. "Islamistischer Terrorismus in Deutschland." *Answer of the Federal Government to the Small Request of the Deputies Stephan Thomae, Renata Alt, Jens Beeck, Further Deputies, and the Faction of the FDP.*

Flade, Florian. 2012a. "Salafisten planen 'Abrechnung' mit Deutschland." *Welt.*

Flade, Florian. 2012b. "'Wandert Aus, Wandert Aus . . .'—Deutsche Salafisten-Kolonie in Ägypten." Terrorismus Und Sicherheitspolitik.

Flade, Florian, and Kristian Frigelj. 2012. "Wie der Staat Salafisten aus Solingen Verjagt: Salafisten-Razzia." *Welt.*

Frigelj, Kristian. 2013. "Hassprediger 'Abu Ibrahim' in Solingen Verurteilt." *Welt.*

Glaser, Barney, and Anselm Strauss. 1967. "Grounded Theory: The Discovery of Grounded Theory." *Sociology the Journal of the British Sociological Association* 12 (1): 27–49.

Hafez, Mohammed, and Creighton Mullins. 2015. "The Radicalization Puzzle: A Theoretical Synthesis of Empirical Approaches to Homegrown Extremism." *Studies in Conflict & Terrorism* 38 (11): 958–75.

Hogg, Michael A., Arie Kruglanski, and Kees van den Bos. 2013. "Uncertainty and the Roots of Extremism." *Journal of Social Issues* 69 (3): 407–18.

Holtmann, Philipp. 2014. "Salafismus: De–Internetaktivitäten Deutscher Salafisten." In *Salafismus in Deutschland: Ursprünge und Gefahren Einer Islamisch-Fundamentalistischen Bewegung*, edited by Thorsten Gerhard Schneiders, 251–76. Bielefeld: Transcript.

Horgan, John. 2008. "From Profiles to Pathways and Roots to Routes: Perspectives from Psychology on Radicalization into Terrorism." *ANNALS of the American Academy of Political and Social Science* 618 (1): 80–94.

Hummel, Klaus. 2014. "Salafismus in Deutschland-Eine Gefahrenperspektive neu Bewertet." *Totalitarismus und Demokratie* 11 (1): 95–122.

Keskin, Hasan. 2013. "No title (April 2013)." YouTube video. Retrieved March 2017.

Keskin, Hasan. 2012a. "Allah Wird Sein Licht Vollenden (02.02.2012)." YouTube video. Retrieved March 2017.

Keskin, Hasan. 2012b. "Mit Jedem Moment dem Tode Näher (21.06.2012)." YouTube video. Retrieved March 2017.

Keskin, Hasan. 2012c. "Wallah Bis Zum Tod—Biidhnillah (03.2012)." YouTube video. Retrieved March 2017.

Lützinger, Saskia. 2010. *Die Sicht der Anderen: Eine Qualitative Studie zu Biographien von Extremisten und Terrroristen.* Munich: Luchterhand.

Malthaner, Stefan. 2014. "Contextualizing Radicalization: The Emergence of the 'Sauerland-Group' from Radical Networks and the Salafist Movement." *Studies in Conflict & Terrorism* 37 (8): 638–53.

Malthaner, Stefan, and Klaus Hummel. 2012. "Islamistischer Terrorismus und Salafistische Milieus: Die 'Sauerland-Gruppe' und ihr Soziales Umfeld." In *Radikale Milieus: Das Soziale Umfeld Terroristischer Gruppen*, edited by Stefan Malthaner and Peter Waldmann, 245–78. Frankfurt: Campus Verlag.

McAdam, Doug, Sidney Tarrow, and Charles Tilly. 2001. *Dynamics of Contention.* Cambridge: Cambridge University Press.

McCauley, Clark, and Sophia Moskalenko. 2017. "Understanding Political Radicalization: The Two-Pyramids Model." *American Psychologist* 72 (3): 205.

Möglich, Manuel. 2011. "Wild Germany Islamistischer Rap. ZDF Neo." YouTube video. Retrieved March 2017.

Religionswissenschaftlicher Medien-und Informationsdienst e.V. (REMID). 2017a. "Die Religionspolitische Dimension von Statistik." https://remid.de/wp-content/uploads/2017/02/Rundbrief-1_2017_14-24.pdf

Religionswissenschaftlicher Medien-und Informationsdienst e.V. (REMID). 2017b. "Mitgliederzahlen: Islam." http://remid.de/info_zahlen/islam

Reynolds, Sean C., and Mohammed M. Hafez. 2017. "Social Network Analysis of German Foreign Fighters in Syria and Iraq." *Terrorism and Political Violence*: 1–26.

Roy, Olivier. 2017. *Jihad and Death: The Global Appeal of Islamic State.* New York: Oxford University Press.

Sageman, Marc. 2008. "A Strategy for Fighting International Islamist Terrorists." *Annals of the American Academy of Political and Social Science* 618 (1): 223–31.

Senatsverwaltung für Inneres und Sport (SenInnSport) Abteilung Verfassungsschutz. 2014. "Denis Cuspert—Eine Jihadistische Karriere." Lageanalyse. (Berlin).

Statistisches Bundesamt. 2017. "Pressemitteilungen—Bevölkerung Mit Migrationshintergrund Um 8,5% Gestiegen." https://www.destatis.de/DE/PresseService/Presse/Pressemitteilungen/2017/08/PD17_261_12511.html

Stichs, Anja. 2016. "Wie Viele Muslime Leben in Deutschland?: Eine Hochrechnung über die Anzahl der Muslime in Deutschland zum Stand 31." Bundesamt für Migration und Flüchtlinge.

Vidino, Lorenzo, Francesco Marone, and Eva Entenmann. 2017. *Fear Thy Neighbor: Radicalization and Jihadist Attacks in the West*. Milan: Ledizioni.

Wiedl, Nina. 2014. *Außenbezüge und ihre Kontextualisierung und Funktion in den Vorträgen ausgewählter salafistischer Prediger in Deutschland: Studie im Rahmen des BMBF-Verbundprojektes Terrorismus und Radikalisierung-Indikatoren für externe Einflussfaktoren (TERAS-INDEX)*. Institut für Friedensforschung und Sicherheitspolitik an der Universität Hamburg.

Wiedl, Nina. 2012. *The Making of a German Salafiyya: The Emergence, Development and Missionary Work of Salafi Movements in Germany*. Aarhus: Centre for Studies in Islamism and Radicalisation (CIR).

Wiktorowicz, Quintan. 2005. "A Genealogy of Radical Islam." *Studies in Conflict & Terrorism* 28 (2): 75–97.

Wiktorowicz, Quintan. 2002. "The Political Limits to Nongovernmental Organizations in Jordan." *World Development* 30 (1): 77–93.

NINE

Spain

Profiles and Patterns of Jihadist Radicalization

Rut Bermejo-Casado

On August 17, 2017, Spain entered the list of Western European countries that have suffered jihadist attacks linked to the Islamic State of Iraq and Syria (ISIS) on their soil. That day, in Barcelona and Cambrils, a cell made up of a dozen terrorists deployed their improvised plans after a sudden change in their plots. The night before in Ripoll, a blast of their explosive devices caused them to alter their scheme. That unanticipated explosion led them to take two vans and emulate previous terror attacks in other European cities, such as Nice or Berlin. Younes Abouyaaqoub drove the first van into a crowded pedestrian area in the city center of Barcelona. Abouyaaqoub's brother and four of his friends perpetrated a car-ramming attack in Cambrils. Those attacks killed 16 persons and injured more than a hundred.

The attacks in Barcelona and Cambrils have been the deadliest terrorist actions in Spain since March 11, 2004. That day Spain suffered the worst terrorist attack, and on that occasion, the assault was not linked to the long-lasting Spanish nationalist terrorism of Euskadi Ta Askatasuna (ETA)[1] but to Al-Qaeda. Terrorists carried and placed their backpacks

---

I would like to thank all the interviewees contacted for this work. I am particularly grateful to CITCO members who have shared their knowledge with me and to my friend and colleague Isabel Bazaga for her academic generosity.

1. "The nationalist and separatist terrorist organization that has been part of Spanish history of terror from 1959 to 2017, the year of its dismantling. The origin of ETA's activities

filled with explosive ordnance on four short-distance trains in Madrid; they killed a total of 191 people and injured more than 1,800. Some of the perpetrators blew themselves up in April that year, and during the trial a total of 21 terrorists were found guilty of perpetration, involvement, trafficking in weapons, or belonging to a terrorist organization.[2]

In two decades, Spanish Courts have indicted nearly half a thousand people for their involvement in jihad-related activities.[3] This chapter analyzes the information about the people mobilized toward global jihad in Spain and the handful of empirical studies that have collected primary evidence on jihadist radicalization in Spain since 2004. After a detailed introduction to the Spanish scene, the first part offers a review of the findings of those studies and a summary of the evidence provided concerning who, how, and why people radicalize in relation to main theoretical approaches identified in this volume. The second section deals with processes of radicalization in order to analyze possible patterns of the "psychological transformations that occur among western Muslims [who have] accepted the legitimacy of terrorism in support of violent jihad against Western countries" (King and Taylor 2011, 603). Nonetheless, the jihad of those radicalized in Western countries does not limit itself to these, with some of these individuals having gone abroad to further the advent of the ISIS caliphate elsewhere. The last section of this chapter discusses the state-of-the-art theories about radicalization processes and profiles in Spain in order to answer the question of whether there is a pattern of radicalization among Spanish jihadists. The answer is based on interviews and meetings with members of security forces and intelligence services as well as prison officers. Secondary open information from newspapers and reports, as well as press releases issued by the Spain's Interior Ministry, are also reviewed.

---

goes back to Franco's dictatorship and the organization perpetrated the last terrorist attacks barely a decade ago. This terrorist organization may be characterized as a typical 'old terrorist' organization due to its nationalist and pro-independence ideology, and its structure and methods of action. Some authors also speak of ethno-nationalism to describe ETA's ideology" (Bermejo and Bazaga 2021, 223). Euskadi Ta Askatasuna (ETA) is sometimes translated as "Basque Homeland and Freedom" (e.g., Alonso 2004; Funes 1998) and others as "Basque Country and Liberty" (e.g., Whitfield 2014).

2. https://www.theguardian.com/world/2007/oct/31/spain.marktran

3. Carola García-Calvo and Fernando Reinares assure that since 2004, 200 individuals have been sentenced by the Audiencia Nacional Courts and 15 lost their lives in terrorist activities (2019, 30). In relation to ISIS mobilization in recent years, 25 persons were sentenced to prison due to their terrorist activities in 2016 and 27 were sentenced in 2017. Those numbers reached a peak of 73 in 2018, which was the highest number since 2007 (when 33 were sentenced due to terrorist offenses) (Fiscalía General del Estado 2019).

Jihadist Violence and Its Threat in Spain

The level of terrorist threat (*Nivel de Alerta Antiterrorista*) in Spain has been rated four (out of five) since June 2015. Nowadays, Islamist-inspired terrorism is considered the principal terrorist threat to Spain as a nation. This type of terrorism has surpassed ETA's nationalist terrorism that has been present in the lives of Spaniards for more than half a century until they ended their "armed separatist campaign" and declared a definitive ceasefire in October 2011. By then, jihadism seems to have taken over terrorist activities in Spanish soil.

Since the Madrid attacks in March 2004, Spanish security forces have detained 931 individuals linked to jihadist terrorism in Spain and abroad in a total of 320 anti-terrorist operations, and 372 of them have been detained since the advent of the caliphate in 2014.[4] In recent years, since 2012, the site with the most detainees (80) and operations (44) is Barcelona, followed by Madrid with 67 detainees. Ceuta and Melilla stand out among the rest of the provinces for the number of arrests, 33 and 32 respectively.[5] Charges against all those suspects have included glorification of terrorism and promulgation of Islamic State (IS) propaganda, recruiting foreign terrorist fighters and facilitating travel to conflict zones, and obtaining or delivering training to commit terror attacks. In the same vein, the Strategic Studies Group (GEES, for its Spanish initials) states that: "If one uses as a reference element both the number of anti-terrorist operations carried out and the number of detainees in these operations, regardless of the judicial results that ultimately derive from such preventive operations, Spain occupies the top place among the other European countries" (Strategic Studies Group 2018, 53).

In spite of those numbers, outstanding experts on terrorism consider that the current situation, in terms of jihadist mobilization for the IS, is not as bad as in other countries of Western Europe; France, Belgium, and even Finland are comparatively worse off. This assessment is based on three factors. Firstly, the number of individuals who have departed from Spain to join the IS in Syria and Iraq is low, estimated at 240, most of them being men.[6] Secondly, Spanish experience in the fight against ETA, in terms of

---

4. This data has been provided by the Minister of Interior and was updated on August 29, 2019.

5. The data was updated on October 7, 2019: http://www.interior.gob.es/documents/101 80/10353119/Infografia+2012+-+Operaciones+y+detenidos+yihadismo+en+España+desde+2 012+%2807-10-2019%29.pdf/f96ec361-6385-4e14-b53a-190805bce2ce

6. Data provided by the Spanish Police for a parliamentary question in July 2019: https://

intelligence and operative knowledge, is perceived as an advantage (Reinares 2016, 161). In that sense, a recent report of the U.S. Bureau of Counterterrorism assured that: "Spain has a mature legal framework for counterterrorism as a result of its long fight against the domestic terrorist group ETA. Spain revised its penal code in 2015, empowering law enforcement agencies to prosecute individuals who glorify terrorism on social media, train remotely, operate without clear affiliation, or travel in support of non-state actors. Spanish Criminal Code specifically punishes any act of collaboration with the activities or purposes of a terrorist organization."[7] Thirdly, many police force actions and detentions are only indirectly related to jihadist terrorist attacks. Thus, they pose a "soft" threat to the country. Such actions intend to detect false documents and stolen vehicles at borders, fight against the financing of terrorism, tighten controls, and detect weapons and explosives. In the same vein, the idea that despite the fact that most of the arrests and accusations of terrorism were related to jihadist terrorism, an analysis of the frustrated, failed, and completed attacks in 2018 shows that, of the eleven plots, one was related to jihadist terrorism, three to left-wing terrorism, and seven to ethno-nationalist and separatist terrorism (Europol 2019, 68).

As for the state's response, the Madrid Train Bombings in 2004 influenced the setup of the Spanish police forces' National Antiterrorist Coordination Centre (known as CITCO since the last reshuffle). This organization succeeded in the coordination of national and autonomous police forces, in different areas of work (penitentiary system and police) as well as at the international level with other countries. They are in charge of implementing the first Spanish Plan for the Prevention and Fight against Violent Radicalization that was passed in 2015, and CITCO is also very active in the European networks as well as in the municipalities of Spain. The southern city of Malaga has served as a pilot site for implementing initiatives to combat violent radicalization.

The Plan meant that Spain embraced the EU strategy of combating terrorism through addressing radicalization and violent extremism and followed other countries "in the emergence of many policies and practices directed toward countering and preventing violent extremism" (Stephens,

---

www.elconfidencial.com/espana/2019-07-09/uno-cada-cuatro-yihadistas-salieron-espana-oriente-proximo-muerto_2114739

7. Country reports on terrorism 2016, July 2017, United States Department of State Publication, Bureau of Counterterrorism: http://www.ieee.es/Galerias/fichero/OtrasPublicaciones/Internacional/2017/DOS_-_Country_Reports_on_Terrorism_2016.pdf. Some countries are still adjusting their legislations (e.g., Austria, Finland, Slovakia, and Sweden) (Europol 2019).

Sieckelinck, and Boutellier 2019). This Spanish Plan does not point to any group, idea, religion, or community because of its tendency toward violent radicalization, but the vast majority of those detained and charged with terrorist offenses in recent years are linked to jihadism. Therefore, nowadays the aim of preventing and fighting against violent radicalization is pretty much focused on radical/jihadist interpretations of Islam. The need for special emphasis on jihadist ideologies was confirmed by the involvement of Abdelbaki Es Satty, the Islamic preacher, in the Barcelona terrorist attacks.

At this point, it should be noted that "Islam" is not at the focus of police or the Spanish policy for the prevention of violent radicalization in general. Spanish authorities and security forces are being especially careful not to criminalize Muslim communities in Spain, which is one the dangers involved when carrying out anti-jihadist policies, as described by Arun Kundnani (2014; 2012). As many authors have stated, religion, or radical views or beliefs, are not a proxy for terrorism (Borum 2011). In Rik Coolsaet's words, "Privileging ideology over context means that all the blame can be offloaded onto the 'radical' individuals and his (or her) ideas" (2019, 10), and accordingly, the society's responsibility in the creation of these breeding grounds for radicalism is diluted, leaving all the blame on the radical ideologues.

The latest report on demographics of the Muslim community in Spain, published by the Union of Islamic Communities in Spain (UCIDE, for its Spanish initials) and the Observatorio Andalusí, dates from December 2019.[8] According to that report, the number of Muslims in Spain amounts to 2,091,656 out of a total population of 47,332,614, which means that the Muslim community living in Spain is around 4% of the total population. However, public opinion greatly overestimates this number. Specifically, a recent study shows that people think 14% of the population is Muslim, when the reality amounts to one third of this percentage (4.4%).[9] The Muslim community in Spain is made up of 42% Spaniards (879,808) and more than 67.5% foreigners, the majority of which (67%) are Moroccans (812,412). Other nationalities include Pakistanis, Algerians, Senegalese, and Nigerians. As for Muslims with

8. Demographic Study of Muslim Population (Estudio demográfico de la Población Musulmana): https://ucide.org/wp-content/uploads/2021/01/Estudio-demografico-2019.pdf

9. See: http://www.ipsos.es/sites/default/files/documents/np_perils_perception.pdf. From 2015 to 2016 there was a total increase in Spanish population of 88,867 individuals. Most of them were Spaniards (81,975) and only 6,892 were foreigners, despite the fact that 112,666 foreigners came as immigrants in one year. So, the difference between those who arrived that year and the number of foreigners in the country has to be explained due to the access to citizenship. In 2016, 150,739 foreigners obtained national citizenship.

Spanish citizenship, in 2019 this group included 352,436 naturalized citizens (mainly from Morocco), 555,266 descendants of naturalized citizens, 64,537 Muslims from Ceuta/Melilla, and 26,072 Spaniards from a Catholic background who had converted to Islam through marriage or personal religious conviction.

The map of Islam in Spain shows that most Muslims live in the autonomous communities of Catalonia (564,055), Andalusia (341,069), Madrid (299,311), and the Valencian Community (221,355). Moroccans, as stated above, are the predominant non-Spanish Muslim community due to geographical proximity and historical links with Spain. Many of them come from the northern part of Morocco, particularly from the former Spanish colonial sites, so they speak fluent Spanish. Moroccans did not require a visa to enter Spain until 1985; men work primarily in temporary agricultural jobs and in the construction sector, while women have mostly incorporated themselves into the domestic and service sectors. Moroccans arrived in large numbers in the 1990s, so they are the oldest and most integrated Muslim immigrant community in Spain.

Despite the importance of the community, the number of Muslims in Spanish society is far smaller compared to other countries, such as Belgium (see chapter 6, this volume). Another feature that distinguishes Spain from other countries such as the United Kingdom, Germany, or Belgium (see chapters 10, 8, and 6, respectively, this volume) is the low rate of political participation and social mobilization compared to other host countries in Europe. The limited involvement of immigrants in general and Muslims in particular is, for instance, observed in that only a handful of them are representatives in regional parliaments. This state of affairs may be due to positive factors such as full integration, which makes representation by communities unnecessary; to other neutral factors such as recent arrival; or to negative factors such as lower qualifications and skills.

As has been said before, Islam cannot be equated to radicalization nor to violent jihadist mobilization. The Muslim population in Spain, mainly Moroccan, is not at the center of the jihadist Salafist currents in Spain. However, there is an overlap between those areas in which Muslim communities are concentrated and reside and the main areas at risk of violent radicalization, mainly the provinces of Madrid, Murcia, and Barcelona. In those areas, arrests have been carried out and individuals and cells have been identified who have mobilized in the name of Salafist currents, or who embraced the postulates of ISIS or other ideological currents and used them as an engine and/or justification for their terrorist actions. The following section analyzes the profiles of these individuals.

Studying Profiles in Spanish Jihadism:
Comparison to a "European Jihadist Profile"

The concept of radicalization and processes of violent radicalization are widespread in the United States and Europe, but they are also the subject of heated debate. Among the critics, the main points of criticism focus first of all on the key role attributed to ideology and religious beliefs ("jihadist" ideology), which are considered the starting points or main driving forces behind radicalization processes (Coolsaet 2019; Ravn, Coolsaet, and Sauer 2019; Crone 2016; Kundnani 2012; Borum 2011). Secondly, the idea of a correlation between extremism and terrorism, that is, the possibility of "identifying individuals who are not terrorists now but might be at some later date" (Kundnani 2014) and who, to a greater or lesser extent, can be discerned by their extremist ideas, is also criticized. In this realm, Randy Borum assures that "radicalization, the process of developing extremist ideologies and beliefs, needs to be distinguished from action pathways, the process of engaging in terrorism or violent extremist actions. Ideology and action are sometimes connected, but not always" (2011, 30). The third point of criticism is the focus on individuals and meso variables, disregarding the importance of a broader context, be it national, global, and mainly political (Coolsaet 2019; Crone 2016; Kundnani 2014) but also economic, social, and cultural.

The focus on individuals' characteristics has led to the search for a "jihadist profile" in order to improve the preventive and anticipatory capacity of responses. Profiling involves identifying all those features, including risk and protective factors, that play a role at the individual level. A well-known problem of profiling, and other explanatory models in the social sciences, is the presence of too many variables, inconsistent with the pursuit of parsimonious explanations. An example of the "too many variables" problem is Edwin Bakker's analysis of the characteristics of individual jihadist terrorists in Europe that studied 15 variables—sex, geographical background, socioeconomic background, education, faith during youth, occupation, family status, criminal record, psychological explanations, age, place of recruitment, faith, employment, relative deprivation, and social affiliation—only to conclude that "there is no standard jihadi terrorist in Europe" (2006, 43).

From the perspective of political science, socioeconomic and political variables have been chosen to center the analysis of jihadist profiles in Spain. However, some voices claim that the large variation in the characteristics of radical jihadists has made the aim of a unique profile unaffordable or even impossible. In different forums, experts "agreed that the attempts to profile extremists on the basis of socio-economic and geographical origins have failed" (European Foundation for Democracy 2017).[10] The heterogeneity of individuals engaging in radicalization processes prevents the development of useful profiles. Marian Misdrahi, at the Center for the Prevention of Radicalization Leading to Violence (CPRLV) in Montreal, also recommends focusing on behavioral and situational characteristics rather than socio-demographic or socio-political profiles.[11]

In Spain, the latest data from October 2019 identified 248 foreign terrorist fighters[12] and 825 people who were arrested for activities related to jihadist terrorism taking place between March 11, 2004, and October 2019.[13] The think tank Elcano publishes nearly every year the profiles of individuals detained for their involvement in jihadist terrorist activities in the country. The most recent analysis of detainees (or deceased) between 2001 and 2017 revealed that they are mainly men (90.7%), half of them married (56.7%) and with an average age of 33.6 years; of those individuals arrested in Spain for Islamic State related activities, 33.2% were Spanish, 40.2% were Moroccan, and 9.8% had converted to Islam renouncing previously held beliefs. When analyzing their level of education, 1.9% lacked a basic education, 70.8% had completed secondary education, and 27.3% held a university degree or had attended tertiary educational institutions (Reinares, García-Calvo, and Vicente 2019).

The attacks in Madrid and Catalonia allow a comparison between the profile of terrorists linked to Al-Qaeda and those of ISIS followers in Spain. Thus, it can be stated that the majority of those who immolate in both attacks are below the average age of 30. Those who immolated in the Madrid 11-M trains and in the Leganes' apartment were between 24 and 39 years old, while terrorists who perpetrated the attacks and died in Catalonia were younger, between 17 and 24 years old. However, those considered ideologues are older than the rest; for example, the ideologue behind

10. At the same time, it was agreed that "the main driving factor of extremism, according to them, is to be found in ideology and the role it plays in radicalizing individuals" (European Foundation for Democracy 2017).

11. Marian Misdrahi, Presentation at Building Resilience to Radicalization and Violent Extremism II. Strong Cities Network Global Summit, May 17–19 2017, Aarhus, Denmark.

12. Secretary of State for Security, Ana Botella, gave that number at the El Instituo El Cano Global Terrorism Forum 2019 in Madrid: http://www.realinstitutoelcano.org/wps/por tal/rielcano_es/actividad?WCM_GLOBAL_CONTEXT=/elcano/elcano_es/calendario/acti vidades/7-foro-elcano-terrorismo-global

13. See http://www.interior.gob.es/documents/10180/10353119/OPERACIONES+Y+D ETENIDOS+YIHADISMO+DESDE+11M+%2807-10-2019%29.pdf/20a82e09-47c2-4a 53-ae0b-d3ecb65e290b

Catalonia's attacks, Es Satty, was 45 years old. Those individuals who made up the 11-M cell were men from Maghreb countries, although since they arrived in Spain very young, they must be considered first-generation immigrants: half of them from Morocco and the rest from Tunisia, Algeria, or Spain, having converted to Islam. Among those related to the attacks on Catalonia were also first-generation immigrants who arrived at a very early age, but the youngest were born in Spain. In this case, they were all of Moroccan origin. Hence, the profiles of those involved in the jihadist terrorist attacks (11-M in 2004 and 17-A in 2017) appear to share a handful of characteristics in terms of age, migrant background, and past; some of them had contacts abroad, although most of the members did not travel to receive training in conflict zones. Most of them were perfectly integrated. This means that they had a "normal life" that included going out, playing football, or drinking alcohol and talking with their friends about relationships and sex. Most of them had completed secondary school and had jobs; some were well paid or ran their own businesses.

Another variable that can be added to socioeconomic profiles is that of criminality, whether for previous terrorist activities or other criminal acts. Some studies have analyzed the new wave of terrorists, foreign fighters, and other radicals linked to global jihadist terrorism in order to explore their "conversion" from other criminal activities to jihadist terrorism throughout Europe.[14] In Spain, an exhaustive analysis shows that some of those who planned and recruited those individuals and some of the executors of the attacks share a profile of criminal and terrorist records (Argomaniz and Bermejo 2019). The Elcano Database on Jihadists in Spain (EDBJS) includes this variable of previous criminal records to conclude that three out of every ten people arrested had some type of criminal record (26.2% of 210) (Reinares, García-Calvo, and Vicente 2019, 62). Regarding the March 11 attacks, it has been proven that the 11-M cell in Madrid was recruited by Amer Azizi, who had broad and deep links with Al-Qaeda organizations in Pakistan and Afghanistan but also with Maghreb terrorist organizations and European jihadist networks such as the Hamburg Cell (Reinares 2016). Other key individuals involved in the March 11 attacks had records of petty criminal activities or trafficking in explosives and illegal arms. On the other hand, Es Satty, planner of the 17-A attacks, was well known to the security forces because of his links with other suspected or convicted jihadists. The analysis of Es Satty's turbulent past and criminal record has

---

14. There has been a pattern of previous criminals being drawn to violent jihad (Rajan Basra, BBC news, March 24, 2017).

centered part of the public debate. This was also the case with the terrorist actions in other several countries: for example, the London Bridge attacks on November 29, 2019, and the Oslo and Utoya attacks on July 22, 2011. In the UK, "one quarter of Islamic-related offences were committed by individuals with a previous criminal conviction" (Stuart 2017, 953).

In terms of foreign terrorist fighter (FTF) profiles, two thirds of those in Germany had criminal records, as did more than half of those in Belgium, and in the Netherlands they shared a similar background. The International Centre for Counter-Terrorism in the Hague collected comprehensive information on the profiles of foreign fighters and concluded that a total of between 3,922 and 4,294 had left Western European countries to fight in international conflict zones (van Ginkel and Entenmann 2016). The locations of the majority of them are unknown (about 30% have returned and about 14% have been confirmed dead). The profile of the EU foreign fighters is that most are men (83%) from urban or built-up areas (90–100%), and less than one in four are converts (6–23%). The Spanish government indicated at that time that Spanish foreign fighters were a total of between 120 and 139, 90% of them male, the majority in their mid-20s to early 30s, and holders of Spanish or Moroccan citizenship (van Ginkel and Entenmann 2016, 38). As indicated above, this figure of FTF has reached 248 Spaniards or residents in Spain. Of these, approximately 19% may have returned to Spain or other European countries, 27% may have died, and the remaining 54% are thought to continue in conflict zones.[15]

As already mentioned here and in other chapters of this book, one of the problems related to this kind of profile is the large number of subjects who fit into these categories, rendering the design of public policies and measures to track or follow possible "radical/jihadist individuals" impracticable. For example, some European countries have registered more than 10,000 individuals whose movements needed to be tracked. Moreover, taking into account human rights provisions, surveillance and prevention action based on these profiles is particularly problematic.

One way to diminish the number of individuals who can fit into categories of violent radicals is to complement socio-demographic profiles with psychological profiles. Attempts to construct such profiles focus on variables such as frustration, identity crisis, or marginalization, or insecure individuals who are easily influenced. Therefore, when added to socio-

---

15. Secretary of State for Security, Ana Botella, gave that number at the El Instituto El Cano's "Foro sobre Terrorismo Global" on October 24, 2019. http://www.realinstitutoelca no.org/wps/portal/rielcano_es/actividad?WCM_GLOBAL_CONTEXT=/elcano/elcano_es /calendario/actividades/7-foro-elcano-terrorismo-global

demographic profiles, these variables might prove helpful in restricting the number of subjects included in surveillance files or prevention programs. In addition, they may be useful for studying causes or driving factors of radicalization processes. In that sense, we cannot claim that an individual's age leads to violence, but some kind of marginalization and frustration may be part of the problem. Thus, psychological profiles can be classified as studies that attempt to answer the question of "why" violent radicalization occurs. Among those studies, Michael King and Donald Taylor's (2011) identified three psychological factors as contributors to radicalization: relative deprivation of certain groups, identity conflicts, and personality characteristics. Identity-related issues are further divided into discrimination, integration, and identity management. However, studies on psychological profiles do not appear much more promising than socio-demographic ones in terms of reducing the number of individuals at risk or who need to be investigated. In this sense, John F. Morrison's chapter on the social psychology of radicalization acknowledges that "there is no psychological profile of a radicalized individual, and/or terrorist actor, and nor will there ever be" (chapter 5, this volume).

Further and more profound criticism arises with the debate about terrorists as abnormal people. Anton Weenink (2015) revived this question when he analyzed a sample of 140 radical Islamists, known by the Dutch Police as violent jihadists (actual or potential). His preliminary findings were that "histories of behavioral problems and disorders are overrepresented." In his follow-up to that research, this time with 319 jihadist travelers, he again assures that a total score of 28% suffers some kind of mental health problem, so his result "appears not to deviate substantially from national averages, considering the European base rate of 27% as provided by the World Health Organization" (2019, 136). However, he proposes a different base rate of 8 to 11%. Then, his findings point to a cluster of individuals with relatively high levels of adversity, distress, trauma, criminality, and mental health problems, compared to their age-matched peers, which "casts doubts on the often-presumed 'normality' of this specific group of 'terrorists'" (Weenink 2019, 130). There seem to be two possible explanations for the "new" overrepresentation of people with behavioral problems and disorders. On the one hand, the role of organizations has changed and so has that of some members. Organizations performed the role of gatekeepers, recruiting only those individuals who were useful for leadership, for designing and preparing explosives, or for organizing and commanding cells. The diminishing role of the organization/structure, but also of recruiters, prevents them from performing this access control goal. On the other hand, the role of the terrorist, particularly in the so-called home-grown jihad, and the new modes of perpetrating terrorist actions (e.g., driving trucks or cars against multitudes) make the possibility of involv-ing abnormal people more feasible.[16] In Spain, a prison psychologist inter-viewed on this issue assures that jihadists are similar to other people; they can suffer minor psychological problems such as anxiety, anger, or depres-sion, but it does not explain their radicalization into violence.[17]

Weenink's results threaten rational choice theory's assumptions in their applications to the realm of terrorism and the longstanding consensus in terrorism studies that "psychologists who have met terrorists face to face have nearly always concluded that these people were in no way abnormal, and on the contrary that they had stable and rational personalities" (Silke 2008, 104); that terrorists do not suffer from mental illness or disorders, but instead, in general, are ordinary people and unremarkable in psycho-logical terms (Silke 2008, 118). These are also key assumptions in the eco-nomic models that consider radicals to be rational actors (see Meierrieks and Krieger, chapter 1, this volume). In Spain, some individuals suffering from lack of social adjustment or psychiatric problems have been arrested, such as the man apprehended in Gerona in October 2007 with a car filled with butane gas cylinders and pyrotechnic material (Jordán 2014, 656). Nevertheless, no mental illness or disorder seems to have been present in those directly involved in the perpetration of large-scale terrorist attacks in this country.

In Spain, the know-how and experience acquired in the fight against ETA support the idea that terrorists are completely "normal" people. In this organization, three types of individuals were differentiated according to their intellectual capacity and role. First, those who were considered the ideological basis of the organization's "creed"; second, those who had been socialized within that context and those ideas; and third, individuals without clear ideas (empty-heads among ETA supporters and members). The interviewee, who is now in contact with jihadists detained in Spain, claims that "the new Islamist jihad is composed of the same three 'types' of individuals."[18] In this regard, several studies have attempted to sepa-

---

16. The emergence of homegrown terrorism in Spain has been studied by Reinares and García-Calvo. They place the blooming of this kind of jihadism in 2013, as far as this is the first year in which nearly half of the individuals detained were Spaniards (2015).

17. Informal interview with a prison psychologist expert on jihadist violent radicalization. Madrid, November 18, 2019. Another two psychologist experts in this field agree with that opinion for the case of jihadists in Spain.

18. Informal interview conducted in February 2017, Member of CGI (Police).

rate the profiles of the members according to their link to certain tasks and activities in the terrorist organizations (Jordán 2014, similar to what Giménez-Salinas Framis, Requena Espada, and de la Corte Ibáñez 2011 did for organized crime). The profiles of the militants (especially age, degree of integration, criminal record, education, and skills) can be very dissimilar, but the logistical tasks to which the militants are assigned or the propaganda received on the internet seem to be more relevant in terms of profiling than if the link is established with one or other of the main terrorist organizations: Al-Qaeda or ISIS. The masterminds of jihadist attacks in Madrid and Catalonia seem to have long links with the global jihad, but they recruited mainly regular young Muslim men to carry out their plots. These people are much more difficult for security forces to detect.

In sum, profiles, whether socio-demographic, criminal, and/or psychological, have been widely analyzed in the last decade of global jihadist terrorism; this trend has also been present in the Spanish case. However, its explanatory capacity for the violent radicalization and mobilization to jihad of young Spaniards is scarce, as is its usefulness in identifying individuals at risk of being recruited or radicalized who must be protected or watched over. Consequently, research tries to move from the study of profiles to the analysis of processes and patterns of violent radicalization applied to the Spanish case, which is the aim of the following section.

Studying Processes of Radicalization in Spain: The Issues of Recruitment, Mobilization, and Self-Indoctrination

A recent report by the European Foundation for Democracy and the Italian ISPI included poverty, unemployment, and lack of job opportunities; juvenile delinquency; trafficking and smuggling; socio-political, economic, and physical marginalization; the role of Salafist ideology; and the influence of brotherhood networks (Varvelli 2016, 153) as variables that can cause, or at least influence, the individual's passage toward violence. The Radicalization Awareness Network (RAN) works with predisposing and precipitating factors and drivers to understand radicalization. The factors include: individual socio-psychological factors, social factors (marginalization and discrimination), political factors, ideological and religious dimensions, culture and identity crisis, and trauma and other triggering mechanisms. Among the drivers, this network includes group and leader dynamics, radicalizers and groomers, and the role of social media.[19]

---

19. RAN research seminar, April 12–13, 2016, Vienna.

The study of violent radicalization processes is frequently linked to recruitment. Social movement theory points to the importance of "forming and motivating recruitment networks, arousing motivation to participate and removing barriers to participation" (Borum 2011, 17). When these two concepts, radicalization and recruitment, are used together, they seem to render complementary but diverse perspectives on analysis. Recruitment places attention on those who recruit a "passive" individual (how they work, what they do), while the idea of a violent radicalization process places the individual in a more active role.[20] Leaving aside the issue of recruitment and focusing on the process in which the individual is subject to radicalization is a matter of debate as it raises the question of whether there can be a process of self-radicalization. Despite the inclusion of the latter as a crime in the penal code reform in 2015 (self-indoctrination in article 575.2) some psychologists doubt the possibility of a complete absence of an "outstanding guide" (interview with psychologist, February 2018).

Javier Jordán's (2009) article on violent radicalization processes in Spain utilizes a three-level model of socio-political analysis as a framework to present concluding recommendations for Spanish public policy. He assures that analysis of those processes should focus on national situations (at macro and meso levels), and therefore the goals and actions of Spanish authorities should be directed toward (1) the involvement of Muslim communities, mainly imams and Muslim leaders, in prevention and awareness activities, (2) the promotion of socioeconomic and identity integration of Muslim immigrants, (3) the prevention and response to radical Islamic views and movements, and (4) the infiltration of police and intelligence services within jihadist social networks.

However, the search for social/causal mechanisms (Elster 1989) that explain any kind of radicalization process must not only identify the underlying factors or root causes but should also offer a response for how those factors directly relate to these effects. To the extent that a different mechanism might intervene, the aim is to determine which ones operate. Along the same lines, Borum asserts that "while the exact mechanisms and sequences of these changes is a matter of some debate, it is certainly clear that different pathways and mechanisms operate in different ways for different people" (2011, 15). Following psychological theories, when talking about processes, the analysis includes different phases. A theoretical perspective distinguishes two parts in the process of radicalization. A first step is the cognitive radicalization. One of the most well-known works

---

20. This issue is deeply considered in chapter 4 on conversion models by Juliette Galonnier, this volume.

on this concept defines cognitive radicalization as "the process through which an individual adopts ideas that are severely at odds with those of the mainstream, refutes the legitimacy of the existing social order, and seeks to replace it with a new structure based on a completely different belief system" (Vidino 2010, 4). The following step, called behavioral radicalization, leads to actions or attacks.

From that bulk of knowledge, other authors differentiate more than one phase. Spanish security forces have developed a model with four phases: pre-radicalization, identification and conversion, indoctrination, and action. They also differentiate and analyze processes of radicalization using something similar to Jordán's three-level analysis. They talk about individual radicalization, group radicalization, and mass radicalization, and all of them can be related to different reasons.

The evidence from the Madrid bombings, gathered during the 11-M trial, indicates that "certain individuals were in charge of planning the recruitment of newcomers who were attracted into their clusters following structured procedures . . . membership of this group would entail regular meetings in order to discuss issues related to Islam, as well as reasons behind the death of 'Muslim brothers' in areas such as Afghanistan, Palestine, Chechnya and Iraq" (Alonso 2008, 111). Reinares points to Amer Azizi as the mastermind of the attacks, acting as a radicalization agent and recruiter (Reinares 2016, 87–121). That role was played by Abdelbaki Es Satty in the attacks in Catalonia to shape the Ripoll cell. The imam of that city of 10,600 inhabitants in northern Catalonia, Es Satty was the recruiter of a group of young and integrated[21] Moroccan Muslims. Some relatives of the immolated young people speak of "brainwashing."[22] Es Satty, who was linked to the global jihad and has been previously investigated by security forces for his links to participants in the March 11 attacks, set up a close group with some sibling pairs who avoided gathering at the mosque in order not to be seen together and avoided internet contact so as not to be detected by law enforcement agencies. Personal, discreet contact was key to that group, as far as is known. This significance of the group and personal contacts is clearly explained in social movement theory and network theory, as Anja Dalgaard-Nielsen says in her summary: "Radical ideas are transmitted by social networks and violent radicalisation takes place within

21. While a debate about their degree of integration arose after the attacks, it is evident that they attended school from an early age, spoke the languages Catalan and Spanish, and performed similar jobs to other young people in their age group.

22. http://www.rtve.es/noticias/20170819/padre-hermanos-oukabir-estado-shock-no-mo straron-signos-radicalizacion/1600300.shtml

smaller groups, where bonding, peer pressure, and indoctrination gradually changes the individual's view of the world" (Dalgaard-Nielsen 2010, 801).

However, recent analyses seem to reveal that recruiters may be losing at least part of their "work" in favor of other processes such as self-radicalization. This issue is due to the fact that some of their "tasks," such as training or engagement with the organization, are not necessary or are not performed directly by individuals. Those who perpetrated the 11-M attacks used web forums and chat rooms, as Akil Awan assures: "The relationship between some users of Jihadist fora and the pursuit of violence or terrorism-related activities is incontrovertible in some cases (the 2004 Madrid train bombings, 21 July 2005 London 'bomb plot' and 2006 Canadian bomb plot are all prime examples)" (2007, 3). Fernando Reinares, Carola García-Calvo, and Alvaro Vicente (2019) have concluded that most radicalization processes have a very relevant offline phase.

In summary, the information reviewed in this section shows that the role of recruiters, who lead individuals through the process of radicalization, may be declining, but it remains clear that they have not abandoned the scenario in favor of online radicalization processes, at least when we speak of professional macro-attacks linked to global terrorist organizations.[23] In order to advance in the knowledge of these processes and phases, in-depth interviews are needed with collaborative subjects involved in terrorist events or who have been radicalized, which is extremely difficult to achieve. The following section goes a step further to unravel the possibility of designing patterns of radicalization.

Patterns of Radicalization among Spanish Jihadists: The Importance of Prisons

Patterns are used to design clothing. The idea behind a pattern is to create a core model that, with slight modifications, everyone could fit into. That pattern may also be used to produce different garments, equal in their essential elements. When it comes to economics, a pattern is a set of data that follows a recognizable form, which analysts attempt to find in the data they observe. A pattern is a series of data that are repeated in a recognizable way.[24] Rogelio Alonso, more than a decade ago, declared that there is "a

---

23. These terms are used in the Strategic Studies Group's report (2018).

24. http://www.investopedia.com/ask/answers/010715/what-are-differences-between-patt erns-and-trends.asp

clear picture of the evolution of jihadism in Spain indicating that the process of radicalization and recruitment generally follows some discernible patterns" (2008, 110). Despite this sentence, he assured that "radicalization and recruitment process was influenced by religious, cultural, social, economic and political factors" (2008, 120). In that process, imams and leaders seem to be essential (Alonso 2008, 120). Are we in the same situation today? The analysis of patterns in the field of violent radicalization is related to processes of radicalization. Qualitative studies focus on "how" radicalization processes work and pay attention to the study of individuals' lives, personal crises, and processes of change. Then, the question could be: Do violent radicalization processes follow one or more patterns, or perhaps no pattern can be glimpsed? This question is discussed here on the basis of interviews conducted with experts on the subject in Spain.

As has previously been stated, it seems that different patterns can be related to the tasks of a criminal or terrorist organization. Terrorists can perform several duties within their organization. Some experts in Spain compare ETA with ISIS to draw different patterns.[25] One interviewee directly associates the role they perform in a terrorist group with the process of radicalization, to conclude that we can discern three distinct patterns. One group, like ISIS or Al-Qaeda or one of their cells preparing independent attacks, is formed by ideologues, those who have a deep knowledge of the ideological basis of the organization. Such ideology leaders are present in each and every terrorist organization and rarely engage in terrorist actions or attacks. A second group of individuals consists of people who have grown up within the organization or who maintain tight ties with its members: They may be children of "combatants," detainees or followers killed in the cause, or have other blood relatives in the terrorist organization. Their knowledge of the ideology is not as relevant as in the first group, but they move into terrorism due to a sense of belonging. The third group of individuals is made up of those who are primarily interested in fighting or who are identified as influential individuals, and they neither possess a sound knowledge of the group's ideology nor share ties of belonging with other members. They may come from "normal" criminal activities or be attracted by an adventurous spirit. In the context of ISIS mobilization, they have been referred to as "cool jihad" or "chic jihad." Evidently, this picture denies the ideas of a single radicalization process in which the individuals follow a pattern ranging from cognitive to behavioral radicalization.

---

25. Interview with police officer, Madrid, April 19, 2017.

The same classification of individuals identified within ETA can be used to distinguish members and supporters of current global terrorist organizations: Daesh or Al-Qaeda. These patterns can be singled out despite the fact that nationalist terrorism cannot be equated to jihadist terrorism in many aspects. The same interviewee asserts that as the scope of action and the number of members of a global terrorist organizations grows, the number of patterns of radicalization increases. Nevertheless, when talking about particular cases of people who had tried to leave Spain for Syria in order to join the ranks of Daesh, these people, after long talks, are described as brainless or knuckleheads.

Following Alonso's work, some others distinguish between two patterns of radicals: recruiters and "the rest." Recruiters seem to be the ideologues of the organization. As in organized-crime groups, their profiles show well-educated individuals with social skills who are older than the rest of the members.[26] The "rest" can be considered vulnerable people. Some interviewees agree with the opinion that the members of that "rest" share a particular characteristic: They suffered a "traumatic life experience." Recruiters know how to reach and approach them by offering what they lack and desire.[27] Both groups of members perform two complementary roles in the organizations: Recruiters perpetuate the existence of the organization, and the rest are in charge of daily actions.

Pattern identification also occurs in the prison environment. The description of processes of violent radicalization in Spanish prisons indicates that they occur in a similar way as outside of prisons, although all interviewees agree that prisons are "special" places in terms of radicalization processes. Radicalization in prisons seems to follow a clear and known trajectory. Prisons are considered "places of vulnerability" (Neumann and Rogers 2007). In their report to the European Commission, Peter Neumann and Brooke Rogers state that "while the role of mosques in Islamist militant recruitment seems to have decreased, the opposite is true for prisons" (2007, 23). Their report draws attention to the growing numbers of Islamic militant inmates and claims that "resources are currently devoted to monitoring the most notorious inmates, the prison system has no capacity to control the activities of those convicted for lesser offences, some of whom are certain to engage in radicalisation and recruitment among

---

26. Prison recruiters are said to follow the above profile. Older jihadists tend to participate more in extremist support networks as radicalizers and recruiters rather than as attackers. In Spain, at least two of the prison recruiters well known to correctional services had mobility problems.

27. Interview with senior police officer chief of an intelligence department, April 27, 2017.

general prison population" (2007, 25). Farhad Khosrokhavar has also analyzed radicalization in prison in his study of the "European model of radicalisation." He asserts that radicalizers opt for very small groups, choose mentally fragile young people, and "cast a spell," which is a particular kind of enchantment on their victims: children and grandchildren of North African immigrants who suffer an identity crisis and account for a large proportion of prison population. He also relates the high prevalence of radicalization in prisons to living conditions and frustration in that environment (Khosrokhavar 2017, 127–36).

A Spanish penitentiary officer relates to the current situation in "his" prison. Most inmates charged with terrorism go to this particular prison for at least two months. He knows perfectly well the recruiting activities and also the radicalization processes inside prisons. In this sense, he is clear that a pattern of radicalization exists in prisons, but also a pattern of recruitment. He talks about the habits and practices inside prisons: "When a new inmate arrives, he usually looks for people and groups of his own nationality or country of origin, and most of them share the same religion. Newcomers need protection and colleagues, which is the reason why they can be easily attracted to religion by recruiters. Recruiters often invite them for coffee or tobacco and after a while propose them to abandon 'non-Islamic' habits for 'real or true Islamic' ones. At that moment, they invite 'the new' to pray or share readings or books."[28] This seems to be the beginning of a process to incorporate new inmates into radical Islamic ideology and possibly into their cells or organizations. Es Satty, the ideologue of the Catalan cell, had been in prison from 2010 to 2014 for drug trafficking, and his stay in prison seemed to provide a starting point on his path to violent radicalization. Some media reported that he was in charge of organizing prayer meetings while others say that he was not religious prior to imprisonment. However, what seems undeniable is that he met Rachid Aglif, alias "El Conejo" (the rabbit), who was serving an 18-year prison sentence for his role in the 2004 bombings.[29] Thus, Es Satty was recruited in prison, and two years later, outside of prison, he was the recruiter of Ripoll's youth group.

In prisons (and elsewhere as well), radicalization entails a change of diet (to avoid prohibited products such as pork), changes in prayer habits, and sometimes changes in clothing. Nevertheless, some experts of the

---

28. Interview with prison security official, May 5, 2017, Prison Madrid V, Madrid.

29. http://www.telegraph.co.uk/news/2017/08/20/imam-behind-barcelona-terror-cell-had-links-madrid-bomber/ and https://politica.elpais.com/politica/2017/08/20/actualidad/1503230607_911490.html

Spanish police services note that individuals immersed in these processes of violent radicalization are trying to avoid these external signs, and they behave, dress, and act as always in order to avoid attracting the attention of neighbors or security forces. That seems to be the case with Ripoll's youth group. Their radicalization processes lasted about a year, and nobody indicated that they suspected their radicalization except for a few comments, made before the attacks, which were deemed irrelevant.

In summary, radicalization in prisons seems to follow a clear pattern. Spanish prison officers are certain that there are radicalization processes in prisons, and therefore it is important to be aware of external changes and habits as indicators of radicalization processes. Officers claim that they are attentive to these processes, but recruiters change their habits. Consider for example prayer activities. Since inmates cannot pray outside their cells and have to go to the common prayer space that is under surveillance, recruiters now try to share cells with those they want to recruit. Compared to previous recruitment activities conducted by ETA, it appears that these organizations function completely differently inside prisons. ETA members did not practice proselytism in prisons. They tried to be alone, and such behavior is rare among jihadists. The total number of individuals in Spanish prisons classified as jihadists convicted of activities directly linked to terrorism (letter A), jihadist recruiters (letter B), and those who have become radicalized in prison or are at risk of violent radicalization (letter C) was between 250 and 300 in 2016.

Conclusion

Despite some exceptions, in Spain the rise of studies on jihadist-oriented organizations can be placed in the aftermath of the March 11 attacks in Madrid, after decades of studies devoted to ETA's nationalist terrorism. Since then, and especially after the definitive ceasefire of this terrorist organization, jihadist mobilization has been the main threat, as has been pointed out at the "threat table" and confirmed by terrorist attacks such as those of August 17, 2017, in Catalonia. The number of people arrested in police operations for jihadism, as well as the number of convicts, also points in the same direction, although other indicators, such as the lower number of foreign terrorist fighters in neighboring countries, point in the opposite direction.

The detailed overview of some of the key studies for the Spanish case, as reviewed in the previous sections, indicates the existence of research on the causes and triggers of radicalization as well as on its processes; but for the most part, research on global terrorism and homegrown jihad is mostly focused on individuals and their profiles, especially on the socio-demographic characteristics that allow individuals to be grouped together. These studies are predominantly quantitative (against the general trend found by Neumann and Kleinmann in 2013) and descriptive, not explanatory in nature; some are comparative. Media and judicial hearings are the main sources used to create profiles and analyze the radicalization processes of jihadist terrorists in Spain. Most academic work is based on secondary data due to difficulties associated with access to information, notably contact with and access to radicalized individuals.

What do we know and what remains to be known about the patterns and profiles of violent radicalization and jihadist mobilization in Spain? The profile of those involved in the two major jihadist terrorist attacks in Spain in 2004 and 2017 shows that they were young people from the Maghreb, mostly of Moroccan descent. The majority of them came to Spain as children and, in the latter case, they seemed to be perfectly integrated in terms of mastery of language, work, education, friends, or habits, as opposed to the former, of whom some lived in marginalized neighborhoods. The influence of organizers and recruiters from the Al-Qaeda network in 2004 or the influence of IS through the Ripoll's imam in 2017 appear to have been decisive and determining.

Concerning radicalization processes, some studies focus on time in order to analyze the duration of the whole process or parts of it. Spanish analysts conclude that these timelines have shortened in recent decades. A radicalization process could last for years in the past, whereas nowadays it can last a few months. Consequently, the processes can be characterized as completely different in terms of time from those of ETA, but also from those related to Al-Qaeda. The reason for this acceleration would appear to be linked to the use of the internet, chats, and forums. The influence of terrorist networks through cyberspace is particularly worrying given the age of the people they recruit, often from 18 to 25 years old. However, Elcano's reports and evidence of the recent terrorist attacks in Catalonia also highlight the importance of face-to-face contact and indoctrination to violent radicalization.

In terms of content and phases of the process, theoretical frameworks propose a path in which the individual is first interested in the ideology/religion, mainly in the extremist visions of Islam, and afterward initiates contact with radical materials, individuals, etc., ending in violence and terrorism. Although this seems a logical image of the radicalization process, some experts deny that this cycle, from cognitive to behavioral radicalization, may be the general or majority rule. As for outward signs of radical-ization, it can be said that in the case of Spain, they are not present in every instance. It is true that several radicals seem to follow a pattern: They aban-don other non-radical friends, change certain dietary habits, or engage in prayer activities. However, once radicals realized these were warning signs, they began to avoid showing external indications of radicalization in order to prevent detection and surveillance.

This chapter has also discussed the issue of lone actors versus terrorist groups and the matter of homegrown radicalization. Most of the jihadists engaged in terrorist attacks in Spain were of Muslim origin, particularly those from Morocco. They or their parents came from a Muslim country, so they can be considered first-generation immigrants. Among Spain's rad-ical Muslim jihadist population is an increasing number of individuals with Spanish nationality who are not descendants of any Muslim ancestor: the converts. In this context, it should be noted that the Muslim community in Spain has neither been identified as a whole nor pointed out for its radical character. Rather, it is composed mostly of moderates from Morocco.

The last part of the chapter deals with radicalization in Spanish prisons. This issue is undoubtedly urgent and worrying. In this scenario, maybe as a result of the constant surveillance and observation of the prisoners, the radicalization does seem to follow a discernible and well-known pat-tern, while the characteristics and circumstances of the individuals who are outside Spanish prisons, and who are suspected of belonging to radical Islamic movements, are too different to speak about in general patterns of radicalization.

REFERENCES

Alonso, Rogelio. 2008. "Jihadist Terrorism and the Radicalization Process of Mus-lim Immigrants in Spain." In *Psychosocial Stress in Immigrants and in Members of Minority Groups*, edited by Michal Finklestein and Kim Dent-Brown, 109–21. Amsterdam, IOS Press.

Alonso, Rogelio. 2004. "Pathways Out of Terrorism in Northern Ireland and the Basque Country: The Misrepresentation of the Irish Model." *Terrorism and Political Violence* 16 (4): 695–713.

Argomaniz, Javier, and Rut Bermejo. 2019. "Jihadism and Crime in Spain: A Con-vergence Settings Approach." *European Journal of Criminology* 16 (3): 351–68.

Awan, Akil N. 2007. "Radicalization on the Internet? The Virtual Propagation of Jihadist Media and its Effects." *The RUSI Journal* 152 (3): 76–81.

Bakker, Edwin. 2006. *Jihadi Terrorists in Europe, their Characteristics and the Circum-stances in which they joined the Jihad: An Exploratory Study*. Clingendael: Nether-lands Institute of International Relations.

Bermejo, Rut, and Isabel Bazaga. 2021. "La Lutte Espagnole Contre l'Extremisme Nationaliste et Indépendantise." In *Le Nouvel Age des Extremes? Les Démocracies Occidentales, la Radicalisation et l'Extrémisme Violent,* edited by David Morin and Sami Aoun, 223–38. Montreal: Presses de l'Université de Montréal.

Borum, Randy. 2011. "Radicalisation into Violent Extremism I: A Review of Social Science Theories." *Journal of Strategic Security* 4 (4): 7–36.

Cano, Miguel Ángel. 2009. "Perfiles de Autor del Terrorismo Islamista en Europa." *Revista Electrónica de Ciencia Penal y Criminología* 11 (7): 1–38.

Coolsaet, Rik. 2019. "Preface." In *Radicalisation. A Marginal Phenomenon or a Mirror to Society?* edited by Noel Clycq, Christiane Timmerman, Dirk Vanheule, Rut Van Caudenberg, and Stiene Ravn, 7–10. Leuven: CeMIS, Leuven University Press.

Crone, Manni. 2016. "Radicalization Revisited: Violence, Politics and the Skills of the Body." *International Affairs* 92 (3): 587–604.

Dalgaard-Nielsen, Anja. 2010. "Violent Radicalisation in Europe: What We Know and What We Do Not Know." *Studies in Conflict & Terrorism* 33: 797–814.

Elster, Jon. 1989. *Nuts and Bolts for the Social Sciences.* Cambridge: Cambridge University Press.

European Foundation for Democracy (EFD). 2017. "Ideology: The Driving Force behind Radicalisation?" February 1, 2017. http://europeandemocracy.eu/wp-content/uploads/2017/01/Policy-Briefing-IN-Design.pdf

Europol. 2019. *Terrorism Situation and Trend Report 2019.* European Union.

Fiscalía General del Estado. 2019. *Memoria de la Fiscalía General del Estado 2018.* https://www.fiscal.es/memorias/memoria2019/FISCALIA_SITE/index.html

Funes, María Jesús. 1998. "Social Responses to Political Violence in the Basque Country: Peace Movements and Their Audience." *Journal of Conflict Resolution* 42 (4) 493–510.

García-Calvo, Carola, and Fernando Reinares. 2019. "Radicalización Yihadista y Asociación Diferencial: Un Estudio Cuantitativo del Caso Español. In *Radicalización Violenta en España: Detección, Gestión y Respuesta,* edited by Rut Bermejo and Isabel Bazaga, 29–42. Valencia: Tirant lo Blanch.

Giménez-Salinas Framis, Andrea, Laura Requena Espada, and Luis de la Corte Ibáñez. 2011. "¿Existe un Perfil de Delincuente Organizado? Exploración a Partir de una Muestra Española." *Revista Electrónica de Ciencia Penal y Criminología* 13 (3): 3:1–3:32.

Jordán, Javier. 2014. "The Evolution of the Structure of Jihadist Terrorism in Western Europe: The Case of Spain." *Studies in Conflict and Terrorism* 37 (8): 654–73.

Jordán, Javier. 2009. "Procesos de Radicalización Yihadista en España: Análisis Sociopolítico en Tres Nniveles." *Revista de Psicología Social* 24 (2): 197–216.

Khosrokhavar, Farhad. 2017. *Radicalization: Why Some People Choose the Path of Violence.* New York: New Press.

King, Michael, and Donald M. Taylor. 2011. "The Radicalization of Homegrown Jihadists: A Review of Theoretical Models and Social Psychological Evidence." *Terrorism and Political Violence* 23 (4): 602–22.

Kundnani, Arun. 2014. *The Muslims are Coming! Islamophobia, Extremism, and the Domestic War on Terror.* London: Verso.

Kundnani, Arun. 2012. "Radicalisation: The Journey of a Concept." *Race & Class* 54 (2): 3–25.

Neumann, Peter, and Brooke Rogers. 2007. "Recruitment and Mobilisation for the Islamist Militant Movement in Europe." King's College London report for the European Commission, December. https://kclpure.kcl.ac.uk/portal/files/57763 21/Pathways_into_Violent_Radicalisation.pdf

Neumann, Peter, and Scott Kleinmann. 2013. "How Rigorous is Radicalization Research?" *Democracy and Security* 9 (4): 360–82.

Ravn, Stiene, Rik Coolsaet, and Tom Sauer. 2019. "Rethinking Radicalisation: Addressing the Lack of a Contextual Perspective in the Dominant Narratives on Radicalisation." In *Radicalisation: A Marginal Phenomenon or a Mirror to Society?* edited by Noel Clycq, Christiane Timmerman, Dirk Vanheule, Rut Van Caudenberg, and Stiene Ravn, 21–46. Leuven: CeMIS, Leuven University Press.

Reinares, Fernando. 2016. *Al-Qaeda's Revenge: The 2004 Madrid Train Bombings.* New York: Columbia University Press.

Reinares, Fernando, and Carola García-Calvo. 2015. "Terroristas, Redes y Organizaciones: Facetas de la Actual Movilización Yihadista en España." *Real Instituto Elcano*, November 16, 2015. https://www.realinstitutoelcano.org/docume nto-de-trabajo/terroristas-redes-y-organizaciones-facetas-de-la-actual-moviliz acion-yihadista-en-espana

Reinares, Fernando, Carola García-Calvo, and Alvaro Vicente. 2019. "Yihadismo y Yihadistas en España: Quince Años Después del 11-M." *Real Instituto Elcano.*

Silke, Andrew. 2008. "Holy Warriors: Exploring the Psychological Processes of Jihadi Radicalization." *European Journal of Criminology* 5: 99–123.

Stephens, William, Stijn Sieckelinck, and Hans Boutellier. 2019. "Preventing Violent Extremism: A Review of the Literature." *Studies in Conflict & Terrorism* 44 (4): 346–61. https://doi.org10.1080/1057610X.2018.1543144

Strategic Studies Group (GEES). 2018. "The Jihad against Spain: Origin, Evolution and Future of the Islamist Threat." February. http://www.gees.org/cont ents/uploads/articulos/the%20Jihad%20against%20Spain%202.0%20low.pdf

Stuart, Hannah. 2017. *Islamist Terrorism: Analysis of Offences and Attacks in the UK (1998–2015).* Henry Jackson Society. http://henryjacksonsociety.org/wp-conte nt/uploads/2017/03/Islamist-Terrorism-preview-1.pdf

van Ginkel, Bibi, and Eva Entenmann. 2016. "The Foreign Fighters Phenomenon in the European Union: Profiles, Threats and Policies." *The Hague: International Centre for Counter-Terrorism.*

Varvelli, Arturo, ed. 2016. *Jihadist Hotbeds: Understanding Local Radicalization Processes.* Milan: Italian Institute for International Political Studies (ISPI) and European Foundation for Democracy.

Vidino, Lorenzo. 2010. "Countering Radicalization in America: Lessons from Europe." *United States Institute of Peace* 262. https://www.usip.org/sites/defau lt/files/resources/SR262%20-%20Countering_Radicalization_in_America.pdf

Weenink, Anton W. 2019. "Adversity, Criminality, and Mental Health Problems in Jihadis in Dutch Police Files." *Perspectives on Terrorism* 13 (5): 130–42.

Weenink, Anton W. 2015. "Behavioural Problems and Disorders Among Radicals in Police Files." *Perspectives on Terrorism* 9 (2): 17–33.
Whitfield, Teresa. 2014. *Endgame for ETA. Elusive peace in Basque Country*. London: Hurst and Oxford University Press.

TEN

United Kingdom

Islamist Radicalization in a Spatial Context

Tahir Abbas

This chapter provides a conceptual and theoretical discussion on the evolution of radical Islamism in the urban centers of Britain. This radicalism refers to toxic Salafism as characterized by particular Islamist groups emerging from the peripheries of politicized indigenous Muslim minority groups. This violent and nonviolent extremism is realized at the local and urban spatial levels due to economic and social marginalization combined with cultural and political alienation. Enforced by state-led narrow definitions of nationalism and citizenship at the national level and challenges to geo-identity politics at the global level, the political rejection of Muslim differences appeals to "left behind" majority group working-class aspirations over their own identity claims. Islamist radicalization in the United Kingdom is therefore sensitive to local socioeconomic challenges, national discourses in relation to citizenship and national identity, and wider issues related to the global "war on terror culture" that dominates foreign policy design and thinking—all of these affirming a sense of Britishness rather than a rejection of it. Islamist radicals in the UK are uniquely a product of British society.

The primary focus of this chapter is to explore the nature of Islamist radicalization as a social process, where the issues relating to the "push" into extremism and radicalization are more often due to the reality of structural and cultural disadvantage, exclusion, and marginalization. While it would be disingenuous to argue that the "pull" of ideology has no role to play, the argument presented here suggests that it is the tipping point into violence in some cases, not the basis for it. This applies in the Global North as much as it does in the Global South. In this regard, it is argued that there is an interconnection between conceptualizations of Islamist radicalization as a reality of failed policy in relation to integration and diversity (Abbas 2011), the objectification of the Islamist Muslim category (Kundnani 2014), and the stoking of far-right extremism through the vilification of Muslims in dominant media and politics. The arguments I am making in this paper focus on the idea that Islamist radicalization emerges from a paradigmatic cycle of cultural and political violence toward young people in the urban centers of Britain. The fundamental argument is thus: Orientalism, xenophobia, and racism are critical factors in the definition and reality of Muslim extremism. At the heart of the malaise, patterns of exclusion persist for all groups, resulting in deep polarizations and the potential for further extremism among existing marginalized minority and majority communities (Social Mobility Commission 2016; Khattab and Johnston 2014). In effect, Islamophobia is actual and symbolic violence from above, socially, culturally, and politically reproduced in various forms. Radicalization among radical Islamists is the response from below among those groups pushed furthest down in society (Abbas 2019; Abbas and Siddique 2012). It is therefore important to appreciate these distinctions, exploring the theoretical dynamics while situating them within wider theories of social conflict, social reproduction, and ethnopolitical relations. It is also necessary to conceptualize and theorize the nature and the characteristics of distinct locally lived experiences that signify Islamist extremisms in various British urban spatial formations.

The relationship between the individual, the urban setting, and the state regarding diverse atomized groups is important to consider. Particular questions on the subject of identity politics and social conflict, especially in light of the social and economic transformation since the era of monetarism and neoliberalism that began in the 1980s, suggests radical Islamists are often drawn from experiences of marginalization and political disenfranchisement (Abbas 2011). The state exercises hard power from the top-down through foreign policy concerning the Muslim world, all the while using nationalism to mollify ethnic majorities at home. This nationalism is assimilationist, and in the post-9/11 climate, the counterterror state apparatus scapegoats and securitizes marginalized Muslim communities in such a charged setting (Mandaville 2009). Since the events of

9/11 and a number of terrorist incidents in the UK, Muslim groups are arguably the most "othered" of all groups. This is partly because of an intensification of caricatures, stereotypes, and generalizations (Lentin and Titley 2012; Open Society Institute 2010; Bhattacharyya 2008; Rai 2004). Muslim groups also receive the brunt of accusations of such iniquities as "grooming" or the subjugation of Muslim women (Cockbain 2013). The objectification of Muslims as "terrorists" occurs when everyday Muslims are thought to be susceptible to radicalization and violent extremism as the new normal (Kundnani 2012). The projection of Muslims as the foremost risk to society, where religion is recognized as a "parallel legal code," magnifies the perception of a "them" and "us" (Lynch 2013; Williamson and Khiabany 2011). The demonization of religious Muslim figures, particularly in the tabloid media, as (a) being representative of a "shadowy community" and (b) thus objectionable figures of loathing through their representation as "hate preachers," for example, further extends the idea that "we" hate "them" because "they" hate "us" (Altikriti and Al-Mahadin 2015). As states legislate against terrorism, which invariably centers on Muslim communities, it leads to perpetuating the view that Muslim communities ought to bear the greatest attention in the determination of everstringent counterterrorism policy developments (Abbas and Awan 2015; Alam and Husband 2013; Choudhury and Fenwick 2011).

First, I provide a conceptual overview of the topics and their definitions. Second, I explore an interpretation of how considerations of Islamophobia and radicalization are characterized in Britain. Third, I analyze the ways in which the authority of the state elites reinforces racial hierarchies among marginalized groups. Extremist Islamist groups exist at the periphery of society. They are excluded and alienated in an enduring cyclical process. Consequently, they are radicalized in response to a simultaneous "left behind" existence, concretized by the authority of state elites. Far-right groups vent their fury against the most "othered" in society, groups perceived as directly pivotal to their own woes. This reaction obtains credibility through the localization of ethnic nationalism driven by the machinations of state elites at the center. In local urban spaces, denial of local and national identity leads to global identity formations among ostracized Muslims, in particular as a response to a geopolitical stance taken toward the Muslim world, especially since the events of 9/11, the war in Iraq, and the emergence and decline of the Islamic State as a specific case. In conclusion, local area urban racial tensions are a microcosm of wider global manifestations. I discuss how the political formations of diverse and excluded communities in inner-city urban areas in Britain, where conflicts between the local, national, and global are played out among variously excluded and marginalized young people in society, and the implications this raises for social cohesion, social trust, and political engagement more generally.

Intersecting Radicalization

Both of the themes *Islamophobia* and *radicalization* are firmly located on the landscape of the human and social sciences. They have also entered into the realms of political discussion and civil society activism. Over the last decade or so, the academy has generated a great deal of output on these topics (Esposito and Iner 2019; Esposito and Kalin 2011; Dalgaard-Nielsen 2010). While there is momentum in utilizing the terms as types of cultural discrimination at one level and racialization on the other, distinct limitations emerge because of a framework pinpointing the contestations as founded within the religion alone. These additional distinctions require consideration, especially in the field of terrorism studies, in particular in how Islamophobia potentially determines the processes of radicalization and vice versa (Abbas 2012). Due to its inherent generalizability, Islamophobia, on the other hand, permits observers to view anti-Muslimism as a function of cultural distinctiveness, denying the fact that it is a variety of racism. It creates the conditions for rendering Muslims invisible as racialized groups, all the while presented as the ubiquitous most different and therefore most undesirable group in society (Kapoor 2013; Tyrer and Sayyid 2012).

Cultural comparisons drawn between radical Islamists and far-right extremists concentrate on the mutual issue of the search for identity (Pisoiu 2015). However, less well understood is the structural contextualization facing both groups. Deindustrialization, postindustrialization, and globalization affect Muslim minority groups in the inner-city areas of major cities across Britain, but these uncertainties also affect majority indigenous groups, the result being that far-right sentiment is further fueled in a neoliberal era that involves all (Saull 2015). However, while majority indigenous communities also suffer from predicaments leading to extremism, radicalization, and violence, media and political discourses rarely concentrate on such groups. Few comparisons between extremist far-right groups and radical Muslim organizations help to explore the synergies between arguably parallel and similar realities (Goodwin 2013). Since 9/11, and in more recent years, far-right extremists have carried out numerous acts, yet states and the media habitually underemphasize or underreport this reality.

As of April 2017, these groups have been responsible for 73% of deadly attacks in the United States (United States Government Accountability Office 2017). The nexus separating white indigenous and Muslim minority groups is the difference between identity formations at the local and global levels, revealing a distinct layer of conflict and locking both groups in intense competition for the least in society.

At the individual level, social, psychological, economic, and structural issues negate a sense of identity and introduce the need for self-actualization among young Muslims faced with many other existing challenges in society. Apprehensions appear over multiculturalism, dislocation, and identity conflict. All are imperative constituents in the causes of radicalization. A lack of hope leads to psychological conundrums, leaving young men vulnerable, exposed, and pliable to external influences. Inadequate education and limited employability, largely because of discrimination and disadvantage, and the uncertain futures facing young people in inner-city areas, for minority and majority, create challenges without real opportunities (Sullivan et al. 2014). Bleak prospects and a competitive environment combine to suppress motivation and desire. At the meso level, nervousness restricts challenges to the dominant institutions of the state or the means to empower individuals. These anxieties affect all communities, but they also reinforce the power, status, and authority of state elites to define the social world in their own image. In exploring these factors that determine minority radicalization and extremism, conflation transpires between structural, cultural, and individual struggles thought to emanate from the religious and cultural characteristics of communities. The motivations of actors exist, arguably, at interpersonal, sociological, and psychological levels, where young men (and women) are reconfiguring, rather than denying, how to be British in various spatial formations. Here, radicalization of British-born Muslims is an aspect of coming to terms with "hegemonic masculinity" and intergenerational disconnect combined with economic insecurity (McDowell 2000). Their masculinities are thus multiple and situational, within the home or in wider society. The transnational sites in which masculinities are constructed interconnect with the local, regional, and global (Hopkins 2006). South Asian Muslims in Britain have withstood being interchangeably characterized as effeminate and hypermasculine. Groups were sissified due to their seemingly "nimble" character but at the same time identified as a threat because of their "dark and handsome" allure throughout the early phases of postwar migration and settlement. The latter ensured these men did not share workspaces with white English women (Kalra 2009). In the post-9/11 climate, British Muslim men are seen as a threat to society, which is directly associated with a projected hypermasculinity that is also presented as menacingly omnipotent (Mac an Ghaill and Haywood 2015).

Britain has profoundly transformed since the advent of monetarism that began in the 1980s (Ferrera 2014). It has led to implications for youth identities in urban spheres (Sassen 1998). The inner cities, long forgotten by urban planners and policymakers until the deleterious conditions facing disadvantaged "underclass" groups could be neglected no further, are sites of diverse communities where a tendency for residential concentration transpires. This can take the characteristics of minorities who cluster in urban areas utilizing the social, economic, and cultural capital of the group for relative advantage, potentially positively contributing to the greater wealth of society. The general dominant discourse is to present "self-styled segregation" as a negative, but it is not always the reality, especially for minorities generally on the receiving end of vilification and discrimination (Peach 1996). Simultaneously, the intensification of deprived marginalized majorities is also an opportunity to protect group norms and values associated with the group identity, which, in the light of present politics, feels threatened by the dominant other. Neoliberalism has combined with ill-fated foreign policy advances in the Muslim world. This social and economic remodeling has led to the reconfiguration of former working classes into various protest resistance movements, frequently centering on the so-called purity of racialized identities, where class identities have failed groups. For disaffected Muslims, where the local has proved futile in the West and in the East, the search for the global enters the frame. All the while, nation-states diminish the position of the welfare state and further embrace neoliberal economics with no obvious future cultural or political direction in a post-truth, post-normal world.

The topics of Islamophobia and its associated concept, radicalization, have received extensive attention in recent periods. Mutually reinforcing discourses perpetuate Islamic extremism as a function of religious norms and values associated within ethnic and cultural groups, namely Muslim minorities. Some of these Muslims hold specific anti-Western attitudes, disengaging them from wider society and thereby further deepening their associations with a complex religious and cultural identity that sets them apart from mainstream society. In these instances in Britain, the media have portrayed groups such as the English Defence League (EDL) and organizations such as Islam4UK, Al Muhajiroun, or Al Ghurabaa, the first historically associated with Tommy Robinson and the latter with Anjem Choudary, in oppositional terms. Elite class structure perpetuates a perennial conflict between different sectors of the working class and the "left behind" of British society. However, national and local identity, social mobility, economic marginalization, political disenfranchisement, and cultural alienation closely connect the ideological concerns affecting white working-class young men and British-born Muslim minorities. In effect, both groups are experiencing similar tribulations produced by various discourses internalized by these groups, who in turn consider their relative counterparts through an equivalent oppositional framework, thereby further legitimizing existing modes of domination and subordination, all of which stem from elite racism.

Islamophobia Revisited

Islamophobia centers on fear and the idea of a threat ostensibly surfacing from otherwise alienated minority groups perceived as not merely antithetical to plural democracies but also a security threat. Part of this view stems from having reached a point in relation to multiculturalism that suggests society has become far too open to differences. This critique is essentially an implicit *misrecognition* of Muslim minorities—a form of structural and cultural racism denying the existence of differences within essentially plural liberal democracies (Lentin 2014). Islamophobia as a means of far-right social, community, and political activism has spread right across Britain and Western Europe. From the EDL in Britain, to the National Front in France, to the Party for Freedom in the Netherlands, to the Northern League in Italy, to the National Democratic Party in Germany, these far-right movements have entered the popular imagination in local area communities and in national politics (World Policy Institute 2011). In this respect, Germany too faces certain concerns in the formation of anti-Muslim racism (Schiffer and Wagner 2011); in particular, after 2015, many migrants fleeing the conflict in Syria came to Germany as part of its then open policy toward these groups, but these policies have retreated to a net restriction of asylum seekers. Similar examples of the resistance toward Muslims are found in Sweden (Roald 2013) and Russia (Arnold and Romanova 2013). A study of 11 EU countries with high GDPs demonstrates that this fear is explicitly cultural-ethnic rather than economic (Lucassen and Lubbers 2012). Similar outcomes exist in Eastern and Central European countries (Mudde 2005), while in some cases, even greater anti-Muslim prejudice appears among these populations (Strabac and Listhaug 2008). Throughout Western Europe, the fear of Muslims concentrates on education and religious practices, a perspective that has remained consistent in the post-9/11 "war on terror culture" (Fetzer and Soper 2003).

While interest in the field of "Islamophobia studies" grows, classification and categorization issues remain. For some, Islamophobia is located somewhere between *outcome* and *process*, where the latter includes history as well as contemporary politics, while the former relates to problematic outcomes measurable as distinct forms of racial, cultural, and religious discrimination. For others, the ambiguity of the concept is its strength, as Islamophobia takes different shapes and forms depending on the milieu, with specific local and global manifestations. It also operates within spheres of intellectual, cultural, and social ontologies (Sayyid and Vakil 2011). Others emphasize Islamophobia's relationship to existing patterns of xenophobia, Orientalism, and imperialism, which affect numerous liberal plural democracies and their constructions of multiculturalism (Esposito and Kalin 2011). The racialization of Muslims through the political and media manufacture of "Muslim as monster" goes beyond imagining extremists through the general signifier of "Muslim as terrorist," "other," or undesirable (Arjana 2015).

A significant element of the current populism in relation to Muslim groups in parts of Western Europe and in Britain relates to worries over population growth of this group. Political elites stoke up these fears while most people in society remain "demographically illiterate" (Kaufmann 2017). It also creates particular issues relating to the responses to violent extremism. The tendency is to ascribe greater weight to radicalization among visibly different groups in society. The invisibility of white extremism and the entry into the mainstream of anti-immigration, anti-Muslim, and anti-other sentiments creates new anxieties. Whiteness remains a privilege in general terms, but also in specific cases regarding the analysis, understanding, and communication of violent extremism per se (Patel 2013). Brown male bodies are regulated within particular spatial contexts, where identities are qualified as global; however, it omits the idea that many British South Asian Muslim men seek a localized realization of identities in context (Isakjee 2016), which is denied due to patterns of "othering" at the national and global levels. On questions of citizenship, visible minorities feel aggrieved at being seemingly targeted by anti-terrorism legislation and state practices, while majority white communities, even though aspects will apply to these groups too, project the issues elsewhere, while remaining "invisible" in the wider discourse (Jarvis and Lister 2013). To improve understandings of radicalization, extremism, and the shaping of identities, there is considerable room for the "spatial turn," particularly in the field of security studies (Adamson 2016).

In the radicalization of British-born Muslims, their coming of age occurs due to various modes of intergenerational change and development, but when exploring the factors determining minority and majority radicalization and extremism, conflation surfaces between structural and cultural anxieties thought to emanate from the religious and cultural characteristics of communities. These motivations nevertheless exist at an interpersonal, sociological, and psychological level, where young men (and women) are reconfiguring how to be British (or English in the light of the Brexit vote of June 2016) rather than denying it. Britain has transformed since the advent of neoliberalism, monetarism, and privatization that began in the 1980s. Brexit has further evoked long-standing claims for sovereignty in Western Europe. During this period, Salafism and (white-indigenous) radicalism have also appeared as corresponding processes at the boundaries of society. Since the events of 9/11, not only has an Islamophobia industry surfaced but also a radicalization/de-radicalization industry, arguably an attempt to placate domestic and foreign policy and converge on group differences as the cause of extremism. The dominant view that violent extremism nevertheless still rests within the religion and culture of specific groups rather than the workings of society and politics takes precedence. It takes tension away from themes relating to structural disadvantage and discrimination, which are arguably pertinent drivers affecting *all* young people in declining urban areas. Local area problems in relation to radicalization and extremism are a function of local area issues and concerns.

In reality, it is important to look at the individual, the social structure, and questions of anomie amongst young Muslims to attain a complete picture. Groups are anti-state, anti-globalization, and pro-localization. They are pro-totalitarian, wish to distill a certain form of identity politics, and have a utopian vision of society. However, they have a narrowly defined vision of the self, which is wholly exclusive of the other. Projected identities are fantasies while facing status inconsistency. An elite media and political discourse creates oppositional perspectives regarding groups in society effectively suffering the same sets of social, economic, and political troubles, fueling Islamophobia *and* radicalization. It disregards numerous social problems facing young people. At the center of the unease is the need for elites to maintain their positions while "othering" others. Although much emphasis is on the incompatibility of Muslim religious and cultural values, the reality tends to be a positive negotiation between superficially conflicting norms. It is precisely a sense of positive British-ness, European-ness, or American-ness that encourages young Muslims to speak out and critically engage with a discourse emphasizing their apparent unassimilability (El-Haj, Renda, and Bonet 2011). Some degree of association with a particular faith identity exists, but the vast majority of British Muslims are pro-integration, where foreign policy is of only marginal interest in their daily lives (Thomas and Sanderson 2011), although a significant motivator for some would-be extremists who join the likes of Islamic State (Schuurman, Bakker, and Eijkman 2016).

Positive approaches to improving ethnic and cultural relations with white majority groups remains a distinct focus for Muslim minority communities in the North of England in particular. These groups are routinely subject to negative attention while facing ongoing challenges of deindustrialization and economic marginalization affecting the entire region. The mode of reform is to introduce soft power, which includes volunteering, civil society, and social work. There is also considerable room for education, engagement, and participation. Policy is an arm of the state but can become an iron fist when instrumentalized unnecessarily or when it is simply not working but forced to do so. Here, soft power can operate to activate positive forms of youth engagement that also functions as deradicalization. Reconfigurations of the ideas of citizenship need to intersect the realities of local area experiences and their implications for an inclusive national identity. For too long governments have toyed with nationhood and belonging as instruments of social policy. Rather than seeing differences as assets in society, political elites have routinely played off groups (Amin 2002; Baeten 2001). In the absence of a national consensus, social conflict in urban centers plays into the hands of right-wing parties and radical jihadi movements. Both are able to instrumentalize grievances, disadvantage, and alienation through politico-ideological perspectives shaped by the urban phenomenon.

The Role of Social Structure

It is important to consider issues of social structure and identity politics when attempting to understand the nature of radicalization and extremism among those who engage in far-right extremism as well as those drawn to Islamist extremism. In the current political climate, the projection is that violent radical Islamism is a reality of Muslim communities, in which lie all the problems and all the solutions. That far-right and Islamist extremists are similarly problematic with distinctively related issues, as the path toward radicalization is local and urban in nature and outcome, is largely true. A need exists to recognize that these kinds of extremism are two sides of the same coin, where limiting one will invariably reduce the other. Both extremisms feed off the rhetoric of the "other," compounded by elite discourse that seeks to maintain a divide and rule approach to dealing with differences in society, combined with the issue of the diminished status of white working-class communities in general terms. Greater understanding of the linkages, interactions, and symbiosis between these two oppositional but related extremisms is crucial. This is especially the case in the current epoch, where a post-truth, post-normal world has gained ascendancy, with expertise derided and the status quo prevailing.

In 2017, there were five terrorist attacks in the UK, with 35 people dead and many others injured. The security services thwarted nine further potential attacks, including one targeting Downing Street and the prime minister. At the same time, Islamophobia is becoming virulent and more aggressive than ever. While investment goes into counterterrorism and combating violent extremist projects, these attacks keep occurring. This is the hyper-normalization of Islamophobia and radicalization, yet we are no closer to solving either of them. With critics of all hues silenced, the average citizen is left confused. It is also an age of rampant disinformation, and there seems to be no escape from it. The current wave of anti-Islam "fake news" or disinformation began immediately after the events of 9/11, although it is clear that Orientalism and Islamophobia have a much longer history in the West. The "weapons of mass destruction" led to the illegal invasion of Iraq, when much of the world argued, with millions demonstrating in cities all over the world, that Saddam Hussein was no threat to the West and going into Iraq was a folly that would cost countless lives and destabilize the region. After numerous pressures derailed the Arab Spring in Egypt, the attacks on Libya and Syria led to the disruption of the entire Middle East/North Africa (MENA) region and the emergence of Islamic State, whose origins lie in Western attempts to arm Sunni rebels in opposition to Bashar al-Assad. The era of UK fakery heightened during the Brexit campaign. Based on huge distortions of fact, it has divided a nation into two, leaving a country stranded.

So-called ethnic "ghettos," where specific Muslim groups are sometimes found living, rarely out of choice, are not a reflection of communities necessarily choosing to live among themselves. Instead, their experience reflects the failures of government policy to implement integration and equality policy and practice. At the same time, former "white" working classes have also suffered because of deindustrialization, technological innovation, and globalization and face ongoing cultural, economic, and political disenfranchisement because of it. Most Muslims retain their ethnic, religious, and cultural norms and values as solace, which some majorities may regard as a retreat into regressive practices. However, though they also suffer from marginalization in society, ostracized "white" groups have the history of their nation, whether imagined or real, and the co-ethnic partisanship of the dominant hegemonic order at their disposal. Combined with this gloomy condition, the dominant political discourse continues to blame the assailants for their "values" or "crises of identity," rarely scrutinizing the workings of wider society to appreciate the holistic character of social conflict. Routinely instrumentalized are issues to do with freedom of expression, or categorizing values as alien, all of which ensure the focus stays on the terrorists. Attacks from 2015 to 2017 by takfiri-jihadis in London, Paris, Berlin, Nice, Barcelona, and Sydney were all carried out by the sons of immigrant minorities caught between cultures. Rather than supported and developed as individuals and communities in society, through mechanisms not always of their own agency, the far fringes of marginalized groups vented their frustrations back toward the center. All of these attackers were the insider-outsiders of society.

Structural crises affect Muslim groups in the Muslim world and in the West. Many of the pre-migration sending countries still have difficulty with trust in the political process, habitually needed for stable democracies. Material and economic issues are also underdeveloped. As young people become vulnerable, they also become outraged. Many of the young men and women who ended up in the Islamic State had little or no real appreciation of Islam at all. In this respect, young people want to develop a sense of themselves for a whole host of reasons, but a specified political Islam provides a pre-prepared model. It is necessary to accept how the lived experience in the West contributes to pushing young people toward extremism (Roy 2010). To look at the structure of societies and their popular culture is vital, where structural disadvantage is measurable, conflated by the extreme center of the political spectrum, which pushes out dissenting voices to the periphery. Opportunities are limited in a climate where the "us and them" dichotomy designed by the powerful affects the most powerless. Those who want to give the impression that everything else affecting people associated with these categories is insignificant in determining both the push and the pull wish to place the spotlight on Islam and Muslims.

Ultimately, those gravitating toward zones of conflict in the Middle East do so because of push and pull factors, but other individuals are also vulnerable. Huge generalizations are dangerous; such is the power of the media that even right-minded people can end up overstating the crises, ultimately fueling a perennial cycle of fear, hatred, and violence. Many other struggles affect Muslim communities across the globe, but misinformation routinely promulgated by self-serving interests fuels protestations on all sides. Muslims have far greater struggles than merely violent extremism. Moreover, around the world today Muslims are the victims of violent extremism more than any other group. Shias, Sufis, Christians, and Jews are all subject to their might. Religion provides the justification, but conundrums of integration, alienation, power, authority, and social class cannot be underestimated. Furthermore, ill-informed policy-making has its unintended consequences. In many of the instances of Muslim-originated violence found in Western Europe in the last few years, the role of the policing, security, and intelligence services remains unclear—not in how they managed to prevent these atrocities or otherwise, but in how many of the young men involved in the violence were on their radars, and in some cases had been picked up and allegedly mistreated by the authorities.

Concluding Thoughts

Muslims in the Global North are young, with one in three under the age of 15, which is consistent with the Muslim world population profiles. This particular dynamic has not shifted over the last decade and a half. Approximately two thirds of all the people on the move in the world today are Muslims, and current conflicts are often in the Muslim world. When the Muslim world is the most affected by neoliberal capitalism, it faces the greatest consequences of the destabilization of capitalism. In addition, while it is inevitable that Islamophobia has the ability to drive different radicalizations that create further Islamophobia, it is important to break this cycle, reverse engineering the process that leads to the deleterious consequences. But before this can happen, Muslim communities need to firmly own both concepts of *Islamophobia* and *radicalization* and define them from within, which means they do need to engage with the state in a meaningful dialogue in order to effectively challenge its workings. Speaking truth to power disrupts the speed, scope, and scale of the uncertainty faced today. However, we also live in the world of great ignorance, surpassed by bundles of arrogance. The consequences of globalization and unfettered capitalism are palpable. The dominant hegemon that is the present world order is bereft of any new ideas, partly based on the failures of ideas of all kinds, as political Islam and Western liberalism have both collapsed. One has a consequence for the "other," and the maintenance of these "self"-"other" identities perpetuates ongoing conflict.

The problems of the hypermasculinity of men and the unreconstructed nature of patriarchy that exists within households is at odds with wider society, where a gradual decline of masculinity and the improving nature of gender equality goes on in earnest in the Global North. A divergence emerges between the Muslim male mind within the home and the workings of wider society with respect to the role and position of Muslim women *and* women in general. Moreover, the "self"-"other" dichotomy remains a powerful force in the minds of people who believe in the absolute truth of their knowledge but without the wisdom or ability to think outside of their own self-contained, self-sealed boxes. This is an issue within all societies and all aspects of society including those with privileged access to power, status, and the ability to define an image of society based on their own self-image. These ongoing trends suggest that there will remain particular challenges of a socioeconomic and sociocultural nature, given the wider forces of hyper-capitalism and neoliberal globalization, and while these powers remain unchecked, Muslim minorities face all sorts of internal challenges as well as the ongoing effects of unreconstructed patriarchy. They are at a real risk of lagging further behind the curve. Assimilation is not an inevitability, but further integration is desirable in order to gain the power, the position, and the potential to bring about positive change to the collective human existence. Revolution can exist within an evolution. In this space, the decolonizing of minds, especially that of the Muslim male, is crucial.

For British Muslim groups, identities are shaped not by religion or minority culture, but by postindustrial spatiality due to the asymmetrical power relations inherent in postwar, post-colonial, and postindustrial societies, especially since the advent of neoliberal economics marking a retreat from the welfare states since the early 1970s. For ethnic minorities in Britain, migration backgrounds, socioeconomic integration, and social policy define the identities of diverse communities. Patterns of Islamization among current generation British-born Muslims, however, are currently at odds with conventional migration-integration theory, which suggests gradual adaptation over time. The arguments presented in this paper provide an opportunity to assess individual, collective, and postindustrial urban spatial formations, helping to understand group dynamics, modes of social conflict, and the development of politico-cultural identities that define the process of Islamized radicalization in an atmosphere of virulent Islamophobia. The challenges of Islamophobia and radicalization are not those that Muslims can undertake to solve by themselves. There are also issues of exclusion and racialization. There is a need for Muslim groups to work alongside each other and with other religious minority groups who face comparable systems of discrimination, intimidation, and violence. The net impact is to reduce the effectiveness of counter-competing narratives, resulting in wastefulness of resources and political opportunities.

REFERENCES

Abbas, Tahir. 2019. *Islamophobia and Radicalisation.* London and New York: Hurst and Oxford University Press.

Abbas, Tahir. 2012. "The Symbiotic Relationship Between Islamophobia and Radicalisation." *Critical Studies on Terrorism* 5 (3): 345–58.

Abbas, Tahir. 2011. *Islamic Radicalism and Multicultural Politics.* London and New York: Routledge.

Abbas, Tahir, and Asma Siddique. 2012. "Perceptions on the Processes of Radicalisation and De-Radicalisation Among British South Asian Muslims in a Postindustrial City." *Social Identities: Journal for the Study of Race, Nation and Culture* 18 (1): 119–34.

Abbas, Tahir, and Imran Awan. 2015. "Limits of UK Counterterrorism Policy and its Implications for Islamophobia and Far-right Extremism." *International Journal for Crime, Justice and Social Democracy* 4 (3): 16–29.

Adamson, Fiona B. 2016. "Spaces of Global Security: Beyond Methodological Nationalism." *Journal of Global Security Studies* 1 (1): 19–35.

Alam, Yunus, and Charles Husband. 2013. "Islamophobia, Community Cohesion and Counterterrorism Policies in Britain." *Patterns of Prejudice* 47 (3): 235–52.

Allen, Chris. 2011. "Opposing Islamification or Promoting Islamophobia? Understanding the English Defence League." *Patterns of Prejudice* 45 (4): 279–94.

Altikriti, Anas, and Salam Al-Mahadin. 2015. "Muslim 'Hate Preachers' in British Tabloids: Constructing the British Self and the Muslim Other." *European Journal of Cultural Studies* 18 (6): 620–38.

Amin, Ash. 2002. "Ethnicity and the Multicultural City: Living with Diversity." *Environment and Planning A* 34 (6): 959–80.

Arjana, Sophia Rose. 2015. *Muslims in the Western Imagination.* New York: Oxford University Press.

Arnold, Richard, and Ekaterina Romanova. 2013. "The 'White World's Future?': An Analysis of the Russian Far Right." *Journal for the Study of Radicalism* 7 (1): 79–107.

Baeten, Guy. 2001. "The Europeanization of Brussels and the Urbanization of 'Europe': Hybridizing the City, Empowerment and Disempowerment in the EU District." *European Urban and Regional Studies* 8 (2): 117–30.

Bhattacharyya, Gargi. 2008. *Dangerous Brown Men: Exploiting Sex, Violence and Feminism in the "War on Terror."* London and New York: Zed.

Choudhury, Tufyal, and Helen Fenwick. 2011. "The Impact of Counter-terrorism Measures on Muslim Communities." *International Review of Law, Computers & Technology* 25 (3): 151–81.

Cockbain, Ella. 2013. "Grooming and the 'Asian Sex Gang Predator': The Construction of a Racial Crime Threat." *Race & Class* 54 (4): 22–32.

Dalgaard-Nielsen, Anja. 2010. "Violent Radicalization in Europe: What We Know and What We Do Not Know." *Studies in Conflict & Terrorism* 33 (9): 797–814.

El-Haj, Abu, Thea Renda, and Sally Wesley Bonet. 2011. "Education, Citizenship, and the Politics of Belonging: Youth from Muslim Transnational Communities and the 'War on Terror.'" *Review of Research in Education* 35 (1): 29–59.

Esposito, John, and Derya Iner, eds. 2019. *Islamophobia and Radicalization: Breeding Intolerance and Violence*. Basingstoke: Palgrave-Macmillan.

Esposito, John, and Ibrahim Kalin, eds. 2011. *Islamophobia: The Challenge of Pluralism in the 21st Century*. New York: Oxford University Press.

Ferrera, Maurizio. 2014. "Ideology, Parties and Social Politics in Europe." *West European Politics* 37 (2): 420–48.

Fetzer, Joel S., and Christopher J. Soper. 2003. "The Roots of Public Attitudes toward State Accommodation of European Muslims' Religious Practices Before and After September 11." *Journal for the Scientific Study of Religion* 42 (2): 247–58.

Goodwin, Mathew. 2013. *The Roots of Extremism: The English Defence League and the Counter-Jihad Challenge*. London: Chatham House Briefing Paper.

Hopkins, Peter. 2006. "Youthful Muslim Masculinities: Gender and Generational Relations." *Transactions of the Institute of British Geographers* 31 (3): 337–52.

Isakjee, Arshad. 2016. "Dissonant Belongings: The Evolving Spatial Identities of Young Muslim Men in the UK." *Environment and Planning* A48 (7): 1337–53.

Jarvis, Lee, and Michael Lister. 2013. "Disconnected Citizenship? The Impacts of Anti-terrorism Policy on Citizenship in the UK." *Political Studies* 61 (3): 656–75.

Kalra, Virinder S. 2009. "Between Emasculation and Hypermasculinity: Theorizing British South Asian Masculinities." *South Asian Popular Culture* 7 (2): 113–25.

Kapoor, Nisha. 2013. "The Advancement of Racial Neoliberalism in Britain." *Ethnic and Racial Studies* 36 (6): 1028–46.

Kaufmann, Eric. 2017. "Why the Fear of Islamization is Driving Populist Right Support, and What to do About it." *LSE British Politics and Society*. March 16. http://blogs.lse.ac.uk/politicsandpolicy/why-the-fear-of-islamization-is-driving-populist-right-support

Khattab, Nabil, and Ron Johnston. 2014. "Ethnic and Religious Penalties in a Changing British Labour Market from 2002 to 2010: The Case of Unemployment." *Environment and Planning A* 45: 1358–71.

Kundnani, Arun. 2014. *The Muslims are Coming!* London and New York: Verso.

Kundnani, Arun. 2012. "Radicalisation: The Journey of a Concept." *Race & Class* 54 (2): 3–25.

Lentin, Alana. 2014. "Post-race, Post Politics: The Paradoxical Rise of Culture after Multiculturalism." *Ethnic and Racial Studies* 37 (8): 1268–85.

Lentin, Alana, and Gavin Titley. 2012. "The Crisis of 'Multiculturalism' in Europe: Mediated Minarets, Intolerable Subjects." *European Journal of Cultural Studies* 15 (2): 123–38.

Lucassen, Geertje, and Marcel Lubbers. 2012. "Who Fears What? Explaining Far-Right-Wing Preference in Europe by Distinguishing Perceived Cultural and Economic Ethnic Threats." *Comparative Political Studies* 45 (5): 547–74.

Lynch, Orla. 2013. "British Muslim Youth: Radicalisation, Terrorism and the Construction of the 'Other.'" *Critical Studies on Terrorism* 6 (2): 241–61.

Mac an Ghaill, Mairtin, and Chris Haywood. 2015. "British-Born Pakistani and Bangladeshi Young Men: Exploring Unstable Concepts of Muslim, Islamophobia and Racialization." *Critical Sociology* 41 (1): 97–114.

Mandaville, Peter. 2009. "Muslim Transnational Identity and State Responses in Europe and the UK after 9/11: Political Community, Ideology and Authority." *Journal of Ethnic and Migration Studies* 35 (3): 491–506.

McDowell, Linda. 2000. "The Trouble with Men? Young People, Gender Transformations and the Crisis of Masculinity." *International Journal of Urban and Regional Research* 24 (1): 201–9.

Mudde, Cas. 2005. "Racist Extremism in Central and Eastern Europe." *East European Politics and Societies* 19 (2): 161–84.

Open Society Institute. 2010. *Muslims in Europe A Report on 11 EU Cities*. Budapest: Open Society Institute.

Patel, Tina. 2013. "Ethnic Deviant Labels within a Terror-Panic Context: Excusing White Deviance." *Ethnicity and Race in a Changing World* 4 (1): 34–49.

Peach, Ceri. 1996. "The Meaning of Segregation." *Planning Practice and Research* 11 (2): 137–50.

Pisoiu, Daniela. 2015. "Subcultural Theory Applied to Jihadi and Right-Wing Radicalization in Germany." *Terrorism and Political Violence* 27 (1): 9–28.

Rai, Amit S. 2004. "Of Monsters: Biopower, Terrorism and Excess in Genealogies of Monstrosity." *Cultural Studies* 18 (4): 538–70.

Roald, Anne Sophie. 2013. "Majority Versus Minority: Governmentality and Muslims in Sweden." *Religions* 4 (1): 116–31.

Roy, Olivier. 2010. *Holy Ignorance: When Religion and Culture Part Ways*. London and New York: Hurst and Columbia University Press.

Saha, Anamik. 2012. "Beards, Scarves, Halal Meat, Terrorists, Forced Marriage: Television Industries and the Production of 'Race.'" *Media, Culture & Society* 34 (4): 424–38.

Sassen, Saskia. 1998. *Globalization and its Discontents: Essays on the New Mobility of People and Money*. New York: The New Press.

Saull, Richard. 2015. "Capitalism, Crisis and the Far-right in the Neoliberal Era." *Journal of International Relations and Development* 18 (1): 25–51.

Sayyid, Salman, and Abdoolkarim Vakil, eds. 2011. *Thinking through Islamophobia: Global Perspectives*. London and New York: Hurst/Columbia University Press.

Schiffer, Sabine, and Constantin Wagner. 2011. "Anti-Semitism and Islamophobia—New Enemies, Old Patterns." *Race & Class* 52 (3): 77–84.

Schuurman, Bart, Edwin Bakker, and Quirine Eijkman. 2016. "Structural Influences on Involvement in European Homegrown Jihadism: A Case Study." *Terrorism and Political Violence* 30 (1): 97–115.

Social Mobility Commission. 2016. *Tenders Sought for Research Project: What Is Breaking the Social Mobility Promise for Young Muslims?* London: Social Mobility Commission.

Strabac, Zan, and Ola Listhaug. 2008. "Anti-Muslim Prejudice in Europe: A Multilevel Analysis of Survey Data from 30 Countries." *Social Science Research* 37 (1): 268–86.

Sullivan, Alice, Samantha Parsons, Richard Wiggins, Anthony F. Heath, and Francis Green. 2014. "Social Origins, School Type and Higher Education Destinations." *Oxford Review of Education* 40 (6): 739–63.

Thomas, Paul, and Pete Sanderson. 2011. "Unwilling Citizens? Muslim Young People and National Identity." *Sociology* 45 (6): 1028–44.

Tyrer, David, and Salman Sayyid. 2012. "Governing Ghosts: Race, Incorporeality and Difference in Post-political Times." *Current Sociology* 60 (3): 353–67.

United States Government Accountability Office. 2017. *Countering Violent Extremism: Actions Needed to Define Strategy and Assess Progress of Federal Efforts GAO-17–300.* Washington, DC.

Williamson, Mary, and Gholam Khiabany. 2011. "State, Culture and Anti-Muslim Racism." *Global Media and Communication* 7 (3): 175–79.

World Policy Institute. 2011. "Anatomy of Islamophobia." *World Policy Journal* 28 (4): 14–15.

Concluding Remarks

Valérie Amiraux

Having reached the end of this volume, several findings now make themselves clear. The first certainly regards the ubiquity of the term "radicalization" in all the European public debates around security issues (internal and external) as well as the question of "living together." This phrase is now part of the public lexicon employed to speak about the relationship between unlike people sharing a particular space (joining other terms such as diversity, social bond, cohesion, living together, etc.). In this instance, however, it is used to talk about something that, in many aspects, doesn't seem to function as it should; when it is used in the context of the social sciences, it is more often than not associated with political rupture, violence, and acts of terrorism. The contributions collected in this volume therefore join two decades' worth of scholarship and serve to confirm the series of lessons contained therein. Notable among these lessons are the unpredictability of how and when agents of political violence in the name of Islam begin acting out, the importance of an interdisciplinary reading of the social trajectory of agents, the futility of looking for a universal "model" to explain the logics behind radicalization, and the fact that ideology alone doesn't explain everything. Since Clark McCauley and Sophia Moskalenko (2008), we know that ideology is at least as important as emotions and affects (love, confidence). In addition, as all the authors in this volume point out, since 2001 radicalization has been first and foremost treated as a security issue and one of international politics. The main contribution of this comparative volume (other than the monographic or conceptual incursions of each individual chapter) is primarily in the attention it pays to two dimensions that are usually underdeveloped or overlooked in most of the works in this field of study: first, the theoretical ambitions that unfold in the first part of this volume through disciplinary entries (Krieger, Meier-rieks, Morrison) and theoretical approaches (Pisoiu, Galonnier, Adraoui), and second, a systematized empirical approach toward national case studies (Teich, Settoul, Pelzer, Moeller, Bermejo-Casado, Abbas).

This volume takes previous work on radicalization into consideration, but distances itself in a constructive rather than critical fashion. Since the beginning of the 2000s, radicalization, whether culminating in violence (Crettiez 2016; Borum 2011a, 2011b) or not (McCauley and Moskalenko 2014; Sommier 2012) has been a subject of exponentially increasing inter-est for the humanities and social sciences (Kundnani 2012; Sedgwick 2010). First linked to the history of religions and theology, then to issues of secu-rity (Bramadat and Dawson 2014) and terrorism (Wilner and Dubouloz 2010; Bigo, Bonelli, and Deltombe 2008; Sageman 2004), it has recently migrated to other fields of application, of which the contributors gathered here are representatives. Since 2010, psychological and psychoanalytical approaches to the subject have multiplied (Lamote and Benslama 2017; King and Taylor 2011; Casoni and Brunet 2003), as have those privileging lexical analyses (Oddo 2014).

Just as in the European contexts discussed in this book, "radicalization" in Quebec, where I am while writing this conclusion, has been introduced into the public discourse in the aftermath of certain events (e.g., the inter-rogation of the cell known as the Toronto 18 in 2006, the foiled attack on Via Rail in 2013, the attack on the Ottawa parliament and in Saint-Jean-sur-Richelieu in 2014, interrogations of youth headed for Syria in 2015, etc.). From January to June 2015, the concept was employed to cover an entire set of wildly variable actualities as a way of qualifying processes that lead to deviant (i.e., criminal) behavior, as the focal point of a "Govern-ment Action Plan" (2015–18); as the raison d'être of the Center for Pre-vention of Radicalization Leading to Violence in Montreal; as a tool for a transnational reading of the individual trajectories of different "youth"; as a motive for the cooperation of public security agencies (provincial, fed-eral, foreign); as a social science concept; and as a category of theoretical consideration for various professional sectors, such as public health, public security, or education (Dejean et al. 2016). Both in politics and in media, the use of the word "radicalization" refers to a security framework and a psy-chologizing and atomized reading of trajectories that are often assessed in terms of a shift toward securitization. As is affirmed by most of the authors in this volume, the term is a contentious one and has lost all nuance. Ely-amine Settoul and Thierry Balzacq describe it as a "catch-all term" in their introduction. For Juliette Galonnier, it's a depoliticizing "buzzword." The contributors as well as the author of this conclusion unanimously see it as an object of disagreement. The ubiquity of its usage, its invocation by all sorts of very different actors, and its circulation in the media is not only apparent in the all the European contexts covered in this volume, but also here in Quebec. The term refers to phenomena as disparate as the radical left, racist hate speech, the rise of the extreme right, and jihadism (Alimi, Demetriou, and Bosi 2015). Deployed at once in the media, in politics, and sometimes in research, the term is summoned so often to describe and analyze that it serves only to confuse social problems with sociological problems (Berger and Luckmann, 1966). Radicalization operates both as a warning and a slogan, taking a common emotion and encapsulating it in technical terms. It works like a "prenotion" as per Émile Durkheim (1982 [1895]) or Pierre Bourdieu, Jean-Claude Chamboredon, and Jean-Claude Passeron (1968) insofar as it encompasses both description and analysis within a normative framework that makes it impossible not just to see, but above all to understand and depoliticize the word (Guibet-Lafaye and Rapin, 2017).

For the contributors to this volume, radicalization is a processual engagement in an extremist, political or religious, ideology. Jihadism, for example, is understood both as a moral performance and political prac-tice (Adraoui). And, as John Morrison explains in chapter 5, radicalization encompasses complex socio-psychological processes that differ from one person to another without necessarily serving as a precursor to any con-crete action. He explains that what one individual creates out of their radi-calization can be very different from the next, which underlines the impor-tance of keeping access open to a "diversity of viewpoints and beliefs" (Morrison, this vol.). As the chapters unfold, radicalization almost becomes a concept designating a form of interaction that generates distance if not outright rupture, as well as a change in an individual's relationship toward the values they hold dear. In this volume, radicalization and terrorism thus overlap only partially.

By setting this common perspective as a base, it becomes possible to build new bridges (e.g., by placing disparate and seemingly disconnected figures side by side: a convert to Islam who approaches his new religious practice with rigorous literalism, a violent terrorist, impassioned adoles-cents, lovers, etc.) and therefore to push the theoretical framework beyond the limited scope within which radicals, as a subject of institutional documentation, are usually interrogated or studied (Bonelli and Carrié 2018). A comparative framework allows for a shift in theoretical perspectives in order to, for example, try and improve the predictive capacity of economic models, which might be made possible by integrating the hypothesis that radicals are in fact rational actors with notions of bounded rationality, information costs, and radical organizations as profit-maximizing firms (Meierrieks and Krieger), or by prioritizing expansions into new, unexpected territories (Galonnier, Settoul). In their chapter dealing with the economic theories of radicalization, Daniel Meierrieks and Tim Krieger examine, for example, the differences in economic calculi depending on the various stages in the process of radicalization, from the perspective of both individuals and organizations. Socioeconomic deprivation, they explain, "may very well be important at the outset of the radicalization process but becomes less important as radicalization progresses" (chapter 1, this vol.).

Since the work undertaken by Donatella della Porta (1995, 2013), a survey of the growth of left-wing terrorist movements in Europe during the 1970s (Germany and Italy) is now practically a must on the theoretical level. Daniela Pisoiu underlines this by taking the contentious approach as her starting point, that is, that part of theory within the study of radicalization dealing with the most mobilized social movements. Simply transposing the theoretical framework of the analysis of social movements to the field of jihadist-inspired terrorism ignores two important dimensions, which Pisoiu describes as possible avenues for theoretical development: not only re-centering focus on the role of the individual and on social bonds, but also on the role of the production of parallel cultures, or alternative cultures within the logics of radicalization. To this end, both Pisoiu's and Morrison's contributions insist on the importance of including psychological processes in any analysis, therefore *also* invoking analytical tools in psychology. Often, individuals who go on to act out in their trajectory to radicalization have already had the experience of belonging to various forms of culture, of other attempts at social belonging in different peer groups. The suddenness of the passage to violence, no matter the scale, is one of the stages in an individual's path where counterculture becomes entangled with viral logic (Adraoui). As an ideology, Islamism has also historically been an "adaptive and flexible" force for mobilization (Akbarzadeh 2020). It is at this epistemological juncture, where the social sciences open up to psychology, that a more granular understanding of both the mechanism through which parallel moral universes are constructed, as well as those proposed and organized by jihadist counterculture, becomes possible.

On the empirical level, Galonnier and Settoul offer the most effective comparative examples, the first through a study of conversions (the different "subtypes of conversion," as they specify), and the second by considering jihadist commitment as a mirror reflection of military commitments in conventional armies. If the trajectories of radicalization can incarnate in violent and deviant expressions of the relationship to the political, such as terrorism, they can therefore also be read as relative and relational. What Pisoiu sketches out on the basis of the theory of social movements, Galonnier and Settoul systematize under different theoretical frameworks based on comparative approaches that allow the reader to understand, among other things, the centrality of collective life as well as the embodied practices and body politics in the socialization process of those who become radicalized. Disentangling radicalization from the readings of it that have dominated for the last 20 years allows us to pay equal attention to interactions, situations and institutions, and emotions (Collovald and Gaïti 2006), and to reconstruct the different levels or junctures where points of rupture might emerge, from moral indignation to racism, from a sense of unease or local discomfort all the way to physical aggression or self-harm behavior. Understanding these socio-spatial scales necessitates recognizing that the direct and mediatized relationship to otherness doesn't always play out in public, in such a way that is visible and accessible to all (Bender 2003; Eliasoph 1998). More often it is behind the scenes, in private, that the discourse, the practice, and also the mechanisms of identification, belonging, and self-worth become susceptible to coalescing around different finely contextualized motives and lexicons (Bayoumi 2015; Kundnani 2014). These elements do not become readable or intelligible until one takes the processes of socialization seriously.

The change in the profiles of those who undertake acts of terrorism in the name of a global jihadist ideology, such as those described in chapter 3 by Mohamed-Ali Adraoui through "spaces of jihadism," is one of the foremost observations of import in this volume. From the transnational and de-territorialized actors who undertook the attacks of September 11, 2001, in the name of a jihadist ideology, to the "lone wolves," "domestic terrorists," and "jihadists" responsible for more recent attacks carried out on both Muslim and non-Muslim territory (Akbarzadeh 2020), the profiles, networks, and even the types of violence are so motley that presupposing a homogeneity of driving convictions is simply no longer possible. Adraoui instead invites us to think about spaces of jihadism to connect the dots that mark the perimeters of adversity within which militants, soldiers, and "squads" embrace a global "mass counterculture" that exists in reference to an "ontological enmity" that in turn helps create a concept of radicalization even before identifying a target. The biggest difficulty for the analyst then lies in identifying what elements specifically pertain to radicalization, that is, pinpointing the quest for significance supported by this specific commitment as opposed to others, as well as the social connections and emotional bonds that drive it. Comparisons between extreme-right groups and radical Islamist ones are more than permissible: They highlight the moments in common along the process, such as the search for an identity. "Less well understood [however] is the structural contextualization facing both groups," as Tahir Abbas emphasizes, based on his work on the evolution of radical Islamism in urban centers in the UK (chapter 10, this vol.).

The authors of part II, dealing with case studies, make a very rich contribution to the volume. In addition to the always-important reminder that context matters, their work, for example, allows for a contrast between the process of framing and that of coding the grievances expressed within the social networks of radicalized individuals across a variety of different profiles (those who are socially marginalized; those who are socially successful) and histories (the quest for romance en route to Syria; the seduction of toxic ideologies in politicized Muslim minority groups). We meet ordinary people on extraordinary trajectories, individuals not just reacting to ideologies, but influenced by emotions, cognitions, and social influences. Social structure and identity politics, after all, are interconnected triggers (Abbas).

Radicalization: What the Word Does to Us, and What It Makes Us Do

Radicalization. In 2020, the word evokes a number of different effects, including fear, anxiety, interest, curiosity, conversation, excitement, and the desire to react, to name only a few. What the word evokes depends on who deploys it (a parent, a teacher, a policeman, a researcher), which social reality it designates (attitudes, words, gestures), and where it is introduced, which can be in any number of different situations and at the heart of multiple institutions (home, school, work, activist groups). All encompassing, the concept of radicalization has become almost generic, deployed both as a descriptor and a form of analysis. In the current context, in Quebec as in Western Europe, radicalization isn't the only term loaded with so much weight. On both sides of the Atlantic, "living together" also functions as a category of public action, a moral and social aspiration, and a norm. It has become at once prescriptive (an exhortation to "do good") and performative (a response modality through which to think about relationships between unlike people sharing a given space). Depending on the circumstances, "living together" can describe a reality, delineate a set of norms and rules that organize the practical conditions of how to accomplish plurality, or refer to a political program. But in this specific case, the effects of language are mitigated by the virtuous nature of the project: Who could possibly oppose the idea of living together? And therefore linking the divisive and alarming term "radicalization" to the euphemistic and consensual "living together,"[1] as in the 2015–18 action plan entitled *Radicalization in Quebec: Acting, Preventing, Detecting, and Living Together* launched in June 2015 by the Quebec government, is not an action without consequences.

As the American sociologist Howard Becker points out, representing social reality in general is the act of an interpretative community, that is, a group made up of individuals (called "makers") who produce standardized representations intended for other people (designated as "users") who will in turn use them routinely (Becker 2007). These representations have different effects depending on the situations in which actors call upon them to make sense of what is happening to them. They can thus be used to validate or invalidate convictions, alter judgments, and influence evaluations. Elsewhere, by using the removal of the headscarf by Muslim women in France, Belgium, and Quebec as an empirical point of reference, I set out the way in which gossip, as a type of discourse (Amiraux 2016), allows for certain types of representations to become fixed, or to be kept active and valid independent of the speaker's authority, thus maintaining their circulation in different arenas of public life.

This reminder with regards to the use of the term "radicalization" in Quebec as in Western Europe allows us to point out, first, the difficult articulation between, on the one hand, a space for public discussion in which the terminologies of government action are established and circulated (for example in the media and in the courts) and, on the other, the experiential contexts within which these same terminologies are experienced in the everyday by different types of actors, from the privacy of the home to the contiguity of urban spaces. A second difficulty arises from this first point. The dominance over the last 20 years of a securitarian definition of radicalization by provincial or federal public security agencies heightens the confusion between what these agencies point to as a social problem (i.e., that which doesn't function the way society ought, or the way official interpretations would have it function) and a sociological problem through

---

1. On the depoliticizing effects of consensual categories (diversity, living together) as compared to programs setting out an action plan to fight discrimination, for example, please see Bereni and Jaunait (2009).

which it would be possible to read the springs and determinants (i.e., that which happens in terms of interactions) (Amiraux and Araya-Moreno 2014).

The political dimension of radicalization runs through all the contributions in this volume. This is probably most clearly expressed in local spaces, particularly around issues of political participation and civic recognition. The texts dealing with national approaches (Belgium, France, Germany, Spain, the UK) elsewhere emphasize the importance of thinking about local situations within larger configurations. The dilemmas and moral puzzles produced by pluralism are simultaneously grasped by institutional actors who disembody them and through the lived experiences of social actors who embody them in concrete ways. Radicalization, as a sociological problem, cannot escape this dynamic. If politicization is constructed in direct relation to the logics of local situations (e.g., the push and pull factors in certain contexts, such as in the Belgian case that became a "major hotbed for radicalization in Europe," outlined by Teich in chapter 6), we must regardless not underestimate the impact of interactions with the state (which Pisoiu emphasizes as a co-creator of radicalization), of the policing of the radicalization of certain movements, and of the general "vilification of Muslims in dominant media and politics" (Abbas, chapter 10, this vol.). In Western Europe in general, debates on radicalization have also served to politicize the entire spiritual realm of Muslim citizens.

The debate might remain strictly theoretical if we don't take seriously the very real effects of the categorization of social problems. The current volume moreover masterfully invites us to reconcile the requirements of description and field work with the aspiration toward a theoretical approach that will dislodge the study of radicalization from its current place: exclusively as a subsection of Muslim minority studies. Trivializing radicalization as a category of public thought about Muslims does not only concern the risk prevention or security management agencies, which in a way set the conditions for any public debate on the subject by helping give a consensual varnish to the issue (fighting radicalization is a priority) without ever straying from the "solvent" effect (diluting issues within a unifying and standardized term). Radicalization, as a "global" category, effectively juxtaposes a multitude of scales and issues, and yet the seemingly reduced number of boys and girls now being identified as supposed "jihadi candidates" cannot but force us to regard them warily. This account sets the stage for the way I would like to invite scholars to "deal with radicalization in its complexity, to situate it as one possible outcome of a reciprocal process of interactions that can potentially increase the distance between groups and harden their representations of their differences" (Amiraux and Araya-Moreno 2014, 99–100). And that, above all, implicates us all as social actors.

REFERENCES

Akbarzadeh, Shahram. 2020. *Routledge Handbook of Political Islam*. London: Routledge.

Alimi, Eitan Y., Lorenzo Bosi, and Charles Demetriou. 2015. *The Dynamics of Radicalization: A Relational and Comparative Perspective*. New York: Oxford University Press.

Amiraux, Valérie. 2016. "Visibility, Transparency and Gossip: How Did the Religion of Some (Muslims) Become the Public Concern of Others?" *Critical Research on Religion* 4 (1): 37–56.

Amiraux, Valérie, and Javiera Araya-Moreno. 2014. "Religious Pluralism and Radicalization: The Missing Perspective?" In *Religion, Radicalization and Securitization in Canada and Beyond*, edited by Paul Bramadat and Lorne Dawson, 92–120. Toronto: University of Toronto Press.

Bayoumi, Moustafa. 2015. *This Muslim American Life: Dispatches from the War on Terror*. New York: New York University Press.

Becker, Howard S. 2007. *Telling About Society*. Chicago: University of Chicago Press.

Bender, Courtney. 2003. *Heaven's Kitchen: Living Religion at God's Love We Deliver*. Chicago: University of Chicago Press.

Berger, Peter, and Thomas Luckmann. 1966. *The Social Construction of Reality: A Treatise in the Sociology of Knowledge*. Garden City, NY: Anchor Books.

Bereni, Laure, and Alexandra Jaunait. 2009. "Usages de la Diversité." *Raisons Politiques* 35 (3): 5–9.

Bigo, Didier, Laurent Bonelli, and Thomas Deltombe. 2008. *Au Nom du 11 Septembre: Les Démocraties à l'Épreuve de l'Antiterrorisme*. Paris: La Découverte.

Bonelli, Laurent, and Fabien Carrié. 2018. *La Fabrique de la Radicalité. Une Sociologie des Jeunes Djihadistes Français*. Paris: Seuil.

Borum, Randy. 2011a. "Radicalization into Violent Extremism: A Review of Conceptual Models and Empirical Research." *Journal of Strategic Security* 4 (4): 7–36.

Borum, Randy. 2011b. "Radicalization into Violent Extremism II: A Review of Conceptual Models and Empirical Research." *Journal of Strategic Security* 4 (4): 37–62.

Bourdieu, Pierre, Jean-Claude Chamboredon, and Jean-Claude Passeron. 1968. *Le Métier de Sociologue: Préalables Épistémologiques*. Paris: Mouton de Gruyter.

Bramadat, Paul and Lorne Dawson. 2014. *Religion, Radicalization and Securitization in Canada and Beyond*. Toronto: University of Toronto Press.

Casoni, Dianne, and Louis Brunet. 2003. *Comprendre l'Acte Terroriste*. Sainte-Foy: Presses de l'Université du Québec.

Collovald, Annie, and Brigitte Gaïti. 2006. *La Démocratie aux Extrêmes: Sur la Radicalisation Politique*. Paris: La Dispute.

Crettiez, Xavier. 2016. "Penser la Radicalisation: Une Sociologie Processuelle des Variables de L'engagement Violent." *Revue Française de Science Politique* 66 (5): 709–27.

Dejean, Frédéric, Sarah Mainich, Bochra Manaï, and Leslie Touré Kapo. 2016. *Les Étudiants Face à la Radicalisation Religieuse Conduisant à la Violence: Mieux les Connaître pour Mieux Prévenir*. Institut de Recherche sur l'Intégration Professionnelle des Immigrants, Collège de Maisonneuve.

della Porta, Donatella. 1995. *Social Movements, Political Violence and the State: A Comparative Analysis of Italy and Germany*. Cambridge: Cambridge University Press.

della Porta, Donatella. 2013. *Clandestine Political Violence*. Cambridge: Cambridge University Press.

Durkheim, Émile. 1982 [1895]. *The Rules of the Sociological Method*. Translated by W. D. Halls. New York: The Free Press.

Eliasoph, Nina. 1998. *Avoiding Politics How Americans Produce Apathy in Everyday Life*. Cambridge: Cambridge University Press.

Guibet-Lafaye, Caroline, and Ami-Jacques Rapin. 2017. "La 'Radicalisation': Individualisation et Dépolitisation d'Une Notion." *Politiques de Communication*. 1 (8): 127–54.

King, Michael, and Donald Taylor. 2011. "The Radicalization of Homegrown Jihadists: A Review of Theoretical Models and Social Psychological Evidence." *Terrorism and Political Violence* 23 (4): 602–22.

Kundnani, Arun. 2014. *The Muslims are Coming! Islamophobia, Extremism, and the Domestic War on Terror*. London: Verso.

Kundnani, Arun. 2012. "Radicalisation: The Journey of a Concept." *Race & Class* 54 (2): 3–25.

Lamote, Thierry, and Fethi Benslama. 2017. "'The Islamo-Occidental Ecological Niche,' The Matrix of Islamist Radicalization." *Research in Psychoanalysis* 23 (1): 15–26.

McCauley, Clark, and Sophia Moskalenko. 2014. "Toward a Profile of Lone Wolf Terrorists: What Moves an Individual from Radical Opinion to Radical Action." *Terrorism and Political Violence* 26 (1): 69–85.

McCauley, Clark, and Sophia Moskalenko. 2008. "Mechanisms of Political Radicalization: Pathways Toward Terrorism." *Terrorism and Political Violence* 20 (3): 415–33.

Oddo, John. 2014. "Variation and Continuity in Intertextual Rhetoric: From the 'War on Terror' to the 'Struggle against Violent Extremism.'" *Journal of Language and Politics* 13 (3): 512–37.

Sageman, Marc. 2004. *Understanding Terror Networks*. Philadelphia: University of Pennsylvania Press.

Sedgwick, Mark. 2010. "The Concept of Radicalization as a Source of Confusion." *Terrorism and Political Violence* 22 (4): 479–94.

Sommier, Isabelle. 2012. "Engagement Radical, Désengagement et Déradicalisation: Continuum et Lignes de Fracture." *Lien Social et Politiques* 68: 15–35.

Wilner, Alex S., and Claire-Jehanne Dubouloz. 2010. "Homegrown Terrorism and Transformative Learning: An Interdisciplinary Approach to Understanding Radicalization." *Global Change, Peace & Security* 22 (1): 33–51.

Contributors

Thierry Balzacq is Professor of Political Science at Sciences Po Paris. He was formerly a Francqui Research Chair (the highest academic title awarded in Belgium) and Visiting Professor at the London School of Economics and Political Science (LSE). He was the Scientific Director of the Institute for Strategic Research (IRSEM), the French Ministry of Defense's research center (2014–2016). Balzacq holds a PhD from the University of Cambridge. A former Postdoctoral Fellow at Harvard, Balzacq held an Honorary Professorial Fellow at the University of Edinburgh, where he was also Fellow for "outstanding research" at the Institute for Advanced Studies in the Humanities. In 2015, he was awarded a Tier 1 Canada Research Chair in Diplomacy and International Security (valued at CAD 200,000 per year). "Tier 1 Chairs are for outstanding researchers acknowledged by their peers as world leaders in their fields." His articles have been published in (or are forthcoming with) *Security Studies*, *Review of International Studies*, *European Journal of International Security*, *International Studies Review*, *Cooperation and Conflict*, *European Journal of International Relations*, *Security Dialogue*, *International Relations*, and the *Journal of Common Market Studies*. He is author/editor of over 13 books in English and French.

Elyamine Settoul is Lecturer at the CNAM in Paris. He holds a PhD of Political Science from Sciences Po Paris (2012). He has been a visiting doctoral student at Oxford University (OxPo 2011), a postdoctoral researcher at the *Institut National d'Etudes Démographiques* (2012–2013), and a Jean Monnet researcher at the Robert Schuman Centre for Advanced Studies of the European University Institute in Florence (2013–2015). His research focuses on security/defense issues, themes related to ethnicity and migration phenomena as well as radicalization. He participated in multiple national and international projects and is a radicalization expert for numerous actors (observatory of radicalizations, ministries, local authorities, prison administration, etc.). He was also Lecturer at Sciences Po Paris. He is a member of the reading committee of the journal *Champs de Mars* (*Presses de Sciences Po*). He created and currently directs the "Prevention of Radicalization" specialization certificate at the CNAM. His latest publication is *Comprendre la Radicalisation: Acteurs, Enjeux et Théories*, Presses Universitaires de France, 2022.

Contributors

Tahir Abbas, PhD, FRSA, is currently Visiting Senior Fellow at the Department of Government at the London School of Economics. Previously, he was Senior Research Fellow at the Royal United Services Institute (2016–17), a Professor of Sociology at Fatih University in Istanbul, Reader in Sociology at Birmingham University, and Senior Research Officer at the Home Office and Ministry of Justice in London. He lived and worked in Istanbul for six years, during which time he was also a visiting scholar at New York University, Leiden University, Hebrew University in Jerusalem, International Islamic University in Islamabad, and the Syarif Hidayatullah State Islamic University in Jakarta. He conducts research on ethnicity, Islam, political violence, and terrorism, publishing *Contemporary Turkey in Conflict* (Edinburgh University Press, 2016) shortly after the failed-coup events of July 2016. He is also editor of the four-volume *Muslim Diasporas in the West* (Routledge, 2017) and co-editor of *Political Muslims: Understanding Youth Resistance in a Global Context* (Syracuse University Press, 2018, with S. Hamid). Abbas has published over 50 peer-reviewed journal articles, book chapters, and encyclopedic entries. He has also published numerous review essays and opinion-editorials. Abbas read Economics at Queen Mary University of London. He has a MSocSc in Economic Development and Policy from the University of Birmingham and a PhD in Ethnic Relations from the University of Warwick. He is a Fellow of the Royal Society of Arts and Associate Editor of the quarterly magazine *Critical Muslim*, published by Hurst and Oxford University Press.

Mohamed-Ali Adraoui was Senior Fellow at the Middle East Institute at the National University of Singapore (NUS). He is now a Marie Curie Global Fellow at the LSE. His research deals with the history and sociology of Salafism, and his doctoral dissertation investigated how this religiosity has gone global from the Gulf to the West over the last decades. This work was published in French in 2013 under the title *Du Golfe aux Banlieues: Le Salafisme Mondialisé*, and an English version is to be published soon. His other work centers on study of historical and contemporary International Relations with a specific focus on the Middle East and Transnational Islamic mobilizations. In 2015, he edited a volume titled *Les Islamistes et le Monde: Islam Politique et Relations Internationales*. This volume raised the issue of the foreign policies of Islamist movements in several Muslims countries (Turkey, Egypt, Palestine, Lebanon, Tunisia, and Morocco). Finally, over the last few years, he has been conducting intense fieldwork about the issue of radicalization of some Muslims in Europe, the Arab world and Southeast Asia. Adraoui holds a PhD from Sciences Po and is affiliated with the "Observatory of Radicalizations" at the EHESS in Paris. He is a former Max Weber Fellow at the European University Institute in Florence. His recent book is titled *Salafism Goes Global* (Oxford University Press, 2020).

Valérie Amiraux holds a PhD from Sciences Po Paris and has been Professor of Sociology at Université de Montréal's Faculty of Arts and Science since 2007. For 10 years, she held the Canada Research Chair for the Study of Religious Pluralism, under which her initial projects involved the transnational mobilization of Islamic political players between Germany and Turkey, and a review of investigation practices in the social science. Since 2007, she has been interested in the place of religious topics, particularly through the study of relations between religious minorities and governments of secular societies. The transfer of knowledge beyond academic circles has a special place in all this work, whether in the form of an exhibition catalogue, a comic strip, or a web documentary. In the Faculty of Arts and Science, Valérie Amiraux served as Vice-Dean of International Partnerships from 2017 to 2020, and Faculty Secretary from 2018 to 2020. She has been the managing editor of the *Sociologie et Sociétés* journal since September 2016 and was elected to the Royal Society of Canada in 2017.

Rut Bermejo-Casado is Associate Professor in Politics at the Law and Social Sciences Faculty (Rey Juan Carlos University-URJC) in Madrid. She holds a PhD from Juan Carlos University (2007), an MA in Politics from the University of Warwick (2004), a BA in Politics and Sociology (1996), and BA in Law (UCM) (1996). She coordinates the MA in Criminal Profiling at the URJC. She has been Researcher on international terrorism at the Elcano Think Tank (2005–2008) and Visiting Research Fellow at the University of Nottingham (2008). Her research areas include justice and home affairs and public policies. She has published dozens of journal articles and book chapters on these subjects. She has participated in national and international projects such as "PRACTICIES: Partnership Against Violent Radicalisation in Cities" (H2020). She has been a member of the Working Group on Training and the Working Group on Strategic Communication since 2014. Both working groups were set up by CITCO (Centre for Intelligence on Terrorism and Organised Crime, Ministry of Interior) in order to implement the Spanish Plan to Fight Against Violent Radicalisation. She is also part of the CITCO's team at the RAN (Radicalisation Awareness Network).

Juliette Galonnier is Assistant Professor in Political Science at Sciences Po/CERI, Paris. She studies the social construction of racial and religious categories, and how they frequently intersect. Empirically, her work has mostly focused on Muslim minorities across various national contexts (India, France, the United States). She received in 2017 a joint PhD in Sociology from Northwestern University and Sciences Po. Entitled *Choosing Faith and Facing Race: Converting to Islam in France and the United States*, her dissertation received the Best Dissertation Award from the American Sociological Association in 2018. This research provides a comparative analysis of the experiences of converts to Islam in France and the United States. On this topic, she has published several book chapters and articles in academic journals such as *French Politics, Culture and Society, Sociology of Religion, Social Compass*, and *Genèses*.

Tim Krieger is the Wilfried Guth Professor of Constitutional Political Economy and Competition Policy at Albert-Ludwigs-University of Freiburg, Germany. He holds a master's degree in empirical economics from the University of Kiel and received his PhD in economics from the University of Munich. He worked as an assistant and interim professor at the Universities of Mainz, Marburg, and Paderborn. His research focuses on economic, social, and education policies in aging and globalizing societies with a special focus national and supranational institutions. In addition, he specializes in the economics of conflict, terrorism, and crime. He has published in international scholarly journals in both economics and political science, including the *Journal of Public Economics*, the *Journal of International Economics*, the *Journal of Conflict Resolution*, and the *Journal of Peace Research*.

Daniel Meierrieks is a senior research associate at the WZB Berlin Social Science Center. After having received a PhD in economics from the University of Paderborn, he held research and teaching tenures at the University of Freiburg and the University of Kiel. His research interests include the economic analysis of terrorism and political violence. His research has been published in leading economics and political science journals such as the *Journal of Peace Research*, the *Journal of Conflict Resolution*, and *Defence and Peace Economics*.

Mika Josephine Moeller is a psychologist and researcher on processes of radicalization, disengagement, and reintegration in the field of Salafist-jihadist extremism. Between 2017 and 2021, she worked as a research associate at the Centre for Technology and Society | Technical University of Berlin in the department of "security, risk and criminology" in various research projects on the subject of (de-)radicalization. Her PhD study focuses on the individual developmental dynamics and biographical pathways of Salafist-jihadist radicalization. She held a lecturer position in qualitative research methods at the International Psychoanalytic University and is a research fellow at Freie Universität Berlin and Technische Universität Berlin.

John F. Morrison is a Senior Lecturer at Royal Holloway, University of London. He is an expert on violent dissident Irish republicanism, organizational fragmentation, radicalization, and broader issues relating to the psychology of terrorist involvement. He is an editorial board member of *Perspectives on Terrorism* and *Behavioral Sciences of Terrorism and Political Aggression* and is the founding director of the Terrorism and Extremism Research Centre (TERC) at the University of East London. In 2016, alongside Dr. Paul Gill of University College London, he co-edited a special issue of *Terrorism and Political Violence* that looked at 100 years of Irish Republican paramilitary activity from 1916 to 2016. In 2014, his first book, *The Origins and Rise of Dissident Irish Republicanism*, was published with Bloomsbury Academic Press and was based on extensive interviews with leadership and rank-and-file members of Irish Republican paramilitary and political groups. Prior to joining UEL John was a postdoctoral research fellow at the International Center for the Study of Terrorism (ICST) at

Pennsylvania State University. Dr. Morrison's current research interests relate to the role of trust in terrorist decision-making, violent radicalization, violent dissident Irish republicanism, and expert novice differences in terrorist activity. Dr. Morrison holds a PhD in International Relations from the University of St. Andrews, an MSc in Forensic Psychology from University College Cork, and a BA in Psychology from University College Dublin.

Robert Pelzer is a postdoctoral researcher at the Centre for Technology and Society (CTS) at the Technical University of Berlin. His main research areas are political violence and terrorism, police research, and reconstructive social research. He studied sociology and criminology and has completed his PhD study at Hamburg University—Institute for Criminological Social Research—on the topic of jihadist attacks in Europe and the patterns of meaning of individual offenders. Between 2010 and 2013, he was a research associate at University of Hamburg in a project on jihadist target selection. Between 2009 and 2010, he worked as a research associate at the Institute for Criminology at Free University of Berlin on a project about violent clashes between the police and protesters during manifestations on the first of May in Berlin-Kreuzberg. In his current research project, he is investigating semantic and interactive patterns of online communication of Salafi-jihadists and right-wing extremists in different stages of radicalization including the transition into violence.

Daniela Pisoiu is Senior Researcher at the Austrian Institute for International Affairs. Before that, she was researcher at the Institute for Peace Research and Security Policy at the University of Hamburg. Her fields of research are terrorism, radicalization, extremism, comparative regional security, and American and European foreign and security policy. She completed her PhD at the University of St Andrews, Centre for the Study of Terrorism and Political Violence, and has conducted fieldwork on the topic of radicalization in Austria, Germany, and France, as well as other European countries. She is the author of *Islamist Radicalisation in Europe: An Occupational Change Process* (2011/2012), and editor of *Arguing Counterterrorism: New Perspectives* (2014), both with Routledge.

Sarah Teich is an international human rights lawyer based in Toronto, Canada. She represents victims of atrocity crimes and human rights abuses including victims of terrorism, and is a legal advisor to the Canadian Coalition Against Terror, a non-profit organization which was founded by terror victims in the aftermath of 9/11. Prior to establishing her legal practice, Sarah conducted research at the Global Justice Lab in Toronto, Canada, on matters relating to the intersection of human rights and counter-terrorism. Sarah holds a Juris Doctor degree from the University of Toronto, an M.A. magna cum laude in Counter-Terrorism from Reichman University, and undergraduate degrees in Psychology and Sociology from McGill University. She also studied law at the National University of Singapore and worked on classified projects at the International Criminal Court in The Hague. She is a senior fellow at the Macdonald-Laurier Institute, and a director of the International Tamil Refugee Assistance Network. Her published works relating to counter-terrorism include "Trends and Developments in Lone Wolf Terrorism in the Western World" (2013), "Islamic Radicalization in Belgium" (2016), "Fighting Back against Global Hostage-Taking" (2021), and "The Troubled Homecoming: Seeking Accountability against Canadian Foreign Fighters Returning Home from Abroad" (2022).

Index

Abaaoud, Abdelhamid, 151–52, 153, 155, 158, 161
Abballa, Larossi, 80
Abbas, Tahir, 17, 237–51
Abdeslam, Ibrahim, 151–52, 155, 160–61
Abdeslam, Salah, 151–52, 155, 160–61
Abou-Nagie, Ibrahim, 191
Abouyaaqoub, Younes, 212
action militarization, 49, 51–52
activism, as stage in radicalization, 30
actor model, devoted, 51
actor-observer effect, 131–32
actors, rational. *See* rational choice
Adraoui, Mohamed-Ali, 15, 68–90, 99
Afghanistan: Afghan War and rise of jihadism, 74–75, 77; and enemy identification, 77; foreign fighters in, 171
age: and Belgium integration, 145–46, 158; and Belgium radicalization, 153, 154; in economic theory, 32; and French radicalization, 169; and German radicalization, 186; and identity-seeking behavior, 177, 182; of recruiters, 229; and Spanish radicalization, 219–20, 224; and UK radicalization, 241, 250. *See also* generational differences
agency: and conversion, 102–3, 109; and recruitment, 225. *See also* rational choice

Aglif, Rachid, 230
Ahrouch, Redouane, 159–60
Algeria: and enemy identification, 77; foreign fighters from, 12
Al Ghurabaa, 242
Ali, Ayanle Hassan, 174
alienation: and conversion, 98; from social ties, 128; in UK, 237, 238
Alimi, Eitan, 4, 54
Allen, Charles, 4
Al Muhajiroun, 242
Alonso, Rogelio, 227–28
Al-Qaeda: and Azizi, 220; and converts, 95; and enemy, 76, 77–78, 81, 84, 88; mechanisms of, 54; September 11 attacks, 78, 88; and Spain, 212, 219–20, 232; sponsorship paradigm, 89; and squad formation, 86
altruism, 62
Altunbas, Yener, 32
Amiraux, Valérie, 17, 255–63
Ansar Al-Sharia, 180
al-Ansariyya, Sayfillah, 197n7
anti-immigration parties, 147, 148, 244
Antwerp: as center of radicalization, 12n4, 153; Muslim population in, 144
Araj, Bader, 57
Armed Islamic Group (Algeria), 77
Asad, Talal, 108

Atran, Scott, 11, 170
attribution error, 131–32
authority: and framing, 63; and Islamic clergy, 9, 82; sacred, 9
Awan, Akil, 227
Azizi, Amer, 220, 226

Bakker, Edwin, 218
El Bakraoui, Ibrahim, 151–52, 153, 155, 161
El Bakraoui, Khalid, 151–52, 155, 161
Bakri, Omar, 60, 148
Balch, Robert, 107
Balzacq, Thierry, 1–17, 257
banlieues, 168
al-Banna, Hassan, 74
Barcelona attack (2017), 16, 212, 216, 219–20, 224, 226, 231, 232
Basque separatists. *See* ETA (Euskadi Ta Askatasuna)
Basuchoudhary, Atin, 35
Becker, Gary S., 24
Becker, Howard, 104, 106
behavioral radicalization, 23, 108–9, 226
Bélanger, Jocelyn, 8–9
Ben Belgacem, Ziyed, 174
Belgium, 143–63; areas of radicalization in, 12n4, 153–54; as center of radicalization, 12, 16; and converts, 95, 144; foreign fighters from, 16, 143, 149, 150, 151, 153–54, 158, 159, 162, 221; government funding of Islam in, 143, 147–48, 158–59; integration in, 143, 145–46, 147, 158, 162, 163; interconnectedness of groups in, 160–62; Muslim population in, 144; and Paris 2015 attack, 16, 143, 148, 150, 151, 159, 162; recruitment in, 148–52, 156–60, 162; and social movement theory, 16, 143–44, 154–62; socioeconomic factors in, 143–48, 153–54, 157–59, 162–63; table of cases, 155
Belgium, attacks in: Brussels (2016), 140, 143, 151, 159, 162; Jewish Museum attack (2014), 16n5, 151; Thalys train attempt (2015), 151, 161
Belkacem, Fouad, 147, 149, 155, 158, 159
Belkaid, Mohamed, 151

benefits and economic theory, 14, 28–31, 39, 40–41, 120–21
Benmelech, Efraim, 38
Bermejo-Casado, Rut, 16–17, 212–33
Berrebi, Claude, 38
bifurcation, biographical, 179
binary thinking: as challenge, 250; and framing, 63; in France, 169; and identity uncertainty, 134; and ideological encapsulation, 52; and military commitment, 178; and permanent state of war, 86; and social conditioning, 9; and social movement theory, 52, 63; in UK, 248, 250
biographical bifurcation, 179
Bjorgo, Tore, 7
Blomberg, S. Brock, 30, 34
body and embodiment: and conversion, 15, 107–9, 110; and military commitment, 176, 179; and radicalization, 108–9, 110, 176, 179
Borum, Randy, 124, 125–26, 130, 218, 225
Bosi, Lorenzo, 4, 54
Bouhana, Noémie, 123–24
Boulahcen, Hasna Ait, 175
boundary activation, 54
bounded rationality, 27, 29, 31, 39
Bourdieu, Pierre, 257
Bouzar, Dounia, 171n3
brainwashing, 58, 96, 100, 102, 171, 226
Brexit, 245, 247
Bromley, David, 107
Bruguière, Jean-Louis, 96
Brussels: 2016 attack, 140, 143, 151, 159, 162; as center of radicalization, 153–54; Jewish Museum attack (2014), 16n5, 151; Muslim population in, 144
Brym, Robert J., 57

Canada: attacks in, 174, 227, 256; policy on radicalization, 256–57
Catalonia attack. *See* Barcelona attack (2017)
causes and goals: desire for, 15; unaddressed causes, 2
causes of radicalization: and facilitating conditions, 6, 7–9; in Radicalization Awareness Network, 224; in social

movement theory, 53–55; theory overview, 6–7

Cavalcanti, H. B., 106

Center for Prevention of Radicalization Leading to Violence, 256

Chalfant, H. Paul, 106

Chamboredon, Jean-Claude, 257

Chand, Steven Vikash, 175

change and conversion, 103–4

chants and songs, 178, 195, 196

Charlie Hebdo attack, 88

Chechnya, 56, 170, 226

Chen, Carolyn, 107

"chic jihad," 228

Choudary, Anjem, 148, 242

CITCO, 215

citizenship: Belgium, 146; Spain, 217; UK, 237, 244, 246

civilians as enemy, 76–78, 80–81, 84–85, 88

clergy, Islamic: and framing, 63; role in countering radicalization, 225; role of authority, 9, 82

closure, 135

cognition: cognitive dissonance, 59; cognitive mechanisms, 53; and conversion, 107–8

cognitive opening, 8–9, 59–60

cognitive radicalization, 4, 225–26

collective action, 31, 48, 125

collective life, 105–7

colonialism, 12

competition: competitive escalation, 14, 49, 50, 188; between groups, 54, 55, 161; within groups, 51, 161

containing, 176

contexts and social psychology, 123–24

convertitis, 97–99, 100

converts and conversion, 93–111; in Belgium, 95, 144; conversion as process, 109–10; conversion term, 94; in France, 95, 96, 99; in Germany, 187, 189; internal *vs.* external, 94; and likelihood of radicalization, 94–101; and liminality, 97–99, 109; mass conversion, 105–6; mechanisms of, 95; numbers of, 95–96, 221; overview of, 15, 93–94; as process, 103–4; radicalization as subtype of conversion,

94, 101–9, 189; second-generation converts, 111; in Spain, 219, 220, 226; in UK, 95, 96

"cool jihad," 228

Cordiez, Cédric, 174

costs: and economic theory, 14, 28–31, 39, 41; opportunity costs, 28–31, 39; and social movement theory, 58

counterculture: jihadism as, 11, 15, 90, 258, 259–60; and social movement theory, 58; viral *vs.* command logic, 15

countermovements: and object shifts, 55. *See also* right-wing radicalization and parties

counter-radicalization and de-radicalization: in Belgium, 162–63; and context, 123; in France, 171; in Netherlands, 206; and socioeconomic conditions, 29; in Spain, 215–16

courage, 62

creativity in attacks, 80, 89–90

Crenshaw, Martha, 69

criminals and criminality: in Belgium, 150–51, 152, 153, 154, 159; as common factor, 10–11, 228; and economic model, 24, 26–27, 40; in France, 169; in Germany, 187, 202–3, 204; radicalization as justification for, 150–51; in Spain, 220–21, 222, 229–31; and youth subculture, 64. *See also* prison

Crone, Manni, 108

Cuso, 196–97

Cuspert, Denis, 16, 189, 193, 194, 198–99, 202–8

Daesh. *See* Islamic State/Daesh

Dalgaard-Nielsen, Anja, 23, 156, 226–27

DawaFFM, 196

da'wa in Germany, 188–94, 198–204

death, fascination with, 10, 11, 167

deconversion, 111

deindividuation, 131, 178

deindustrialization, 17, 240, 246, 248

de Koning, Martijn, 206

della Porta, Donatella, 48–52, 54, 57–58, 60, 128, 157, 188, 207

demand: in economic theory, 24, 36–39, 40; and opportunistic terrorism, 90

Demetriou, Chares, 4, 54

demographic factors. *See* socioeconomic factors

demographic stress, 35

Denis, Jean-Louis, 149–50, 151, 154, 155, 159, 161

deprivation: and quest for significance, 133; relative, 124–25, 222

de-radicalization. *See* counter-radicalization and de-radicalization

Deso Dogg. *See* Cuspert, Denis

deviance: and identity, 104; and relative deprivation, 125. *See also* criminals and criminality

devoted actor model, 51

Dewinter, Filip, 147

Diaby, Omar, 130, 172–73

Die Wahre Religion, 191, 193, 196

diffusion, 54

discipline: and conversion, 104, 108; and German radicalization, 189; and military commitment, 176

discrimination: in Belgium, 143, 145, 146–47, 158, 162, 163; and economic theory, 35; in France, 168; as general factor, 224; and geographic differences in radicalization, 12; and social psychology, 124–25, 128–29; in UK, 238–39, 241, 242. *See also* Islamophobia

disinformation, 247, 249

Doosje, Bertjan, 2, 135–36

Dumont, Lionel, 175

Durkheim, Émile, 257

duty, 81–85, 171, 191, 205

economic policy, 34–35, 40–41

economic theory, 23–41; and demand, 24, 36–39, 40; economic calculus, 27–31, 35, 120–21; overview, 14, 23–26; socioeconomic factors in, 14, 24, 26, 29–30, 31–36, 38–40; and supply, 24, 26–36, 37, 40. *See also* rational choice

education level as factor: in Belgium, 143, 144, 145, 153, 154, 157, 162, 163; in economic theory, 32–33; of recruiters, 229; and recruitment, 38–39, 40; in Spain, 219; in UK, 241

Egypt: escalating policing in, 49; and Muslim Brotherhood, 73–74; rise of jihadism in, 74, 76

Einladung zum Paradies, 190–91

Elcano, 219, 220

embodiment. *See* body and embodiment

employment as factor, low: in Belgium, 143, 144–45, 153, 154, 157, 158, 162, 163; in France, 168; in UK, 241, 242

enclosure, militant, 49, 51–52

enemies: civilians as, 76–78, 80–81, 84–85, 88; co-religionists as, 81–82, 84–85; demonization of, 9; depersonalization of, 60; identifying, 71, 72–73, 75–81, 84–85; and identity, 82, 134; as open-ended/indiscriminant, 76, 79, 80–81, 84–85; radicalization before identifying, 80–81, 89, 90; states as, 76, 77, 78, 79, 88

English Defence League, 242

enrollment *vs.* recruitment, 84, 87

entrepreneurs, terrorism, 23–24, 36–39, 40

environmental mechanisms, 53

escalation: competitive escalation, 14, 49, 50, 188; escalating policing, 49–50, 188, 207, 208; and social movement theory, 49

Es Satty, Abdelbaki, 216, 220–21, 226, 230

ETA (Euskadi Ta Askatasuna): and escalating policing, 49; mechanisms in social movement theory, 54; patterns of radicalization, 228–29; recruitment by, 231; terrorism by, 16–17, 212, 214–15, 223–24

ethnic tensions, 35

Europe: converts in, 95–96, 221; increase in radicalization, 24; Islamophobia in, 243–44; Muslim population in, 95–96; radicalization as Western phenomenon, 9–10, 26; socioeconomic factors in, 224; terrorism attacks in, 24, 25

exception and jihadism, 70, 71–73

extremism, as stage in radicalization, 30

factors. *See* causes of radicalization; socioeconomic factors

family: fathers, 11, 172–73, 176, 177–78; and military commitment, 176–77, 182; and recruitment, 50–51, 226; siblings, 51, 152, 161; and social movement theory, 50–51, 57–58; and Spanish radicalization, 226. *See also* social networks

fathers, 11, 172–73, 176, 177–78

Fer, Yannick, 106

Finn, Thomas, 103

Flower, Scott, 95

foreign fighters: in Afghanistan, 171; from Algeria, 12; from Belgium, 16, 143, 149, 150, 151, 153–54, 158, 159, 162, 221; differences in place of origin, 12–13; diversity of, 166; from France, 16, 130, 166–74; from Germany, 16, 186–87, 188, 191, 192, 198, 207, 221; increase in, 26; motivations of, 10, 11, 169–74; from Netherlands, 221; patterns in, 229; religious knowledge of, 159, 248; from Spain, 16, 213, 214, 219, 221; use of as cannon fodder, 38n7; in Yugoslavia, 171

framing theory, 48, 60, 62–63, 156–60

France, 166–82; as center of radicalization, 12, 16; centers of radicalization in, 12n4, 130; colonialism, 12; and converts, 95, 96, 99; as enemy, 88; foreign fighters from, 16, 130, 166–74; influencers in, 130; military commitment comparison, 16, 167, 173–82; Muslim population in, 168; secularism policy, 167–68; socioeconomic factors in, 166, 168, 176–77, 182

France, attacks in: beheading of Hamel, 81; *Charlie Hebdo* attack, 88; Nice truck attack, 130; Paris 1995 attack, 10n1, 77n10; Paris 2015 attack, 16, 24, 25, 143, 148, 150, 151, 159, 162; on police, 80; on soldiers, 174–75

Freytag, Andreas, 30, 34

friendship, 50–51, 57–58, 127–28. *See also* social networks

fundamental attribution error, 131–32

Gaibulloev, Khusrav, 35n5

Galonnier, Juliette, 15, 93–111, 257

Gambetta, Diego, 32

García-Arenal, Mercedes, 94

García-Calvo, Carola, 213n3, 223n16, 227

Gelowicz, Filiz, 197n7

Gelowicz, Fritz, 197n7

gender: and Belgian discrimination, 146; and Belgian integration, 145, 158; and economic theory, 32; and German radicalization, 186; hegemonic masculinity, 241–42, 250; and patriarchy, 250; and Spanish radicalization, 219, 220, 221, 224; and UK gender equality, 250

generational differences: in Belgium, 145–46, 158; and converts, 111; in France, 177–78, 182; radicalization as youth movement, 64; in Spain, 16–17; in UK, 241, 245, 250

Germany, 186–208; attacks and plots in, 186, 197n7; foreign fighters from, 16, 186–87, 188, 191, 192, 198, 207, 221; and Millatu Ibrahim, 188–89, 192–208; Muslim population in, 190; right-wing radicalization and parties, 64, 191, 192, 195, 243

Ghlam, Sid Ahmed, 151

globalization and UK radicalization, 240, 245, 248, 249–50

Goodin, Robert, 53–54

Government Action Plan (Canada), 256

Gries, Thomas, 35n5

grievances: as common element, 2, 6, 57, 181, 260; and framing, 63; group, 125–26, 137, 154, 157–62; personal, 125–26, 133, 137, 154, 157; and quest for significance, 133; and recruitment, 154; removing economic, 34; and right-wing radicalization, 246; and social movement theory, 48–49, 63, 157–62; and social psychology, 125–26, 130, 137

group identity. *See* identity, group

Gunaratna, Rohan, 8–9

Gusse, Isabelle, 181

habits, hiding of changes in, 230–31, 233

Hadden, Jeffrey, 106

El-Hamahmy, Abdallah, 174

Hamel, Jacques, 81

headscarf bans, 149

hegemonic masculinity, 241–42, 250

heroism: and framing, 62; and recruitment, 11, 180, 181, 182; self-perception of, 60

Hertog, Steffen, 32
Hervieu-Léger, Danièle, 105, 176
Hess, Gregory D., 30, 34
hijrah, 10, 79, 170–71, 193, 197
Hilafet Devleti, 199
Hogg, Michael, 133–35
Horgan, John, 7, 119, 120, 169
Hughes, Seamus, 95
humanitarian motives, 169–70
humiliation: and Belgium radicalization,
    147; and *Charlie Hebdo* attack, 88;
    direct, 56; as motivation for foreign
    fighters, 10; and quest for significance,
    133; and radicalization, 8, 10–11, 56;
    vicarious, 56
Hussein, Saddam, 247

identity: and appeal of radicalization, 10,
    11, 15, 224; and conversion, 106; and
    deindividuation, 131, 178; and devi-
    ance, 104; and enemies, 82, 134; and
    French radicalization, 169, 172–73,
    176–78; and German radicalization,
    189, 192; global Muslim identity, 239–
    40; and military commitment, 176–78,
    182; and organizational compartmen-
    talization, 51; and prison popula-
    tion, 230; and second-generation
    immigrants, 177–78, 182, 248; and
    social movement theory, 58–59, 60;
    and social networks, 58–59, 60, 106,
    178; and social psychology theory,
    15, 122, 131, 132–35, 178, 188; and
    Spanish radicalization, 222, 226; and
    UK radicalization, 17, 239–40, 241,
    245–46, 250; and uncertainty, 98, 109,
    122, 132, 133–36, 177–78, 189
identity, group: and conversion, 105;
    and deindividuation, 131, 178; and
    prejudice toward out-groups, 134,
    135; songs and chants, 178; threats
    to, 135–36; and UK radicalization,
    239–40, 242
identity, national, 237, 238
ideology: and converts, 102, 107, 109,
    110; encapsulation, 49, 51–52; and
    framing, 48, 60–61; as general factor,
    171, 181, 224; over-focus on, 5, 16,
    93, 109, 110, 136, 144, 216, 218, 255;

and patterns in members, 228–29;
    relationship to violence, 4; and social
    movement theory, 48–49; and social
    psychology, 120, 122–25, 127–29, 131,
    134–36; and spaces of jihadism, 69–70,
    72–81, 84, 86, 87, 89–90
immigrants, first-generation: in France,
    177–78; in Germany, 190; in Spain,
    220, 233. *See also* generational differ-
    ences; integration
immigrants, second-generation: and
    conversion, 98–99, 100; in Germany,
    187; and identity uncertainty, 177–78,
    182, 248; and military commitment,
    175–79, 182; and prison, 230; in
    Spain, 233. *See also* generational dif-
    ferences; integration
individuals. *See* micro level
influencers: and identity uncertainty,
    134, 172–73; role of, 129–30, 136
in-group: isolation and social ties,
    128–29; and justification of violence,
    128–29, 131–32; prejudice towards
    out-groups, 125, 134, 135; and threats
    to identity, 135–36
Institute for Creative Technologies, 181
institutional variables *vs.* economic, 35
integration: in Belgium, 143, 145–46,
    147, 158, 162, 163; economic, 34–35;
    role in countering radicalization, 225;
    in Spain, 217, 220, 225, 226, 232; in
    UK, 238, 247
interaction, arenas of, 54–55
International Brigades, 171
intra-movement interactive arena, 55
Iraq: US as enemy of, 78; US inva-
    sion of, 247. *See also* foreign fighters;
    Islamic State/Daesh
Irish republicanism, 129
Islam4UK, 148, 242
Islamic Salvation Army (Algeria), 77
Islamic State/Daesh: as business or
    firm, 37–38, 40; and converts, 95–96;
    diversity of recruits, 166, 169; and
    enemy identification, 78–81, 84–85,
    88; heroism as motivation in, 11, 180,
    181, 182; patterns of radicalization,
    228–29; and permanent state of war,
    78–80; rise of, 247; and Spain, 212,

214, 219–20, 232; and squad formation, 86–87; videos, 172, 173, 180;
violence as central to, 71. *See also*
foreign fighters
Islamization of radicalism, 64, 97, 167,
181–82
Islamophobia: in Belgium, 147; defined,
243, 244; and geographic differences
in radicalization, 12; in Germany, 243;
in UK, 238–39, 240, 243–47, 249–51.
See also discrimination
Islam Party (Belgium), 159–60

Jessen, Tina Gudrun, 103
Jewish Museum attack (Brussels), 16n5,
151
jihadism: "chic/cool jihad," 228; as
counterculture, 11, 15, 90, 258–59;
hijrah merging with, 79, 170–71,
193; historical concept of, 71–72; and
permanent state of war, 78–80, 84–85;
rise of modern, 73–75; scope of, 71;
terms for, 74n6. *See also* spaces of
jihadism
Jihadist centers (Varvelli), 13
Johnston, Hank, 56
Jordán, Javier, 225

Kelkal, Khaled, 10n1
Kepel, Gilles, 10, 167
Keskin, Hasan, 16, 189, 193, 194, 196,
197, 198–202, 205–7, 208
el-Khazzani, Ayoub, 151
Khosrokhavar, Farhad, 4, 10, 56, 68, 172,
230
King, Michael, 124, 222
Kleinmann, Scott, 13–14, 95
Krieger, Tim, 14, 23–41
Krueger, Alan, 32
Kruglanksi, Arie, 8–9, 126–27, 132–33,
135, 178
Kundnani, Arun, 4–5, 69
Kwakkel, Jan, 30

Laachraoui, Najim, 151, 155
left-wing radicalization, 2, 35n5, 36, 49,
64
legitimacy: and clergy, 82; and converts,
99; and framing, 63; and role models,

129; and social psychology, 129; and
spaces of jihadism, 68, 69, 73, 75, 82,
85, 87–88; and theology, 73, 75; and
viral paradigm, 87–88
Lesaca, Javier, 180
LIES! campaign (Germany), 191, 195,
196
liminality and conversion, 97–99, 109
living together concept, 255, 260–61
locale and geography: centers of radicalization, 12; differences in, 12–13;
global goals, 75–76, 77–78, 81–82, 87;
and opportunism, 75–76; and radicalization in Belgium, 153, 154
local space and UK radicalization, 245,
247
Lofland, John, 107
London: 2005 bomb plot, 227; 2017
attack, 80; London Bridge attack,
221
lone-wolf radicalization, 39, 105, 225,
227
Long, Theodore, 106
Loseman, Annemarie, 135–36
love: and quest for significance, 133;
and radicalization of women, 172; and
social movement theory, 59; and social
psychology, 125, 126, 129, 133

Machalek, Richard, 107
macro level: and collective life, 105–6;
defined, 7; socioeconomic factors at
country-level, 33–36; in Spain, 225
Madrid 2004 attack, 16, 88, 212–13, 215,
219–20, 226, 227
Mahmood, Saba, 108
Mahmoud, Mohamed, 193, 194, 196,
198
Malečková, Jitka, 32
Malthaner, Stefan, 110
al-Maqdisi, Abu Muhammad, 191, 193,
197
Marchal, Roland, 101
martial law, 70, 72, 73, 89
masculinity, hegemonic, 241–42, 250
Mauss, Marcel, 108
McAdam, Douglas, 52–53, 54
McCants, William, 167–68
McCarthy, John, 156

McCauley, Clark: on mechanisms, 12–13, 59, 125–26, 127, 133, 255; mechanisms and Belgium radicalization, 143–44, 154–56, 160, 161–63; mechanisms table, 161; on small groups, 157, 160, 162
McGinty, Anna Mansson, 103
meaning-seeking and conversion, 102–3
mechanisms: and Belgium radicalization, 143–44, 154–56, 160, 161–63; cognitive mechanisms, 53; and conversion, 95; defined, 53; environmental, 53; overview of, 6, 8–9, 13; relational mechanisms, 53, 54; and social movement theory, 12–13, 53–55, 58–60, 161; and social psychology, 125–37; and spaces of jihadism, 71; table of, 161
media: in France, 178; media policy, 41. *See also* social media
Meierrieks, Daniel, 14, 23–41, 35n5
mental illness, 11, 27, 119–20, 222–23
Merah, Mohammed, 174, 175
Meserole, Christopher, 167–68
meso level: and conversion, 105–7; defined, 7; over-focus on, 218; in Spain, 225; and spatial regulation in UK, 239–40, 241, 245
Mezroui, Adel, 158
Mezroui, Soufiane, 158
micro level: and conversion, 105–6; and creativity, 80, 89–90; defined, 7; and indiscriminate targets, 80–81; and social movement theory, 57–63; socioeconomic factors at individual level, 36
militant enclosure, 49, 51–52
militant networks, activation of, 49, 50, 188
military: attacks on, 80, 174–75; military recruitment comparison, 16, 167, 173–82; military service by jihadists, 175
Millatu Ibrahim, 188–89, 192–208
Moeller, Mika, 16, 104n1, 186–208
Moghaddam, Fathali, 8, 124
monetarism. *See* neoliberalism and spatial regulation in UK
El Morabit, Saïd, 158
Mormonism, 106

Morocco: as center of radicalization, 12; Moroccan immigrants in Belgium, 144, 152, 155, 161; Moroccan immigrants in Spain, 216–17, 219–21, 227, 232
Morrison, John F., 15, 98, 107, 119–37, 222, 257, 258
Moskalenko, Sophia: on mechanisms, 12–13, 59, 125–26, 127, 133, 255; mechanisms and Belgium radicalization, 143–44, 154–56, 160, 161–63; mechanisms table, 161; on small groups, 157, 160, 162
mosques, 148, 152–53, 159; influence of Saudi Arabia on, 152; recognition of in Belgium, 148, 159; role in radicalization in Belgium, 152–53
Mossière, Géraldine, 108
Muslim Brotherhood, 49, 73–74
Muslim co-religionists: antipathy to in Germany, 190; as enemies, 81–82, 84–85
Muslim Executive of Belgium, 148, 158

Al-Naji, Abu Bakr, 79n16
nasheeds. *See* chants and songs
national identity and UK, 237, 238, 239
National Socialist Underground (Germany), 64
negative influencers, 129–30
Nemmouche, Mehdi, 16n5
neoliberalism and spatial regulation in UK, 238, 240, 242, 245, 249, 250
Netherlands: counter-radicalization in, 206; foreign fighters from, 221
Neumann, Peter, 2, 4, 13–14, 23, 24, 109, 229
new religious movements, 101, 111
new social movement theory, 156
Nice, France: 2016 attack, 130; as center of radicalization, 12n4, 130
19HH, 130, 180
Norway, attacks in, 221

obedience, 82–83, 176
Oberschall, Anthony, 48
object shift, 55
Omsen, Omar. *See* Diaby, Omar
opening, cognitive, 8–9, 59–60

opportunity costs, 28–31, 39
opportunity spirals, 55
Orehek, Edward, 135
organization: capacity to organize, 48; and compartmentalization, 49, 51; radicalized groups as business or firm, 37–38, 40; and social movement theory, 48, 49, 51; and squads, 86–87
Orientalism, 96, 238–39, 244; and converts, 96; in UK, 238–39, 244
Oslo attack (2011), 221
otherness: of Muslims in UK, 239, 244, 245; and spaces of jihadism, 73, 75–81, 259. *See also* binary thinking
outbidding, 50, 55
out-groups: harm from, 126, 198; prejudice against, 125, 134, 135; and relative deprivation, 124–25; role in radicalization, 126, 128–29, 131–32, 137, 205, 207
Özyürek, Esra, 96

Paris: 1995 attack, 10n1, 77n10; 2015 attack, 16, 24, 25, 143, 148, 150, 151, 159, 162; *Charlie Hebdo* attack, 88
Passeron, Jean-Claude, 257
patriarchy, 250
patriotism, 180
patterns in radicalization in Spain, 227–31
Paul (Saint), 103, 105
Paveau, Marie-Anne, 178
Pelzer, Robert, 16, 104n1, 186–208
physical training, 179. *See also* body and embodiment
Pisoiu, Daniela, 14, 46–65, 60, 61–63, 121
policing and police: attacks on police, 80; escalation of policing, 49–50, 188, 207, 208; as factor in violence, 249; in Germany, 188, 195, 196, 199, 200, 201, 204; interaction arena, 55; and radicalization as term, 4–5; in Spain, 215–16; in UK, 238
policy: economic policy, 34–35, 40–41; and funding of Islam in Belgium, 143, 147–48, 158–59; and geographic differences in radicalization, 12;

integration policy in Belgium, 145–46; radicalization policy in Canada, 256; radicalization policy in Spain, 215; secularism policy in France, 167–68; weapons policy, 41
politics and political variables: *vs.* economic variables, 35; as motivation in radicalization, 169, 170–71, 224; political instability as factor, 35; political participation, 35; in social movement theory, 48–49, 55, 58–59; in UK, 237, 238. *See also* right-wing radicalization and parties
positive influencers, 129–30
post-feminism motivations, 169, 172
power: competition between groups, 55; and framing, 62; as reserved for clergy and princes, 82; soft power, 246
prayer, 108
prediction: and conversion, 102, 103; in economic theory, 24, 29–30, 32, 33, 36, 39, 258; and facilitating factors, 7; and focus on causes, 6; limits of approach, 4, 5, 6, 7, 124–25
prenotion, 257
pre-radicalization, 226
prestige in framing theory, 62. *See also* status
price of radicalization, relative, 29
prison: and hiding of change in habits, 230–31, 233; and Millatu Ibrahim, 193; overcrowding, 153; and recruitment, 17, 229–31; role in radicalization, 11, 152, 153, 161, 229–31, 233
probation before God, 192–94, 200–202, 205–6
profiling: as flawed, 102, 109, 121–22, 218, 222, 224; and psychopathy, 11
profits and economic theory, 14, 37–38
Pro NRW, 196
propaganda: and contexts, 123; and creativity, 80; and economic theory, 39; and skills, 224; and social media, 180, 181; and social movement theory, 49, 51–52; video games, 180–81; videos, 172, 173, 180
proselytizing. *See* da'wa in Germany
Pruyt, Erik, 30

psychology. *See* mental illness; social movement theory; social psychology theory
psychopathy, 11

Quayle, Ethel, 131
quest for savagery, 79–80
quest for significance, 8–9, 122, 132–33
Qutb, Sayyid, 74

racism. *See* discrimination; Islamophobia
radicalization: behavioral, 23, 108–9, 226; beyond jihadism, 1, 2; centers of, 12; cognitive, 4, 225–26; degrees of, 126–27; forms of, 2; as global, 75; lone-wolf, 39, 105, 225, 227; radicalization of Islam concept, 10, 167, 181–82; scholarly interest in, 256; scholarly methods and rigor, 13–14, 15; self-radicalization, 225, 227; shortening of period of, 17, 232; stages of, 30–31, 59–60, 226; before target, 64, 80–81, 89, 90; violence as central to, 2, 70–71, 84, 85; violent, 4; as Western phenomenon, 9–10, 26. *See also* causes of radicalization; converts and conversion; counter-radicalization and de-radicalization; economic theory; mechanisms; right-wing radicalization and parties; social movement theory; social psychology theory; socioeconomic factors; spaces of jihadism
radicalization as term: and conversion model, 93; and economic theory, 23; and indicator paradigm, 4–5; as linked to terrorism, 24; multiple meanings of, 255–63; need for clarity on, 17; overview of, 2, 3–5; and social movement theory, 46, 54, 64; and social psychology, 120; and spaces for radicalization, 68, 71; as stigmatizing/cohering, 2
Radicalization Awareness Network, 224
rational choice, 23–41; and abnormal behavior, 223; and economic theory, 14, 23, 26–31, 33, 35, 37, 39–40, 120–21; and social movement theory, 47, 56, 60–63, 160; and social psychology, 120–21
recognition in framing theory, 62

recruitment: in Belgium, 148–52, 156–60, 162; and conversion, 106; and economic theory, 37–39; and education level, 38–39, 40; *vs.* enrollment, 84, 87; by ETA, 231; and family, 50–51, 226; in France, 172–73; and friendship, 50–51; and gatekeeping, 222–23; and heroism, 11, 180, 181, 182; military recruitment comparison, 16, 167, 179–82; patterns in radicalization and, 228–29; patterns in recruiters, 229; and prison, 17, 229–31; role of influencers, 129–30, 136, 172–73; and social media, 180, 181; and social movement theory, 156–60; and social networks, 58–59, 125, 126; in Spain, 17, 225–27; videos, 130, 172, 173, 180
Red Army, 48, 127–28
Red Brigades, 48, 54, 128
refugees, 243
Reinares, Fernando, 213n3, 223n16, 226, 227
relational mechanisms, 53, 54
relative deprivation, 124–25, 222
relative price of radicalization, 29
religion: and focus on enemy in theology, 72–73; lack of religious knowledge, 63, 153, 159, 248; and legitimacy, 73, 75; as motive, 69–70, 169, 170–71, 224
religious conversion. *See* converts and conversion
religious violence. *See* violence
repression: defined, 54; and German radicalization, 188, 197–208; as opportunity for *da'wa*, 200–202, 205–8; reactions to, 206; selective *vs.* generalized, 54; in social movement theory, 49, 51–52, 54, 64
resource mobilization, 48, 156
Resto du Tawhid, 148, 149–50, 151, 155, 159, 161
reward in framing theory, 62
Richards, Anthony, 100
Richardson, James, 102
Rigby, Lee, 174
right-wing radicalization and parties: in Belgium, 147; and common elements of radicalization, 2; in Germany, 64,

191, 192, 195, 243; invisibility of violence by, 240–41, 244; tolerance of, 64; in UK, 238, 240–49; in US, 241
Robinson, Tommy, 242
Rogers, Brooke, 229
role models, 129
Roy, Olivier, 11, 64, 97, 167
Roy, Quentin, 175
rupture commitment, 176
Russia: Islamophobia in, 243; USSR as enemy, 77
Russian Orthodoxy, 106

Sageman, Marc, 11, 27, 58–59, 101, 102, 128
Salafism: and Belgian radicalization, 148, 152; as contributing to radicalization, 10; and converts, 99; in France, 167; in Germany, 187, 188–92, 194, 196–97, 203–8; prohibitions on suicide, 11; rise of, 10, 64, 74–75; in Spain, 217, 224; in UK, 237, 245. *See also* Millatu Ibrahim
Salafism, Takfir. *See* Millatu Ibrahim
Salem, Zekeria Ould Ahmed, 101
salvation, 60, 61, 104, 194, 201
Sandler, Todd, 35n5
Saudi Arabia: influence on mosques in Belgium, 152; as "renegade" state and enemy, 78
security forces. *See* policing and police
Sedgwick, Mark, 9
self-actualization. *See* quest for significance
self-concept, 132–35. *See also* identity
self-esteem, 125, 182
self-interest in social movement theory, 61
self-persuasion, 59
self-purification, 189, 190, 194, 203
self-radicalization, 225, 227
September 11 attacks, 4–5, 78, 88
Settoul, Elyamine, 1–17, 166–82, 257
Shakur, Abdul, 175
Sharia4Belgium, 16, 147, 148–49, 150, 155, 158, 159, 161, 162
Shughart, William, 35
Shupe, Anson, 107
siblings, 51, 152, 161, 226

significant quest theory, 8–9, 122, 132–33
Situational Action Theory (SAT), 123–24
slippery slope, 125, 126
Snow, David, 107
social media: and German radicalization, 194–205; and recruitment, 180, 181; role of, 11, 224; and self-radicalization, 227; and shortening of radicalization period, 232
social movement theory, 46–65; and arenas of interaction, 54–55; and Belgian radicalization, 16, 143–44, 154–62; and culture, 56–57; development of, 48–52, 128, 156; future research areas, 63–65; and German radicalization, 188, 207; and mechanisms, 12–13, 53–55, 58–60, 161; overview of, 14, 46–47; and rational choice, 47, 56, 60–63, 160; shortcomings of, 57–65; and Spanish radicalization, 226–27. *See also* framing theory
social networks: and activation of militant networks, 49, 50, 188; and commitment, 50; and context heterogeneity, 123–24; and conversion, 15, 105–7, 110; and diaspora, 11; and framing, 62–63; and identity, 58–59, 60, 106, 178; and military commitment, 176–77; and quest for significance, 133; and recruitment, 58–59, 125, 126; role of, 107, 127–30, 187, 224, 226–27; and siblings, 51, 152, 161; in social movement theory, 49, 50–51, 58–59. *See also* family; social psychology theory
social psychology theory, 119–37; and context, 123–24; defined, 120; and identity, 15, 122, 131, 132–35, 178, 188; and mechanisms, 125–37; in military commitment comparison, 16, 176–77, 178, 188; overview of, 15, 119–22; and social movement theory, 47, 57–59
social welfare, 34
socioeconomic factors: in Belgium, 143–48, 153–54, 157–59, 162–63; country-level, 33–36; in economic theory, 14, 24, 26, 29–30, 31–36, 38–40; in

socioeconomic factors (*continued*)
Europe, 224; in France, 166, 168, 176–77, 182; individual-level, 36; and military commitment, 176–77; and popular support for terrorism, 33, 34; and right-wing radicalization, 240–41; and social psychology, 124–25; in Spain, 218–22, 224; in UK, 17, 32, 237–38, 240–43, 245–50

soft power, 246

songs and chants, 178, 195, 196

spaces of jihadism, 68–90; historical jihadism, 71–73; and identifying enemy, 71, 72–73, 75–81, 84–85; overview of, 15, 68–71; rise of contemporary, 73–75, 81–83; and role of all Muslims, 81–85; and techniques, 85–90; violence as central to, 70–71, 84, 85; viral paradigm, 15, 87–90. *See also* spatial regulation in UK

Spain, 212–33; arrests and detentions in, 213, 214, 219, 231; centers of radicalization in, 214; as enemy, 88; escalating policing in, 49; foreign fighters from, 16, 213, 214, 219, 221; increase in terrorism in, 231–32; integration in, 217, 220, 225, 226, 232; International Brigades, 171; Muslim population in, 216–17; patterns in radicalization, 227–31; prisons in, 229–31, 233; process of radicalization in, 223–31; rise of radicalization in, 16–17, 212–14; socioeconomic factors in, 218–22, 224; terrorism laws in, 215

Spain, attacks in: Barcelona (2017), 16, 212, 219–20, 224, 226, 231, 232; Gerona (2007), 223; Madrid (2004), 16, 88, 212–13, 215, 219–20, 226, 227

spatial regulation in UK, 237–51; and Islamophobia, 238–39, 240, 243–46, 247, 249–51; local space, 245, 247; meso level, 239–40, 241, 245; overview of, 237–43; and right-wing radicalization and parties, 238, 240–49; and socioeconomic factors, 17, 237–38, 240–43, 245–50

spirals, opportunity/threat, 55

sponsorship paradigm, 87–90

sports, 173, 179

squad formation, 86–87

standing in framing theory, 62

Stark, Rodney, 107

state: and escalating policing, 49–50, 188, 207, 208; funding of Islam in Belgium, 143, 147–48, 158–59; as interaction arena, 55; renegade/corrupt states, 78, 79, 170; role in social movement theory, 14, 55, 59–60, 64; role in spatial regulation in UK, 239–40, 245; states as enemy, 76, 77, 78, 79, 88; and tolerance of right-wing radicalization, 64

status: of immigrant fathers, 177–78; as motivating factor, 135, 173; and prestige in framing theory, 62; and social psychology, 125, 126, 134, 135. *See also* socioeconomic factors

steadfastness, 200, 201–2, 204, 205, 206, 207

Straus, Roger, 102, 103, 104, 106

suicide: prohibitions on, 11; and rationality, 56

supply: in economic theory, 24, 26–36, 37, 40; and opportunistic terrorism, 90

Sweden, Islamophobia in, 243

Syria. *See also* foreign fighters; Islamic State/Daesh

Takfir Salafism. *See* Millatu Ibrahim

Taras, Raymond, 12

tarbyia, 61. *See also* salvation

Tarrow, Sidney, 52–53, 54

Tauhid Germany, 202

Taylor, Bryan, 102

Taylor, Donald, 124, 222

Taylor, Max, 119, 120, 131, 178

Teich, Sarah, 16, 143–63

terrorism: as collective action, 48; creativity in attacks, 80, 89–90; economic theory, 23–41; entrepreneurs, 23–24; by ETA, 16–17, 212, 214–15, 223–24; as linked to radicalism, 24; outbidding thesis, 50; popular supprt for, 33, 34; processes in Wiktorowicz, 59–60, 187; radicalization before target, 64, 80–81, 89, 90; and rational choice, 23–41, 120–21; Spanish laws on, 215; as stage in radicalization, 30; as term,

2, 46; tolerance of right-wing, 64; viral paradigm, 15, 87–90
terrorism entrepreneurs, 23–24, 36–39, 40
Thalys train attempt (2015), 151, 161
theory: overview of, 5–9, 14–15. *See also* converts and conversion; economic theory; social movement theory; social psychology theory; spaces of jihadism
Thornton, John, 32
threat spirals, 55
Tilly, Charles, 8, 52–54
time and conversion, 103–4, 109–10
Trigeaud, Sophie-Hélène, 106
trust: and identity uncertainty, 136; in political process in UK, 248; and recruitment, 58, 59; and social psychology, 122, 126, 128, 129, 136
Tunisia, as center of radicalization, 12
Turner, Karen, 98
Turner, Victor, 97–98

UCLAT (Unité de Coordination de la Lutte Antiterroriste), 169
umma: as term, 70n2; unification of as goal, 70
uncertainty: and converts, 98, 109; and probation before God, 194, 200–202, 205–6; and second-generation immigrants, 177–78, 182, 248; uncertainty-identity theory, 98, 122, 132, 133–36, 189
unfreezing, 125, 126
Unité de Coordination de la Lutte Anti-terroriste (UCLAT), 169
United Kingdom, 237–51; and Brexit, 245, 247; converts in, 95, 96; integration in, 238, 247; Islamophobia in, 238–39, 240, 243–46, 247, 249–51; national identity, 237, 238; and right-wing radicalization and parties, 238, 240–49; socioeconomic factors in, 17, 32, 237–38, 240–43, 245–50
United Kingdom, attacks in: in 2017, 80, 247; London bomb plot (2005), 227; London Bridge attack (2019), 221; on soldiers, 80, 174
United States: converts in, 95, 96; embassy attacks, 78; as enemy, 78, 88;

and Iraq, 78, 247; and military recruitment, 181; Muslim population in, 95; right-wing radicalization and parties in, 241; September 11 attacks, 4–5, 78, 88; socioeconomic factors in, 32
USS *Cole*, 78
USSR, as enemy, 77
utility, 27–30, 39
utopia, 170, 181, 245
Utoya, Norway attack (2011), 221

van den Bos, Kees, 135–36
Van Nieuwkerk, Karin, 108
Van Son, Marion, 95
Van Vlierden, Guy, 147
Vicente, Alvaro, 227
video games, 180–81
videos: and German radicalization, 194–205; military recruitment, 181; recruitment, 130, 172, 173, 180
Vidino, Lorenzo, 95
violence: assumption of causal relationship to radicalization, 2, 4; as central to radicalization, 2, 70–71, 84, 85; and deindividuation, 131; in economic theory, 30, 31; elimination of barriers to, 125; fascination with, 172–73; invisibility of white, 240–41, 244; justification of, 48, 69, 125, 128–29, 130–32; policing as factor in, 249; and quest for savagery, 79–80; radicalization as cover for innate, 64, 97; and radicalization as term, 4, 120; and terrorism as collective action, 48; use of indiscriminate, 52, 80–81; violent extremism as stage in radicalization, 30
violent radicalization, 4
viral paradigm, 15, 87–90
Vlaams Blok/Belang (VB), 147
Vogel, Pierre, 191, 203
vulnerability: and contexts, 124; and converts, 97, 100, 102; and identity uncertainty, 134; and incarceration, 153, 229; and socioeconomic factors, 241, 248

war, permanent state of, 78–80, 84–85
Wasmund, Klaus, 127–28

weapons of mass destruction, 247
weapons policy, 41
Weenink, Anton, 222–23
Weerapana, Akila, 30, 34
whites: invisibility of violence by, 240–41, 244; working-class whites in UK, 247–48
Wikström, Per-Olof, 123–24
Wiktorowicz, Quintan, 8, 59–60, 61, 157, 187
Winchester, Daniel, 108
Winter, Timothy, 97, 98
women: concerns about in UK, 239, 241; and French radicalization, 166, 169, 171–72, 175; and gender equality in

UK, 250; and German radicalization, 197n7; strategic use of by Islamic State, 172. *See also* gender
Woods, Orlando, 105

xenophobia, 238, 244

Yugoslavia, foreign fighters in, 171

Zald, Mayer, 156
Al-Zawahiri, Ayman, 79n14
Zehaf-Bibeau, Michael, 174
Zerkani, Khalid, 150–51, 155
Zerkani network, 143, 148, 150–52, 153–55, 159, 160–61, 162